'Irish Blood, English Heart'

'Irish Blood, English Heart'

Second-generation Irish Musicians in England

Sean Campbell

CORK UNIVERSITY PRESS

First published in 2011 by
Cork University Press
Youngline Industrial Estate
Pouladuff Road, Togher
Cork, Ireland

© Sean Campbell

British Library Cataloguing in Publication Data
A CIP catalogue record for this book is available from the British Library.

ISBN-13: 978-185918-461-5

Typeset by Dominic Carroll, Co. Cork
Printed by CPI, UK

www.corkuniversitypress.com

For my mother,
and in memory of my father

Contents

List of Illustrations

Acknowledgements

I have benefited enormously from the support and advice of many people while researching and writing this book. In particular, I would like to acknowledge the musicians who gave so generously of their time in interviews: Shane MacGowan, Johnny Marr, Kevin Rowland and Cáit O'Riordan spoke thoughtfully and at length about their lives and work, and provided an abundance of original material; Philip Chevron also offered invaluable help and support, and answered numerous questions via e-mail. Dialogues with friends and colleagues have sparked illuminating insights and helpful advice. My warm and sincere thanks to Aidan Arrowsmith, Philip Bohlman, Barbara Bradby, Ruth Davis, Simon Fletcher, Mary Hickman, Joel Isaac, Keith Khan-Harris, Mairtin Mac an Ghaill, Martin McLoone, Jon Savage, Alison Stenning, Bronwen Walter and Nabeel Zuberi. Colin Coulter and Gerry Smyth kindly read draft chapters, and made precise and incisive comments. The anonymous readers for Cork University Press offered helpful advice on the manuscript. The staff at Cork University Press – especially Sophie Watson, Maria O'Donovan and Mike Collins – have been generous, encouraging and patient. I am extremely grateful to the Arts and Humanities Research Council, which supported this project with a period of research leave. The Department of English and Media at Anglia Ruskin in Cambridge has also offered help in myriad ways. Thanks to my colleagues and students for providing such a vibrant and friendly research environment.

A number of people were very helpful in co-ordinating interviews and locating unpublished material. I am particularly grateful to Joey Cashman, Carol Clerk, Daryl Easlea, John Foyle, Simon Goddard, Paul Gorman, Barney Hoskyns, Phil King, Joe Moss, Paul Nolan, Pete Paphides, Johnny Rogan, Jon Savage and Ann Scanlon. The staffs of the British Library and Cambridge University Library were extremely helpful (and patient) in dealing with my requests for archive material. Many thanks to the photographers who kindly gave permission for their work to be reproduced in this book: Peter Ashworth, Bleddyn Butcher, David Corio, Colm Henry, Steve Pyke, Tom Sheehan, Paul Slattery, Ian Tilton and Russell Young.

I am especially grateful to my family in England, Ireland and America, whose warmth and generosity helped sustain me throughout the writing of this book. Most especially, I would like to thank my mother, Margaret, and my late father, Sean, to whom this book is dedicated. The Loughnanes of Illinois have been unceasingly kind in their support, and

I cannot thank them enough. Warm thanks (and appreciation) also to the Fishers of Wiltshire and Spain, the Jordans of east Galway, and the Campbells of Thurles and Naas. Conversations with my brother Fergus have helped to clarify much of my thinking on this book. His astute insights and incisive advice have been invaluable. Most of all, I want to thank my wife and best friend, Leah, for her love and patient support, which has nourished me more than she knows, and which has helped bring this book about migration home.

'Dwellers on the Threshold':
A Prologue to the Book

this century will see the evolution of the Anglo-Irishman in a new sense – a man with a legitimate pride in his Irish ancestry and contributing his own distinctiveness to English life

Donogh O'Malley, Irish minister for health, 17 March 1966[1]

The significant thing about the second-generation Irish is their contribution to British *culture. The fact that we're all, you know ... up the front*

Kevin Rowland[2]

it is in the interstices between cultures that some of the most exciting things happen

Michael D. Higgins, Irish minister for arts, culture and the Gaeltacht[3]

The dominant forms of popular music in most contemporary societies have emerged, notes Simon Frith, 'at the social margins – among the poor, the migrant, the rootless'.[4] This has certainly been the case in Britain, where, as one high-profile magazine put it, a 'potent shebeen of home-grown music' has been ensured only by a 'multi-ethnic mix' in which 'the immigrant Irish have proved most crucial'.[5] The vital role played by musicians of Irish descent in the history of British pop is as enduring as it is diverse, spanning such figures as Lonnie Donegan, McCartney and Lennon, Dusty Springfield (Mary O'Brien), John Lydon, Kate Bush, Elvis Costello (Declan McManus), Shane MacGowan, Kevin Rowland, Boy George (George O'Dowd), Morrissey, Johnny Marr (born Maher) and Noel and Liam Gallagher.[6] Despite the vast amount of attention that has been paid to these figures, there has been relatively little address – in either popular or scholarly work – to their Irish context.[7] This has obscured the role of Irish ethnicity in the musicians' lives and work, and has masked the diverse ways in which the offspring of Irish migrants have shaped popular music in Britain.[8]

The presence of the second generation at the hub of British popular culture became most striking in the 1980s, the period addressed in this book.[9] This presence was registered not only via their high visibility (in the mainstream media) but also through their address to Irish ethnicity in their personas and creative work.[10] This address took a wide range of forms (across the musical, visual and verbal realms), via diverse registers, from the abstract to the essentialist, and from the upfront to the oblique. Such efforts were staged, moreover, at a time when Irish ethnicity was less than fashionable. Thus, while Irishness became, in the 1990s, an increasingly marketable commodity,[11] it was, in early Eighties Britain, a much less profitable enterprise. As Shane MacGowan's English band-mates have explained, it was 'quite difficult' – and 'definitely not a good thing' – to be Irish in early-Eighties London, and it was observed by certain critics at the time that Irish musicians who eschewed Irish styles were more likely to find success.[12] Indeed, at least one of the musicians surveyed in this book was advised, in the Eighties, to avoid Irish sounds and styles on the grounds that they might not be popular.[13]

In addressing this particular period, the book takes a case-study approach, exploring three high-profile projects: Kevin Rowland and Dexys Midnight Runners (1978–86), Shane MacGowan and The Pogues (1982–91), and Morrissey/Marr and The Smiths (1982–87). These figures were preceded by John Lydon, who came to prominence (as the face of punk)[14] in the late 1970s, and in certain ways informed these post-punk projects.[15] Lydon's significance is therefore cited throughout. The book affords a comparative view of the diverse 'routes' pursued by second-generation Irish musicians,[16] exploring their different styles and personas, and discrete social locales, from London (MacGowan and Cáit O'Riordan) to the Midlands (Rowland) and Manchester (Morrissey/Marr).[17] Rather than seeing their work as either 'Irish' or 'English', the book views second-generation Irish music-making as a complex cultural process that exceeds both Irish ethnicity and English assimilation, and points to an often intricate accommodation of Anglo-Irish issues (marked by 'in-betweenness'). The book's title therefore serves to invoke the dilemma faced by second-generation Irish people, many of whom locate themselves as 'half and half' and 'very much both', or 'caught right down the middle'.[18] The musicians thus adopt a range of hyphenated positions (such as 'London-Irish' or 'Mancunian-Irish'), and inflect their affinities uniquely (Kevin Rowland, for instance, maintains an 'Irish heart' *in* an 'English culture').[19]

The book deploys – in its account of the musicians – diverse approaches, including biography, musicology and cultural history. It draws on original interviews with the key figures (including Kevin Rowland, Shane MacGowan, Cáit O'Riordan and Johnny Marr) as well as extensive archival research of print and audio-visual media (based on a systematic trawling of British and Irish newspapers, and colla-tion of broadcasted material and popular-cultural paraphernalia).[20] The book also makes use of pertinent scholarly work, drawing on sources and methods from diverse fields, including cultural studies, popular music studies and Irish studies. The chapters offer new analyses of the musicians, addressing songs and salient ancillary 'texts' (such as record sleeves, videos and interviews), as such sources serve – along with the songs themselves – to shape the œuvre of a musician. Such texts are viewed less as 'authentic' expressions of experience (offering unmediated 'truths' about a musician's life) than as creative acts that take shape through performance. The book does not see this body of work, then, as a mere reflection of second-generation life; rather, it seeks to explore how issues of Irish ethnicity were invoked and inflected in the popular-musical realm.

Irish ethnicity is, of course, only one aspect of the musicians' lives and work, which can be viewed – and scrutinised – through the prism of diverse issues, not least gender, region and class.[21] Indeed, some of the figures discussed here have been addressed from such perspectives.[22] Scant attention has been paid, however, to the ethnicity of the second-generation Irish in accounts of British popular music; hence my wish to privilege this particular issue in the present book.[23] The critical elision of this issue has been evinced at key points in British popular music history, not least the celebrated 'Britpop' period of the mid-1990s.[24] At this time, the rock group Oasis, led by the second-generation Irish brothers Noel and Liam Gallagher, became the focus of Britpop, a 'defiantly nationalistic'[25] discourse that emerged in the London-based music press,[26] and which was predicated on the notion of an ostensibly homogeneous white Englishness (rather than a multi-ethnic Britishness). In much Britpop discourse, then, Oasis – a band of self-confirmed 'Irish Mancunians'[27] – were viewed as Anglo-Saxon archetypes ('as English as Yorkshire pud', as the *New Musical Express* (*NME*) put it).[28] Meanwhile, other second-generation musicians were seen as Britpop's predecessors, particularly John Lydon and The Smiths, who were conscripted for what the press called the 'home guard' of Britpop.[29]

Coinciding with such critical views, though, was an attempt – by the musicians – to assert Irish difference in the face of Anglocentric appropriation. Thus, at the height of Britpop, in the summer of 1995, Oasis dismissed claims that they would record a song for the England football team with a robust assertion of Irishness: 'Over my dead body', said Noel Gallagher; 'we're Irish'.[30] Meanwhile, the former Smiths guitarist Johnny Marr (who had been honoured in the press as a 'Britpop icon') expressed his 'despair' at the 'nationalism' of Britpop, whilst pointing to his personal experience of anti-Irish prejudice.[31] At the same time, John Lydon – who re-emerged in the 1990s for the Sex Pistols' reunion

– published an autobiography entitled *No Irish, No Blacks, No Dogs* that offered a striking account of second-generation Irish experience.[32] Even (the post-Smiths) Morrissey, who had engaged with the iconography of English nationalism in the early 1990s, invoked an 'Irish defiance' as part of his persona.[33]

Such assertions of Irish difference drew attention to the role of second-generation Irish musicians in British pop culture. This point was, however, routinely ignored in contemporary accounts, which viewed the musicians as unequivocally English.[34] Whilst this view was most conspicuous in mainstream media discourses, it was also evident in academic accounts. Thus, at a major conference on popular music in the mid-1990s, a panel on national identity featured a paper on Englishness that made reference to numerous second-generation Irish figures without once mentioning their Irishness.[35]

Also at this time, the Commission for Racial Equality (CRE) published a high-profile book (and organised an associated touring exhibition) entitled *Roots of the Future: Ethnic Diversity in the Making of Britain* in a bid to address the 'striking contributions' made to British life by 'post-war immigrants and their descendants'.[36] However, while this work made a point of acknowledging the presence of Irish migrants (who are often overlooked in such accounts), it failed to register a single second-generation Irish contribution in its long section on popular music, instead recruiting such musicians for a de facto Anglo-Saxon 'centre' against which to differentiate more identifiably immigrant-descended figures. Thus, it set up a discursive binary between Oasis and a contemporary indie band, Echobelly, in which the latter – described as 'Britpop superstars [who] enjoy massive chart and critical success with their unique brand of guitar-driven pop' – function as 'ethnic' (against the assumed Englishness of Oasis) on the grounds that their vocalist was of 'Asian descent' and their guitarist was of 'Caribbean origin'. The fact that all five members of Oasis were second-generation Irish was clearly insufficient – despite the CRE's acknowledgement, in *Roots of the Future*, of Irish migration – to view them as migrant-descended.[37]

Thus, the increasing visibility of the second generation in the realm of British pop coincided with a conspicuous silence about their ethnicity in popular and scholarly accounts. This silence was informed by a certain assumption that the second generation were an indistinguishable part of the white English host populace, who instantly assimilated, and identified unambiguously, with the host country.[38] This view has been evidenced on both sides of the Irish Sea. The Irish sociologist Liam Ryan, for example, has argued that assimilation – for the Irish in Britain – was 'practically complete in a single generation'.[39] Meanwhile, sociologists of ethnicity in Britain, such as John Rex, have claimed that 'the incorporation of the Irish into the [English] working class [has been] relatively easy'.[40] Such views have, then, informed the abiding silence about this generation in the popular and scholarly realms. This silence is starkly at odds, however, with ethnographic work on England's Irish, who constitute the largest migrant minority in western Europe, with almost two million people of immediate Irish descent (in addition to one million Irish-born).[41]

The first survey of the second generation was conducted at a north London school (attended at the time by John Lydon) in 1970.[42] The respondents made clear their investment in Irish ethnicity: most had visited Ireland several times, and when asked whom they would support in a football match between Ireland and England – a useful index of allegiance in an urban English milieu – the majority chose Ireland (despite England's success in the 1966 World Cup). Such findings were, as the survey explained, a 'very strong indication' of the alliances of the second generation, who were 'strongly aware of their links with Ireland'.[43]

Such conclusions were underlined by ethnographic research in the 1980s. One such project detailed the extent of this generation's identification with Irishness: more than three quarters felt 'half-Irish' or 'mainly Irish'. In addition, this survey explained that

> anti-Irish prejudice was widely experienced [and] questions relating to identity formed a major issue in the lives of many of these people. It was clearly not the case that they had been assimilated to a greater extent than other minorities, or that they had escaped the many problems associated with second-generation youth.[44]

Striking evidence of second-generation difference emerged in the 1990s, when an account of second-generation Irish health – published in the *British Medical Journal* – explained that the English-born offspring of Irish migrants had experienced disproportionately high instances of ill health, having 'significantly higher mortality [rates]' than the host population 'for most major causes of death'. The report elaborated that, at working ages, the 'mortality of the second generation Irish in every social class ... was higher than that of all men and all women in the corresponding categories'.[45] This 'very unusual' finding in migrant health research[46] implied that crucial differences 'remain in place' for the second generation,[47] who had not, it seemed, been subsumed by the host populace.

Such claims of Irish difference – which clearly refute the assimilationist view – have been augmented by further studies.[48] Even so, it is worth considering here an example of the assimilationist view. One of the best-known advancements of this view was published in the *British Journal of Sociology* in the late 1980s: in an article entitled 'The assimilation of Irish immigrants in England' the authors explored the academic performance of the second generation.[49] What they set out to find, then, was 'a *convergence* in the levels of education achievements' of the second-generation Irish with those of an English control sample.[50] What they went on to discover, though, was that the second-generation Irish actually '*exceed*[ed] the educational qualifications held by their English counterparts'.[51] However, despite the fact that this evidence was at odds with their own criterion of assimilation, which required a 'substantial convergence' between the second-generation Irish and the English control sample, the authors nevertheless saw this educational success as evidence of second-generation Irish assimilation.[52]

It seems, then, that when the second generation exceed the educational achievements of the English group, they become invisible and are understood in terms of assimilation. Yet, when they exceed standard mortality rates, they become visible and are seen in terms of Irish difference. Of course, this makes sense for a number of reasons. For instance, the parents of this generation generally achieved low levels of educational success, and experienced high instances of ill health;[53] consequently, the second generation would appear to be closer to their parents in terms of health patterns, and closer to the host population in terms of academic performance. In addition to this point, migrant 'success' is often seen as assimilation, and thus disadvantage as 'difference'. Such assumptions are, however, quite reductive, as they restrict our view of ethnicity to only problem-centred issues (hence, poor health but not educational success). Indeed, the editorial that framed the *British Medical Journal* article explained that the 'persistence of excess mortality into the second generation … suggests that some important elements of *being Irish* persist long beyond the initial migration'.[54] An address to other aspects of 'being Irish' might, then, enhance our conception of the second generation.

This suggests a critical question for how we conceive of the second generation. For instance: should the Irishness of this generation be conceived *only* in terms of disadvantage? Do 'positive' divergences, such as educational achievement, *necessarily* signify Irish assimilation? If only 'negative' divergences, such as poor health, are used to demonstrate Irish difference, this constricts our conception of the second generation, who become construed as a problem-centred presence. Thus, while existing accounts of the second generation are highly valid and useful, the overall field has clustered around a narrow range of problem-centred issues.

We have come to know, then, about ill health, alcohol abuse, anti-Irish prejudice, the difficulties of identifying as Irish in England, and state attempts at incorporation.[55]

This body of work has been essential – and also illuminating – in the endeavour to detail the (otherwise overlooked) specificities of second-generation life. However, it has, with a few exceptions, neglected to consider the possibility of second-generation cultural *agency*, and has instead assumed their passivity.[56] This has served to confirm, of course, the assimilationist view, in that it assumes that the host culture will *act upon* the migrant group – for example, by incorporating or assimilating them – whilst overlooking the possibility that the migrant group may not only resist this, but might also *act upon* the host culture. The high-profile forms of creative work that are explored in this book thus serve to illustrate this agency, drawing attention to the diverse ways in which the second generation have acted upon the host culture.[57] Their cultural efforts also shed light on the role played by Irish ethnicity – as a creative wellspring *and* a psychic burden – in the lives and work of the second generation. Thus, the book views the second generation as a highly active and creative presence that has engaged with Irish ethnicity *as well as* the host culture, supplying – in the process – a striking counter to those that have seen this generation as simply passive or assimilated.

This address to second-generation Irish creative 'success' could, then, reshape our conception of the Irish in England, who might be seen less as a peripheral (and problematic) presence than as centre stage and productive. With this point in mind, it is perhaps unfortunate that some of the most vocal resistance *to* acknowledging the second generation as Irish has come from many Irish-born people, an issue that is worth addressing here.

A number of debates about the perceived Irishness of this generation have been staged in the Irish community press, such as the *Irish Post*, the chief newspaper for the Irish in Britain.[58] In many such debates, the term 'plastic Paddy' has been used to denote the children of Irish immigrants in England. This term, which found currency among Irish-born migrants in 1980s England,[59] can refer, in certain contexts, to the adoption of essentialist forms of Irishness among the second genera-tion.[60] While this practice might exasperate Irish-born migrants, the label 'plastic Paddy' is, fundamentally, a derisive allusion to the perceived *inauthenticity* of the second generation's identification with Irishness.

A noteworthy rendition of this view has been evinced in the realm of sport, a highly potent site of national identification. In an ethno-graphic account of Republic of Ireland football supporters, Marcus Free observes the means by which Irish-born fans have sought to distance themselves from the second generation.[61] During an international game in Portugal in the 1990s, Irish-born fans expressed 'hostility' and 'rejection' towards the second generation.[62] In one particular scene, a group of fans from Dublin respond to the presence of second-generation supporters by mocking their English accents, and displaying a 'degree of bitterness' towards them.[63] What is most remarkable about this, of course, is the fact that supporting a sports team typically involves an unambiguous assertion of group homogeneity. Here, however, the Irish-born fans chose to deride a section of their own support, even in the face of the sporting 'opposition' (a number of Portuguese supporters were also present).

This policing of ethnic boundaries (which the second generation have implicitly transgressed) suggests a desire amongst some Irish-born people to deride the English-born offspring of Irish migrants. This desire has been observed in a range of situations,[64] many of which occur when the second generation are seen as 'English' and seek to correct this view. It is striking, though, that this should emerge when the second generation have expressly designated themselves as Irish, as was clear in Portugal. The territorialist stance of some of these Irish-born fans was, moreover, somewhat ironic, as the 'authentic' Irish football team that they were so anxious to protect from the (hybrid) second generation itself contained many second-generation players.[65] What this incongruity points to, of course, is the untenability of such exclusivist claims to authenticity. As David Morley and Kevin Robins have explained: 'In a world that is increasingly characterised by exile, migration and diaspora, with all the consequences of unsettling and hybridisation, there can be no place for such absolutism of the pure and authentic', and thus 'no recovery of an authentic homeland'.[66] The second-generation Irish are clearly alert to this point, and have stressed the untenability of such essentialist views. A study of the Irish in 1980s London detailed a 'prevailing second-generation attitude', articulated by one respondent:

> We are a different breed from that of our parents. Of course we know and enjoy Ireland, but London is our home, our city. We can't try to recreate a lost Ireland in the midst of 1980s London. Neither are we prepared to put up with the shabby treatment once meted out to our parents.[67]

Such comments were not, it seems, born of a wish to eschew Irishness, for this respondent would conclude: 'we believe that the only way the Irish community in London will ever be treated on a par with the home nation is through asserting its Irish identity'.[68]

This standpoint has been echoed by other second-generation Irish people, not least those who have engaged in the various debates staged by the *Irish Post*. In the midst of one such debate in the late 1990s, a Leeds-Irish letter-writer intervened by explaining:

> we are Irish but not in the sense of our parents or people in Ireland today. The identity of the Irish in Britain is an extension of the Irish in Ireland but it's not the same – there is a clear divergence. We have to recognise this.[69]

Such views had, significantly, been presaged by the *Irish Post* in its first editorial of the 1980s, which announced that

> The Eighties for us must be a decade of encouraging the second generation to grow up securely and unapologetically Irish abroad. This means no disloyalty to the country of their birth. Rather does it mean a *healthy sense of duality* ...[70]

This invocation of 'duality' was, of course, aimed at Irish-born people in England, who – as Breda Gray explains – often expect their offspring to polarise and 'identify as *either* English *or* Irish'.[71] This viewpoint has also informed the agencies of the British state, who in the 2001 census forced the second generation to 'choose between accepting the notion of complete assimilation and becoming simply "British" or rejecting the land of their upbringing [and] citizenship ... by asserting that they were unequivocally "Irish"'.[72]

It is perhaps time, then, that this section of the Irish diaspora was conceived beyond the narrow frames of, on the one hand, a wholly assimilated Englishness and, on the other, an essentialist Irishness. Such quasi-Celticist binary divisions are, of course, relics from (at least) the nineteenth century, and are consequently oblivious to the hybrid identities that marked the second half of the twentieth century.[73] In the very first survey of the second-generation Irish, conducted in 1970, the majority viewed themselves as 'neither Irish [n]or English, but as a mixture of both nationalities'.[74] Thirty-five years later, a survey of second-generation Irish adults observed that the majority sought 'recognition of [their] hybridity', with respondents wishing for 'a way of articulating allegiances to *more than one* domain' rather than insisting on being seen as *either* Irish *or* English.[75] What such conclusions point to, then, is a hyphenated Irish-Englishness that is not reducible to either dimension, and which facilitates a flexible, fluctuating and (sometimes) fractious identification with both.

The chapters that follow thus provide an account of the different means by which second-generation musicians have engaged with this 'in-betweenness' through their creative work and their engagements with audiences, the media and the music industry. The complex and nuanced picture of the second generation that emerges throughout the chapters serves to confound the simplistic view of this generation as either essentialist or assimilated. The book begins with an account of intervention and ethnic 'recovery' in the work of Kevin Rowland and Dexys Midnight Runners.

1

'Here is a Protest':
Intervention and Recovery in Dexys Midnight Runners

I had a need, in me, to find a way of saying that 'I'm Irish and I'm not shit'
Kevin Rowland[1]

In the closing moments of 'The Waltz', the final track on Dexys Midnight Runners' third and final album, *Don't Stand Me Down* (1985), the group's lead singer, Kevin Rowland, emits a striking gesture of unambiguous dissent. Mixed to the fore of the track's sparse sound (comprising guitar, violin and slow-paced snare), Rowland forcefully reiterates, in spoken-sung form, a simple vocal phrase – 'Here is a protest' – drawing out the sonoric contours of the latter word before an upbeat coda. Described by Sean O'Hagan as the album's – and thus the band's – 'defiant parting shot', this overt gesture of refusal served as a remarkably apposite postscript to Rowland's Dexys venture, which comprised a series of self-conscious interventions on Irish–English affairs.[2] This project was ensconced on the group's debut single, 'Dance Stance' (1979), in which Rowland's austere chorus – an unadorned litany of well-known Irish authors – supplied a strategic antidote to prevailing conceptions of the 'thick Paddy' in popular discourses.[3] Meanwhile, *Too-Rye-Ay* (1982), the group's second LP, offered a celebratory re-working of traditional Irish sounds as part of a self-conscious effort – on Rowland's part – to offset the negative value bestowed on Irishness in early Eighties Britain (an attitude encapsulated in Rowland's statement cited in the epigraph to this chapter). This interventionist ethos attained critical mass, however, on Dexys' third and final collection of songs (the aforementioned *Don't Stand Me Down*), which staged an oblique and emotive address to second-generation experience – and Anglo-Irish issues in general – before the upfront assertion of 'protest' outlined above.

This chapter explores the diverse means by which Rowland invoked and articulated Irish ethnicity in the work of Dexys Midnight Runners

(1978–86). There are currently no scholarly – and scarcely few 'serious' journalistic – accounts of Rowland's work in the vast body of writing on popular music. Moreover, in the few essays in which the singer has been cited or discussed, issues concerning Irishness are either sidelined or overlooked.[4] This is a remarkable oversight when one considers the salience of Irish concerns in Rowland's œuvre (not to mention the high level of attention the singer has enjoyed in popular music culture).[5] Rowland's significance for the present study cannot be overstated: he was unarguably the first second-generation Irish popular musician to deploy overtly Irish themes and styles, with Dexys' 'Dance Stance' predating the first Pogues record (usually credited with this achievement) by nearly five years.[6]

Charting the diverse modes of ethnicity that Rowland invoked in the Dexys project, the chapter discerns six key impulses that took shape across the band's output: first, a public rebuttal of popular prejudices about the Irish in England; second, a veneration of Brendan Behan, who emerges as a special figure of ethnic identification; third, a visual evocation of diaspora in the band's ancillary media; fourth, a wish to evoke Irish issues, in the face of a perceived repression or silence; fifth, the cultivation of an expressly 'Celtic' aesthetic during the group's second major period (1982–83); and sixth, the figuration of nostalgia, resistance and recovery – alongside overt assertions of Irish ethnicity – during the group's third and final phase (1983–86). Before I begin my account of Dexys' creative work, though, the chapter first locates Rowland, the band's lead singer, chief songwriter and 'major driving force', in his social and cultural context.[7]

Introducing Kevin Rowland and Dexys Midnight Runners

Kevin Rowland was born in Wolverhampton in the English Midlands in 1953. His parents, who had first settled in England at the end of the 1930s, came from Crossmolina in County Mayo. Like many Irish migrants of the period, Rowland's father found work in Britain's construction industry. However, after a decade and a half's English residence, the family returned (with five children, including a twelve-month-old Kevin) to Mayo. There they would remain for a further three years, moving back to England when Kevin was four. The youngster appears to have been somewhat unsettled by this relocation to the English west Midlands, suggesting that his mother's assurance that this was his birthplace only perplexed him further.

There was also, he recalls, a palpable tension on the streets of their new neighbourhood, and he immediately became aware of certain differences between his family and the other households in the street. Notwithstanding such feelings of dislocation, though, the Rowlands would settle in England for the long term, setting up home (once again) in the west Midlands before putting down more permanent roots in an Irish area of north London (to where they moved in 1964).[8]

After the family's relocation to England, Kevin attended Catholic schools, initiating an aspect of his upbringing that comprised long periods of service as an altar boy together with an apparently sincere attempt to join the priesthood. The singer would later explain that ten years of his life had been 'spent as a member of the Catholic Church', during which time he 'became about as close to the Church as a layman possibly can without actually taking the cloth' (the singer failed to pass an exam that was a prerequisite for priest-training college).[9] One of the principal functions of the Catholic education system in England has been to assimilate the English-born children of Irish migrants, converting second-generation pupils into what Mary Hickman calls 'useful citizens, loyal subjects … and good Catholics' by accentuating their religion at the expense of their ethnicity.[10] Nevertheless, Rowland's early dedication to Church life evidently failed to distract him from the expressly Irish aspects of his milieu. The singer would explain, for instance, that during his formative years in England he enjoyed a distinctively Irish upbringing, taking part in migrant cultural activities (such as Irish dancing), whilst being informed that he was Irish by his parents.[11] This experience was underlined by family visits to Ireland. 'I really liked it over there', Rowland recalls, stressing that he 'really connected with it'.[12] Back in England, meanwhile, the youngster acquired a keen sense of ethnic difference. This first emerged in Irish social clubs, where Rowland became aware of a migrant culture.

> It was the early 1960s, and I'm sitting in St Teresa's social club in Wolverhampton … And then all of a sudden there's all these sad, melancholy faces around, and they're drinking, and there's smoke everywhere, and they played 'Kevin Barry'. And my mum says to me, this song's banned in England. And I'm saying how can a song be banned? And she says, because it's about what the British did to the Irish. And then I realised, OK, we're kind of cut off a bit.[13]

This sense of being 'cut off' was underlined in English schoolrooms, where Rowland observed certain differences amongst his classmates.

> I was aware that some of the other kids at school were Irish, and yet

some of them were English. And the English kids seemed smarter dressed. They seemed to have more money. The Irish kids had bigger families. The English kids looked more sedate. They looked more calm, settled. The Irish kids were a bit more lively, less contained, and scruffy generally.[14]

This sensitivity to Irish difference was heightened by the prejudice that Rowland saw his parents encounter in England.[15] Such experiences – in which the second generation see their parents being subjected to anti-Irish expressions – have had what Hickman et al. call 'a searing impact' on this generation's consciousness.[16] An awareness of such prejudice did not, however, prevent Rowland from identifying with Irishness in his adult life, with the singer maintaining Irish citizenship, receiving Dublin newspapers at his London home, and visiting Ireland on a regular basis.[17]

Prior to becoming a professional musician, Rowland had followed his father into the construction industry, receiving tuition at the Willesden School of Building (in north London) before working – in his words – as a 'navvy on a building site'.[18] The singer's first experience of musical performance thus came at the (relatively late) age of twenty-one, when Rowland took on guitar-playing duties in his brother's country and western band (a genre especially popular with the Irish in Britain).[19] Although music does not appear to have been central to the family's daily life, Rowland does recall his parents occasionally singing Irish songs, which he says he enjoyed.[20] 'My mum used to sing all them old songs', he explains, noting 'those things got quite deep in, I suppose.'[21] This exposure to Irish music was enhanced during visits to Ireland, where he heard records by The Clancy Brothers, as well as Irish songs sung by his cousins, which he enjoyed and was 'interested to hear'.[22] Despite this awareness of Irish music, when Rowland came to perform music professionally he had little interest in pursuing an overtly Irish style. 'I couldn't have done just an Irish thing', he explains;

> I couldn't have done it. This country's [Britain] had too much of a massive influence on me. I loved this country. I loved growing up here. I loved all those cool kids in north-west London who were all listening to black music, underground music. It's a massive part of me, all that.[23]

In this context, Rowland points to the multi-ethnic matrix of his metropolitan milieu, in which the second-generation Irish mixed with working-class English as well as second-generation Greeks and Italians, all of whom shared an attraction to reggae and soul. For Rowland, then, the encounter between a certain Irish migrant culture and the diverse aesthetic forms of (multi-ethnic) Britain would play a crucial role in moulding the tastes of the second generation. 'It shaped us', the singer explains, with reference to the urban culture of his English milieu. 'We embraced it.'[24]

With the sounds, styles and subcultures of post-war Britain – alongside a migrant Irish dimension – shaping Rowland's peculiar habitus, it was the host country's popular music culture (rather than an Irish 'traditional' culture) that he sought as an expressive platform. 'I wanted to be part of it', he explains, 'and up the front of it, what was going on here [in England]', noting that 'second-generation Irish Catholics, from John Lydon on, have been at the cutting edge of British popular culture', rather than allied to an Irish ethnic culture. Indeed, the 'significant thing' for Rowland 'about the second-generation Irish is their contribution to *British* culture. The fact that we're all, you know ... up the front.'[25]

This desire to be at the 'front' of contemporary British culture did not, however, equate with a wish to eschew Irish ethnicity. Thus, while Rowland felt an ambivalence towards the more essentialist aspects of Irish migrant culture, he nevertheless sought to maintain an affiliation with Ireland alongside his engagement with urban England (hence the singer's wish to have 'an Irish heart *and* [be] part of what's going on here').[26] With this dynamic in mind, then, it made little sense for Rowland to pursue an expressly Irish aesthetic in his early musical endeavours. His work on the country-music live circuit was therefore followed by a range of diverse projects, including a short stint with 'art-rock' act Lucy and the Lovers, before Rowland turned – like Shane MacGowan and Steven Morrissey – to England's punk scene during its watershed year of 1977.[27] Rowland's attraction to punk centred, says Richard White, on the figure of John Lydon, and Rowland would go on to be viewed as Lydon's 'post-punk, voice of protest successor'.[28] Lydon's Irish ethnicity was, it seems, not lost on the young Rowland. 'I must have read somewhere that he was Irish', the singer explains, 'and I was pleased about that, because you weren't hearing about people who were second-generation Irish.'[29] Rowland's own contribution to punk, however, was a somewhat undistinguished genre single by Birmingham-based band The Killjoys. With Rowland supplying guitar and lead vocals, this song – 'Johnny Won't Get To Heaven' (1977) – issued a rejoinder to Lydon's 'Johnny Rotten' persona whilst appearing to ape the latter's vocal style. Although they generated a fair amount of press attention, the band remained a minor punk presence, and by the middle of 1978 The Killjoys had dissolved.[30]

By this stage, punk's vitality had fallen into decline, with its ostensibly dissident sounds being incorporated into the mainstream culture industries.[31] Against this post-punk backdrop, Rowland sought out fresh musical avenues, cultivating an unexpected (and, at the time, highly unfashionable) interest in Sixties soul acts such as Otis Redding, Geno Washington and Sam and Dave. During the early months of 1978, the singer drafted plans with fellow west Midlands musician Kevin Archer for an eight-piece soul-based band (comprising saxophone, trumpet and trombone, as well as standard rock instrumentation) based on the 1960s ensembles associated with Stax and Tamla Motown. After an array of painstaking auditions – for a projected 'new wave soul group' – in the summer of 1978, the new outfit began rehearsals at Rowland's parents' house, before making their live debut (as Dexys Midnight Runners) at Digbeth Irish Centre in December of that year.[32] Taking their name from an illegal amphetamine called Dexedrine that had been popular with followers of northern soul (the drug apparently supplied worn-out dancers with a source of late-night energy – hence, 'midnight runners'), the pharmaceutical provenance of the band's moniker was somewhat at odds with Rowland's puritanical stance on alcohol and recreational drugs, a point to which I shall return.[33] Leaving aside such incongruities, the emergent Dexys had, by the end of 1979, secured a recording contract with Oddball, an independent label licensed to EMI.[34]

With unfashionable Sixties-style horns at the fore of the new group's sound, this first incarnation of Dexys was largely of a piece – despite Rowland's claim that they had 'nothing in common with other musical groups'[35] – with the late-Seventies 'mod resurgence', a passing revival in which, as Simon Reynolds explains,

> Taut and punchy horns replaced screeching, self-indulgent guitars as the lead instrument – trombones and trumpets in 2-Tone's case, mass brass with Sixties soul-inspired bands like Dexys Midnight Runners ... Keyboards came next in the hierarchy, supplying a choppy Hammond organ pulse, or rollicking, rinky-dinky embellishments. Guitar was mostly relegated to a minor role – low in the mix, scratchy rhythm playing, *no* solos.[36]

Within this broad framework, Dexys sought to combine – in the words of bass player Pete Williams – the 'brassy sound' of soul with the 'aggression and immediacy of punk',[37] yielding what Reynolds has termed a 'toughened version of the high-energy, horn-driven Atlantic–Stax/Volt-style soul of the mid-Sixties', with 'staccato brass blasts and jabbing, jousting fanfares' effecting a 'pugilistic' sound.[38] This somewhat improbable fusion of punk and soul offered a unique backcloth for Rowland's highly mannered – and often quite abrasive – vocal style, leading critics to note Dexys' 'iconoclastic conflagration of Stax horns and Anglo-Irish angst'.[39] Rowland's singing (which evinced an obvious debt to the 'wavering yelp' of Chairmen of the Board vocalist General Johnson)[40] was, as Reynolds suggests, 'neither strong nor pleasing' but conveyed, say Rowland's band-mates, 'forcefulness' *and* 'vulnerability'.[41]

Perhaps betraying his apprenticeship in punk, Rowland's vocal also evinced an audibly regional inflection, with his west Midlands accent becoming especially pronounced during Dexys' numerous spoken-word sections.[42] On occasion, however, the singer's idiosyncratic amalgam of melancholy and rage (his early vocals were heard as a 'howl of anguished, angry lyrics'[43]) rendered certain song words incomprehensible.

With regard to his public persona, meanwhile, Rowland cast himself as a serious, combative and somewhat morose figure situated on the margins of popular culture (Dexys had a policy, according to *NME*, 'of wanting nothing to do with the rest of the pop and rock world').[44] In early interviews, then, Rowland was described as 'stubborn' and 'uncompromising', with his contrary persona being likened to that of Johnny Rotten.[45] Despite such prickliness, the 'physically unprepossessing' singer also managed to exude, notes Reynolds, a 'weird charisma'.[46] If this charisma was in evidence at the group's live shows, it was often counterpoised by confrontation, with Rowland insisting that fans pay close attention to the group's performance instead of engaging in discussion, dancing or drinking. Occasionally, this led to the singer physically threatening hecklers and jumping into the audience to challenge disobedient fans.[47]

The singer's recalcitrance towards professional orthodoxies was best evidenced, however, by an outright refusal to partake in media interviews throughout much of his career with Dexys, with the band instead issuing a series of polemical communiqués in the pages of the music press.[48] The oppositional persona fashioned by these press messages was only exacerbated by Rowland's repute for physical violence (the singer attacked one journalist that he felt had distorted his views).[49] A rather more subtle means by which Rowland signalled his dissent from pop convention was through a public disavowal of drink and recreational drugs, with the singer invoking a highly unpopular alcohol ban on both musicians and fans during Dexys' live shows. He would thus 'go mad' – explain former band-mates – if he discovered them drinking, and issued press releases warning that 'light refreshments' only would be sold at concerts, stressing that Dexys' shows would be 'completely "dry" … with

Photograph: David Corio

no alcoholic beverages on sale at any of the venues'.[50] In stark contrast
to the scenes of excess more commonly associated with rock musicians
backstage, Rowland engaged in a strict period of fasting for several hours
prior to live performance, with the only sanctioned stimulant being a
supply of hot tea, a beverage with which Dexys would become inextrica-
bly associated through consumption of the drink during interviews, and
via a formal demand for large quantities of it in their backstage 'rider'.[51]
Thus, when journalists enquired about the lack of booze in the band's
dressing room, Rowland replied 'we're big tea drinkers'.[52]

The group's visual style, meanwhile, was at variance with the norms
of late-Seventies pop, drawing on a self-conscious 'New York dock-
ers' look (comprising woollen hats, hard boots and donkey jackets that
Rowland had sourced from films such as *Mean Streets* (Scorsese, 1973)
and *On the Waterfront* (Kazan, 1954). While the latter film had overtly
Catholic (and covertly Irish-American) characters and themes, Rowland
seems to have been more interested (at this particular time) in staging
a vaguely Italian (rather than distinctly Irish) ethnic style, adopting
the stage name Carlo Rolan, and employing Italian national colours in
the group's visual media, prompting critics to speculate on the implied
Italian provenance of his 'dark pigment': 'is Kevin Italian, Irish or both?'
asked one writer.[53]

Despite Rowland's attempt to evoke an Italian-American docker
aesthetic, critics would discern, in Dexys' attire, the style of 'itinerant
labourers', and Rowland would concede that his band resembled, for

certain observers, a group of 'navvies', a vernacular term used to denote the stereotypical Irish male in post-war Britain.[54] With this in mind, the public perception of Dexys as navvies is particularly noteworthy, not simply for Rowland's earlier experience as a 'navvy on a building site' but also – and perhaps more importantly – because the band's first recorded output, 'Dance Stance' (1979), was a self-conscious riposte to popular (mis)conceptions about the Irish in 1970s Britain.[55]

'Dance Stance', anti-racism and the 'Irish joke'

A particularly virulent strain of anti-Irish humour gained currency in the 1970s, with 'thick Paddy' jokes becoming prevalent in popular discourses. A scholarly survey of language and humour at this time explained that

> [the] most pervasive humour theme in Britain today … is centred upon the supposed simple-mindedness of the Irish population. Irishmen feature as fools in a vast number of so-called 'Irish' jokes; these jokes would be more appositely labelled '*anti*-Irish'. On the surface at least, the success of the most modern Irish jokes depends upon a salient stereotype concerning the low intellectual prowess of the Irish.[56]

This purported 'humour theme', which was particularly evident in popular entertainment, became a special source of anxiety for Rowland, who felt affronted by the casual expression of anti-Irish sentiment in everyday English life, not least in the work places and social spaces of his (then) home town of Birmingham.[57] The singer recalls that inhabitants of this city would call Irish people 'pigs' or 'duck eggs' (the latter have thicker shells than hen eggs), and his residence in this locale appears to have supplied an 'extra edge', as Shane MacGowan puts it, to Rowland's outlook.[58] This west Midlands city had been the target of a vicious IRA bomb attack in 1974, which killed twenty-one and injured 162 of the city's inhabitants.[59] In the immediate aftermath of the bombings (described by Robert Kee as 'the most savage act of terrorism ever experienced in Britain'[60]), Irish people were subjected to increasing discrimination. In Birmingham, Irish organisations and individuals became, explains K.I. Ziesler,

> the targets for abuse and obscene phone calls; stones and a petrol bomb were thrown through the windows of the Irish Centre; an Irish pub …

was badly damaged by another petrol bomb; two lorries belonging to an Irish construction firm were damaged; and a Roman Catholic junior school and a church, the Holy Family in Small Heath, were attacked. At the British Leyland works in Longbridge, where some 3,000 Irish were employed, there was a walk-out by car assembly workers.[61]

Such forms of prejudice (which conflated IRA actions with Irish ethnicity) made little attempt to distinguish between Irish-born migrants and their English-born children. An Irish mother in Seventies Britain thus explained to a survey on migrant housing conditions that after the Birmingham bombs her children had not been able to 'play outside the house' as they were likely to be 'attacked by British children and beaten'.[62] Similarly, the sociologist John Gabriel records that Irish-descended people became 'the object of attacks' in English schools both 'during and after IRA bombing campaigns'.[63] Second-generation Irish people have also recalled the physical abuse that they faced in the period after the Birmingham bombs.[64] It seems clear, then, that Irishness came to accrue, in late 1970s Britain, especially negative values (not least the 'horrible evil thing' of IRA bomb attacks, as the Birmingham-born, second-generation Irish politician Clare Short would put it), with public displays of Irish ethnicity, such as St Patrick's Day parades, consequently becoming less common.[65]

The associated expressions of anti-Irish sentiment – which found a socially acceptable outlet in the so-called 'Irish joke' – became a cause of concern for Rowland, who felt compelled to register his 'sick[ness]' and 'disgust' at the comic rendering of the 'thick Paddy' in contemporary British life.[66] This 'humour-theme' had now extended beyond the realm of comedic entertainment (such as television shows and live stand-up routines)[67] into the popular music culture with which Rowland was engaged. Indeed, one of the singer's early band-mates is alleged to have displayed a penchant for 'Irish jokes'.[68] More significant, though, was the upfront exposition of pernicious Irish caricatures that emerged in the British music press, a branch of the mainstream media that had aligned itself with anti-racist politics.[69] The high-profile paper *Sounds*, for example (which published a special 'anti-racism' issue in 1978), rehearsed a plethora of 'Irish jokes' during the late 1970s, printing sketches of an 'Irish' skateboard (with square-shaped wheels), expressing overt antipathy to Irish people en masse, and mocking the country's best-known rock musicians as (variously) 'bog trotters' and 'mad Paddies'. An especially telling review of Dublin punk band The Radiators From Space scoffed at the very notion of Irish people performing popular music, enquiring: 'Irish punks? Will it start "One, tree, faw, two"?'[70]

Such humour was evidently well received by large sections of the British public: one publishing house sold nearly 600,000 'Irish joke' books between 1977 and 1979.[71] As the anthropologist Edmund Leach would explain – at the time of the release of 'Dance Stance' – the prototypical 'Paddy' that emerged in such books was

> not so much a figure of fun as an object of contempt merging into deep hostility. He is a drink-addicted moron, reared in the bog, who wears his rubber boots at all times, cannot read or write, and constantly reverses the logic of ordinary common sense.[72]

The prevalence of such caricatures served to engender, as Liz Curtis points out, 'an instantaneous association' in the popular consciousness 'between Irish nationality and stupidity'.[73] This was especially true of British youth, who perceived the Irish to be 'ignorant' or 'thick'.[74] Such was the conflation of Irishness and idiocy in daily life that many second-generation Irish people would begin to introject ideas of Irish obtuseness, a point confirmed by the sociologist Marie Gillespie and the popular singer Siobhan Fahey (of the 1980s girl group Bananarama), who recalls that she 'absorbed some pretty negative messages' about herself from the host culture, particularly the incrimination: 'You're a paddy, you're thick.'[75] In a similar vein, Rowland would go through 'a process of wondering if it was true' (that the Irish were innately unintelligent), even asking his parents: 'Are Irish people supposed to be stupid?'[76] The singer also notes that many second-generation people would seek to perform 'Irish jokes' (which arguably points to the internalisation, amongst this generation, of ideas of Irish idiocy). With this point in mind, Rowland would increasingly feel that he had 'kept quiet too many times' in the face of anti-Irish asides, which by the late 1970s had become, for him, intolerable.[77]

It was in this hostile context, then, that Rowland deployed his band's debut single 'Dance Stance' as a strategic public riposte, assailing the myth of the 'thick Paddy' by issuing what Gavin Martin called 'the most simple [and] direct … thing anyone has had to say about "Ireland" in the past few years', with Rowland 'set[ting] the country's solid literary heritage against the devious and supercilious practice of telling "Irish jokes"'.[78] Impelled by exultant brass motifs, Rowland's 'anguished vocal' and 'finger-pointing lyrics' convey, for Richard White, a 'menacing air of injustice'.[79] The song's memorable centrepiece, though, is the collectively-sung chorus section in which Rowland catalogues well-known Irish authors, such as Oscar Wilde, Brendan Behan, Seán O'Casey and Edna O'Brien. Although such listing activities can be seen as chauvinistic in certain contexts (in that they serve to chronicle, in the words of Sabina

Sharkey, 'so many great Irish personae' to '"prove" to "outsiders" how gifted, clever or musical the Irish are'),[80] Rowland's endeavour was born of a rather different desire, being prompted by the fact that people were 'still calling us [the Irish] stupid', as Shane MacGowan relates.[81]

Thus, Rowland's song words – which punctuated the writers' names with briskly delivered spoken-sung interjections ('They never talk about …'; 'They don't know about …'; 'They don't care about …') – 'savaged people', says Reynolds, 'who tell jokes about stupid Irishmen but don't know about Oscar Wilde, Samuel Beckett, Brendan Behan and the rest'.[82] Rowland laid stress on the song's 'message' in interviews, expounding, in the aforementioned *Sounds*: 'I wrote [the song] because Irish jokes made me sick. A lot of people believe all that stuff. I'm sure the BBC or Lew Grade could stop it but they won't. Anyway that's what the lists of great Irish authors are in it for – to show the other side.'[83] Elsewhere, the singer would state that the song was 'about how everybody in England talks about the Irish like they're not human', adding that the country was 'saturated with all these comedians telling jokes about thick Irishmen', a humour-theme that, for Rowland, was 'really malicious'. 'It's supposed to be light-hearted', the singer relayed, 'but underneath the surface, it's not.'[84] This interventionist stance – described by White as an 'act of catharsis' – was underlined by a set of press adverts that featured graphic illustrations of well-known books by Irish writers.[85] Consequently, 'Dance Stance' came to be viewed by critics and fans as Rowland's pop-cultural 'protest against "Paddy" jokes',[86] with its title serving as a pun on the notion of 'stance' as physical pose and critical position.[87]

Released as a single in November 1979, Dexys' debut disc would reach number forty in the British singles chart in February of the following year, occasioning a television appearance on the BBC's *Top of the Pops*.[88] The success of the single was assisted by Dexys' participation in the celebrated 'Two Tone Tour' of 1979. Originating in the west Midlands city of Coventry, the Two Tone record label and associated 'scene' was centred on two multi-ethnic ska-based acts, The Specials and The Selecter.[89] With its 'ideals of racial harmony and musical hybridity', Two Tone became identified with the anti-racist initiatives of Rock Against Racism and the Anti-Nazi League, offering a popular-musical riposte (that, for Reynolds, 'did more for anti-racism than a thousand Anti-Nazi League speeches') to far-right organisations such as the National Front, which at the time was seeking to increase its appeal among white British youth.[90] The anti-racist ethos of Two Tone became pronounced during the label's nationwide tour in autumn 1979 (by which time it had gained a mainstream profile), on which Dexys appeared as the opening act for scene leaders The Specials and The Selecter.[91] The obvious disparities between Dexys and the other acts (Rowland's band were neither ska-based nor on Two Tone) were assuaged by shared regional affiliations (in the English Midlands) and ideological concerns (such as anti-racism). Despite Simon Frith's claim that Dexys were incongruous on the tour, the band were largely embraced by the Two Tone audience, and were expected to record a single for the label.[92]

Dexys' appearances at the Two Tone concerts coincided with the release of 'Dance Stance', and the song – with its 'searing indictment of anti-Irish racism'[93] – thus became associated with the scene's anti-racist ethos, serving as a specifically Irish intervention in its multi-ethnic scheme. Rowland's colleagues recall his 'very strong anti-racist streak', suggesting that the singer was 'very conscious that what people had said [in the 1950s] about black people was being said about Irish people coming [to Britain]'.[94] Two Tone participants also recall that 'Dance Stance' furnished the project with 'an uncommon angle on the race issue', noting the record's 'outraged attack on the bigotry directed at the Irish community'.[95] In a similar vein, fans of Dexys would stress that 'Dance Stance' prompted them to reconsider their views not only of the Irish but also of other ethnic groups.[96] This point was noted at the time by certain journalists, who saw the song's response to 'Irish jokes' as a comment on 'the whole set of attitudes in Britain towards other minorities'.[97] Indeed, Rowland would confirm this view, extending his account of the Irish towards other minority groups: 'I know loads of people who believe that Irish people are thick', he explained. 'It's fucking *ridiculous*, like the thing that Jews are tight, or Pakis [a pejorative term for South Asian people in Britain] smell – England is riddled with that kind of shit.'[98]

In the ethical matrix of Two Tone, then, Dexys served to emphasise the issue of anti-Irish prejudice, evoking the (often overlooked) experience of the immigrant Irish in a multicultural frame. From an expressly second-generation perspective, 'Dance Stance' would subvert the ideas of Irishness that prevailed in the popular realm. Rather than acceding to this negative charge, the song inverted the alleged inferiority, supplying an emphatic antidote to hostile caricatures, and imparting an alternate mode of Irishness based on esteemed qualities (such as literariness, creativity, erudition). In a setting (1970s Britain) that offered the second generation 'no positive reinforcement' of Irish ethnicity,[99] 'Dance Stance' appeared to express – as Cáit O'Riordan would explain – 'so much' about 'finding out who you are' as a second-generation Irish youth.[100] This is particularly noteworthy, as Rowland had sought, in his work, to engage an expressly *second-generation* perspective on Irishness (distinct from that of Irish-born migrants, and the Irish in Ireland).[101] In the process, his œuvre would serve as a source for other Irish-descended people (such as O'Riordan).

Despite this point, though, Rowland had not contrived to become an icon for the second generation, and was more concerned, it would seem, with a broader (British) audience. He recalls, for example, being told that he had become 'a bit of a hero to the second-generation Irish':

> And I was thinking, 'oh, wow', but that wasn't my aim. That wasn't what I was trying to do, at all. I remember thinking 'oh, that's a nice thing', a by-product of it, really. It certainly wasn't what I was trying to do.[102]

What Rowland was rather more interested in, then, was 'trying to show some of this [Irish] culture' to the British so as to – in his words – 'correct the misunderstanding'. He was especially gratified, therefore, to see his British fan base noting the list of Irish authors that he had composed for 'Dance Stance'. 'I remember walking through a university bar', the singer explains, 'and people didn't really know who we were, and a female English student was singing the chorus [of "Dance Stance"]. I remember just getting a real buzz out of that … the fact that she was singing Irish writers.' He was similarly pleased to hear his English band-mates, at least one of whom had a taste for 'Irish jokes' – and was thus part of his reason for writing the song – singing the writers' names.[103] Other English fans felt compelled to consult the Irish writers who were cited in the song. In this context, John Aizlewood recalls that he 'started to discover these people, most of whom [he'd] never heard of'. He says, 'I read Behan's *Borstal Boy*, Beckett's *Waiting for Godot*, and anything I could find by Edna O'Brien', adding that he also 'discovered who Laurence Sterne and Seán O'Casey were'.[104] The song's refashioning of Irish culture would come to be seen as a sort of signal post for the subsequent reassessment of all things Irish in Britain. As Charlie Reid (of the Scottish folk-rock band The Proclaimers) has explained: 'In 1980, in Britain, the Irish were despised. Now [in 2007] everyone's proud of that culture. Dexys led the way by championing Irish culture on "Dance Stance".'[105]

Press protests, public personae and 'pissed Paddy'

The interventionist signal of 'Dance Stance' was followed by a chain of supplementary gestures throughout the early 1980s. The best known of these was an exchange between Rowland and the English journalist

Julie Burchill. The latter's repute was largely based on public contrariness, but she showed a special predilection, during the early 1980s, for anti-Irish commentary via a series of adverse editorials on the Irish in the celebrated 'style bible' *The Face*.[106] These ill-tempered expositions were underlined by the upfront expression of anti-Irish sentiment, not least Burchill's announcement in the London journal *Time Out* that 'I hate the Irish, I think they're appalling.'[107]

Interestingly, this journalist's polemic had first taken shape as a critique of 'Dance Stance', with Burchill issuing an acerbic satire of Rowland's list of authors, supplanting this litany with a catalogue of Welsh cultural figures (her article was written on St David's Day). What the occasion of this Celtic festival afforded Burchill, then, was a chance to expound her ideas on Irish inferiority. 'The merits often ascribed to the Southern Irish', she explained – citing 'literacy, articulacy, drunkenness, recklessness [and] rebellion' as purportedly 'Irish' characteristics – actually 'belong to the Welsh'. The cultural achievements of the 'Southern Irish' since the end of the Second World War ('the one when the Southern Irish sided with Mr Hitler, *that* War') were thus reduced to the caricatures of 'Edna O'Woman and Phil O'Lizzy' – in other words, 'a real wagonload of slop, schmaltz and slush'.[108] This diatribe would later extend to the Troubles in Northern Ireland via a scathing attack on the then recent IRA 'dirty protest': according to Burchill, this was a 'quite dazzlingly typical Catholic indulgence with all the overtones of babyishness and self-loathing'.[109] Meanwhile, the Catholic Church was zealously (and erroneously) taken to task for – in her words – 'never com[ing] anywhere near excommunicating the butchers of the IRA'.[110]

This serialised tirade on Irish issues eventually received a sharp riposte from Rowland, with an open letter to *The Face* serving as the singer's most overt mode of intervention yet. 'I was just boiling over with rage reading that stuff', Rowland recalls. 'I just had to write it. It made me really angry.'[111] Deploying a rather polemical – not to say essentialist – position of his own, the singer boldly assailed the 'inbred aversion to all things Irish' in British culture, registering his rebuttal of Burchill's biased affront: 'one can only take so much bullshit', he said, 'even from one as blundering, brutal and ineffectual as your "Little England" self'. Contesting the journalist's errors on Irish issues, Rowland again invoked the literary figures that he had extolled on 'Dance Stance', making special reference to Brendan Behan, who would serve as a key icon of Irish affinity in Dexys' œuvre.[112]

I will return to the theme of Behan shortly. First, I will address what might be seen as an ancillary aspect of Rowland's interventionist outlook:

his well-known abstemiousness. As already mentioned, Rowland would choose to abstain from alcohol and recreational drugs before and during Dexys' live shows, adhering instead to a fitness regime that often comprised public displays of group exercise.[113] This incongruous display of self-discipline and restraint was partly born, for Rowland at least, of his allegiance to Catholicism, or what he has called his personal 'understanding' of what it meant to be Catholic.[114] Notwithstanding the provenance of this purportedly 'Catholic' sensibility, it would become a crucial strand of Rowland's persona, receiving special emphasis in interviews and song lyrics, as well as in the group's visual style. Rowland would inform critics, for instance, of the 'pure Catholicism' of his psyche, insisting: 'it's there for life in me, the Catholic religion. I'll defend it against anybody.'[115] Meanwhile, songs such as 'Let's Make This Precious' (1982) and 'Until I Believe In My Soul' (1982) implored their addressees to 'bare' their 'hearts' and 'cleanse' their 'souls', evincing a highly disciplined stance on spiritual self-sacrifice ('I will punish my body, until I believe in my soul').[116] Such sentiments – described by White as a 'personal entreaty on Catholicism' – were also invoked by the group's sartorial codes, not least the austere hooded coats that Rowland felt conveyed a 'monastic' look to complement what he called the 'religious feel to some of the music'.[117]

Quasi-Catholic evocations of faith, temperance and the 'soul' were somewhat at odds with the norms of Britain's popular-cultural milieu in the early 1980s. The self-conscious asceticism that Rowland pursued at this time might, however – like 'Dance Stance' and the 'open letter' – be seen (at least in part) as a response to notions of Irishness in British culture, not least the stock Irish drinker in popular discourses.[118] The singer's abstinence could, of course, have been born of diverse issues, but Rowland would make clear his distaste for displays of Irish inebriation. 'I detest all that', the singer announced with reference to The Pogues. 'It's just playing the drunken Paddy for the Saxon and I detest it. I find it personally repulsive. Irish people have never been about that, it's just a British myth.'[119] Leaving aside this citation of the 'Saxon', the point to note is that Rowland's sobriety, when viewed in the light of these comments – and the interventionist schemes he employed elsewhere – appeared to act as a rejoinder to the 'drunk Paddy' caricature that prevailed in popular culture. The singer felt that there were 'more dimensions' to Irishness than such caricatures allowed, and with this in mind he sought 'to do something different'.[120] Thus, if 'Dance Stance' fashioned 'literary Paddy' as a critical rejoinder to 'thick Paddy', then its singer's pious persona supplied an attendant ascetic riposte to the associated typecast of 'pissed Paddy'.

Rowland's two-pronged counter-attack on popular Irish caricatures (with idiocy and alcoholism displaced by the erudite and ascetic) was itself indebted to rather essentialist – though conceivably less disabling – ideas about Irishness distilled in the hubristic concept of 'saints and scholars'.[121] It would be churlish to rebuke Rowland for unwittingly reviving this benign old stereotype in his obviously earnest endeavour to cancel out another, especially in the milieu of Eighties Britain. Nevertheless, there was – at the very least – an obvious discrepancy between Rowland's dislike of the 'drunken Paddy' and his concomitant wish to revere one of that type's most famous purveyors, Brendan Behan, who became a special figure of Irish identification in Dexys' output.

Behan, 'boozing' and migration

Behan played a crucial role in Rowland's association with Irishness, with the name-check in 'Dance Stance' being followed by an advert for the group's second single 'Geno' (1980) featuring the cover of *Borstal Boy*. Meanwhile, the sleeve art of Dexys' debut album, *Searching for the Young Soul Rebels* (1980), included a brief citation of Behan's text.[122] Rowland would go on to extol *Borstal Boy* as his favourite book, and to record a song – 'Reminisce Part One' (1983) – that addressed his quest to locate 'the spirit of Brendan Behan'.[123] Such was the extent of Rowland's association with this writer that Britain's leading music paper, the *NME*, assigned a full-page article to the Behan–Dexys nexus. 'Who was this loud-mouthed Irish drunk and why does Kevin Rowland keep going on about him?' asked the paper lightheartedly before detailing numerous Behan references in Rowland's songs.[124]

Interestingly, another English-born musician of Irish descent, Shane MacGowan, would embark on his own revival of Behan in the early 1980s, and it is perhaps worth noting that MacGowan felt that it was his – rather than Rowland's – literary allusions that had led to the writer's recuperation in popular-cultural discourses.[125] Dexys' debut single had, however, preceded the first Pogues release by nearly five years. In any case, a succession of further articles continued to trace Behan's influence on both MacGowan and Rowland, with the *NME* suggesting that while Behan had served as a 'guiding light' for Dexys and The Pogues, it was clearly the latter that had come 'closest to the Behan lifestyle, moving twixt Camden Town and King's Cross, dazed, drunk and inspired'.[126]

There is little doubt that MacGowan took the Behan template rather more literally than Rowland, as the latter espoused a far more sober form of literary homage. Indeed, the shared concerns of these respective musicians belied their bands' radically different approaches and styles. Dexys' highly choreographed live shows thus had little in common with the alcohol-fuelled ambience of Pogues concerts, with the former being staged in theatrical venues at which fans were often denied the opportunity to imbibe.[127] With this in mind, it would seem that Rowland's interest in Behan was based more on the writer's repute as an 'Irish-in-England' cultural figure than in the mere fact of Behan's Irishness or his notoriety for heavy drinking (which MacGowan, in stark contrast, would take on wholesale).[128] As Niall Cunningham explains, Behan enjoyed a special 'resonance' with the second generation, and many Irish-descended creative figures, not least the actor/director Kathy Burke, have expressed an identification with the writer.[129] 'If you were second-generation Irish', Burke explains, 'there was enough great writing and enough great people to choose from if you wanted to understand your roots and my main man was Brendan'. Dismissing the writer's 'drinking' and 'rebellion', Burke relates that it was Behan's 'warmth' and 'wit' that drew her to his work.[130] In a similar vein, Rowland's investment in Behan lay in the affinity that the author had expressed, in *Borstal Boy*, towards his English peers. 'One of the interesting things', recalls Rowland, 'was that he really related to those English guys in the borstal, who were kind of cool, street, London kids.'[131]

An attendant concern with transient life in England was evinced in Dexys' visual media, which often evoked the themes of migration and displacement. A particularly notable instance of this trope was based in a pervasive motif (across an array of sleeves, iconography and attendant paraphernalia) that offered an overt – and in the first instance Irish – evocation of displacement. The striking green-tinted sleeve of the group's debut album, *Searching for the Young Soul Rebels* – based on a black-and-white photograph of a Belfast boy carrying a suitcase and holdall bag – served as the first illustration of this itinerant symbol. Rowland had asked the band's art director to locate 'a picture of unrest' for the record sleeve, and added that an image with Irish resonance would be ideal. He was, then, 'secretly glad' that the sleeve image had been sourced from Ireland.[132] Anthony O'Shaughnessy, the boy in the photograph, would later explain that the picture was taken during the turbulent days that followed the British government's introduction of internment (in which suspects could be held without trial) in 1971, which prompted one of the greatest residential evacuations since the Second World War, with large numbers of people fleeing their homes across Belfast.[133] The photograph – which, as O'Shaughnessy points out, provoked a clear set of questions: 'Where was I going? Where was I going to sleep? What does the future hold?' – was taken during a shoot-out between the IRA and the British army, and the original image featured, as Aizlewood notes, a now absent group of soldiers 'wielding guns at the boy', who many felt bore a resemblance to 'the young Kevin Rowland'.[134]

Leaving aside the implied association between Dexys' lead singer and the Irish evacuee, this photograph set up a ubiquitous visual trope in the group's graphic style, featuring a dislocated figure – like the boy on the album sleeve – carting luggage in the midst of flight. Its emphasis on transience and travel – a central motif, as Avtar Brah has explained, of diaspora experience – would, then, come to imbue the band's visual media.[135] The trope in question (which can also be seen in the work of second-generation Irish visual artists) is evinced on the labels and sleeves of numerous albums and singles, as well as in attendant ephemera, such as tour programmes and press adverts.[136] Meanwhile, the videos for 'Geno' (1980), 'Celtic Soul Brothers' (1982) and 'Come On Eileen' (1982) portray the band as nomads, while 'Knowledge Of Beauty' (1985) depicts Rowland as an itinerant loner.[137] Such was the extent of this trope in the band's visual media that they even considered calling one of their albums 'Hey, Where Are You Going With That Suitcase?', a self-consciously jocular comment on the import of this object in Dexys' graphic style.[138] Such evocations of travel and flight served to conjure the dynamics of diaspora life, enacting a ceaseless condition of movement in which there was – quite literally – no *place* like home.[139]

Rowland explains that he felt, at this time, that nowhere was 'home' to him, and adds that he felt drawn to images of movement and dislocation. And if such transient motifs were only obliquely Irish, they had been born – at least in their first incarnation (on the debut LP sleeve) – of Rowland's wish to evoke Irish issues in a manner that was somewhat covert. 'I wanted to get in anything Irish that I could', he recalls (of the album sleeve), without 'doing an Irish thing': 'I wanted to express it', he reflects, suggesting that 'it felt subversive' because of (what he viewed as) the prevailing repression, at that time, of all things Irish in Britain.[140]

An additional means by which this wish was materialised was in the unusual choice of venue at which Dexys concluded their 1980 UK tour, with Rowland electing to stage this show at an Irish dance hall in north London.[141] Such venues had served, as Enda Delaney explains, as a communal 'focal point' for the Irish in post-war Britain.[142] It is clear that Dexys would have had access at this time to several mainstream theatres, having recently achieved a number-one single in the UK chart.[143] However, Rowland insisted on playing the London show in an Irish community venue, the National Ballroom. Located in Kilburn, the capital's best-known Irish district, it had never before hosted a rock event (Dexys played between shows by Frankie McBride and the Polka

Dots and Philomena Quinn and the Gamblers).[144] While the show was widely advertised in Irish community media, the British press felt compelled to explain that this 'obscure venue in Kilburn' was 'a London-Irish ballroom'.[145]

Prior to the Kilburn show, the band had played a seven-date Irish tour that went beyond the established circuit of Dublin, Belfast, Limerick and Galway – itself fairly unusual for visiting acts of this period (who typically only performed in the capital) – to include the smaller towns of Sligo, Dundalk and Tralee.[146] Like the Kilburn date, the Irish trip was born of a wish, explains Rowland, to 'connect with Irish people', as well as to 'get in anything Irish that [he] could'.[147] The latter point also informed the apparel worn by the band at the Kilburn show, with Rowland exchanging the group's 'navvy' style for a quasi-military garb that intentionally echoed Irish 'rebel' attire. 'One of the things we did on that Irish trip', the singer recalls, 'is we bought some trench coats and some berets. And a couple of us wore those at the National. I certainly did. I came on wearing one.'[148] This gesture, for Rowland, was not intended as 'an out-and-out thing' (by which he means an overt endorsement of IRA action), and it was evidently not perceived as such at the time (critics felt that the band looked like 'pseudo revolutionary army guerillas').[149] However, the outfit was an attempt, says Rowland, to evoke an experience that he felt was unfairly repressed: 'There was so much fucking repression here [in Britain] at that point that it made you want to fucking do it [wear the beret and trench coat at Kilburn]. It made me.'[150]

This feeling of repression pertained in part to the constraints that Rowland felt on (what he calls) his 'Irish side', which he sensed he 'wasn't allowed to express'. However, it was also informed by what he saw as the silencing of Irish Catholics in Northern Ireland. 'I could identify with [their] anger and frustration', Rowland explains. 'Nobody was listening to them [in Britain]. They weren't allowed a point of view. They weren't allowed to have an opinion.'[151] With this context in mind, Rowland composed a lyric ('The only way to change things is to shoot men who arrange things') for the Dexys song 'There, There, My Dear' – a top-ten UK hit in 1980 – that was informed by the Northern Troubles.[152] Once again, Rowland's wish seems to have been to express a certain viewpoint that he felt was unfairly repressed, rather than to endorse paramilitary action. 'I went through so many different feelings about it all', he says of the Troubles. However, he did feel a degree of sympathy with militant republicans. 'I suppose at that point [1980] I did believe the only way to change things is to shoot those who arrange things. I did believe that. I wouldn't have written it otherwise.'[153] Although the lyric was sufficiently vague to not be linked with Northern Ireland (critics heard it as a 'classic class-war couplet'),[154] the sentiment was underlined by a gesture in the group's 1980 tour programme, which took on the trite music-press discourse of listing 'likes' and 'dislikes' by including – amongst the former – 'The Irish Republican Army'.[155] (Remarkably, this appears to have gone unnoticed at the time, despite the band's visit to Belfast.) 'I agreed with what their aims were', Rowland explains, 'and you weren't allowed to say it. And I wanted to say it.'[156]

Such gestures were, then, born of an inchoate wish to invoke Irish issues in an environment in which they were, for Rowland, repressed, rather than to articulate anything more specific. 'I wanted to say something, anything really, about Ireland. Every chance I got, I wanted to. I just felt that need to do it. I think it probably was because [there was] so much repression', he explains.[157] The singer's comments on Northern Ireland, then, were perhaps informed less by contemporary events in Ulster than they were by second-generation Irish repression, and the sense that Irish expression (at least in England) had been constrained or disavowed. The extremity of Rowland's gestures thus appears to have been born more of a wish to express the inexpressible (and open a space for Irish issues) than to endorse paramilitary action. A less contentious, and less overt, means by which this was achieved was through the band's deployment of a tricolour flag (in red, white and green – effectively, an inverted Italian flag) as a stage backdrop for their 1980 tour. This gesture was, of course, consistent with the vague evocation of 'Italianicity' that Rowland had evidenced elsewhere. For the singer, though, this modified flag had been shaped by a different desire: he had thought about using green, white and gold, but felt it was 'going a bit far'. However, when the customised flag was draped onstage and bathed in strong light, it evidently looked somewhat like an Irish tricolour, and thus caused provocation at certain venues. 'The roadies wouldn't put it up in Belfast', recalls Rowland. 'And in Glasgow we were told that the bouncers were going to rip it down.'[158]

The flag's reception at the National Ballroom was presumably somewhat different. Indeed, it is worth reflecting here on the image of Rowland, in trench coat and beret, offset by a tricolour flag, singing songs shaped by the Troubles and 'Irish jokes', in an Irish dance hall in Kilburn, promoting an album with a cover shot of Belfast, on a tour whose programme endorsed the IRA. On this occasion, which marked the end of the band's first major tour, Rowland's wish to 'get in anything Irish that [he] could' without 'doing an Irish thing' (a not inconsiderable balancing act) seems to have reached its limits.

The show would certainly signal the end of the group's first phase, and over the next few months Dexys underwent a period of radical change (with personnel shifts, record-company switches, and a short stint that some critics see as Dexys Mark II), before Rowland informed the group's manager, in 1981, that he wanted 'to push the Irish thing'.[159] Despite being advised against this, on the grounds that it could prove unpopular, the singer pursued his idea, launching a new Dexys project in 1982, with a fresh ensemble marking a striking shift in sound and style.[160] Introducing an audibly Irish folk aesthetic into their Sixties soul template, the newly remodelled Dexys overlaid fiddles, banjos and accordions onto their previously brass-based sound. With the newly installed strings section performing under the openly Irish appellation of 'The Emerald Express', Rowland re-designated Dexys as 'Celtic' on a new single – 'Celtic Soul Brothers' (1982) – the first fruits of the band's second phase.[161]

Underscoring this shift was a new set of stage attire, with Rowland's navvy, docker and rebel looks being unexpectedly exchanged for a rustic gypsy style based on dungarees, stubble and sandals. Such a dramatic change of approach took the band's audience – as well as the wider pop industry – by surprise, with observers noting its 'radical departure into Irish waters' and 'curious blend' of folk and soul, suggesting this had been born of Rowland's 'suddenly remembered ... Irish ancestry' via 'memories of ceilis [sic] and informal pub sessions'.[162] How had this peculiar change of style come about? And what was the particular context in which this desire to be Celtic was staged?

'Celtic soul', 'roots rock' and the Ulster crisis

The period immediately prior to – and coinciding with – this self-conscious Celtic turn was marked by a number of crucial shifts in British political and popular culture that would have a significant bearing on the new direction of Dexys. Perhaps the most obvious of these was a burgeoning trend in the popular-musical milieu for what Allan F. Moore has termed 'roots rock'.[163] With its stress on 'authenticity', this roots vogue offered a stark alternative to the hegemony of British synth-pop, which had embraced the values of artifice.[164] The roots scene was closely related to the concomitant 'world music' project, as evidenced by the inaugural WOMAD (World of Music, Arts and Dance) Festival in 1982, which showcased a collection of 'ethnic' sounds.[165] The contemporary interest in roots sounds would serve to heighten the profile of Irish folk music, with records such as The Fureys and Davy Arthur's 'When You Were Sweet Sixteen' (1981) and Clannad's 'Theme From

Photograph: Getty Images

Harry's Game' (1982) gaining chart success in the UK.[166] Coinciding with this development was an increasing awareness among musicians of Irish descent of the roots music of their specific milieu – hence Shane MacGowan's decision at this time to pursue an 'ethnic' style.[167] In this context of diverse roots styles – and emergent Irish sounds – in the popular-musical sphere, it was perhaps not entirely surprising that Rowland would assume an Irish folk aesthetic, a development that was seen at the time as a 'movement back to his roots', as well as an 'indictment [of] synth pop'.[168]

An interest in Celtic expression appeared to be in the ascent in British rock culture at this time, with a number of musicians broaching Celtic styles. Perhaps the best known of these was Big Country, a Scottish group that sought to evoke such a sound within a rock framework, an endeavour they launched in London at the start of 1982.[169] The band's leader, Stuart Adamson, explicated their aesthetic in interviews. Dismissing the notion that he had 'decided to sit down and write something *really ethnic*', he would locate the band's style in a certain Celtic habitus:

When I was growing up, my mum would always have a lot of old

Irish and Scottish folk records lying around, so it's something that I've been brought up with. There would always be folks around on Friday and Saturday night after the pubs and dance halls shut and everyone would have to get up and sing or play a song. There would be guys up there playing guitars, bagpipes, accordions and fiddles, so I suppose some of the things that I write go right back to that.[170]

This vogue for Celtic rock was also evinced by Van Morrison's (then) current album, *Beautiful Vision* (released in February 1982), which was seen at the time as an integration of Celtic and rock styles, and featured a song called 'Celtic Ray' that would play a role in the new Dexys scheme.[171] Rowland had sought to find a suitable name for his new project, through which he could make 'a connection between Irish music and soul music'.[172] This connection, for Rowland, was born of his reflection on an earlier Van Morrison song – 'You Don't Pull No Punches, But You Don't Push The River' (1974) – that made reference to the 'real soul' found on the 'west coast', which Rowland took to mean the west of Ireland.[173] With this in mind, 'Irish soul' was explored as a potential name for the group's new style.

> I was trying to find out the Irish word for 'soul', and that's what I was going to call our music: 'Irish soul'. I don't think I liked the sound of it, or something, I was hoping it would be a different spelling but that you could recognise that the word was 'soul'. That's what I was hoping for, and I was going to call it that.[174]

The substitution of 'Celtic' for 'Irish' was, interestingly, drawn from Morrison's 'Celtic Ray', which Rowland had heard at the start of 1982.[175] Consequently, 'Celtic Soul' (despite Rowland's own doubts about the term) was settled on as the name by which the band's new aesthetic would be known.[176]

It is clear, then, that this self-consciously Celtic turn correlated quite clearly with contemporary *musical* conditions. (Indeed, for Johnny Marr, Rowland's new style was 'very typical of the times'.[177]) However, its relation to immediate *political* shifts was rather more abstruse. Questions of nation, 'race' and ethnicity had acquired a certain significance at this time via a series of critical events, including the widespread 'race' riots of 1981, and Britain's military ventures in the Falklands/Malvinas, which effected a conspicuous increase in patriotic sentiment in popular discourses.[178] In a major interview at this time, Elvis Costello drew connections between the (then) current crisis about 'race' and the experience of the Irish in England:

You can point fingers and say, 'These are the people who are the source of all your problems: it's the black people' ... I'm English, but my ancestry is Irish, and they used to say the same about the Irish as well. My wife's Irish. Sooner or later, we'll probably have to leave England – because I'm sure the people of England will try and send the Irish back.[179]

While such comments were overblown, it is clear that issues of Irishness had come into notably sharp relief, with a succession of IRA bomb attacks (including strikes on Oxford Street, Hyde Park, Regent's Park and Chelsea) and the deaths of ten IRA/INLA hunger strikers dramatically focusing attention on this fraught period in Irish affairs.[180] Also at this time, the historic visit of the Pope to Britain increased the profile of Roman Catholics in England, the vast majority of whom were – as was made clear at the time – of Irish descent.[181] However, this did little to quell expressions of anti-Irish thought, with even the liberal *Guardian* attacking the 'un-English' character of the Catholic reception, alleging that it 'smack[ed] of strange proceedings over in Ireland, a country that no one can understand'.[182] Meanwhile, the right-wing *Sun* denounced the Irish, in this same period, as 'treacherous', before the London *Evening Standard* issued an especially noxious cartoon (a mock film poster advertising 'The Irish: The Ultimate in Psychopathic Horror') that went on to gain, as Martin McLoone points out, 'notoriety among the Irish communities in Britain' for 'exacerbating the anti-Irish prejudice with which they were already trying to cope'.[183]

In this context of, on the one hand, ethnic tensions and, on the other, roots-rock sounds, Rowland felt a need to intervene, and was compelled to 'find a way of saying' (as he put it almost two decades later) that he was 'Irish' and 'not shit'.[184] From Rowland's perspective, then, Dexys' Celtic turn was shaped by a wish to claim Irishness in the face of its negative status. While a range of additional factors no doubt also played a part in the group's dramatic change, it is worth stressing that Rowland's wish to express an Irish affiliation at this time was unlikely to have been born of commercial concerns, as Irishness was regarded – in the early 1980s – as neither profitable nor popular.[185] Indeed, when the singer informed his management that he wished to pursue an 'Irish thing', he was advised against the idea on the grounds that it would be unpopular ('English people don't really like Irish', explained his manager).[186] Thus, while scholars such as Bill Rolston suggest that it has been strategic for Irish pop musicians – in the post-1980s period – to lay stress on their origins, it is clear that, in the context of Thatcher's Britain, Irish ethnicity was not yet a desirable commodity.[187] With this in mind, it is worth noting that the first recorded product of Dexys' Irish experiment, the 'Celtic Soul Brothers' single, was – on its initial release – a commercial failure, falling short of the British Top 40 (which the bulk of Dexys' records had easily achieved).[188]

Notwithstanding this poor response, Rowland continued with plans for an album of Celtic-style tunes. At the same time, the singer eschewed an overt assertion of Irishness, evincing a highly ambiguous subject position in which he downplayed Irish ethnicity at the very moment in which it was invoked. In press interviews to promote *Too-Rye-Ay*, the vinyl centrepiece of the group's Celtic scheme, Rowland was often erratic on the issue of its (and his) Irish provenance, drawing attention, on the one hand, to the 'long process' involved in 'getting the Irish element into the group' whilst, on the other hand, stressing that this 'Irish element … really isn't very important'.[189] In a similar vein, the singer would divulge that his mother was Irish (yet strangely failed to mention his Irish father), and openly discussed his childhood residence in Ireland (and ongoing interest in Irish music), but with the cautionary caveat that he was 'born over here [in England]', insisting: 'I don't see myself being Irish or anything.'[190] Consequently, while the singer was willing to admit to being 'part Irish', he would typically qualify this by stressing that it was something from 'a long way back' that had no great bearing on his current life and work; 'I don't want people to make too much of the Celtic thing', he informed one interviewer.[191] This caution was compounded by the coy allusions to Rowland's provenance in the band's auxiliary media, not least the nonchalant note on the sleeve of 'Celtic Soul Brothers' that the singer 'claims to be of Celtic origin'.[192] Journalists, in turn, discerned that the singer had 'some vague Celtic roots'.[193]

The indeterminate subjectivity of Rowland's persona at this time was, of course, consistent with the ambivalence that has been observed in ethnographic work on the second-generation Irish. Indeed, Rowland would later admit to the 'mixed feelings' that he had about his Irish upbringing, stressing the 'ambivalence' that he felt towards Irishness (especially its more essentialist forms) during the *Too-Rye-Ay* period.[194] In addition, the singer has explained that his reluctance to overtly align himself with Irishness during this period was born of circumstantial concerns, not least the 'snobbery' that he had discerned in Ireland's view of its own diaspora: Irish-born people had, he said, been keen to 'take the piss' out of second-generation Irish people like him.[195] It is also worth noting, in this regard, that any expression of Irish ethnicity amongst the English-born diaspora in the early Eighties was likely to be contentious. In this context, Rowland's wish to both invoke and conceal ethnicity (in the space of a single interview) meant that he was able to resonate with multiple constituencies (not least English, Irish-born and second-generation Irish) in a single communicative act. Such inconsistency, though, was also an attempt to evade strict forms of press categorisation: 'I never wanted to be pigeon-holed in any one thing', he later said; 'I always tried to skirt around it.'[196]

Regardless of Rowland's uneven allegiance to an Irish position, it is clear that the singer was perceived – in the midst of this Celtic project – as broadly Irish. Thus, he was described in press profiles as a 'second hand' (implying imperfect or indefinite) Irishman, whilst Irish-themed editions of British TV shows, such as *The Tube*, featured music by Dexys.[197] Moreover, when Rowland was interviewed in the Irish media during the *Too-Rye-Ay* tour, programme hosts would extend an important greeting, announcing: 'Welcome home, Kevin.'[198] With this view of Rowland (as 'Irish') in mind, I will address the particular modes of Irishness that the singer acquired in his Celtic period. How was this evocation of ethnicity conceived? And in what ways did the band's new approach serve to register – as well as resonate with – the political and pop-cultural contexts outlined above?

Celticism, essentialism and *Too-Rye-Ay*

Perhaps the most prominent aspect of the band's new persona was its fresh (and unexpected) gypsy look. This highly choreographed rehearsal of 'shabby chic' served to dissociate Dexys from the showy glamour of their pop milieu (which had become increasingly glitzy in 1982), whilst signalling the group's dramatic shift from their earlier incarnation. A key function of this new attire, though, was its role as a visual corollary of the group's folk-inflected songs, affording them a vaguely Celtic image to augment an expressly Celtic sound.[199]

With its suggestion of a pastoral lifestyle, Rowland's threadbare attire conjured ideas of 'Celticism', a term historically associated with highly sentimental conceptions of Irish life.[200] The nineteenth-century critic, Matthew Arnold, a noted exponent of 'Celticism', saw the Irish as an inherently poetic 'race', setting the mystical (and thus less rational) Celt against the prosaic (and therefore practical) Anglo-Saxon, in a discourse that supplied succour to English power. Irish culture, in this context, came to be seen as a 'primitive' endeavour, and was condensed – by 'Celticists' – into a 'politically neutered aestheticism'.[201] Certain strands of this 'Celticist' view would emerge in Dexys' new work. In the videos for 'Celtic Soul Brothers' and 'Come On Eileen', for example, the group were located in highly urban – and obviously contemporary

– English geographies. In such metropolitan settings, the band's faux-rustic attire – and informal set-dance moves – offered a playful pastiche of Victorian Irish street singers, imparting a gentle critique of English urbanity via a saccharine show of Celtic charm.[202] In this sense, Rowland's means of asserting Irish difference (in late-twentieth-century Britain) was curiously antiquated (not to say rather regressive). Indeed, certain second-generation people expressed antipathy towards this Celtic project, with Shane MacGowan, for example, stressing his distaste for what he saw as Rowland's 'pathetic attempt' to 'incorporate some kind of Celtic bit – with the fake wearing of dungarees and berets and growing stubble and walking round without any shoes and straw hanging out of [his] hair'. For MacGowan, this peasant-style persona served as an 'insult' to 'the whole [Irish] thing'.[203] MacGowan's colleague Cáit O'Riordan has confirmed that the former was 'pissed off and disappointed' with this incarnation of Dexys, explaining that the second-generation Irish had, in the early 1980s, 'been going through this thing of saying "we're not animals or idiots, we're people with pride"', before Rowland came to accent his Irishness with the aid of 'dungarees and straw in his hair'.[204]

Sections of the Dexys fan base were quick to defend the band from such accusations, and these fans would often make reference to the group's ethnic credentials. Thus, one follower sought to counter MacGowan's critique by stressing, in the *NME* letters page, 'that with names like O'Hara, Kilkenny and Brennan, Dexys have some right to introduce an Irish element into their looks'.[205] Such defenders were, however, oblivious to Rowland's chicanery in concocting Irish nomenclature for his band-mates during the Celtic project. New recruits such as (the Bristol-born) Helen Bevington, for example, had been transformed by Rowland's Gaelicising process, being renamed O'Hara, the 'Ballymena Belle'.[206] This quixotic contrivance – in conjunction with a Celtic attire – would leave the singer open to charges of ersatz Irishness. Certain critics, such as Ian O'Doherty, claimed that this phase of Rowland's career was '"Oirish" rather than Irish', suggesting that the 'silly clothes and complete change from his urban image of previous years … looked somewhat contrived', and noting that the singer 'never looked as comfortable as [Irish-born musicians such as Van Morrison] did with the whole notion of the Celtic revival'. For O'Doherty, this was 'largely to do with the fact that Rowland was trying to adopt an image which was false. That aspect of Irish culture was as alien to him as it was to young indigenous Irish people who felt embarrassed by the whole "diddly-eye" movement.'[207]

Notwithstanding that the idea of 'authenticity' that informs such critical views is itself a particular 'effect' of popular music practice, it is worth stating that the character assumed by Rowland during the band's Celtic phase was an expressly self-conscious and highly choreographed persona (critics discerned its 'almost vaudeville amateur dramatics').[208] Moreover, when taken in the light of Dexys' earlier address to Irish issues, this persona seemed to function as yet another instance of intervention (in this case, in the concomitant crises of the hunger strikes and the bombing campaign, and against the backdrop of a malicious press discourse). Rather than censuring Rowland for his contrived take on Irish ethnicity, then, his short-lived Celtic venture might instead be observed as an openly constructed (and shamelessly anodyne) response, offering benign conceptions of Irishness (as playful, lightweight, upbeat) to offset the more ominous impressions that occupied the public domain. 'It's the misunderstanding [about the Irish in England] that drove me', he recalls, noting that when he read Irish literature, or listened to Irish music, he encountered 'something else entirely' to the dominant conception of Irishness in Britain.[209]

Irishness as self-conscious in(ter)vention

The heavily theatrical character of Rowland's Celtic persona was such that any conflation of the singer's 'stage' and 'actual' selves was largely kept in check. This is not to suggest that Rowland set up any clear-cut distinction between his life experience and his band's new aesthetic. In fact, he would stress various ways in which Irish ethnicity had informed their sound, advising the press that this was a 'reflection of his past', and affirming that the 'Celtic Soul Brothers' appellation had alluded to his friendship with the band's Scottish trombone player, Jim Patterson. Similarly, the singer would reveal that the title of his new album – *Too-Rye-Ay* – contained a phonetic allusion to the sounds of his childhood. 'We used to sing those songs', he explained, intoning the words of J.R. Shannon's 'That's An Irish Lullaby' (which includes a phrase that approximates to 'too-rye-ay'). 'That's one of my earliest memories', Rowland observed.[210] With such comments in mind, it would seem that Rowland's new work was born in part of a wish to evoke his early life in general, rather than Irish ethnicity specifically. It is, of course, difficult to de-couple these issues, as confirmed by the singer's claim that his song words for 'Come On Eileen' – the major hit that marked the peak of Dexys' commercial success – were born of an adolescent liaison with a second-generation Irish girl.[211]

This theme was drawn out by Rowland in a series of interviews at the time of the single's release. Thus, the singer spelt out that the song's eponymous female 'also came from an Irish background', adding that he and 'Eileen' had shared certain Irish customs before the onset of adolescence and youth: 'we used to sing those [Irish] songs [together] and then we grew up. And there was a time, about 14 or 15 … [when] … sex came into it and our relationship had always been so clean. It seemed at that time to get dirty and that's what [the song is] about.'[212] Expanding on this theme, Rowland detailed:

> Eileen is a girl that I grew up with … my Dad used to sit both of us on his knee and sing … 'it's an Irish lullaby'. And we just grew up together, and by the time we came to about thirteen or fourteen, sex came into it, sex *reared its ugly head.*[213]

Such distaste for sensual pleasure was less than common in mainstream pop, and echoed the ascetic sentiments expressed by Rowland elsewhere. In this context, 'Come On Eileen' came to be viewed as 'one of the great Catholic guilt love songs'.[214]

Despite Rowland's claim – at the time of the song's release – that it cited a specific person (one Eileen McClusky, played in the song's video by Maire Fahey, sister of Bananarama singer, Siobhan), he later explained that its lyrics were informed by a broader dynamic of desire among second-generation Irish youth.[215] Such was the song's association with this second-generation theme that when 'Come On Eileen' was reissued as an Old Gold classic in 1989, the sleeve notes explained that Rowland's 'Irish-Catholic upbringing and its affect [*sic*] on an early relationship' had shaped the lyrics.[216]

There is little doubt, then, that Rowland's Irish upbringing had some bearing (and was *perceived* to have had some bearing) on the band's Celtic project. Nevertheless, a perceived gap between the singer's actual and stage selves was in large part maintained by the highly choreographed means by which Rowland performed his personas, switching from docker to gypsy and (later) yuppie in the course of Dexys' relatively short career. This ceaseless sartorial flux – and regular turnover of colleagues – meant that it was difficult to locate any stable 'authentic' presence at the heart of Dexys' work. Indeed, in the midst of his band's Celtic endeavour, Rowland outlined future plans for an 'ever-changing' – and, hence, conceptually unfixed – creative persona.[217]

This desire for dramatic artifice had been unveiled at the start of the Celtic period, with Rowland announcing, in the prelude to 'Celtic Soul Brothers' (which served as both the project's lead-off single and the opening track on *Too-Rye-Ay*), a formal and highly staged spoken preface to the group's new guise ('Ladies and gentleman, I give you: the Celtic Soul Brothers ...'). Such upfront self-reflexivity was also evident in the group's liner notes, with the sleeve of the above-mentioned single detailing semi-fictive profiles of the individual group members. Rowland was thus assigned a history as a 'failed priest', 'tramp' and 'wandering minstrel' (connoting numerous Celtic caricatures), while fiddle player Steve Brennan displayed his alleged pedigree as an heir of George Bernard Shaw (a writer who had, of course, been cited in the lyrics of 'Dance Stance').[218] This highly stylized side of the group's new project was also evinced in live performance, with the openly contrived *Too-Rye-Ay* shows (described by critics as 'pure panto') being staged in theatre spaces (as opposed to rock venues), where a formal compère and raised curtain would signal the beginning of each performance.[219] As if to clarify the point, a Dexys spokesperson had announced – several months prior to the tour – that the group's live shows had 'more in common with theatre than rock'.[220]

This theatrical staging of Irishness was – in terms of style, tone and content – overtly upbeat and bright, hence the songs' 'melodic playfulness', 'bouncy pace' and 'jaunty', 'uplifting style'.[221] Rowland would later confess to the project's 'lightweight' and 'shallow' character, and critics singled out its 'romantic, tourist-eye view', describing the tour as 'a merry hoedown' and the band's new sound as 'a watered-down version' of Irish folk styles.[222] It is clear that Dexys' pop/soul approach and quasi-classical strings section bore little relation to Irish traditional music. Thus, Johnny Marr – who admired the quality of song-writing on *Too-Rye-Ay* – viewed the project as a soul/pop synthesis with 'an Irish tinge', observing that Rowland infused his work with 'an aesthetic that meant something to him ... It was just a different kind of flavour.'[223] Elsewhere, musicians such as MacGowan would take issue with Dexys' 'bland' – and allegedly tokenistic – 'few fiddles', explaining that the classically-trained Emerald Express failed to 'even play them like fiddles', employing them instead as 'orchestral instruments'.[224] In fairness to Dexys, their new material also comprised distinctively Irish sounds, not least the tin-whistle melody that served as a prelude to the centre-piece track, 'Until I Believe In My Soul', as well as the Irish-language words that Rowland read at the end of 'All In All'. Nevertheless, it was felt by (otherwise supportive) critics, such as Colin Irwin, that Dexys' accretion of Irish influences was 'incidental and not a little clumsy': their Celtic instrumentalists 'would be lynched', said Irwin, 'in any self-respecting Irish pub in Kilburn'.[225] Rowland had little interest in engaging an exclusively Irish aesthetic,[226] however, and instead set out to evoke Irish sounds in a much broader template, drawing on the diverse musical forms (such as soul, jazz and pop) of his contemporary milieu. As he made clear at the time, the 'Irish feel' of *Too-Rye-Ay* was merely 'a part of the whole'.[227]

While Rowland's pop/folk project was not unpopular with the Irish in Britain (the *Irish Post* praised it as 'a striking reflection' of the singer's 'preoccupation with his Irish roots'), it does seem to have been enjoyed by a much broader demographic: Reynolds notes the 'new MOR [middle-of-the-road] audience' that the band accrued, a constituency that came to be evident at the *Too-Rye-Ay* live shows.[228] (Critics observed the absence of any 'fad or faction' amongst the audience.[229]) In this sense, Rowland's shows were markedly different from those of MacGowan's Pogues, whose shows enabled fans to 'articulate' – in the sense of a conjunction or interface – with a collective Irish ethnicity. (This notion of 'articulation' is elaborated by Richard Middleton to make sense of musical processes in which two discrete elements that are not innately attached – such as 'performer' and 'fan' – become symbolically conjoined at the juncture of production and consumption (such as live performance). In the midst of this crucial moment, then, the distinct constituents of band and audience – though not intrinsically entwined – can affectively join and therefore 'articulate'.[230]) Rowland explains, however, that he had no interest in offering 'an all-out Irish thing' for an exclusively Irish (or second-generation Irish) audience. 'It wasn't what I wanted to do', he recalls, and despite feeling envious of The Pogues for 'getting all of that Irish acclaim' (MacGowan would displace Rowland, after 1983, as the popular-musical figurehead of the second generation), he 'didn't want what they had' – hence Dexys' orientation towards a broad pop/rock demographic.[231]

This is not to say that Rowland sought to evade Irish audiences. Earlier in their career, Dexys had performed at Irish clubs in Birmingham, and they had, of course, concluded their 1980 tour at an Irish ballroom in north London, following several shows in Ireland, all of which was born of a wish to connect with Irish audiences.[232] The London date of the *Too-Rye-Ay* tour would, however, be staged at the Shaftesbury Theatre (rather than an Irish-associated venue), and onstage Irish signals were confined to minor features, such as the insertion – in the slow-paced middle-eight of 'Come On Eileen' – of the phrase: 'it's an Irish lullaby', or the Irish folk songs that appeared on a pre-recorded tape prior to the band's arrival onstage.[233] Nevertheless, what the *Too-Rye-Ay* show seemed to offer Dexys' broad-based audience was a means to partake in putatively Celtic (unreserved, quixotic, exuberant) pursuits in the leisure-based confines of a concert arena, rather than a direct address to overt aspects of Irish ethnicity.[234]

The highly palatable brand of Irishry that was staged in this context was underlined by the anodyne themes of Rowland's song lyrics and media interviews at this time. Exchanging his trademark press communiqués for a series of mainstream interviews, Rowland was 'more relaxed' and 'less irascible than before', remarked critics.[235] He certainly showed little concern for Irish political issues, despite their prevalence during this period. There was no engagement, for instance, with the contemporary Troubles, or with Irish diaspora affairs, other than vague allusions to inter-Celtic camaraderie ('Celtic Soul Brothers') or intra-Irish romance ('Come On Eileen'). Even 'Dance Stance', the band's signature song on Irish issues, was expunged from their live shows for the duration of this phase.[236] Rowland's Celtic effort was, then, shaped less by contemporary Irish experience, or traditional Irish sounds, than by a wish to invoke – in a highly accessible (and culturally acceptable) way – certain ideas of Irishness for a mainstream audience.

Like Rowland's other interventionist acts, his Celtic endeavour would arguably serve as a sort of response to Anglo-Irish issues. Thus, if his earlier attempts to address such issues ('Dance Stance', press protests, public temperance) were prompted by prevailing forms of popular prejudice ('thick Paddy' jokes, 'drunken Irish' stereotypes, pernicious press discourse), Rowland's Celtic stage ethnicity offered a quiet corrective to the highly charged conceptions of Irishness that circulated in early Eighties Britain (often informed by IRA violence and associated issues), enacting innocuous ideas of Irishry as a cordial counterpoint. 'I was trying', explains Rowland, 'to show Irishness to the English … I was directing it at them', he reflects, 'because of the misunderstanding'.[237] (Such was the degree of 'misunderstanding', however, that Dexys' Celtic work would itself become bound up with IRA actions: when 'Come On Eileen' was played on a British radio station shortly after an IRA attack in England, the broadcaster issued an immediate on-air apology in case listeners had taken offence at the song's Irish aspects.[238])

Rowland's effort to assail one reductive archetype would, in any case, have the effect of reviving another, for while the singer had previously displaced 'thick' with 'literary', and 'drunken' with 'dry', he was now projecting 'mystical' as a well-meaning curative to 'mad'.[239] This ethereal antidote was, moreover, drawn from a conspicuously Celticist set of ideas and associated stage-Irish codes. The sleeve notes for *Too-Rye-Ay*, for example, featured a brief extract of 'Believe Me, If All Those Endearing Young Charms' – a song sung by Rowland a cappella in the album's untitled coda – by the Victorian Irish writer Thomas Moore. The latter's œuvre, as Harry White points out, evinced a 'romantic perception' of Ireland's 'ethnic repertory', evoking 'a version of ancient Ireland' that found favour in England's (middle-class) parlours, where 'pseudo-Celtic elements' were well liked.[240] Moore was thus chastised for privileging 'non-Irish' audiences, and was accused, as Leith Davis explains, of 'selling out' Irish culture 'in order to enjoy commercial success'.[241] Like Moore, Rowland also faced a trenchant critique – from certain second-generation figures – for drawing on such parlour-room songs.[242] Rowland was 'disappointed and upset' by such attacks,[243] particularly as they came from people with whom he had assumed a degree of (second-generation) solidarity. 'It really annoyed me', the singer explains. 'It really got to me at the time.'[244] Nevertheless, Rowland would later defend his use of the Moore material:

> I had and have no idea if that song found favour in Victorian England and I don't care. I'm the son of an Irish builder, not an Irish intellectual. What I do know is that hard-working Irish people all over Britain like my Mother and my Uncle Tommy loved the song and sung it beautifully.[245]

He adds, 'It was great for them', and says that '*I* loved it. It was a beautiful song.'[246]

While it is, of course, the case that certain songs become detached from their original context, accruing new meanings and significance over time, the special purchase of stage-Irish codes for Dexys' Celtic venture should not be underplayed: *Too-Rye-Ay* was originally to be titled after the Moore song before it took its name (as well as the hook line of 'Come On Eileen') from an analogous American tune, 'That's An Irish Lullaby' (1914), by J.R. Shannon.[247] Elsewhere, Rowland displayed his unashamed attraction to the more kitsch aspects of Ireland's stage canon, not least in the brief allusion (in 'Reminisce Part One') to 'Delaney's Donkey' (1964), a song by the popular entertainer Val Doonican, as well as via Dexys' rendition of 'Kathleen Mavourneen', a song from the 1920s by the Irish tenor John McCormack.[248]

As explained above, such gestures did not go unnoticed by Rowland's second-generation peer group, at least one of whom expressed disquiet at Dexys' stage-Irish ethos.[249] Rowland was impenitent, however, about the kitschiness of his source material and its 'low' value in Ireland: 'I like songs that [people in Ireland] consider corny', he divulged, expressing a fondness for tunes such as 'I'll Take You Home Again Kathleen' and 'Danny Boy'. There was, it seems, a certain migrant provenance to such 'corny' tastes: these were the songs, Rowland said, that were popular with his parents 'when they were young people coming over to [England]'.[250] (This point was confirmed by Irish critics, who saw the songs that Rowland enjoyed as having 'a far more emotive appeal' for the 'Irish exile' than for the 'inhabitants of [Ireland] themselves'.[251])

If migrant Irish song culture has comprised, as Phil Eva explains, 'both "sentimental" and "political" inflections', then Rowland's pop/folk project would pursue the former, displaying – in the manner of certain migrant ballads – 'depoliticised' forms of 'sentimental cliché'.[252] As Rowland later explained, the Celtic project had been 'very light, in a very lightweight way', and he would concede to his own 'sentimentality'.[253] In this regard, Rowland's debt to Thomas Moore was arguably greater than he realised: Moore's work offered 'an essentially non-threatening view' of Ireland, eschewing reference to contemporary events whilst serving as 'a reaction to negative stereotyping by the English'.[254] In fairness to Rowland, he had made some reference in the Celtic phase to Irish experience, not least his overt reference in 'Reminisce Part One' (B-side of the re-released 'Celtic Soul Brothers') to the (then) Greater London Council (GLC) leader Ken Livingstone, whose left-wing multiculturalism had provided, in the early 1980s, 'a significant impetus for the increased activism of the Irish in London by recognising the Irish as an "ethnic minority", thereby legitimating the funding of specifically Irish welfare and cultural projects'. In this regard, Livingstone's GLC had, as Breda Gray observes, directly 'contributed to the visibility of Irishness in England' via its leader's 'strong and public support for Irish groups'.[255] Most significant, perhaps, was Livingstone's highly public intervention against anti-Irish prejudice through his withdrawal of GLC advertising (then worth a considerable amount) from the London *Evening Standard* after it had printed anti-Irish material. 'We will not put another penny into the *Standard* while they continue to vilify the Irish', Livingstone announced, in a stance that was seen by many as 'the greatest gesture of support ever towards the Irish community in [Britain] by a major, elected authority'.[256] In the context of this public protest, Rowland paid a playful tribute, with his spoken-word song lyrics praising Livingstone as a modern-day 'folk hero' ('*You know* what I'm talking about', intones the singer, teasingly.[257]) A less oblique allusion to Irish issues in England was evinced in the video for the song's A-side – the 1983 re-release of 'Celtic Soul Brothers' – which comprised footage of Irish life in London, tendering a portrait of an ordinary (rather than a 'suspect') community, with work and sociality (rather than violence and stupidity) at its heart.[258] The video includes scenes of migrant Irish labourers setting out for work in the metropolis before enjoying refreshments at a well-known Irish dance hall (The Crown) in north London.[259] ('I just wanted to show the culture', says Rowland of the video, 'because it is so rich.'[260]) This visual exposition of an actual Irish milieu was accentuated elsewhere by Rowland's public endorsement of associated ethnic venues, such as the Shamrock Club in Birmingham (which, as the singer explains, had become less popular in the years after the Birmingham bombs).[261] This affiliation with an overtly ethnic 'scene' appeared to increase awareness of an *actual* Irish presence, offering an image of the Irish as a settled community pursuing 'normal' lives. The 'Celtic Soul Brothers' video was, then, part of Rowland's wish, as he puts it, to 'correct the misunderstanding' about the Irish in Britain.[262] Even if this invoked an existing set of Irish caricatures (pertaining to manual work and alcoholism), the singer's effort served to acknowledge the lives of the Irish in England, presaging the more nuanced approach to Irish ethnicity on Dexys' next major project, *Don't Stand Me Down*. Signalling another dramatic switch of style, this record (the band's third, and final, LP) would offer a far more dense address to Irish issues than its predecessor. The album would stand, moreover, as Rowland's most substantive engagement with second-generation concerns, and the Anglo-Irish relationship in general.

Introducing *Don't Stand Me Down*

After the commercial achievements of the Celtic period, Rowland withdrew his band from public view, taking time to reflect on the feats and frailties of this project (he had tired of the 'teeny fame' and 'wanted to make it serious'),[263] before drafting ideas for Dexys' next phase. During this self-imposed hiatus, Rowland became – in his words – 'obsessed with Irish politics'.[264] The early 1980s was a particularly 'polarised moment' (as Seamus Heaney would put it) in Anglo-Irish affairs, with the H-Block dirty protests and IRA hunger strikes being followed – during the years in which *Don't Stand Me Down* (henceforth *DSMD*) was written, conceived and recorded (1983–85) – by large-scale IRA attacks (including the bombing of Harrods and the Thatcher Cabinet), before the historic Anglo-Irish Agreement in 1985.[265] This context clearly informed Rowland's new (and more sombre) persona, which eschewed the sentimental folk Celticism of *Too-Rye-Ay* for a far more difficult and demanding address to Irish ethnicity and associated issues. (In contrast to its predecessor's warmth and conviviality, *DSMD* was, as Dermot Stokes explained, 'awkward, opinionated and annoying'.[266]) Rowland had started to read books on Irish history, and became 'immersed' in this subject.[267] His interests were not confined to scholarship, however, for the singer's reading (which included Kevin Kelly's *The Longest War* and Eamonn McCann's *War and an Irish Town*) was augmented by more active pursuits. As well as visiting Irish social clubs and attending concerts by The Wolfe Tones, the singer made trips to Belfast and Derry in 1983. 'I wanted to find out what was going on', he recalls, citing the 'very difficult situation' at that time.[268] Following the trip, the singer began to attend Irish political demonstrations in England.

> I started going on marches in Birmingham, in 1983, '84. I contacted Troops Out, and started going to their meetings, going on marches. And there would be other people on these marches, there'd be Sinn Féin on the march, there'd be Troops Out, there'd be socialists, there'd be the Irish in Britain Representation Group. And I got to know a few of those people, and one of the Sinn Féin guys contacted me and said 'Do you want to come and have a chat?', and he just said: 'I heard you're going on marches, but be careful: one extra person on a march isn't really going to make a massive difference, but your face … [could make such a difference].'[269]

After this discussion, Rowland was invited to Belfast with a view to performing a concert for the republican movement.

> [The Sinn Féin representative] just said: 'The leadership are wondering if you might do a gig for them', and he said: 'Do you want to go over to Belfast', and I said: 'Yeah.' So me and a mate went over for a weekend, and we met with a guy, Richard McCauley, who was the press guy for Gerry Adams, and also we met with Danny Morrison, who was, like, head of communications at that point.[270]

Plans were soon hatched for a Dexys concert in west Belfast (to raise funds for an Irish-language school), and though this show would fail to transpire (due to administrative problems on the band's next tour), Rowland's involvement with political activists would undoubtedly play a role in the formation of *DSMD*.[271]

With its emphasis on resistance, recovery and recuperation, *DSMD* staged an introspective (and often oblique) excursion into second-generation life, alongside polemical commentary on Anglo-Irish affairs. Its key tracks, 'Knowledge Of Beauty' and 'The Waltz', enact a renewal of Irish ethnicity in the face of enforced assimilation, while 'One Of Those Things' offers a critique of what Rowland saw as the British left's silence on Irish affairs. The album's unusually serious tenor – and comparatively complex character – was not easily accommodated in the structural confines of the traditional pop song, and Rowland sought appropriately challenging forms (theatrical dialogue, ornate arrangements, extended tracks) in which to stage his address.[272] How might we make sense of this album's invocation of Irish issues and sounds, and particularly its endeavour to speak to certain second-generation concerns?

Recuperation, identity politics and *Don't Stand Me Down*

If the Celtic orientation of *Too-Rye-Ay* had been impelled by Rowland's wish to announce his ethnicity in the face of its socially negative status, then *DSMD* would be born of Rowland's 'urge' – in Hutcheon's terms – 'to reconcile himself with his Irish roots' (the singer recalls that it emerged from 'a real yearning for Ireland' and a wish 'to do something for Ireland').[273] In contrast to his Celtic persona, however, Rowland was markedly keen, at the outset of this new project, to assume an expressly Irish subject position, discarding the ambiguity of his previous incarnation. 'I'm Irish', he stressed unequivocally to the UK media, adding that he had an 'Irish upbringing', and visited Ireland often.[274] The singer also made clear his concern for Northern Ireland, explaining that he had become 'very, very interested in what's going on there'.[275]

This newly resolute mode of ethnic self-ascription met with significant press criticism, with journalists inviting Rowland to partake in the often absurd forms of identity-contestation that have marked debates about second-generation life in England. Tackling a succession of questions about the frequency with which he visited Ireland, the number of close relatives that continued to reside there, whether he defined himself as British or Irish, and how his ethnic allegiance could be reconciled with his place of birth, the singer was insistent on his adherence to Irish ethnicity.[276] One such interrogation occurred during a fractious exchange with *Melody Maker* in 1985.

Melody Maker: 'Do you go back there [to Ireland] much?'
Rowland: 'Yes.'
MM: 'Family?'
Rowland: 'Yeah.'
MM: 'Are you British or Irish?'
Rowland: 'I am an Irish citizen. I am an Irish passport holder.'
MM: 'But you were born in England.'
Rowland: 'Just because you were born in a stable doesn't make you a horse.'[277]

Such insistence on Irish ethnicity provoked overt forms of ridicule, with the music press issuing a number of satires of Rowland's identity politics. Most striking was a caricature of the singer that appeared in an ironic Christmas cartoon entitled 'Snow White and the Seven Anglo-Irish Dwarves', in which Rowland was assigned the role of 'Grumpy'. 'None of you people are truly Irish', his character informed the other dwarves, asserting: 'I'm the only proper Irish person in the world, and it's about time people appreciated me for it.'[278]

Rowland could not have been more serious, however, and he went on to launch a physical assault on one journalist who contested his claims to Irish ethnicity.[279] The theme of contested identity was also invoked – via songs about ancestry and assimilation – on the new album. Before presenting my analysis of this material, a certain strand of the *DSMD* project requires some consideration. To announce the record's release in September 1985, the band (again) adopted an entirely new set of stage attire. Exchanging the shabby chic of *Too-Rye-Ay* for pinstripe suits and ties (courtesy of Brooks Brothers, a high-end business-wear retailer), the group looked conservative. The new record's artwork was especially unusual, with the band adopting solemn facial expressions and excessively formal poses (legs crossed, hands clasped) in a self-consciously posed shot that seemed almost corporate. And while the singer would insist that this look was simply a reflection of the band's off-stage appearance,[280] there were a number of more likely explanations for this striking sartorial shift. Perhaps most obviously, the new outfits served to signal the band's wholesale eshewal of their nouveau-gypsy phase, whilst stressing the expressly 'serious' nature of their new songs. Rather ironically, their sharp-tailored suits and corporate body postures also evoked the harsh sartorial codes of Thatcherite Conservatism, and, consequently – despite Rowland's claims that this wardrobe offered a timeless 'Ivy League' aesthetic – many critics felt that it veered precariously close to the Stock Exchange styles of the Eighties UK yuppie.[281]

The unusual attire may also have been conceived as an ocular adjunct to the new Dexys sound, with its highly decorous formality matching the meticulous production and refined performances of the new material. The band's conservative veneer was at odds, however, with Rowland's song lyrics, which staged a highly charged act of ethnic 'recovery'. In this sense, his prim apparel appeared to obfuscate his more headstrong lyrics, evoking ideas of decency and decorum – values that Rowland would extol in the *DSMD* period, not least through the band's 1985 tour programme, which detailed (beneath a photograph of the well-groomed singer) his parents' evolution from immigrants 'with little money, but a lot of ambition' to 'successful' people who had earned 'respect'.[282] In the

light of this stress on 'success' and 'respect', the band's new suits conveyed a certain social esteem, recalling the look of black American acts in the 1960s whose 'Ivy League clothes – snug Brooks Brothers blazers or tweed jackets, button-down shirts and ties, horn-rimmed glasses, slim grey flannel trousers and brown loafers – embodied', for Joe Boyd, 'a confident new ethos in the black community'.[283]

Perhaps with such propriety in mind, the more political aspects of the new Dexys album were somewhat less than upfront. Critics discerned its 'obliquely political' themes, noting the 'buried clues' that Rowland's 'obtuse [*sic*] imagination' had 'scattered' across the album's 'obscure landscape'.[284] The record's often veiled address to Irish issues was an effect of the unease that the singer had felt towards its lyrical themes. In this context, he became anxious about the album's reception, and chose to withdraw certain titles and words that engaged with Irish themes. 'I bottled out of some of the original Irish titles on the album', he later explained, 'and I cut out some lyrics about hunger strikes. I thought the press would crucify me.'[285] Elaborating on this withdrawn lyric about hunger strikes, Rowland recalls:

> I was afraid to say it. I was afraid of what people would say to me. I wasn't afraid of losing my career, of losing money or anything. That wasn't the fear. It was more that they'd go: 'Who are you to fucking say that? You haven't got the right to say that. You're not even Irish. You were born here.'[286]

With such concerns in mind, a song that had been called 'Elizabeth Wimpole and Kathleen Ní Houlihan' was re-titled 'The Waltz', whilst 'My National Pride' became 'Knowledge Of Beauty'. Rowland explained that 'for most of its life during the recording', the latter song was called 'My National Pride': 'That is its true title, I just didn't have the courage to title it that when it came around to the artwork, because I didn't believe … that I had the right to be Irish' (by which he seems to mean 'publicly' – rather than 'privately' – Irish).[287]

To compound this concern about claiming Irish ethnicity, Rowland also felt that such a frank invocation of patriotism was simply 'too strong' a gesture in the charged political climate of mid-1980s Britain.[288] Apart from the intimation of far-right rhetoric contained in the title 'My National Pride', the singer's deployment of this term as an expressly *Irish* gesture was likely to have been viewed, in the context of the time, as support for political violence.[289] With this in mind, one critic has explained that Rowland's 'urge to reconcile himself with his Irish roots' on *DSMD* was 'perceived in England as tantamount to wearing a balaclava and carrying a machine gun'.[290] In light of this point, it was perhaps understandable that Rowland withdrew certain references that he had made to Anglo-Irish affairs.

This caution was also evident in Rowland's press interviews. He refused to deal with questions about Irish issues, and asked that whatever remarks he had made be withdrawn from printed copy. During one interview, for example, the singer declined to elaborate on the record's Irish themes, refusing outright to answer a question on the topic of Northern Ireland. Only when he was faced with the charge of 'running away from the political situation in Ireland' did Rowland feel obliged to respond. 'I've said more about Ireland than any other musician, Irish or otherwise', he would claim.[291] Nevertheless, the singer refused to offer any extended commentary on the matter, and recanted any comments that he had made. In the immediate aftermath of another interview, Rowland made contact with the journalist to express his regret that he had 'let [his] own personal political views about Ireland be known', adding that such views 'don't matter', and advising the reporter to 'dilute' his remarks 'a bit'.[292]

There is little doubt, then, that Rowland felt reticent about the ethnic orientation of this project. The caginess that he displayed about the record's reception was, moreover, not without foundation. It would be wrong to infer from this, though, that *DSMD* was wholly abstract in its address to Irish issues, for there were many overt signals in the song words, and these were drawn out by Rowland in interviews, videos and attendant media. An Irish theme was invoked, for example, in 'One Of Those Things', in which Rowland's spoken-sung dialogue assails the (alleged) silence about Northern Ireland amongst Britain's political left (or 'public ignorance over Belfast', as one critic explained at the time).[293] Rehearsing an imaginary exchange between the song's narrator and 'a couple of so called socialists', Rowland makes audible reference to 'Ireland' and 'Belfast', before inviting his addressees to elaborate on the apparently elusive issue of Northern Ireland. The lyrics were partly drawn, it would seem, from the singer's personal experience. 'I'd be talking to supposed socialists', Rowland later recalled, 'and I'd say, "Do you know what's happening in Ireland?" and they'd say "What?" and I'd say, "It's being occupied, by the army of this country!"' Leaving aside this claim of 'occupation', Rowland's quarrel was that the crisis in Northern Ireland 'should have been top of their priorities', rather than 'way down there'.[294] In the song, then, Rowland sought to 'make a very definite point', namely 'that it is very easy for most British socialists who pontificate about revolutions far away not to recognise the very obvious point that the most important problem facing them is what is going on in Ireland'.[295] Rather than viewing the Troubles as social turmoil, the left in Britain had, for Rowland, reduced the Irish to mere 'gangsters'.[296]

As well as addressing the disinterest in Irish affairs in British political life, 'One Of Those Things' introduced Irishness as one of *DSMD*'s central themes, setting up the fuller (if less overt) engagement on its two key tracks, 'Knowledge Of Beauty' and 'The Waltz'. In these companion pieces, the singer conveys an account of second-generation life through the tropes of resistance, recovery and assimilation. If this marked a thematic departure from the lightweight lyrics of *Too-Rye-Ay*, then the languid pace and reflective tenor of these new songs deviated starkly from the buoyant mood of 'Celtic Soul Brothers' and 'Come On Eileen'. The words for 'Knowledge Of Beauty' had, as Rowland explained, sprung from a feeling of being 'misplaced', with the singer stressing – in interviews – its theme of 'roots' and 'parents': 'Ireland is obviously there', he made clear.[297] (Critics, in turn, noted that the song 'reflects on heritage, on roots, on *Irishness*'.[298]) The song enacts a symbolic resolution of second-generation angst, with its narrating first-person subject (described by White as 'a searcher devoid of ties and sense of belonging') reverting – in the face of unfulfilled assimilation – to ethnic 'roots' and 'heritage'.[299]

This 'magical recovery' of Irish ethnicity offers more than mere subjectivity though, for the singer's provenance also functions, in this scenario, as a recuperative well spring, supplying psychic rejuvenation in the face of emotional decline.[300] Like other second-generation Irish figures who have sourced their upbringing for its 'strength and sense of historical solidarity',[301] Rowland's narrating persona, in a quest for psychic 'strength' (to 'take bad on') elects to 'look back to where [he] came from', effecting a thematic closure that prompts the relief of the chorus. In this regard, the track bears a resemblance to other accounts of Irish ethnic 'recovery', not least John Ford's *The Quiet Man* (1952), in which the figure of Sean Thornton (John Wayne) forsakes the anguish of urban America for ancestral restitution in a curative Irish west.[302] The analogies between these (otherwise) disparate texts are realised in the video for 'Knowledge Of Beauty', which details Rowland's return to the parish of his Mayo-born parents.[303] There are profound differences, of course, between Ford's film and Rowland's song, with the sombre intro-spection of Rowland contrasting starkly with Ford's Hollywood whimsy. The slow-paced 'Knowledge Of Beauty' thus unfolds almost inaudibly, with a sparse piano supplying colour to a simple bass and gentle snare. While sliding steel guitars conjure a distinctly country and western style, a picked mandolin serves as a clue to the song's setting. In this mood of what White calls 'convivial warmth',[304] Rowland emits a low, softly controlled vocal, offering nostalgic gestures towards his speaker's homeland. This sets the scene for an address to Ireland's diaspora (to whom the song has been seen as a 'tribute'),[305] who 'these days' dwell in 'US and Britannia care'. Imparting an oblique critique of England, the speaker stages a sort of abdication, journeying west (beyond 'hollow words' and 'the "now" generation') to reconnect himself with the 'wisdom and warmth' of his 'past generations'. ('Hardly a hip statement', as one critic observed at the time.)[306]

It is in the song's final chorus, however, that the speaker unveils (in quietly mixed, spoken words) the track's resolution, which White views as 'an awakening'.[307] 'I've denied my beautiful heritage, gone away from my roots', Rowland narrates, stating a desire to 'come back home again'. If this 'home' was harmonically evoked by a distinctly Irish fiddle part, it was more conspicuously evinced in the aforementioned video, which literally relocates (the emotionally displaced) Rowland in the spatial terrain of Ireland's west coast, with shots of the singer voyaging through a series of Irish vistas in a physical manifestation of the song's symbolic passage.[308] Shots of Rowland gazing at an ancient family tombstone in County Mayo and bowing at Catholic icons in a rural Irish church convey the quasi-religious aspects of the singer's ancestral voyage, whilst lingering views of archetypal Irish scenes (including a thatched cottage, stacked turf and the Cliffs of Moher) forge a sentimental portrait of Ireland. This is offset, though, by the video's slow pace and artfully unfocused images, which – like the visibly solemn Rowland and his song's reflective tenor – conjure melancholy more than schmaltz.

More problematic, perhaps, is the hook that Rowland intones in the stern lyrical coda. Here, as frantic brass figures and busy percussion urge the track to crescendo, the singer – who has hitherto been restrained – emits the abrasive words that gave the track its original title ('My national pride is a personal pride'), with Rowland asserting Irish ethnicity in what John Mulvey has called 'one of the most uncluttered outpourings of emotion ever recorded by a British singer'.[309] By taking on the argot of Britain's far right, however, Rowland had effectively assailed *one* sort of nationalist enterprise (via his speakers' refusal to assimilate) by extolling another (through a reverence for 'roots' and 'heritage'). And though this gesture was intended, as Hutcheon has explained, to urge exilic Irish listeners to be 'proud of [their] roots',[310] it effectively effaced the motif of diaspora that was invoked at the start of the song, with its de-territorial impulse now displaced by an expressly nationalist outlook. This was at odds, moreover, with earlier aspects of Rowland's work, such as the critique of patriotism that he had expressed in certain songs (including 'There, There, My Dear' and 'Old' (1982)), as well as in interviews and ancillary media ('one thing I detest is patriotism', he had told the Irish music paper *Hot Press*).[311] In the course of 'Knowledge Of Beauty', though, Rowland had aligned himself with Irish nationalism and (what he called) 'nationalist music'.[312] The singer would later concede that he became 'very nationalistic' during this period: 'I did get into that thing then', he explains, 'of "everything Irish is great and everything English is shit".' He suggests that he 'retreated too much into that', viewing this standpoint as a withdrawal.[313] As Malone and Dooley have explained, certain sections of the second generation have sought – in the absence of their own sense of 'home' – an idealised Irish elsewhere that was 'separate in time and place from the demands of everyday existence', and served 'to obviate the need to be thoroughly engaged in the "here and now"'.[314] This is certainly how Rowland came to view the ethnic nationalism of his mid-1980s self: 'It's a way of disengaging … because you're here [in England]', he says. 'It's denying that you're *here*' – something he sees as a 'really negative thing'.[315]

The 'national pride' song lyric, then, suggests that Rowland's dislike of patriotism was less of an aversion to nationalism per se than a response to British nationalism from an outsider's (quasi-nationalistic) view. This view was occasionally evinced in Dexys' œuvre, not least in their 1980 tour programme, which concluded with a refusal of patriotism and yet began with an endorsement of the IRA, a paradox also present in 'There, There, My Dear', which rebukes a 'dumb, dumb patriot' before issuing allusive succour to Irish nationalist actions.[316] Reflecting on this point, Rowland notes that he set out to find an identification that was distinct from that of Irish-born migrants and the Irish in Ireland. Seeing the second generation as 'a breed apart', he explains, 'We're so different from the first-generation Irish', laying special stress on the fact that 'we're much angrier than them'. Whether or not this helps to explain the IRA allusions outlined above, it evidently informed the singer's approach to Irish issues. 'I wanted to find out my *own* Irishness, not my dad's Irishness', he explains.

> I wasn't saying what my dad was saying about Ireland. I wasn't saying that the Irish flag is great. I wasn't saying that just because it's Irish it's good. I was saying '*This* is important.' I was kind of finding my own way.[317]

This notion of 'finding your own way of being Irish' is one that appears in many second-generation accounts.[318] In this context, John Lydon recalls that a lack of access to Irish culture in his early milieu left him feeling 'isolated and shallow inside', and prompted him to 'find out about [his] own Irishness'.[319]

This sort of symbolic journey – towards a second-generation subjectivity – would be explored on *DSMD*'s final (and de facto title) track, 'The Waltz'. Tackling similar thematic terrain to 'Knowledge Of Beauty', it adheres to that song's pace, tenor and instrumentation. Rather than staging a recovery of Irish ethnicity, though, 'The Waltz' pursues the quandary of dual identity as a dysfunctional tryst between its subject and two mythical women, presented here as sisters. The song's original title had been 'Elizabeth Wimpole and Kathleen Ní Houlihan', and although concerns about its reception had led the singer to 'change the title and make some of the lyrics more vague', the latter figure is present in the revised song words (albeit in the truncated form of 'Kathleen') – an estranged 'sister' to the addressee.[320] If Ní Houlihan acts as an embodiment of Ireland, then 'Elizabeth' serves, in the song, as an index of England (Rowland had heard someone refer to Elizabeth Windsor as 'Lizzie Wimpole' – hence the name in the song's original title).[321] It is 'Elizabeth', in any case, to whom the speaker projects, with Rowland recounting his regret at being tricked by her 'strategy' and for pursuing her 'course'. Evoking themes of assimilation, Rowland's speaker goes on – in the double-length third, and final, verse – to assail such English schemes, lamenting how he had 'swooned to the stories of Royal victories', before reproving England's dreaming ('your books of history were fairy tales'). The track thus acts as a critique of the 'imperial mentality' that, for Bhikhu Parekh, 'penetrated everyday life, popular culture and consciousness' in post-war Britain.[322] The song also attacks, as White points out, 'all things monarchical', questioning the 'propagators' and 'historical fallacies' of 'British myth'.[323] Amidst this admonition of England as Elizabeth, the singer cites Ireland – via the 'good sister', Kathleen – as an absent presence, a figure rendered invisible ('She's nowhere to be seen'), thus evoking the silence about Ireland in English textbooks.[324] (This resonated with Rowland's experience of school history lessons: 'There was no mention of Ireland', he recalls.[325])

While 'The Waltz' registers the 'doubt' and 'confusion' of second-generation life, there is no curative reversion, here, to the ancestor lore of 'Knowledge Of Beauty'. What the song offers instead is a lament for the silence on Irishness in the speaker's milieu ('They don't talk of Kathleen, things are not how they seem'). Rowland would explain that the track had been shaped by his 'strong feelings for Ireland and what was going on there'.[326] However, the song's only discernible theme is that of English incorporation and Irish ethnicity, with the latter theme staged as a kind of return of the repressed ('She won't wait anymore', the singer strains anxiously, prior to the heartfelt middle-eight). Later on, in a gentle refrain that restores the song's tender prelude, the speaker declares his allegiance to the unseen figure of Kathleen ('Don't stand me down ... for I'll never stop saying your name'), with Rowland reflecting in interviews that this lyric, which had supplied the album with its title, was an appeal from the diaspora to not be abandoned by 'home'.[327]

Such gestures had, however, been rendered oblique by Rowland's wish, in the latter stages of production, to make the song lyrics 'more vague'. Nonetheless, the singer's final words – in the closing moments of what would become Dexys' last album – were unambiguous, distilling Rowland's long-term address to Irish issues. With his controlled delivery at the fore of the track's sparse mix – with violin, guitar and slow-paced snare as accompaniment – the singer enunciates a simple vocal phrase, 'Here is a protest', dwelling on the contours of the latter word before the song's emphatic coda in which blue-note brass motifs and improvised singing supply a markedly upbeat mood. Like its companion piece, 'Knowledge Of Beauty', then, 'The Waltz' enacts a certain closure, renouncing assimilation whilst revering roots (and thus assuaging the ambivalence that is associated with second-generation life).

In light of Rowland's concerns about the silence on Ireland in contemporary British life, it is somewhat ironic that *DSMD* was so veiled and oblique. The singer would defend this abstraction, explaining that the 'best' forms of 'nationalist music' had historically been 'the stuff in disguise when you don't know that it is actually about Ireland at all'.[328] As allusive as they no doubt were, the tracks on *DSMD* nevertheless comprised the most substantive address to second-generation Irish experience in the realm of popular song. With this in mind, it is worth noting that the album received a largely hostile response at the time of its release, with poor sales and mixed reviews leading to a low turn-out at the group's 1985 live shows.[329] The album thus became, as Hutcheon explains, an 'object of derision',[330] a fate born of a range of factors (not least the band's unusual appearance and ornate songs, as well as the broader shifts in popular music since their last incarnation). However, the record's vexed address to Irishness arguably also played a part in its poor reception, which, in turn, as Mulvey explains, 'effectively destroyed' the group's career.[331] Rowland's forthright recovery of Irish ethnicity thus signalled (and perhaps helped to bring about) the end of the Dexys project.

Conclusion: 'It was like this'

In this chapter, we have seen how Kevin Rowland invoked various sorts of Irish ethnicity in the work of Dexys Midnight Runners. This invocation coalesced around the themes of protest, intervention and recovery, taking both overt and oblique forms, from the candour of 'Dance Stance' to the riddle of 'The Waltz'. These highly 'serious' interventions served to bookend the incarnation of Dexys that was most obviously Irish and yet least *engagé*. It appeared, then, that Rowland found it easier to engage with Irish issues when dressed as a yuppie or docker in a brass-led soul ensemble than when clothed as a Celtic gypsy amidst fiddles, banjos and whistles. If this was a symptom of genre (and the limits of aesthetic style), it was also born of the journey (a key trope in Dexys' output) on which Rowland's venture was mapped. This began with a gesture of 'passing' – or Anglo-Italian pretence – that would act as a platform of protest for expressly Irish concerns (via 'Dance Stance', temperance and Two Tone, and attacks on the 'Irish joke'). This position would then be vacated for an openly Celtic style, with Irishness placed at the forefront, but only in fanciful form (saccharine sounds and rustic attire, 'Celtic Soul Brothers' and 'Come On Eileen'). While this project comprised a riposte to prevailing conceptions of Irishness (with their emphasis on violence and alcoholism), it took on a sort of 'Celtitude' – assuming the essentialist ethos of 'Celticism' – in its staging of ethnic difference. Realising the frailties of this persona, Rowland acquired a far more serious, controlled and engaged (as well as much less conventionally 'Irish') mode of expression for the final Dexys project (with its sombre expressions and heavy suits, ornate songs and slow tempo). Presenting the singer's most extensive (if somewhat veiled) address to second-generation experience – and Anglo-Irish issues in general – this project eschewed both 'passing' and 'acting-out' as ways to assert ethnic difference. However, its hard-line identity politics met with considerable public disdain, and precipitated the end of the Dexys project in 1986. In the next chapter, we shall see how another evocation of Irishness – launched at the same time as *Too-Rye-Ay* – sought to stage a different type of ethnic recovery, with its own distinct aesthetic character and deeply contrasting effects.

2

The Importance of Being (London) Irish:
Hybridity, Essentialism
and The Pogues

[Shane] MacGowan was the first voice ... that arose from within [the London-Irish] to give defiant and poetic expression to a community which had never really felt able to proclaim itself

Eamonn McCann[1]

[The Pogues] were the first people who helped define what you could be as a second-generation Irish person in this country

Martin McDonagh[2]

Off-stage and on, The Pogues disported themselves like archetypal Paddies, with a reputation for hard drinking, bad manners, and disdain for personal appearance

Nuala O'Connor[3]

In 1988, at the height of The Pogues' commercial success, the late Irish journalist Bill Graham offered a compelling account of the group's appeal, arguing that their œuvre equipped Ireland's exiles with a means by which to 'reclaim *and* reorder their inheritance'.[4] This succinct observation remains the most insightful précis of The Pogues' expressive project, which refracted strands of Irish folk music through the prism of English punk, fashioning a vibrant new aesthetic that was viewed by observers as 'a lively manifestation of second-generation Irish in Britain'.[5] The band's (highly audible) synthesis of both the 'English' and 'Irish' aspects of second-generation life offered a striking illustration of what Josh Kun has called 'audiotopia', a term that he uses to describe a musical space in which 'contradictions and conflicts do not cancel each other out but coexist and live through each other'. Audiotopias in this way serve, then, as

> identificatory 'contact zones,' in that they are both sonic and social spaces where disparate identity-formations, cultures, *and* geographies historically kept and mapped separately are allowed to interact with each other.[6]

Such 'contradictions and conflicts' were, of course, often experienced *within* the lives of second-generation Irish people,[7] and in this context what The Pogues seemed to offer was a sort of symbolic accommodation, with their work serving to reconcile the contemporary pop-cultural and historical folk-cultural strands of 'Irish-English' life. Rather than retracting into either side of the ethnic-national binary, then, The Pogues took on a certain *Irish-in-England* subject position, locating themselves as irreducibly 'London-Irish'.[8] In the process, Irish ethnicity was reordered – in the group's œuvre – as an attribute to be audaciously paraded, instead of a flaw to be anxiously concealed.

The band's project would effect, however, both regressive and regenerative ends: for while The Pogues conveyed an Irishness that was confidently cosmopolitan and contemporary – evincing a London-Irish outlook that had not yet been evident in popular song – they simultaneously served to reactivate archaic ethnic roles, evoking the inebriated archetype outlined by O'Connor above, prompting claims that they were 'nothing more than a bunch of stereotypical second-generation Paddies'.[9]

This chapter will seek to make sense of The Pogues' antithetical drives, addressing, in the first instance, the more inventive aspects of MacGowan's project, including his formation of a second-generation Irish subject position and London-Irish imaginary. These pioneering efforts are set against the less novel components of The Pogues' persona, not least their activation of the age-old 'drunken Paddy' and associated ethnic tropes. While such tropes often seemed to eclipse the band's more innovative impulse, MacGowan's wish to stage a hybrid (London-) Irishness was contingent on the singer being *seen* as Irish, and one of the few available means by which an English-accented (and London-raised) figure could achieve this was through the exposition of existing archetypes, perhaps the best known of which (in the popular-cultural context of 1980s Britain) was the 'boozy' migrant 'Paddy'. The chapter explores these different strands of The Pogues, whilst charting the band's highly charged reception. Throughout, the discussion will focus on The Pogues' founder, chief songwriter and lead singer, Shane MacGowan.

Most scholarly work on MacGowan has viewed his œuvre from a general – rather than a specifically second-generation – frame of Irishness.[10] In marked contrast, this chapter locates the singer as an expressly second-generation figure whose work with The Pogues supplied the first explicitly *London*-Irish intervention in popular music culture. Before presenting my analysis, however, I will outline the particular contexts from which the singer, and his work, would emerge.

From the broad majestic Shannon to the old main drag: the early years of Shane MacGowan

While many accounts of MacGowan's life suggest that he was born on the banks of the River Shannon in County Tipperary, he was in fact born in the small English town of Tonbridge, Kent, on Christmas Day 1957.[11] MacGowan's Irish-born parents had been visiting relatives in south-east England, where they would remain for several months. Within the year, however, the family had settled on a farm owned by MacGowan's grandfather in Puckaun, County Tipperary.[12] In common with Kevin Rowland, then, MacGowan would spend a sizeable part of his childhood in Ireland, with the youngster 'going backwards and forwards [between the two countries] many times'.[13]

In Tipperary, MacGowan lived amongst an extended family of uncles, aunts and cousins, and frequently attended, as well as participated in, 'open house' sessions of traditional Irish music and dance. His mother, an Irish dancer and fluent Irish speaker, later explained that Shane had 'absorbed all that ... traditional Irish music and singing ... through his pores when he was at a very formative age', noting that this had 'a tremendous influence on him'.[14]

Despite the apparent sparseness of life in rural Ireland (the family had no television, cooker or running water),[15] MacGowan recalls that he had an idyllic childhood. This is not to say that he became prey to that amnesic illusion of Ireland so often associated with its diaspora, for the singer has also acknowledged the less attractive aspects of Irish life (including what he calls the 'small mindedness', the 'sadism' and the 'brutality').[16] Nevertheless, his abiding memory of this period is of what he calls 'happy times.'[17] This enjoyable Irish infancy was evidently sundered, however, when MacGowan's father took up an administrative post with the British clothing firm C&A in the early 1960s, precipitating the family's transfer to London.[18] The transition from Ireland to England was quite traumatic, with MacGowan describing the passage as an 'horrific ... change of life'.[19] The youngster, who was now of school-attending age, recalls 'crying [himself] to sleep' at night whilst 'thinking about Ireland', noting the 'anxiety, depression, and ... paranoia' that this experience induced.[20] This distress was only made worse by MacGowan's English classmates, who, he claims, 'kicked' the more overt forms of Irishness 'out of [him]'.[21] At the same time, the singer's parents were evidently unhappy at being stationed in England, a point underlined by his father's admission that he 'never really settled' there.[22]

The alienation that MacGowan felt in England was alleviated to some extent by his attending Irish social clubs, as well as by regular visits to Ireland. '[B]ecause there's an Irish scene in London', he later explained, 'you never forget the fact that you originally came from Ireland. There are lots of Irish pubs, so there was always Irish music in bars and on jukeboxes ... Then every summer I would spend my school holidays back in Tipp.'[23] The Irish aspects of MacGowan's upbringing would leave what he calls 'a strong impression' on him.[24] ('You don't stop being Irish when you leave [Ireland]', he later explained, adding 'you increase being Irish when you leave it', implying that life in England had made him more aware of his Irish identity.[25]) Nevertheless, the singer was forced to confront the more fraught strains of identity politics that have marked second-generation life.[26] Recounting the fractious intra-generational tensions that engaged his London-Irish peers, MacGowan recalls their differential responses to the Irish–English quandary, explaining that the second-generation Irish in 1970s London 'got split down the middle, really heavily' between one set of youngsters who 'decided that they would never be English' ('however long they spent in England, they would always be Irish') and another strand that was 'ashamed of their own parents and their own roots', and consented to 'the general belief that Paddies were stupid and violent and drunken and that that was all there was to them'.[27] MacGowan's affiliation was undoubtedly with the former: he 'went through a stage', he explains, 'of thinking that every-thing that was Irish was great and everything else [was] shit'.[28]

Notwithstanding such intra-ethnic issues, MacGowan achieved exceptional academic success, attaining a highly competed-for schol-arship (via an essay-writing contest) at Westminster, one of Britain's most prestigious private schools. His attendance at this esteemed institution would be relatively brief, however (he was expelled for pos-session of drugs within his first year), and after a short period at Brook Green College in Hammersmith, the sixteen-year-old withdrew from formal education.[29] A period of alcohol and drug abuse followed, before MacGowan was admitted to the Bethlem Royal Hospital, a well-known psychiatric institution in London. The singer later explained that his symptoms were not confined to the effects of substance abuse, with a series of 'acute anxiety attacks' pointing to what he calls a 'mental breakdown'.[30]

After his spell in hospital, MacGowan worked as a warehouseman, porter and barman, although his attentions had become focused on London's nascent punk scene.[31] The highly visible presence of a second-generation Irish singer, Johnny Rotten, at the forefront of the punk subculture heightened the scene's attraction to MacGowan. The latter witnessed several Sex Pistols shows, and 'admired' what Clerk has called 'the Irishness he came to see in Rotten'.[32] 'I probably wouldn't have been that interested if Johnny Rotten hadn't been so bloody obviously Irish and made a big noise about it and made such anti-English records', explains MacGowan.[33]

It is worth stressing that England's punk scene – with its assemblage of various outsiders – included what MacGowan calls a 'Paddy mafia', with numerous London-Irish figures performing key roles.[34] This point often went unacknowledged in England, despite John Lydon's upfront evocation of Irish ethnicity. In the face of attempts by the far-right National Front to appropriate English punk, Lydon openly cited his Irishness: 'I'm Irish', he explained, 'and if they took over I'd be on the next boat back. I believe you should be allowed to live where you want, when you want and how you want.'[35] This aspect of Lydon's character did not go unobserved by his English band-mates (who called him 'Paddy'), nor by Britain's far right, some of whose adherents physically attacked the singer shortly after his anti-racist remarks.[36]

If English punk had served, then, as a haven for marginalised youth (a point that Jon Savage has maintained), its emergence would coincide (as Bill Graham has explained) with the coming-of-age of the second generation.[37] In this context, punk supplied MacGowan (in the words of Sean O'Hagan) with a crucial 'sense of belonging' (or what Clerk has called a 'home').[38] The youngster certainly became a visible (and highly active) participant in the scene, publishing a noted fanzine (called *Bondage*) whilst working at the in-vogue Rock On record store and attending numerous punk gigs.[39] Rather ironically, MacGowan would announce his presence at many punk events with a conspicuous Union Jack shirt, a garment that seems somewhat curious in light of his Irishness.[40] The Union flag had been subjected – within punk's visual economy – to a radical *détournement*, not least through the Sex Pistols' iconoclastic appropriation of the red, white and blue during Queen Elizabeth's silver jubilee in June 1977.[41] Despite punk's seditious revision of the symbol, MacGowan would be taken to task by the scene's de facto spokesman, John Lydon, for his Union-flag adornment. 'Shane MacGowan used to come and see [the Sex Pistols] play all the time', Lydon has explained, recalling that the youngster was typically 'pissed out of his head' in a 'Union Jack T-shirt'. From Lydon's perspective, this gesture would render MacGowan's shift from English punk to Irish folk somewhat disingenuous, with Lydon dismissing this transition as an 'instant nationality swap'.[42] MacGowan, in turn, would deny the allegation that his Union-flag attire signalled an affiliation with Britain. 'I was accused by Johnny of being a Brit', the singer later explained, 'because I wore a Union Jack shirt, and then of changing into an Irish republican, to be fashionable'. MacGowan would insist that 'nothing could be further from the truth', noting that he had (in the mid-1970s) appeared in public with the initials 'IRA' inscribed on his forehead.[43]

Notwithstanding the veracity (or indeed the ethics) of MacGowan's gesture, it is clear that his punk pseudonym (Shane O'Hooligan) signalled a desire to announce (rather than conceal) his Irishness.[44] This peculiar alias deviated starkly, moreover, from the music industry custom of migrant-descended performers effacing ethnic difference through 'stage' nomenclature. As Dave Laing explains, there is 'a long history of performers of Jewish, Italian or German origin acquiring Anglo-Saxon names for their show-business career'.[45] Similarly, many English-born musicians of Irish descent have assumed non-'ethnic' stage appellations – hence, 'Dusty Springfield' (Mary O'Brien), 'Elvis Costello' (Declan McManus) and 'Boy George' (George O'Dowd). The central function of the punk pseudonym was, however, rather different, for its designations stemmed from public insults that were, as Savage points out, 'taken on board and flaunted as a badge of pride' in a self-conscious strategy that 'not only turned the insult on its head' but also 'meant that the owners of these pseudonyms were often required to act out the pejorative definitions of others'.[46] Whether or not MacGowan's persona had served to enact such derogatory meanings, it is clear that his 'O'Hooligan' pseudonym conveyed a certain conception of Irishness, and the singer was in turn perceived – at least by his punk contemporaries – as Irish.[47] Acquaintances of MacGowan from this period have confirmed that he was 'unassailably proud of his Irish background', noting that he had a 'focused sense of what it was to be Irish', and frequently 'talk[ed] about what it was to be Irish in London'.[48] This affiliation with Irish ethnicity was underscored by the youngster's punk-informed accessories, which, according to Clerk, drew on 'the imagery of his Catholic background with crucifixes and rosary beads teamed with a beret'.[49] MacGowan was also subjected, at this time, to a series of violent attacks that observers would put down to 'Paddy-bashing'.[50]

However, while MacGowan's 'O'Hooligan' persona evinced an expressly Irish invocation of disorderliness (and one that was, of course, compatible with punk), the singer made little attempt, at this time, to deploy Irish sounds or styles, drawing instead on a punk/rockabilly hybrid whilst using an 'exaggerated Cockney accent'.[51] It was, moreover, in this context – as vocalist/lyricist with The Nips (c. 1977–81; originally The Nipple Erectors) – that MacGowan made his first mark on popular culture.[52] Though this group enjoyed a moderate amount of success, they had begun to disband by the start of the Eighties, by which time Shane had observed, in the words of McAnailly-Burke, a 'tendency toward ethnicity in the contemporary rock scene', whose burgeoning roots milieu supplied a striking antidote to the then ubiquitous sounds of synth-pop (which the singer had been censuring since 1979).[53] In the face of this binary between, on the one hand, folk authenticity and, on the other, pop artifice, MacGowan turned to the specific variety of roots music that he 'felt naturally emotionally involved with' (in other words, Irish folk).[54] Despite the multicultural character of the metropolitan roots scene, it had yet to properly register the 'ethnic' music that lay in what MacGowan calls its 'own backyard', with the immigrant Irish folk scene remaining, in his words, a 'totally ignored subculture'.[55] It was at this crucial juncture, then, that the singer embarked on a profound shift in orientation: 'I just thought ... if people are being "ethnic", I might as well be my own "ethnic".'[56]

With this as his guiding principle, MacGowan went on, in the words of Colin Irwin, to 'cull' his 'Irish ancestry in a harsh and highly deliberate rejection of modern pop'.[57] Thus, The Pogues' first output – a promotional film for 'Streams Of Whiskey' (1983) – lampooned the styles of British 'new pop' via a parody of glitzy videos such as that for 'Club Tropicana' by Wham! (1983).[58] With a drained and grimy canal functioning as a surrogate hotel swimming pool, and MacGowan accessorising with a humble pint pot (rather than showy cocktail flute), the band's free-form Irish step dancing supplied an ironic 'folk' rejoinder to the stylized disco pose of George Michael et al.[59] Such gestures did not signal tactical alliance, however, with England's burgeoning roots-rock scene, for MacGowan was also keen to distance The Pogues from that aesthetic milieu, with songs such as 'Connemara Let's Go' (1983) secreting a critique of contemporary roots-based acts such as Havana Let's Go, who MacGowan admonished as an 'annoying, ethnic, world music group'.[60] Positioning themselves against both roots rock and synth-pop, The Pogues staged a startling fusion of folk and punk, becoming 'an unlikely meeting point between The Clancy Brothers and The Clash'.[61] In this regard, the band had revived a style that was, for Clerk, 'unfashionable and widely unloved' by infusing it with 'the spirit, the spontaneity, the attitude and the language of punk', bequeathing a brand of Irish music that was 'relevant' and 'exciting'.[62]

While the ethnic orientation of this project was in little doubt, MacGowan made it clear that he was *London*-Irish, laying stress on his second-generationness.[63] ('My parents are Irish', he explained in 1986. 'I come from an immigrant background.'[64]) Such assertions of Irish ethnicity were, however, a not unproblematic endeavour in early-Eighties Britain, where anti-Irish prejudice had been intensified by the IRA's 'mainland' bombing campaign.[65] In this context, MacGowan's colleagues recall that it was 'definitely not a good thing to be Irish' in early-Eighties London, noting that 'there was a lot of racism against Irish people'.[66] This is a point confirmed by observers, who explain that the band's allegiance with Irishness seemed – in the context of IRA violence and anti-Irish sentiment – somewhat incongruous.[67] 'I really can't stress enough how *other* that was', suggests Dee O'Mahony with regard to MacGowan's identification as Irish-in-London, seeing this as 'a completely different take' on ideas of Irishness at the time.[68]

Interestingly, it was the old-fashioned 'folk' (rather than the more contemporary punk) aspects of the new group's sound that were considered most contentious (one of MacGowan's band-mates recalls that Irish rebel songs were one of the few musical forms capable of causing indignation at the time).[69] There is certainly little doubt that the band aroused hostility: an early live show came to an abrupt conclusion when a group of off-duty British soldiers (apparently on leave from Northern Ireland) reacted angrily to their set, and pelted the band with food.[70] The music business was also quite unreceptive. As Stan Brennan, The Pogues' first manager, recalls, 'negativity [towards the band] was enormous', and there was 'real shock' that MacGowan had turned to 'this Irish thing'.[71] How, then, did this curious punk-folk project materialise? And how did MacGowan and his band seek to stage it?

Irish ethnicity, English punk and The Pogues

MacGowan had first conceived of The Pogues' aesthetic as a hypothetical style he called 'Paddy beat', a projected synthesis of Fifties rock and traditional folk.[72] One of his key reference points in devising this 'beat music based on Irish music' was Jimmy Lydon (the younger brother of John), with whom MacGowan would occasionally drink and sing Irish songs.[73] Lydon's band, The 4Be2s, would, as Ann Scanlon explains, subvert the 'immigrant put-down "No Irish, no blacks, no dogs" by fusing Irish music with dub'.[74] However, what most impressed MacGowan about the group was their desire to incorporate a 'traditional Irish tenor banjo' (played by one of Lydon's uncles) in their post-punk style. Recalling that Jimmy Lydon was 'the actual obnoxious London-Irish cunt that Johnny was posing as', MacGowan explains that the 4Be2s performed Irish rebel songs in an 'obnoxious' and 'entertaining' manner, thereby serving as a template for his notion of 'Paddy beat'.[75] Significantly, then, while John Lydon had played a crucial role in attracting MacGowan to punk, it was Lydon's younger sibling Jimmy who sparked MacGowan's idea for a folk-punk fusion act.[76]

Rather appropriately, this formative 'Paddy beat' scheme was publicly showcased in the Lydons' home district of Finsbury Park, where MacGowan played 'shambolic' versions of nationalist songs – under the appellation of The New Republicans (*c.* 1981) – in the local train station.[77] Over the next eighteen months, the singer would recruit two musicians of Irish descent, Cáit O'Riordan (bass) and Andrew Ranken (drums), alongside three non-Irish associates: Jem Finer (banjo), Spider Stacy (tin whistle) and James Fearnley (accordion).[78] O'Riordan notes that it was her ethnicity (more than her musical aptitude) that led to her conscription by MacGowan, who viewed the bassist as 'very important' to The Pogues.[79] Like MacGowan, O'Riordan had been raised in an Irish family in London (with whom she attended the city's Irish clubs and annual St Patrick's Day parades) before moving into an Irish hostel in Kilburn. O'Riordan had also been active in the Troops Out Movement, attending demonstrations in Belfast and Derry prior to joining The Pogues.[80] This early Pogues ensemble was augmented (in 1985) by two Irish-born musicians, Philip Chevron (guitar) and Terry Woods (bouzouki), before O'Riordan departed and was replaced on bass (in 1986) by the group's English 'roadie', Darryl Hunt.[81]

It was an embryonic Pogues line-up, however, that made their live debut as Pogue Mahone (Irish for 'kiss my arse', and thus a 'dual expression', as Clerk points out, of 'attitude *and* Irishness') on 4 October 1982 at the Pindar of Wakefield pub in King's Cross, north London.[82] As Scanlon explains, early Pogues shows were often 'drunken' and 'shambolic', with critics observing the group's 'scrappiness', 'disorganisation' and 'sizeable alcohol intake'.[83] Nevertheless, the distinctive aspects of The Pogues' aesthetic were already in evidence at this stage, with the band performing traditional songs in a fast-paced, frenetic manner.[84] In this respect there was a curious synchronicity between The Pogues and the (then) current incarnation of Dexys Midnight Runners, who had released the year's best-selling single, 'Come On Eileen' (1982).[85] MacGowan was apparently 'furious' when he first heard Rowland's Celtic sound, believing that the singer had 'stolen his idea'.[86] However, despite being 'shocked and horrified' at Dexys' new style, MacGowan soon incorporated 'Come On Eileen' as a light-hearted live encore.[87] Moreover, his band-mates would explain that The Pogues' concurrence with 'Celtic'-era Dexys was simply a 'bizarre coincidence', and the two projects were – in any case – highly disparate in execution, with critics noting the difference between The Pogues' 'punchy, wholly revitalised pub folk format' and Dexys' 'lavish showband revue'.[88]

Retrieving the 'raw' forms of folk that MacGowan had observed on the London-Irish pub circuit, The Pogues accrued a conception of Irishness that was accommodated easily in the ethos of punk – hence their penchant for shouting, swearing and rowdiness (while Stacy struck metal beer trays against his head as a form of percussion, MacGowan and O'Riordan traded insults and, occasionally, blows).[89] Consequently, the band's repertoire of traditional songs was radically reconfigured by their brash and boisterous delivery, with high-speed melodic lines set against a punchy electric bass and minimal stripped-down kit (initially restricted to floor-tom, crash cymbal and snare, which Ranken would play standing up).[90]

The band's style has been outlined by the musicologist Allan F. Moore, who discerns a 'well rehearsed carelessness' that is 'derived from punk'; unusually hectic speeds ('the up-tempo numbers ... are in the region of 150 beats to the minute, which is very fast indeed'); and a 'complex, energetic interplay of instruments' that 'connotes informal dance' whilst belying 'simple' song 'structures'. MacGowan's vocal style, meanwhile, displayed a 'carelessness' that, for Moore, was redolent of punk. Thus, as Moore observes, the words in Pogues songs 'tend to be spat out', with 'the voice having no resonance, no vibrato and no sense of shaping of phrases'.[91] Joe Cleary confirms the band's indebtedness to punk, noting, in The Pogues' œuvre,

> a sense of low-tech but high-energy rough musical improvisation; a demotic taste for the trashy and vulgar; a tendency to favour cacophonous and abrasive musical textures over refinement and melody (a feature of their style that extended to MacGowan's smoke-scarred, alcohol-slurred vocals); near-chaotic sets ... and a backbeat dominated, hook/riff-based musical language.[92]

However, Cleary also notes The Pogues' sourcing from *céilí* and Irish ballad groups: from the former the band would draw 'their basic instrumentation, a pounding collective beat, and a flair for musical speed that prized vigour and verve above polish and sophistication', whilst the latter would supply a model of 'rabble-rousing music' that combined 'old street songs, rural and industrial folk songs, nationalist rebel music, and a broadly leftist or populist politics'. Amidst these different styles, MacGowan's voice functioned as 'a point of lyric identification', supplying 'some sort of vocal core to an otherwise shambolically centrifugal line-up'.[93] If the singer's delivery was drawn in part from punk, it was also indebted to Irish folk – hence descriptions of the singer as 'emerging at the point where Luke Kelly collided with Johnny (Rotten) Lydon', or as 'Johnny Rotten's kid brother, jacking up on Celtic lilting'.[94] (This aspect of MacGowan's vocal was underlined by an Irish-inflected accent, which deviated from his previous singing style and served – for MacGowan – as an effect of Irish-based songs.[95])

Photograph: Bleddyn Butcher

In terms of visual style, MacGowan devised an idiosyncratic ensemble called 'Paddy chic', based on the plain black suits and tie-less white shirts of writer Brendan Behan, an homage that was not lost on critics, who observed in The Pogues a 'dissolute image of a squad of Brendan Behans'.[96] Contrasting starkly with the nouveau-gypsy attire of Dexys' Celtic phase, MacGowan claimed that his band's garments were drawn from a 'classic Paddy' look that 'could have come from any decade'.[97] However, such Behan-esque garb clearly conjured the styles of migrant Irish labourers in 1950s London,[98] and accrued a late 1970s inflection when set alongside the group's ruffled hair and facial sneers. In a similar vein, the band's display of tartan (through Ranken's chequered ties and O'Riordan's plaid skirts) signalled both their Celtic provenance as well as their punk credentials.[99]

It is clear, then, that The Pogues' expressive style – at both the sonic and sartorial levels – was indebted as much to Irish folk as it was to English punk (two ostensibly incompatible codes that, for Cleary, had something in common: both were 'aggressively "low cultural" and trashy', as well as 'intensely rebellious and anti-authoritarian').[100] This unusual fusion, which some critics felt was 'schizophrenic',[101] made for a compelling new aesthetic, with the band's accommodation of folk and punk serving, for Chevron, as 'an expression of what it was to be second-generation Irish at that time in England'.[102] The band's work would certainly resonate *with* the migrant Irish, who emerged as The Pogues' early fan base: the London-Irish, recalls MacGowan, 'came out in force, out of the wood-work' to attend the band's concerts, with many displaying visible symbols of Irish ethnicity (such as Glasgow Celtic banners and Irish tricolour flags).[103] MacGowan's point is confirmed by Stan Brennan, who explains that the group found an audience in the English-born offspring of Irish migrants: 'They'd heard The Dubliners, they'd heard Willie Clancy and loved it, although they were too embarrassed to play this sort of music at parties with their mates. But they also loved punk, and they got the Pogue Mahone synthesis very quickly.'[104] Nuala O'Connor extends this point, suggesting that the second generation heard in The Pogues a music that was both 'contemporary' and 'culturally familiar', and thus 'showed a way in which they could be Irish in Britain'.[105]

It is perhaps worth noting, however, that the group would attract a myriad of other constituents ('you definitely don't have to be Irish to enjoy [their shows]', explained critics).[106] Musical forms that are associated with specific ethnic groups can, of course, offer pleasure to listeners from other social groups (and thus, in turn, invite identification from non-members),[107] with the fan's investment in a band being based less, as John Waters explains, on the musicians' 'roots or nationality' than on 'a relationship suggested by the music'.[108] Reflecting on this point, Scanlon relates that The Pogues' audience displayed a 'cross-cultural identity of its own: from punks, football supporters, psychobillies, students and folk fans to anyone with a tint of green blood'.[109] It was undoubtedly with the latter strand of listeners, however, that the group became associated, and The Pogues would go on to 'articulate' with the second-generation Irish (a point I develop below). This constituency would remain, moreover, a 'vocal' and 'important' element of The Pogues' audience.[110] Indeed, certain critics would claim that the band's live shows had the effect of 'excluding … non-Catholic/Irish Pogues fans' (although it could also be argued that such fans took the band's concerts as a means by which to adopt recreational modes of Irish ethnicity).[111] The point to note, in any case, is that a second-generation Irish identity was at the forefront of the group's persona, and in this regard The Pogues were unarguably without precedent.

Assembling a second-generation Irish speaking position: articulation, catharsis, critique

The band's adoption of a second-generation Irish speaking position has been noted by many observers, not least McDonagh and McCann (see the epigraphs that preface this chapter). And while MacGowan suggests that John Lydon was the first singer to address the London-Irish experience,[112] the former's colleagues insist that it was him. O'Riordan, for instance, explains that prior to The Pogues, 'no one talked about us [the second generation]', and consequently 'You didn't know how to articulate what *your* life was like', referring to the 'very difficult' experience of 'growing up London-Irish in the 1970s, having this funny name and parents who had this funny accent, with bombs going off'. In this context, The Pogues offered 'focus' and 'pride', with MacGowan serving as a 'figurehead' that came, for O'Riordan, to 'crystallise' second-generation life.[113] In a similar vein, Chevron claims that The Pogues spoke for 'this huge group of people that were second-generation Irish', not least by engaging with 'the anger and the frustration that people felt growing up Irish in London.' This constituency had, for Chevron, been 'doubly disenfranchised, once by the lingering strains of the "no blacks, no Irish, no dogs" mantra of their British upbringing, and then by the "plastic Paddy" taunts that greeted their accents on holiday visits "back home"'. Consequently, such people had become used to 'cowering in corners pretending not to be Irish or sublimating that completely' before MacGowan 'gave them a voice', becoming 'the first person to stand up and not be embarrassed about it and shout about it'.[114]

In light of this ground-breaking effort to, in O'Hagan's terms, speak both 'to – and for – a whole subculture that history and culture ignores',[115] it is surprising that scholarly work on The Pogues has failed to register the second-generation issue in precise terms. McLaughlin and McLoone, for instance, lay stress on the variegated modes of Irishness that were evoked in the group's work (recording its 'full range of characterisation', including 'drunken Paddies, sentimental Paddies, homesick Paddies, pathetic and nostalgic Paddies') but fall short of actually specifying what was arguably the most salient mode of Irishness in The Pogues' persona, which was expressly second generation and overtly English-based.[116] How, then, was this second-generation subjectivity evinced in the band's work? And in what ways did The Pogues 'articulate' – in the sense of a conjunction or interface[117] – with a second-generation audience?

Acts of musical expression are, for Simon Frith, best understood less as a transparent reflection of a fixed a-priori identity than as a symbolic (and highly practical) means by which participants (such as listeners and players) can take on, inhabit and re-work identities that are always already in process. The issue as far as Frith is concerned, then, is not so much 'how a particular piece of music or a performance' simply '*reflects* the people', as how that event '*produces* them'. In elaborating this point, Frith – significantly – makes reference, by way of illustration, to the immigrant Irish pub scene in England's metropolitan centre.[118]

Frith's line of reasoning certainly helps to make sense of The Pogues' early live shows, which afforded second-generation listeners with a means by which to access and express Irish ethnicity. Observers of the band's early concerts recall that The Pogues 'affected a lot of Irish people in London … just by *making it possible* to claim back some sense of pride in being Irish', with the band supplying their fan base with a 'vital, *accessible* link to ancestry'.[119] The second-generation figures in the group were keenly aware of their capacity to foster communal identification. MacGowan, for instance, would claim that his band acted as a locus around which the second generation coalesced, with The Pogues providing a forum in which this generation could display Irish difference without inhibition.[120] This view was confirmed by journalists, who saw the group as 'cheer and tear-leaders for the disaffected Anglo-Irish community'.[121] O'Riordan, meanwhile, explains that the exhibition of Irish ethnicity that characterised Pogues concerts was comparable to a sporting event: 'It was like being a football team more than a band', she recalls, 'it was like your supporters came along.' Invoking the sense of 'community' that was evident at such events, the bass player argues that the band and their audience were 'in the same boat' by virtue of a shared upbringing, background and experience.[122] However, for O'Riordan, the charged ambience of Pogues shows surpassed the simple act of staging communality. Instead, what such events offered was 'a positive release' of the 'tension' experienced by the second-generation Irish, whose experience required both 'release' and 'expression' – hence the 'joy and passion' that was evident at Pogues shows. 'It's not just that you've got the same experience', she recalls, 'it's that you need some catharsis because [being London-Irish at that time was] kind of a soul-bending experience that could break you if you [couldn't] let it out. And that's why … our audiences were so amazing, because it was cathartic.' What this 'release of tension' afforded, then, was a means to 'let go' of (rather than 'internalise') the 'anger' of second-generation life, enabling this constituency to 'become more positive' about their experience by showing that 'there was a way to be who you were and proud of who you were and proud of your cultural background, and for it to be a *cultural expression*' rather than one marked by either violence or sublimation. Pogues concerts thus allowed the second generation to find expression for their experience

Photograph: Paul Slattery

(instead of simply 'lash[ing] out'), and showed that Irish migrants were not merely 'thugs or weirdos'.[123]

This view of Pogues concerts as a form of collective catharsis was shared with other band members. Ranken, for example, would claim that the group's live shows functioned as a pressure valve in which an otherwise 'suppressed' identity could be discharged.[124] MacGowan, meanwhile, saw such events as a means of 'letting ... out' shared 'frustrations', suggesting that the 'very close' bond between band and audience was based on common experience.[125] In a similar vein, critics observed a 'forged-steel pact of unquestioning loyalty' between the group and their fans, with their respective 'attitudes, aspirations and mutual requirements interlock[ing]' with 'microscopic accuracy', yielding 'an eerie quality of crowd communication' that went 'much further than audience participation'.[126] Others confirmed that they had 'never been at a gig ... where the mood and the music and all the expectations and underlying assumptions seemed so exactly in tune', and had 'never been part of an audience that felt so ... *validated* by being there'.[127] Fans of the group also detailed the 'spirit and vigour' of Pogues concerts, viewing such events as an outlet for second-generation Irish identity. As one audience member explained: 'What is striking on such occasions is the number of

second-generation Irish at these concerts – all united in asserting their
Irish identity ... There are so many pressures today on second-generation
Irish to assimilate and become British that the existence of an outlet'–
such as The Pogues – 'whereby the second generation can stand up and
show their Irishness, should not be dismissed or treated lightly.'[128]

Notwithstanding such suggestions of catharsis and collectivity, there
are obvious economic (as well as crucial symbolic) discrepancies between
professional onstage musicians and their auditorium-bound audience.
Consequently, such impressions of communality can often belie pop's
commercial process, masking material forms of monetary exchange
(through the consumption of concert tickets and other products) with
imagined forms of (psychic) solidarity. With this point (about the une-
venness of the performer–fan nexus) in mind, I think the concept of
'articulation' – as outlined in the previous chapter – provides a more
useful means of conceiving the charged communal dynamics that characterised Pogues live shows.

As Richard Middleton explains, 'articulation' can occur when two
discrete constituents in the musical process (such as 'performer' and
'fan') become conjoined at the moment of consumption (such as live
performance). In the midst of this material event, then, the different
elements of band and audience – though not innately conjoined – are
seen to (symbolically) coalesce, and in this way 'articulate'. Middleton
observes that 'articulative relationships' become 'established' when 'two
or more different elements [such as band and audience] are made to
connote, symbolise or evoke each other', an effect that works especially
well when 'the pattern of elements that it organises comes to seem
"natural"'.[129] It is clear that the work of The Pogues evinced such 'articulative' qualities, and these were often augmented by acts of affiliation
towards the migrant Irish community. The group thus performed at
benefit shows for London-Irish welfare funds, and staged promotional
films, press interviews and launch parties at Irish social venues in the
English capital. (The band even supplied the soundtrack to British
television commercials for Gaelic-sports events.)[130] The extent of this
association was perhaps best evidenced during the annual enactment
of Irishness that marked St Patrick's Day in England, with the band
assuming a totemic role during this openly ethnic social event. In this
context, Clerk has claimed that The Pogues played a vital role in the
revival of this festival in pre-Irish-theme-pub Britain.[131]

In light of such points, it would perhaps not be unreasonable to claim
that the second-generation fan base that emerged as The Pogues' audience had come into being (at least as a recognised constituency) through
the presence of The Pogues in the popular-cultural sphere. (For the

Irish Post, The Pogues were 'as much a part of the ethnic identity of the second generation as the Irish football team and school summers spent in Ireland.'[132]) MacGowan certainly invoked this generation – which he described as a 'subculture' – in interviews, outlining their claims to ethnicity and arguing that the English-born offspring of Irish immigrants had 'got as much right to call [themselves] Irish as anyone with an Irish accent'.[133] At the same time, however, the singer expressed a reluctance, as Merrick has explained, 'to be used as a figurehead for second-generation orphans', a point confirmed by O'Riordan, who notes that 'no one ever asked [MacGowan] to speak for the second generation', stressing that the singer was not a formal 'spokesperson'.[134] In a similar vein, MacGowan would insist that his fan base was not made up solely of Irish-descended advocates. 'They're not *all* second-generation Irish', he told *Sounds* in 1985.[135] Nevertheless, MacGowan would become – as O'Riordan has explained – the public 'representative' of the second-generation Irish in England, and the presence of The Pogues in the popular-cultural sphere would have the effect, as McDonagh has maintained, of *making* a second-generation identity, a filament of immigrant life that had previously gone uncharted in mainstream media discourse.[136]

After The Pogues' first single, the media acquired a keen awareness of the second-generation Irish. This acknowledgement first emerged in Ireland, where *Hot Press* informed its readers, in an article on The Pogues: 'Most Irish families have at least one relative who emigrated to Britain in the first dismal 15 years after the war. But we forget their children. They haven't all been assimilated so completely as to blot out their parents' culture.'[137] In England, meanwhile, publications as unlikely as the *Mail on Sunday* (a right-wing paper not noted for its interest in Irish issues) invoked London's second-generation Irish populace in a short profile of The Pogues.[138] In a similar vein, music papers such as *Sounds* observed, in the band's œuvre, 'a *second-generation* Paddy punch'.[139] Elsewhere, 'style' magazines such as *The Face* (which had previously been a vehicle for Julie Burchill's anti-Irish tirades) dispatched staff to well-known social establishments in London's Irish quarters, where they observed 'youngsters with the uniform of any young Londoner and accents wider than the Holloway Road out to enjoy a culture that's been carried intact across the Irish Sea'. Such reports also catalogued that

> A Saturday night out in Cricklewood or Kilburn, Camden Town or Kentish Town is a night out amongst the ethnic community that time forgot but the Special Branch didn't. Immigrants from Ireland and their second-generation offspring have been part of the fabric

of Britain's major cities for so long now, such an integral part of our urban character that we don't notice how successfully they've maintained their separate identity in every city they've settled.

With special reference to the second generation, *The Face* explained:

> Their experience is a London one: the Sex Pistols and Sergio Tacchini, Soho and shitty comprehensives just like anybody else. But it's flavoured with a peculiarly durable respect for the old ways which brings them out in their thousands on a Friday and Saturday night to waltz and jive to imported showbands in vast velveteen dance halls.

Acknowledging that, prior to the 1980s, 'no band [had] tried to capture this romantic mood', this article concluded by announcing that 'Shane MacGowan and his beat combo ... are changing that.'[140]

Not everyone was receptive to MacGowan's project, however, and his band would face hostility on both sides of the Irish Sea. Amongst sections of the British press, The Pogues were viewed as 'spoilt, lying Londoners' performing a 'pale, anaemic imitation' of a music 'they really have *nothing in common* with'.[141] Meanwhile, the group's second-generation audience was rebuked as a pack of 'pseudo-Irish ... drunken moron[s]'.[142] Elsewhere, belittling terms such as 'leprechaun rock' and 'leprechaunabilly' were used (even by 'progressive' London journals like *Time Out*) to describe the band's style, which evinced, for certain critics, a 'touch of blarney'.[143] Fellow musicians also critiqued the band's claim to ethnicity, with one well-known singer of the period dismissing MacGowan's 'unconvincing Irish accent'.[144] Readers of the music press expressed similarly censorious views, claiming that MacGowan's decaying dental profile was a contrived attempt to look like an Irish folk musician.[145]

More serious was the assumption (at least in Britain) that the band's allegiance with Irish ethnicity implied support for violent sectarianism. Certain observers alleged, for instance, that The Pogues had sanctioned anti-Protestant bigotry and endorsed the Provisional IRA, with their work being viewed as an expression of 'hate' towards non-Catholics, and of 'support' to 'cold-blooded killers'.[146] Such accusations were not uncommon: the band often met claims that they were 'some sort of IRA support team', an allegation that led to MacGowan being assaulted.[147] In light of such attacks, it was ironic that, in Ireland, the band were accused of being 'anti-Irish racists', trafficking in 'some wicked manifestation of cultural imperialism'.[148] Such critiques were based, it seemed, on musical-aesthetic, as much as national-ethnic, considerations. Well-known figures on the Irish traditional scene thus took umbrage with The

Pogues' folk-punk style. Philip King, for instance, issued a 'vitriolic' critique of the band on a live radio show.[149] King's much-vaunted interest in transcultural exchange in Irish music had evidently not extended eastwards (across the Irish Sea); he 'went bananas' when he first heard The Pogues, and launched a 'ferocious' attack on the band in the Irish media.[150] Prior to King's attack, The Pogues had appeared at the 1985 Cibeal Cincíse, a major folk festival in Kenmare, County Kerry, where a large number of musicians had expressed negative views of the group, and where Kevin Conneff of The Chieftains had walked out of their performance.[151] One observer explained at the time that they had 'never heard such venom spewed upon a popular band by traditional musicians'.[152]

It was not only musicians that had problems with The Pogues, however, for the Irish media were also quite unsympathetic. The *Irish Times*, for instance, viewed the band as an 'Irish joke', claiming that MacGowan '*play-acts* as the emigrant casualty' (implying inauthenticity of experience), and dismissing his œuvre as 'Oirish' (invoking inauthenticity of style).[153] Elsewhere, the Irish rock paper *Hot Press* found The Pogues 'amusing' but remained 'dubious' about them 'ever making it as recording artists'.[154]

The most notable event in the band's Irish reception was a radio interview staged by RTÉ in September 1985.[155] This event, broadcast on the *BP Fallon Orchestra* (a popular music show hosted by a well-known critic and disc jockey), featured The Pogues alongside a number of Irish journalists, traditional musicians and members of the public. The dynamic between the band and the invited audience was openly fractious, and the session 'broke down several times as tempers became frayed'.[156] Attendees have confirmed that the 'sense of hostility' between the group and their critics was 'stifling', describing the event as an 'hour of ... attrition'.[157] A key theme in the debate was the issue of the band's Irishness. Thus, the band members – who had been described in the *Irish Times* as 'second-generation Irish from London'[158] – were asked to account for their precise volume of 'Irish blood', and to ponder if their 'not being ... *thoroughbred*' (i.e. Irish-born) should bar them from Irish music.[159] This view of the band as outsiders was underlined when their Irish-born manager Frank Murray was singled out by the host as 'Irish': Fallon made a point, in the show, of framing Murray as 'an *Irish* gentleman' and 'an *Irish* voice', thus distinguishing him from the (English-accented) musicians. This stress on 'voice' was quite significant, for accent has (in the absence of more phenotypic distinctions) served as a key marker of Irishness.[160] Indeed, it has been claimed, in this context, that the view of the second generation as 'not

Irish' pertains more to the sound of their English accents than the fact of their place of birth.[161] This issue has, moreover, been explored – as a crucial source of anxiety – in accounts of second-generation life. In Maude Casey's (semi-autobiographical) novel, *Over the Water*, for example, the chief protagonist Mary, a London-Irish youth, relates that when she speaks amongst Irish-born people her 'voice', as she hears it, is 'flat and awkward with the dead vowels of London': 'it sounds so weird', she explains, 'in among the rising falling song of the way they talk'.[162] Thus, when she converses with people in Ireland, Mary's accent, at least for her, 'feels all wrong'.[163] This sense of feeling 'wrong' was born, it would seem, of the disjuncture between, on the one hand, the girl's affective affinities (with Ireland), and, on the other, her expressive qualities (as English); for while she might *feel* at home in Ireland, her *speech* marks her out as 'English'. This issue has surfaced in other London-Irish literary texts, not least John Walsh's memoir, in which he details a similar dynamic: 'every time I open my mouth', he explains whilst speaking with his family in Ireland, 'I'm reminded how much I don't fit in'.[164] John Lydon, meanwhile, relates that his English accent was a problem for his Irish relatives, not least his (nationalist) grandfather. 'He hated the English', Lydon says, 'and probably hated me and my brother Jimmy.' He points out that 'We spoke with thick cockney accents that he could not stand.'[165] Lydon's accent also caused problems when he was detained in an Irish jail after a scuffle in the country in 1980. He recalls: 'I would get IRA chaps coming up and saying, "You're with us," but then they copped my accent, and suddenly I wasn't. Then the UDA came over and they said, "But your name's Lydon." I'd lost both ways because of my Irish name and my English accent. I was a doomed gang of one.'[166] Such perspectives (however embroidered) underline the significance of voice (via accent) in marking 'Irish' off from 'English', highlighting the fraught (and unstable) status of the second-generation Irish when they perform acts of speech in Ireland. One highly audible means by which to offset this issue of accent, of course, is through the adoption of an Irish musical style; for the performance of Irish music supplies the second generation with a means to actually *sound* Irish. The awkward tension between affinity (feeling Irish) and expression (sounding English) can, in this way, be assuaged.

For The Pogues' Irish critics, however, the band's 'non-indigenousness' remained – despite their Irish *sound* – a rather vexed issue. (This was perhaps an effect of the band's *London*-Irish persona, as well as their fusion of folk with punk, which imbued The Pogues' œuvre with, as it were, an English accent.) With this issue in mind, the traditional musician Noel Hill pressed The Pogues – at the BP Fallon event – on their pursuance of an Irish style: 'But where is that Irish music *rooted*?' Hill asked the band anxiously, implying that their displaced stance was an aesthetic flaw. The band had made clear in interviews that the Irish aspects of their work had been drawn from the particular migrant milieu of north London. 'Our stuff is based on the sound of Kilburn', MacGowan had explained the previous year, making a point of the distinction between migrant styles and those located within Ireland.[167] The musical cultures of the London-Irish were, though, of little value to Hill, who had a rather different view of The Pogues' sources: the style on which they drew was, Hill explained, 'a terrible abortion' of Irish music.[168]

The band's response to such attacks was one of incomprehension. Thus, when Fallon informed the group that certain people in Ireland had been displeased (as well as perplexed) by The Pogues' efforts, MacGowan expressed bafflement. 'I just don't understand what's so surprising about a group playing what we're playing', the singer explained. 'I don't understand why people are so confused by it.'[169] Notwithstanding that the band's punk/folk fusion was, in 1985, still quite novel, the singer's incredulousness points to the profound incommensurability that marked the gap between The Pogues and their Irish critics. This disjuncture (or what Stuart Hall might call a 'lack of fit' between 'the two sides in the communicative exchange'[170]) was patently clear at the BP Fallon event: questions from the floor, and answers from the band, were invariably misconstrued and instantaneously dismissed. The 'lack of fit' between the two parties pertained, at least in part, to their contrasting modes of Irishness, for while MacGowan and O'Riordan saw themselves as (London) Irish, and had identified themselves as such, not least through their musical style, they were viewed – at least by some – in Ireland as suspect interlopers, making unwelcome incursions into Irish culture.

This was not an uncommon dynamic, as many second-generation people have, as Bronwen Walter explains, had their Irishness challenged in Ireland.[171] This challenge (which relates to the issue of accent) has ranged from gentle mocking to verbal abuse, and threats of physical violence.[172] Thus, the London-Irish writer John Healy (who had grown accustomed to being called an 'Irish cunt' in England) was construed as the quintessence of Englishness in Ireland: 'Go back to England, John Bull', he was advised on one visit.[173] Significantly, second-generation musicians have not been exempt from such treatment. As Kevin Rowland explained – in an interview published on the same day as The Pogues' BP Fallon broadcast – Irish people in Ireland had been keen to 'take the piss out of the second[-generation] Irish like [him]self'.[174] In such contexts, then, the feeling of being in-between was less a productive dynamic than a disheartening flaw.

The Pogues were undoubtedly upset at their Irish reception, and angry at Hill's remarks. 'That was very depressing', says O'Riordan of the BP Fallon event, noting that the criticism the band faced in Ireland was a 'harsh realisation'.[175] MacGowan (who had previously said that the 'only people [he'd] worry about giving [The Pogues] a bad reception would be first-generation Irish') was also, he explains, displeased.[176] Feeling somewhat 'ambushed' by their Irish critics,[177] then, the band would become quite defensive – as well as rather hostile – at the BP Fallon broadcast. O'Riordan, in particular, had been enraged by Hill's remarks: 'It's hard for me to believe how upset I was about Noel Hill', she recalls. 'I was furious.' The bassist would later reflect on the possible causes of Hill's attack, putting it down to a misconception, in Ireland, about the second-generation Irish: 'we had to think', she explains, 'we *weren't* Irish, we were *London*-Irish, so why should some Irish guy [such as Noel Hill] ... be any more receptive to us than some English person ... It was so far beyond anything he could grasp. It was new. And why *would* he know what it felt like to be London-Irish?'[178]

At the time of the event, however, O'Riordan was rather less reflective, and rebuffed Hill's remarks with her own obnoxious retorts. 'If you don't like it', she said of The Pogues' aesthetic, 'you know what you can do.'[179] Such belligerence (which owed more to John Lydon than John Bull) was evidently viewed by certain critics as anti-Irish: as the show came to an end, the Irish journalist Joe Ambrose claimed that O'Riordan had, through her irate manner, 'more or less chosen to say "you're nothing but a crowd of Paddies, I don't give a tuppeny damn what you think"', implying that O'Riordan had been 'racist' in her 'attitude toward Irish people'.[180] Such indictments point, once again, to a view of the second generation as not-Irish; for this London-Irish figure had, on visiting Ireland, not only had her ethnicity challenged, and her musicianship condemned, but had also – in her defensiveness – been construed as anti-Irish. The degrees of 'misunderstanding' were, then, quite profound, and seemed based on the fact that people in Ireland viewed The Pogues – as Barbara Bradby explains – as 'not Irish'.[181]

In response to the charge that she was not only not-Irish but also *anti*-Irish, O'Riordan would issue an upfront assertion of ethnicity. 'Listen', she explained coldly, 'you say I'm sitting here acting as if I'm talking to a room full of Paddies. I have an Irish passport, and it says I'm Irish.'[182] What this retort (which sought to correct the view of O'Riordan as non-Irish) confirmed, of course, was the very logic of the preceding critique, for the hybrid ethos of The Pogues had, in the face of fraught questions (born of binaristic assumptions and territorialist views) been eschewed in O'Riordan's agonistic response, which reduced the diaspora to the nation, with a state-issued certificate being cited as proof of identity. If this gesture had echoes of Kevin Rowland's response ('I am an Irish passport holder') to a similar enquiry that same year,[183] then O'Riordan would, like Rowland, augment her retort with a physical comeback, launching an attack on Joe Ambrose the following day.[184]

Irish antipathy towards The Pogues would continue, however, for several years, as evinced by the late folk musician, Tommy Makem, who described the band, at the end of the 1990s, as 'the greatest disaster ever to hit Irish music'. Such was Makem's contempt for The Pogues that he would see them as 'a political plot':

> You see, Irish culture was getting extremely popular [in the 1980s], and Mrs Thatcher's government knew it – now this is my own view – but I am convinced that they were released to do as much damage as they could to Irish culture. And they managed to do more damage than the British government ever could.[185]

Perhaps with such critiques in mind, Philip Chevron has claimed that The Pogues were 'reviled' in Ireland. 'Nowhere in the world do people "get" The Pogues less than they do in Ireland', he explains.[186] This aversion to the band was, though, also evident amongst sections of the Irish in Britain, some of whom saw The Pogues as 'an outrage to Irish music'. 'The Pogues have taken *our* traditional music', announced one irate letter-writer in the *Irish Post*, 'and dragged it in the mire.'[187] This claim provoked a certain amount of discussion in Irish community forums, with respondents noting that The Pogues 'could have turned their backs on Ireland' but chose instead to 'reflect the bridging of traditional Irish music and contemporary popular music'.[188]

Beyond the immigrant Irish, the bulk of criticism in Britain would centre on MacGowan's wish to square his audibly English accent with an expressly Irish ethnicity. As Hebdige (citing Barthes) has explained, a common response to such anomalousness is that in which the object of 'otherness' is 'trivialised, naturalised' and 'domesticated', with the fact of its 'difference' being 'denied'.[189] This particular tactic was deployed with frequency in accounts of The Pogues, through a variety of narrative forms. In a 1988 issue of *Melody Maker*, for example, the singer's life was satirised in a cartoon chronicle comprising fictionalised exchanges between MacGowan and his caricatured 'Cockney' parents. In this parodic scenario, the singer's father (who appears as an archetypal Londoner) is baffled at his son's contrivance to be Irish. ''Ere, you're not still pretending to be a Mick, are you?' he snaps at the youngster, inquiring: 'Why can't you admit you're a Cockney through and through, like your dear old dad?' The cartoon incarnation of MacGowan in turn lets slip that he has 'never been to Ireland before', imparting ill-informed impressions of contemporary Irish life ('I hear that [they] still get about by dog-cart and pony trap.')[190] An especially noteworthy instance of this trivialising tactic later appeared in the rock magazine *Q*, which claimed – in an account of the former Spice Girl, Geri Halliwell – that the latter was (by virtue of her mother's Spanish birth) *'more justified* in her excursion into Samba than Shane MacGowan is for his *half-baked* Irishness'.[191] Notwithstanding the absurd logic of this claim (with one Spanish parent ensuring Halliwell's Latin 'authenticity', while two Irish parents merely annul MacGowan's Irishness), the point to note is the desire – in mainstream media discourse – to deny (and deride) second-generation Irish ethnicity.

Part of this ridiculing strategy, it might be argued, sprang less from MacGowan's simple claim to Irishness than from the ostensibly excessive manner in which this claim had been staged. Impelling many critiques of The Pogues, then, was an assumption that their work had been shaped by an unhealthy obsession with Ireland and its historical past. Thus, certain critics discerned, in The Pogues' œuvre, 'a cloud of nostalgic sentiment' – evoking 'a million tears cried into a pint mug' – and a lack of 'hope' amongst the band's tropes of 'drunkenness, death and disaster'.[192] From this standpoint, The Pogues were marked by a gloomy refusal of 'where they were at' and a naive celebration of 'where they were from' (to borrow Paul Gilroy's phrase).[193] There was undoubtedly a degree of truth to this critique, and MacGowan would admit to his own sentimentality,[194] a condition that rendered him susceptible to that quixotic migrant mindset in which an idealised Hibernia acts as Edenic 'other' to Albion's assumed dystopia. The singer would therefore explain that the reason his adaptations of traditional songs were, as he put it, 'so fucked up' was because 'you *are* more fucked up if you live in London than say Tipperary'.[195] Such pronouncements (which had resonance with MacGowan's personal life) elide not only the assets of the host environment but also the drawbacks of 'home', and would confirm – for certain observers – the band's retrogressive standpoint. However, while the outlook of The Pogues was in large part 'rooted' in an expressly Irish past, it was no less overtly 'routed' in a distinctly English present.

Making a London-Irish 'home' with The Pogues

The sleeve art for The Pogues' second album, *Rum, Sodomy and the Lash* (1985), offers a self-conscious adaptation of Géricault's *Raft of the Medusa*: it features, as McLaughlin and McLoone point out, 'the members of the band out at sea, "in between worlds", looking for land'.[196] Despite this graphically implied quest for terra firma, though, MacGowan was keen to distance himself from territorialised conceptions of identity. In early interviews, for instance, the singer would insist that The Pogues were '*not* an Irish folk band', explaining that most of their songs were 'about London'.[197] Emphasising that he was 'London Irish' (rather than Irish-born), MacGowan would even suggest that The Pogues were 'a London band' that happened to 'play Irish music', laying stress on the diasporic features that had shaped the group's work.[198]

While the majority of traditional songs that The Pogues performed evoked displacement and itinerancy (for example, 'The Leaving Of Liverpool', 'The Wild Rover', 'Poor Paddy', 'Kitty', 'Muirchin Dirkin', 'The Parting Glass'), the vast bulk of original songs recorded by the group contained an address to migrant life.[199] Perhaps with this in mind, The Pogues' work has been viewed as an expressly diasporic inflection of Irish aesthetic forms. As Chevron has explained, The Pogues 'could never have happened in Ireland', and thus could only 'happen from the diaspora'.[200] This point has been confirmed by other band members, such as Spider Stacy, who feels that people 'tend to sort of look at the Irish side of the equation and possibly not give enough importance to the London side of the equation':

> And I think if anything the London [side] is probably more important or at least equally important because the Pogues could NEVER have come out of Ireland … The point about the Pogues is that they weren't actually Irish, they were in fact a London band. With very strong London Irish elements. But first and foremost they're a London band.[201]

MacGowan's second-generation Irish contemporaries, such as Johnny Marr, appear to agree. 'The Pogues could only have happened in London', reflects Marr. 'They couldn't have happened in Dublin', he explains, 'because they needed that objectivity, they needed to see it through a refracted standpoint.'[202] In a similar vein, Robert Elms would maintain that The Pogues' debut album 'wasn't an Irish album, but it *was* a London-Irish album', and 'probably the first ever'.[203] Andrew Ranken bears this out, noting that it was 'the Irish experience in London' that impelled the band, a point evidenced by the title of their first single, 'Dark Streets Of London' (1984).[204] This expressly English perspective on Irish immigrant life was undoubtedly one of the more pioneering aspects of MacGowan's project. Re-imagining the metropolitan centre as a site of insubordinate Irish ethnicity, The Pogues interweaved Britain's popular-cultural fabric with a uniquely Irish immigrant thread, epitomising – in the process – Avtar Brah's idea of 'diaspora space', in which a complex web of migrant forms conjoin (and thus serve to remake) the 'indigenous' national life.[205]

Traditional forms of migrant cultural expression, particularly among the Irish, have been marked by an often disabling obsession with the lost ancestral 'home', making a fetish of what Roy Foster calls (in an account of historical memory) the 'perspective over one's shoulder', imparting a perpetual 'parting glance'.[206] Studies of Irish migrant song culture have thus observed a penchant, in such forms, for 'bitter anguish', 'profound melancholy' and 'homesick' remorse.[207] Such tropes, which seem to enact a rejection – on the part of the migrant – of life in the host-culture realm, have often been associated with the Irish in London, whose imaginary is thought to be imbued, as Fintan O'Toole has explained, with the 'melancholy allure of a lost paradise'.[208] When viewed in the light of this context, MacGowan's songs signalled a striking disruption of Irish migrant tradition, for they conveyed less a sentimental image of an absent ethnic 'home' than a vivid (and markedly vibrant) evocation of the host milieu, evincing as much concern for England's present as they did for Ireland's past. In this context, Chevron points to MacGowan's 'love for the oppressor, England', which is 'expressed in so many of his songs'.[209]

Whether or not this is the case, it is clear that urban England (much more than rural Ireland) shaped The Pogues' imaginary. 'Transmetropolitan' (1984), the opening track on the group's debut album – and thus a sort of index of the band's ensuing œuvre – is illuminating in this regard.[210] With its titular intimation of excursion and urban space, the song sets an Irish folk aesthetic against an English narrative frame. The slow-paced opening bars, featuring a gently strummed banjo and rather languid accordion, invoke the maudlin nostalgia typically associated with migrant song. However, this sombre tenor is abruptly undercut when the speaker's upbeat lyric ('In the rosy parks of England') unexpectedly 'drops' into the mix, prompting a sudden acceleration of tempo and the track's ensuing fissure of Irish migrant lament. In contrast to the sorts of migrant song culture that have eschewed the urban host milieu for an exalted rural 'homeland',[211] 'Transmetropolitan' stages an exhilarating, upbeat eulogy for inner-city London. As McLaughlin and McLoone have explained, The Pogues 'twist and bend sentimental ballads to rearticulate feelings of alienation in London', wrenching the 'nostalgic associations' of traditional songs 'out of their context' via the 'irreverent way' in which they were rendered.[212] Throughout the course of

'Transmetropolitan', then, the band's sprightly pace and jaunty harmonic pattern provide the backcloth for MacGowan's speaker, who casually poeticises the mundane terrain of his urban locale, yielding unlikely (and not entirely ironic) exaltations of well-known English place names in an audibly Irish idiom. Although the singer would later claim that these song words were tongue in cheek,[213] his paeans to Brixton ('lovely boulevards'), Hammersmith ('sightly shores') and King's Cross nevertheless highlight the significance of the host space in MacGowan's imaginary. This emphasis on host culture sites does not suggest, however, any clearcut wish to assimilate, for its first-person speaker retains – throughout 'Transmetropolitan' (and beyond) – an openly Irish subject position, augmenting the ethnicity that infused the group's aesthetic with semiotic ciphers in the song words. Most striking in this regard is MacGowan's deployment of the abbreviation 'KMRIA', a contraction of 'Kiss my royal Irish arse', drawn from Joyce's *Ulysses*.[214] While this gesture clearly alluded to the name of the nascent Pogues project ('Pogue Mahone', a phrase that also appears in Joyce's work), the abbreviation principally functions, in the context of this song, as a playful sign of defiance, insisting (if somewhat cryptically) on the inassimilability of MacGowan's speaker. What the song's narrator seeks to reconcile, then, is an embrace of the English host culture with a display of ethnic difference. This impulse resonates with those forms of diaspora consciousness in which the subject maintains an affinity with both the absent 'homeland' and the host milieu.[215] As scholars of migration have observed, such forms of ethnic consciousness can often comprise a desire – whether actual or imagined – for geographical or spatial 'return'.[216] This 'desire' was often evinced by the Irish in post-war England: as Enda Delaney explains, the 'possibility of return to Ireland' – and a 'redemptive homecoming' – 'loomed large in the social imaginaries of the expatriate Irish', even 'after decades of living in Britain'.[217] This impulse is less evident, however, in 'Transmetropolitan', which is more a critique (than a celebration) of so-called ethnic 'return'. Thus, while the song's speaker is not entirely at ease in the host milieu – MacGowan offers allusions to ethnic disadvantage (not least via the reference to Arlington House, a shelter for the Irish in London)[218] – there is little interest in ethnic 'return', with the song's narrating subject laying stress on the fixed location of the 'we' for whom he speaks ('we've been here for a long time/ And we'll be here till we die', the singer snarls ahead of the final restorative chorus). Such gestures of ethnic settlement invoke a wish to stake out space in the host milieu, and strategic incursions are therefore launched, by the song's subject, on important cultural (BBC) and political (Whitehall) sites. In this regard, MacGowan's speaker seems to demonstrate the condition of 'dwelling in displacement' that is associated with migrant groups, including the second-generation Irish, in which people maintain psychic attachments to an absent 'homeland' whilst physically settling in the host culture.[219]

This 'settling' stance would arguably imbue The Pogues' œuvre. Thus, while the speaker occasionally dreamt of an 'escape' from urban life ('The Old Main Drag') or yearned for an absent 'home' ('NW3'), this was allayed by an embrace of the here and now (hence the upbeat jauntiness of a song titled 'London Girl'). This embrace was underscored by an awareness of nostalgia's pitfalls. Early Pogues tracks such as 'Connemara Let's Go' offered a riposte to quixotic conceptions – nurtured outside Ireland – of 'a nice little place full of donkeys and carts', a sentiment also invoked in 'The Body Of An American', which critiques, says Prendergast, the 'empty sentimentality' of certain Irish emigrés.[220] Meanwhile, 'The Broad Majestic Shannon' tackled the migrant's longing for things that are 'changed' or 'gone', and was, for the band, 'about trying to look ahead', beyond the 'cloying' and 'sentimental' aspects of ethnicity.[221] MacGowan made it clear that this song was born of the experience of

> meeting people that you knew then and there [in the past in Ireland] and seeing them again now in London, and the way that all the stuff that we loved when we were kids has gone. It's basically just about the good old days and they're gone, and we've got to accept it ... I've got to accept it.[222]

In this respect, the song served a remedial function, affording both speaker and listener a means by which to reconcile to the 'here and now' of host-culture life. Such gestures were redolent of certain African-American blues songs, which staged, for Albert Murray, less an act of 'self-commiseration' than a means to 'get rid of' the very sorrows they sought to express.[223] Thus, while 'The Broad Majestic Shannon' was, at times, ambivalent – the subject neither mocks nor mourns his origins ('it's stupid to laugh and it's useless to bawl') – it nevertheless sought accommodation with the psychic effects of displacement (not least via its hook line: 'There's no pain, there's no more sorrow'), thereby easing the speaker's transition.[224]

If this idea of 'dwelling in displacement' was first staged in 'Transmetropolitan', then another key aspect of The Pogues' London – its multi-ethnicity – also emerged in this song, with citations of Brixton and the GLC invoking a multicultural impression of the English capital.[225] The London that unfolded in Pogues songs was, then, multi-ethnic, with MacGowan's migrant imaginary engaging an array of nationalities and ethnicities, and evoking England – once again – as a 'diaspora space'. In this context, the singer has maintained that his lyrical interests exceeded the confines of the Irish-English milieu, evoking the experience of 'all sorts of people, from a London-based emigrant's point of view'.[226] The singer also espoused, in the 1980s, the view that it was 'far better to have a cosmopolitan outlook' than any inward-looking standpoint on Irish migrant life.[227] Similarly, fans of the group (who were themselves described as 'cosmopolitan') saw The Pogues as accessible to 'young people in Britain of all ethnic backgrounds' (despite the band's link with the second-generation Irish).[228]

As the opening track on their debut album, 'Transmetropolitan' was emblematic of the unfolding Pogues project, presaging the tropes and sensibilities of the band's ensuing œuvre. The song's instalment of a London-Irish imaginary (and evocation of multi-ethnicity) would thus be extended in subsequent material. Most noteworthy in this regard was the sheer volume of Pogues songs that cited the English capital in song titles ('Dark Streets Of London', 'London Girl', 'A Rainy Night In Soho', 'Lullaby Of London', 'NW3', 'London, You're A Lady', 'White City') or song words ('Transmetropolitan', 'Sea Shanty', 'Streams Of Whiskey', 'The Old Main Drag', 'The Sick Bed Of Cuchulainn', 'Boat Train').[229] This catalogue of London songs supplied an expressly Irish impression of the city at the level of both harmonic signification and semantic association, not least via MacGowan's habit of name-checking areas linked with Irish settlement, such as Hammersmith ('Transmetropolitan', 'Dark Streets Of London'), Camden Town ('Transmetropolitan', 'London Girl') and north London ('NW3'). His evocation of the capital was (as noted above) also multi-ethnic, with the narrating subject in Pogues songs fashioning alliances with other ethnic positions ('The Sick Bed Of Cuchulainn') whilst occupying immigrant social spaces, such as Greek eateries ('The Broad Majestic Shannon') or cosmopolitan cafés ('London Girl'). Such spaces serve as inter-ethnic 'contact zones', a concept used by post-colonial theorists to invoke 'the spatial and temporal copresence of subjects previously separated by geographic and historical disjunctures, and whose trajectories now intersect'.[230] This notion of 'contact zones' has special resonance in musical life, where different cultures and styles can perhaps convene more readily than in other expressive forms.[231] Thus, the multicultural mindset of The Pogues' protagonist was underscored by forays into 'ethnic' sounds, not least zydeco ('London Girl'), Spanish ('A Pistol For Paddy Garcia', 'Fiesta'), Arabic ('Turkish Song Of The Damned') and jazz ('Metropolis'), evincing an idea of 'audiotopia', as outlined above.[232] This point was expounded by MacGowan in interviews, in which he stressed the place of Irish music in the multi-ethnic metropolis:

Half the pubs in North London in the Sixties and Seventies had
a lot of Irish records on the juke-box, and at least half the pubs in
London must be Irish-run. So you had blacks, Italians, English and
Irish in there and there would be Irish music playing along with soul
and rock 'n' roll. It's a real melting pot, especially in North London,
of musical types.[233]

This musical 'melting pot' was also observed by journalists, not least Bill
Graham, who saw The Pogues as symptomatic of 'that section of North
London where the Irish mingle with Greeks, Rastas and a host of other
minorities', effecting an 'Irish music' that was 'viewed through the prism
of a North London sensibility that includes bluegrass, bluebeat, cajun,
rockabilly, punk, ska [and] Greek'.[234]

The 'London' evoked by The Pogues, then, surpassed the simple
binary of the English–Irish interface, with the band's persona being
propelled by a more complex range of coordinates.[235] This is not to suggest, however, that the English capital that was staged by The Pogues
was a naively multicultural utopia, for while this imagined metropolis
was explicitly multi-ethnic, it was equally multi-racist. The speaker in
Pogues songs thus made reference to the prejudice faced by other ethnic
groups ('The Sick Bed Of Cuchulainn'), and acknowledged the racist
attitudes held by sections of the Irish in Britain ('Boat Train'), a point
elaborated by MacGowan in interviews: 'Some of the Irish are very
racist', he observed. The singer was also keen to downplay the prejudice
experienced by Irish migrants. 'There is a lot of racism in England',
he explained, 'but the Irish get very little of it compared with other
groups.' Rather than making special claims about Irish victimhood, then,
MacGowan (who had experienced anti-Irish prejudice first hand) would
qualify English views of the migrant Irish:

> There's a section of English people who are actually anti-Irish. There's
> a larger section of people who tell Irish jokes and that, but it's just a
> joke. But if you're talking about people who really look down on the
> Irish and treat them as maybe blacks are treated in the South [of the
> United States], there's really very little of that. It's exaggerated. There's
> a lot of them [anti-Irish perceptions] around the IRA, but that's a
> different thing.[236]

Despite such disclaimers, though, the bulk of The Pogues' address to
prejudice was focused on the case of the immigrant Irish, extending the early allusion, in 'Transmetropolitan', to dispossessed Irish in
London. Indeed, Chevron would later suggest that '[t]he only politics

that counted in the London-Irish scene were the politics of being Irish in a place that was innately racist towards the Irish'.[237] Songs such as 'The Old Main Drag' – which addressed what O'Hagan calls the 'flotsam and jetsam' of Irish in London – thus detailed the harsh aspects of immigrant life.[238] Meanwhile, 'NW3' (the title of which denotes a north London postal-code area) offered a bleak rendition of Irish experience, with MacGowan expounding – in interviews – its account of an Irish labourer who feels that 'England's fucked him over' and 'let him down'.[239] The song also espoused a somewhat gloomy view of second-generation life, with its narrator protesting: 'My kids will never/ Scrape shit around here'. An even more contentious account of Irish experience emerged in 'Birmingham Six' (1988), a song described by the band as a 'vengeful' address to the mistreatment of Irish migrants by Britain's judicial system.[240] With this intervention in mind, it is worth exploring the band's handling of Anglo-Irish political themes.

Political Pogues: between prejudice and partisanship

With its citation of the trials of the Birmingham Six and the Guildford Four, 'Birmingham Six' comprised a protest against the British government's Prevention of Terrorism Act (PTA), which had been introduced in 1974 in the immediate aftermath of IRA bombings in Birmingham. As Hillyard explains, this hastily conceived piece of legislation gave the secretary of state 'considerable new powers to control the movement of people between Ireland and Great Britain', including 'the power to remove people who are already living in Great Britain to either Northern Ireland or the Republic of Ireland'. The Act would come to be seen as a 'discriminatory piece of law' in that it was 'directed primarily at one section of the travelling public', with Irish people being subjected to a 'more restrictive set of rights than other travellers' – hence Hillyard's conclusion that 'the Irish community as a whole' had been viewed as 'suspect'.[241]

This claim (that the PTA impacted on the migrant Irish 'as a whole') gains support from the fact that almost ninety per cent of those detained under the Act between 1974 and 1991 were eventually released without charge.[242] Many of these individuals were second-generation Irish, the most high-profile of whom were the London-Irish teenagers Vincent and Patrick Maguire, who were arrested in 1976 under the provisions of the PTA before being (wrongly) convicted of involvement in the 1974 Guildford pub bombings.[243] The brothers' London-Irish peers would respond to this miscarriage of justice by concealing their Irishness in

strikingly literal ways. 'A friend of ours', Vincent says, 'went out to his
garden and buried anything to do with Ireland – records, everything,
in the garden in case the police came and gave his place a spin. He was
second generation, same as us.'[244] Such reactions were a not uncommon
response to anti-Irish prejudice, and call to mind earlier accounts of
second-generation life, in which discrimination has provoked a desire
to 'put away' things Irish.[245]

This practice of secreting Irish things (in the face of prejudice) was,
of course, the very thing that The Pogues had sought to challenge.
Within this project, moreover, they had addressed some of the issues
– such as the view of the Irish as 'suspect' – that had led certain sections of the second generation to conceal their Irishness. MacGowan
thus makes reference, in 'Birmingham Six', to this specific context: the
singer (who had first-hand experience of security inspections[246]) cites
the alleged crime of 'being Irish' in the 'wrong place' at the 'wrong time'.
In this sense, MacGowan's song, like Rowland's 'Dance Stance', was
one of the few pop-cultural protests against anti-Irish prejudice, issuing a 'comment', as Clerk explains, 'on the perceived victimisation and
oppression of Irish people by the British'.[247] At Britain's Independent
Broadcasting Authority (IBA), however, this gesture was viewed as
support for a proscribed paramilitary organisation (the IRA) on the
grounds that it offered 'general disagreement with the way in which
the British Government responds to, and the courts deal with, the terrorist threat in the UK'.[248] Notwithstanding the tacit conflation, here,
of Irish migrant and 'terrorist threat', the IBA issued a memorandum
to all independent radio stations advising that the track should not be
played because of its alleged suggestion 'that all Irish people are always
at a disadvantage in any dealings they may have with the British legal
system'.[249] The Pogues thus became the first major act to be restricted by
the 1988 broadcasting ban, which 'prohibit[ed] the broadcast of direct
statements by representatives or supporters of eleven Irish political and
military organisations'.[250] MacGowan's account of Irish disadvantage
was therefore perceived, as David Miller explains, as 'identical to supporting Sinn Féin or the IRA'.[251]

Aside from the fact that the song was an address to the imprisonment of innocent people (not the crisis in Northern Ireland), the
allegation that The Pogues were militant republicans was clearly at odds
with their (public and private) stance on Irish affairs. In interviews,
for instance, they were 'anxious not to be considered a political band',
with MacGowan confessing to being 'confused' about the Troubles,
whilst denouncing the 'fierce defensive nationalism' that he had felt
in his youth.[252] Elsewhere, he condemned IRA actions as 'stupid' and

'revolting'.[253] Such comments were underscored by anti-sectarian gestures, not least the band's involvement with peace initiatives in Northern
Ireland, as well as MacGowan's plans to fuse the Lambeg drum (an
instrument associated with Protestant marching bands) with the
bodhrán.[254] The singer was also keen to point out that supporters of both
Celtic and Rangers (Glasgow's rival Catholic-related and Protestant-
related soccer clubs) had attended The Pogues' Belfast and Glasgow
shows.[255] There is little doubt, however, about which of these constituencies was most evident at Pogues concerts, as the band's shows were
often adorned with the paraphernalia of Glasgow Celtic (a club publicly
associated with Irish Catholics in Britain) – hence the 'myriad green-'n'-
white-hooped Celtic shirts' and Irish tricolour flags that critics observed
amongst the group's audience.[256] (With this in mind, The Pogues were
once described as 'the musical wing of the Celtic team'.[257])

This association of The Pogues with Catholic interests had been augmented by the (highly unfashionable) affiliation to Catholicism that
MacGowan had expressed in interviews. The singer stressed that he had
been a 'very religious kid', recalling the Catholic iconography of his early
milieu: 'Crucifixes, rosary beads, a red lamp for the Sacred Heart, a blue
lamp for the Virgin Mary.'[258] This Catholicity had, moreover, endured
into his adult life: 'I'm still a Catholic', he explained in 1987:

> What my Catholic upbringing means to me now is, I have an idea
> of the connection between the physical world and the supernatural
> world ... and a lot of things still really move me. I occasionally go to
> Mass and that still moves me. Things like the rosary still move me.
> There's a lot of different ways of appreciating life: through music, or
> nature, or through people whether it's conversationally or sexually ...
> A very deep, heavy, powerful, symbolic religion like Catholicism is
> another way of appreciating that.[259]

Such comments, when taken alongside the band's musical style and
political stance, were often viewed (particularly in cities such as Belfast
and Glasgow) as an exclusivist assertion of Irish Catholic identity –
hence the group's (assumed) association with Celtic.[260] However, The
Pogues, as Eamonn McCann would explain, were 'unhappy about the
one-to-one identification of the band with Celtic', and informed the
press that this was 'none of their making', whilst requesting that fans
refrain from passing Celtic scarves onto the stage.[261] The band made
clear, then, their wish to not be associated with 'anything even slightly
sectarian'.[262] Regardless of the band's wish, their invocation of Irish
ethnicity (however inclusive in intent) had, through its reception, been

subsumed by existing discourses of Irishness, which were often bound up, in 1980s Britain, with Irish republicanism.[263] Despite The Pogues' anti-sectarian stance, certain sections of their audience would – in the midst of live concerts – express support for paramilitary violence (critics claimed to hear shouts of 'Up the IRA!' from audience members), and the band had to admit to 'an element of real partisanship' amongst their fans.[264] For MacGowan, however, there was 'nothing intentional' about The Pogues 'becoming partisan' or attracting 'a partisan audience'. 'We never came out with any bigoted statements', the singer insisted.[265] This was arguably true, as the band had, in the words of Jack Barron, never 'deigned to openly court or espouse Republican sympathies'.[266] Moreover, The Pogues had 'explicitly refused', as Prendergast notes, 'to support the actions of the IRA and those that financed them'.[267] Thus, if the band came – through the course of their consumption – to 'articulate' with certain concerns (in which Irish nationalism prevailed), this was not, it seems, always endorsed (or even welcomed) by the band themselves.[268]

MacGowan's public claims of non-partisanship are underlined by the fact that he seems to have been, in private, a less than ardent nationalist. Friends of MacGowan from the pre-Pogues period have confirmed that while he was 'defiant' in his Irishness, he was not 'overtly nationalistic'.[269] Within The Pogues' circle, meanwhile, MacGowan sought to moderate the less temperate views of certain colleagues. In this context, O'Riordan explains that – prior to joining The Pogues – she had been 'a London-Irish extremist' (seeing this as a symptom of 'living in a racist, oppressive society'). Rather than nurturing this position, however, MacGowan teased the bass player away from what she calls her 'angry', 'warped' views on the Troubles, and convinced her that violence was 'wrong'. Thus, while The Pogues expressed broad support for a united Ireland, this did not equate with an endorsement of militant nationalism. 'We were never "up the RA" [IRA]', relates O'Riordan. 'We were never pro-Sinn Féin.'[270] Claims that The Pogues were an 'IRA propaganda tool' were therefore 'complete rubbish', as Finer explains.[271]

The band's politics – which were broadly liberal-left – emerged in opposition to what MacGowan called the 'new Toryism' of the 1980s, a point confirmed by O'Riordan, who sums up their stance as 'anti-Thatcher'.[272] This perspective was clearly evinced in the band's video for 'A Pair Of Brown Eyes' (1985), which, as Clerk points out, portrayed Thatcher's Britain as a 'police state', and featured shots (removed at the record-company's request) of The Pogues spitting on pictures of Thatcher.[273] In this respect, The Pogues oriented themselves less as ardent patriots than as ethnic outcasts, a point borne out by the narrating protagonist in Pogues songs, who, for Finer, was more of 'a displaced person' than 'a native of a place'.[274] Critics also observed that the band's work was 'steeped in the language of the outsider', noting – in particular – its 'outsider' account of London.[275] Rather than being seen as ethnic jingoism, then, The Pogues' work would arguably serve as a 'national anthem for the dispossessed'.[276]

Despite such observations, many critics would view The Pogues as regressive essentialists who acted out an age-old 'anarchic/mystical Celtic dialectic' in which MacGowan played 'the quintessential hooligan'.[277] In light of the band's pioneering character, this was a rather narrow conclusion. However, one aspect of the group's persona that undoubtedly provoked such adverse critiques was their engagement with the 'drunken Irish' stereotype.[278] The Pogues' association with this clichéd trope was such that journalists would habitually relate that '[t]he criticism … most often levelled at [the band] … is that they re-enforce the stereotype of the "drunken Irishman"'.[279]

Reviving the 'drunken Paddy'
In stark contrast to Kevin Rowland, who sought to confound conceptions of Irish intemperance, MacGowan seemed happy to conform to this age-old ethnic stereotype, appearing to many observers as 'the drunken Paddy re-incarnate'.[280] This motif of inebriation was evinced at various levels of the group's œuvre. At The Pogues' first photo session, for example, MacGowan would insist (according to the photographer) on including his pint glass in the frame (see photo overleaf), and the band would 'rarely [be] photographed', notes Grainne Ni Scanlain, 'without an accompanying glass or bottle'.[281] This association with drink-related objects also extended to The Pogues' live shows – hence the 'ever-present cigarette and glass' and general 'onstage drinking habits' that reviewers would routinely observe.[282] While such objects served as props in The Pogues' staging of what Gerry Smyth calls 'Celtic chaos', the band often seemed inebriated during live performance, creating the impression of a 'great big boisterous bar-room', as *Melody Maker* put it.[283] In this context, Clerk has detailed the group's capacity for 'sustained intoxication and riotous behaviour', noting that this led to 'serious alcohol problems'.[284] O'Riordan, meanwhile, confirms that 'there was a lot of drinking involved' in The Pogues, a view corroborated by other band members, as well as their staff and acquaintances.[285]

The band's onstage condition was only exacerbated by alcohol-fuelled audiences, who sought to dispatch further drinks to the stage.[286] In turn,

Photograph: Bleddyn Butcher

MacGowan would claim that his onstage inebriation was born of an obligation to his less sober fans: 'our audiences drink a lot and I feel we owe it to them to stay drunk', he explained.[287] There can be little doubt, however, that the fans' 'boozy' etiquette had sprung in no small part from the singer himself, whose link to excessive drinking was at the fore of the group's persona. The Pogues' first concert tour was thus called 'Lock Up Your Drinks Cabinet', a gesture that made clear the distinction between MacGowan and Rowland (who famously demanded abstemiousness, both onstage and in the auditorium, during Dexys' live events).[288] Such titles were underscored by the band's penchant for issuing bogus on-the-road stories (via their record-company press office) claiming that The Pogues had been banned – as a result of their excessive drinking – from every temperance hotel in Britain.[289]

In numerous interviews, MacGowan detailed his fondness for heavy drinking, explaining that The Pogues 'drink more than other bands', and stressing that 'the way we perform depends entirely on how pissed we all are. We are trying now to reach that perfect state where we are pissed enough to play well and enjoy ourselves.'[290] Such pronouncements would occasionally extend to the singer's admission of alcoholism as a personal lifestyle choice, with the singer confessing: 'I just drink slowly, all day and all night.'[291] In this context, MacGowan revealed, in 1985, that he was 'under medication for alcohol abuse'.[292] However, while the singer expressed concern for Irish migrants that 'go off the rails' after moving to England, he was insistent that alcohol had acted, at least for him, as 'the path to awareness'.[293] When asked why life was 'worth living', then, MacGowan uttered the pithy (and pre-*Father Ted*) riposte: 'Drink'.[294]

If such comments provoked suggestions that The Pogues had perpetuated the 'drunken Paddy' stereotype, this was only augmented by the band's evolving repertoire, which made reference, notes Ni Scanlain, to 'whiskey and beer' in 'every other song'.[295] MacGowan would admit that the band's set list was based around what he called 'drinking songs',[296] with the bulk of tracks performed by the group conjuring alcohol in various ways. Their suite of traditional songs, for instance, laid stress on the act of drinking, as evinced by 'Waxie's Dargle', 'Whiskey, You're The Devil' (1984) and 'I'm A Man You Don't Meet Every Day' (1985).[297] This drink motif was even evident in the titles of the band's instrumentals (such as 'Repeal Of The Licensing Laws' (1984)) and album collections (*Rum, Sodomy and the Lash*).[298] Even more significant, perhaps, was the theme of inebriation that emerged in the bulk of songs composed (or co-written) by MacGowan for The Pogues, with only one of the singer's original tracks, prior to 1988, failing to conjure this lyric-theme.[299] 'Drink is a central motif in Shane's work', observed Spider Stacy in 1984.[300]

This motif was openly evident in the group's debut single, 'Dark Streets Of London', but emerged most strikingly in 'Streams Of Whiskey' (1984), the first song that The Pogues performed onstage and which was originally intended as their debut single – hence its choice as their first video.[301] The track – which has been viewed as a 'statement of purpose'[302] – was eventually issued as the opening track of side two of The Pogues' debut album, and exemplifies the symbolic flip side of their more regenerative impulse, which had been set up by 'Transmetropolitan', the opening track on side one. Introduced by MacGowan as a 'blatant defence of heavy drinking', 'Streams Of Whiskey' has an exceptionally upbeat tenor (Clerk notes its 'galloping *joie de vivre*'),[303] with its fast-paced single snare supplying a backcloth for banjo, accordion and tin whistle (whose sprightly melodic lines are mixed to the fore of the track's bright preface). During the contrasting low-key verses – when Ranken reverts to a single tom, and the banjo and tin whistle pause for respite – MacGowan's speaker relates a dream in which Brendan Behan 'advises him', as Dorian Lynskey explains, 'that the answers to all of life's problems do indeed lie at the bottom of a glass' (which perhaps accounts for the track's status as a celebrated 'drinking song').[304] Amidst the accordion's jittery lines, however, MacGowan's harried delivery and erratic leaps in range render many of his song words incomprehensible. What the discernible segments of verse lyrics seem to offer, though, is a recital of life's anxieties, alluding to sadness, suicide and the search for meaning. Such concerns are clearly assuaged in the collectively-sung chorus section, which restores the song's jaunty prologue via a vocalisation of Behan's sage-like words. The homespun counsel offered to the song's subject is in this way rendered as a folk mantra ('I am going, I am going/ Where streams of whiskey are flowing'). The fretful voice of the subdued verse is thus replaced by jovial group hollering and upbeat harmonic adornments, with any disquiet being thrown into sharp thematic relief. Adhering throughout to a regular pattern of major chords (D–G–A), the subtle harmonic shifts outlined above highlight the fissure between verse and chorus sections, with the restless figure of the former finding a carefree moment of drunkenness in the latter's warm sociality. This point is most clearly rendered in the closing couplets of the final verse, when the song's narrating speaker – seeking shelter from a world that is 'too dark' – re-ignites 'the light inside of [him]' by consuming 'fifteen pints of beer'. In this way, 'Streams Of Whiskey' staged, as Clerk points out, a 'fantasy of escape' in which 'alcohol' acted as 'refuge'.[305] In marked contrast to Rowland, then, who staged his defection from England by retreating (in the lyrics and video for 'Knowledge Of Beauty') to a curative Irish coast, MacGowan sought the space of the pub and the effects of heavy drinking as a means to escape from host culture life.

The Irish pub in England has, of course, been 'a long-standing element of the social landscape of Irish migrants', and has served, for Liam Ryan, as 'the one place where [Irish migrants] could find' what he calls 'a substitute for home'.[306] This view of the Irish pub as a space for what Walter terms 'self-segregation' extends to the second generation, who have seen such venues as a means by which Irish migrants can achieve a 'communal sense of belonging'.[307] Notwithstanding the obvious issues that this invokes about alcoholism amongst the Irish in Britain, including the second generation (who have been amongst the heaviest drinkers in England),[308] it is clearly this view of the pub (as a site of ethnic respite) that informs MacGowan's speaker in 'Streams Of Whiskey'.

Like 'Transmetropolitan', 'Streams Of Whiskey' served as a sort of signal for the band's ensuing œuvre, with its drink-fixated lyric theme infusing the group's persona (Kieran Keohane suggests that The Pogues' 'text' was 'soaked in alcohol', while Clerk detects 'the whiff of the barroom wafting through their lyrics') – hence the hook lines of songs such as 'Boys From The County Hell' (1984), 'Waxie's Dargle', 'I'm A Man You Don't Meet Every Day' and 'Sally MacLennane' (1985), the latter a 'song about alcoholism', according to Gerry Smyth.[309] This issue would steadily saturate the group's reception, with critics spotlighting

drink in interviews, articles and reviews. Early coverage thus described
the band's work as a 'boozy Irish ... trash-out', while interviews would
often begin by explaining: 'The best known thing about [the band] is
that they drink like fish.'[310] Elsewhere, critics noted the 'drunkenness'
that The Pogues '[wore] as a badge', and claimed that MacGowan was
not merely 'propagating the image of the soused but poetic scoundrel'
but was 'living it too'.[311] Meanwhile, journalists would observe the 'vast
phalanx of bottles' festooning the singer's apartment, associating his
abode's odour with that of a brewery, and noting its occupant's custom
of drinking 'all day, every day'.[312] Newspaper copy-editors also concocted
corny drink-themed strap lines for the band's press reportage – hence
'The booze brothers', 'A fair intake of ale in New York', 'For a few ciders
more' and 'I drink therefore I am'.[313] It was clear, then, that The Pogues
would find it difficult to shake off the view, expressed in 1984, that
'Pogue music is drinking music'.[314]

Such was the extent of this emphasis on alcohol in coverage of The
Pogues that journalists would themselves concede that the press 'harps
on about one particular aspect of The Pogues' lifestyle to the exclusion
of everything else', this of course being 'the demon drink'.[315] As this
issue began to obscure the more innovative aspects of the band's project,
the group would start to object to what they saw as the press' default
'drinking angle', and especially the criticism that they had re-enforced
'the stereotype of the "drunken Irishman"'.[316] This grievance was at least
partly understandable. It was clearly unreasonable, for instance, to dis-
miss MacGowan as a 'moronic pisshead', or to write off The Pogues as 'a
drunken novelty act'.[317] There were perhaps certain grounds, moreover,
for MacGowan's claim that public typecasting of the band as 'drunken
Paddies' had sinister associations ('it suits certain people to have all
the Irish portrayed as drunken yobs', he explained).[318] In this context,
O'Riordan would suggest that a 'very casual racism' informed press
accounts of The Pogues, explaining that if 'English people get drunk,
they're just English people getting drunk', yet when 'Irish people get
drunk', they are seen as the 'drunken Irish' due to the perceived affirma-
tion of an imagined ethnic trait.[319] Clerk confirms this point, arguing
that The Pogues 'were by no means the only outfit' to consume alcohol
in excess, but were 'singled out for special treatment' due to what she
calls the 'Paddy factor'.[320] Any difficulty that the media encountered in
making sense of the band's pioneering (London-Irish) impulse could
therefore be assuaged by laying stress on a facet of their work that correlated with received ideas of Irish ethnic behaviour. It would thus be
drinking rather than diaspora – and alcohol instead of ethnicity – that
supplied the most expedient angle in media coverage of The Pogues.[321]

This undoubtedly reductive commentary had the effect of 'belittling' a project that was, for the late Pogues collaborator Kirsty MacColl, 'very powerful' and 'very creative'.[322] Nevertheless, it was perhaps somewhat disingenuous for MacGowan to maintain that the 'drunken Paddy' image that the group accrued had been 'laid on' them by the press.[323] Equally, the singer's insistence that The Pogues 'never had anything to do with [this]' Irish stereotype seems – in light of the array of drink-related signifiers in their songs and ancillary media – at odds with actuality.[324]

To be fair, The Pogues made occasional efforts to correct this image of excess, not least by imposing 'drinks bans' on group members.[325] In addition, the band's record company would ask The Pogues to be 'less openly enthusiastic about drinking', and advised journalists to steer clear of this topic.[326] When the band had signed their first record contract, they had, said MacGowan, 'to pretend we'd stopped drinking'. During photo sessions, he explains, 'we had to hide our drinks behind our backs'.[327] The group's management revived this policy (of concealing alcoholic drinks during press encounters) later on in the group's career.[328] Rather ironically, this would only serve to accentuate the group's hard-drinking reputation, as their teetotal pose was routinely undermined by editorial captions unveiling the contrived strategy. A major article on the band thus explained: 'These days, when The Pogues have their photograph taken in a pub they clear the glasses away and pose behind empty tables. It looks ridiculous but, they claim, "it will help calm down the boozy image."'[329] In light of the band's ubiquitous evocation of drink – not to mention the correlation, in popular discourses, between Irishness and alcohol – it was perhaps unlikely that such a gesture would reduce the group's 'boozy' reputation. With this point in mind, it is worth considering why the band had allowed the issue of drink to attain such a prominent role in their persona in the first place. In photo shoots and live performance, as well as interviews and song lyrics, the figure of the 'drunken Paddy' was actively conjured. What, then, was the value (the significance, attraction and function) of this figure for MacGowan's aesthetic scheme? And how might this figure pertain to the band's more regenerative impulse?

Notwithstanding the obvious point that MacGowan was in fact a heavy drinker[330] (an aspect of his personal life that he could, perhaps, have concealed), Irishness has often functioned (in Britain) as an 'hedonistic opposition' to 'British rationalism'.[331] In this context, The Pogues' 'pissed Paddy' persona was perhaps – in part – an effect of performing Irish ethnicity in England. A certain penchant for 'playing the fool' (through the enactment of stage-Irish caricatures) has been observed amongst the second-generation Irish.[332] This has been seen as a means by which the (English-born) offspring of twentieth-century migrants have sought to celebrate their Irishness.[333] However, this practice appears to have a somewhat older provenance, for, as Terry Eagleton explains, such traits were evinced in the persona of the nineteenth-century artist (and alcoholic) Patrick Bronte, who lived 'a flamboyant stage-Irish existence, obediently conforming to the English stereotype of the feckless Mick'.[334] MacGowan's attraction to this type was, perhaps, only heightened by the denial of difference that met second-generation claims to Irishness, and aroused excessive displays of ethnicity. Amidst a perceived reluctance to recognise second-generation Irishness, then, MacGowan would insist on making it overt. This is, of course, a well-known practice amongst minority ethnic figures, and was memorably expounded – in a different context – by Frantz Fanon, who, in the face of a refusal to recognise his difference, explained that 'there remained only one solution: to make myself known' – hence his decision to assert himself 'as a BLACK MAN'.[335] MacGowan was, it seems, propelled by an analogous desire to announce his Irishness, with his performance of the 'Paddy' persona attracting – above all else – recognition. This wish to insist on Irish ethnicity was unveiled in the singer's account of England's popular music culture, which, despite its embracing of diverse 'ethnic' sounds, had ignored, from his standpoint, Irish-related styles: 'there's ethnic [i.e. Irish] music in their own local fucking pub', MacGowan detailed, 'and they're ignoring it'. In this context, then, the singer had sought to 'shove it [Irish music and its associated ethnicity] down their fucking throats'.[336] With this in mind, it was perhaps not surprising that The Pogues' early work was heard as 'a raucous bellow of identity'.[337]

The more overblown aspects of MacGowan's Irishness were, then, shaped in part by his context, for assertions of ethnicity become raucous when that identity is either weak or under threat.[338] In this context, what the 'Paddy' figure offered MacGowan was a means by which to magnify his image as Irish, attaining a highly amplified ethnicity. In the complex effort to lay claim to a contested and hybrid identity, MacGowan thus felt the need to act out more orthodox ethnic codes. It has, of course, been difficult in the realm of popular culture to assert ethnic difference without recourse to archetypes.[339] Such assertions might originate in what John Nagle has called (in an account of Irish ethnicity in England) 'an important politics of recognition', but often become susceptible to 'a dangerous reification of culture and ethnicity'.[340] This quandary pertains, in part, to issues of style and aesthetics with regard to the standardised ways of *performing* Irish identities in the popular-cultural realm. In this context, the essentialist aspect of The Pogues was one of the few available ways in which to be *recognised* as Irish in the popular-cultural matrix of 1980s Britain. Moreover, such essentialist modes of ethnicity can – in certain contexts – supply what Sonia Kruks describes as a source of pride, and are thus 'at once untenable and yet necessary'.[341]

There are associated ideological issues concerning the adoption of prescriptive subject positions (including putatively 'negative' ones) by minority group members. With this in mind, MacGowan's adoption of an ethnic stereotype might be seen as a form of interpellation, in which the singer was 'hailed' by a derogatory role that he was only too willing to perform.[342] This is certainly the view of MacGowan's critics, who observe in his work 'all the stereotypes regarding the Irish in Britain' – including 'the drunkenness [and] the aggression' – bequeathing Irish audiences 'a badge of permanent cultural disability.'[343]

McLaughlin and McLoone expound a rather different view, suggesting that The Pogues' re-enactment of existing ethnic types offered a means by which to 'parody and interrogate' orthodox 'aspects of Irishness' in 'complex and confusing ways'. While it is clear that 'blatant Irish stereotypes' – as the above-mentioned authors maintain – were 'rearticulated' by The Pogues in 'interesting ways',[344] the ubiquity of alcohol in the band's live shows, song lyrics, personal lives, interviews and photographs (not to mention their occasional attempts to obscure this theme) would indicate that their 'drunk Paddy' persona lacked the requisite self-reflexivity to be seen as parodic. It is, perhaps, rather more likely that this figure provided The Pogues with a means of asserting ethnic difference in a way that was both recognisable *and* recalcitrant (the band's 'excess' was, Cleary argues, 'anarchic' and 'subaltern'[345]).

Conclusion: from fixity to flux

In an account of England's Irish folk scene in the early 1990s, Smyth outlines the obstacles that he faced as a singer confronting competing conceptions of Irishness at assorted concert venues. Recounting the divergent expectations of the scene's key constituents (including fellow musicians, audience members and venue proprietors), Smyth explains that different musical repertoires comprised attendant – and often conflicting – ideas of what it meant to be Irish. Most obviously, there was, he suggests, a highly fractious contestation between, on the one hand, his own wish for the diaspora Irish to 'signify something different from the old stereotype', and, on the other, the audience's desire for songs of nationalism, alcoholism and nostalgia. Smyth's immediate problem, then, was 'how to be Irish and not Irish at the same time; that is how to announce my Irishness but not perpetuate or become victim of these other disabling discourses'.[346] The quandary outlined here encapsulates the tension contained in The Pogues, for while they would radically fissure accepted notions of Irish ethnicity, they also seemed to authenticate age-old conceptions of Irishness.

The second-generation Irish persona that emerged in The Pogues' œuvre thus evinced both regressive *and* regenerative desires. These incongruous urges were, it seemed, equally crucial for the band's project: it is difficult to de-couple, for example, the London-Irish imaginary of 'Transmetropolitan' (and associated songs) from the evocation of alcohol in 'Streams Of Whiskey' (and related tunes); indeed, these songs, and several others, contain strands of each impulse. It is clear, however, that the band's initially playful celebration of drinking (as dramatised in the 'Streams Of Whiskey' video) became a somewhat clichéd aspect of their œuvre (and its reception) that would gradually detract from, and eventually destabilise, their innovative impulse. In this context, Stan Brennan explains that the 'interesting synthesis' that shaped the group's project 'got lost the longer the band went on'[347] (which might be taken to mean that the productive tension between the group's urges became less balanced over time). Most obvious in this regard was MacGowan's ongoing alcoholism, which for Clerk would start to 'obscure', where it had once served to 'illuminate', the band's project.[348] This point is confirmed by MacGowan's band-mates, who explain that he went 'off the rails' and became 'hell-bent on destroying himself', leading to 'unreliable' and 'erratic' performances, weakened song-writing skills, and spells in rehabilitation clinics and police cells ahead of his unscheduled absence from a prestigious US tour (supporting Bob Dylan).[349] Such problems would only persist, with critics noting MacGowan's 'severely slurred' vocals and habit of 'lurching' around concert stages with 'a drink in each hand and mis-tim[ing] things to a comical degree'.[350] Matters came to a head when a binge in the early Nineties led to the singer being hospitalised, and MacGowan parted company with The Pogues.[351]

Rather than viewing The Pogues' fixation with drink as a form of postmodern 'parody', then, it would seem that this attribute functioned as a strand of the group's persona that both announced their Irish ethnicity and ensured their eventual demise. In this regard, the band's re-enactment of an ethnic stereotype would in the end eclipse their innovative impulse, which had staged a second-generation Irish speaking position and installed a London-Irish imaginary. This symbolic dialectic – between the fixity of 'roots' and the flux of 'routes' – is one that is notoriously difficult to navigate, and would be mapped out very differently – though with notable concurrency – by The Smiths, who are the focus of the next chapter.

3

'Oscillate Wildly':
Ambivalence, Elusiveness
and The Smiths

*I think I had the best of both places [Dublin and Manchester] and the best of both
countries [Ireland and England]. I'm 'one of us' on both sides*

Morrissey[1]

*I don't consider myself either [Irish or English] ... I hate nationalism of any kind.
I feel absolutely nothing when I see the Union Jack, except repulsion ... and I don't
feel Irish either. I'm Mancunian-Irish*

Johnny Marr[2]

*[Music] can stimulate inter-cultural understanding at a deeply personal level,
with the result that a person is no longer a member solely of one culture*

Catherine Ellis[3]

In December 2004 Morrissey concluded his most successful worldwide
tour for several years with a concert at Dublin's Point Depot. Adorned
in the vestments of a Catholic priest, the singer made a series of playful
references to local places (showing his affinity with Ireland) before performing the tour's signature song, 'Irish Blood, English Heart', which
invoked his ethnic provenance.[4] This display of Irish Catholic ethnicity
was in marked contrast with Morrissey's earlier persona as frontman of
The Smiths (1982–87), which appeared to evince little sign of his – or
his fellow musicians' – immigrant Irish origins. The vast bulk of scholarly (and journalistic) writing on the group has, in turn, shown scant
concern for this aspect of The Smiths, with most accounts stressing the
group's Englishness while making little or no reference to their Irish
ethnicity.[5] The band would often be seen, moreover, as an archetype of
Englishness in rock. Michael Bracewell, for instance, has claimed that
The Smiths were 'organically English', deeming Morrissey the pop-
cultural 'embodiment' of 'English sensibility'.[6] Mark Sinker, meanwhile,
maintained that The Smiths 'sang for or of England ... with a music
that could only come from the urban heart of England'.[7] Elsewhere, the

NME inferred, from the band's œuvre, 'avowedly Anglo-Saxon' qualities, arguing that The Smiths had aspired to a 'myth of English purity'.[8]

Such readings did not go unnoticed by The Smiths themselves. 'It was always odd', explained Morrissey of The Smiths' reception, 'when I was described as being "extremely English" because other people would tell me that I looked Irish, I sounded Irish and had other tell-tale signs.'[9] Notwithstanding this, it is clear that The Smiths eschewed Irish sounds and styles in their eclectic venture into 'independent' rock (which drew on pop and funk as well as folk and country music).[10] Moreover, their work would often evoke an expressly English milieu via the citation of local places in song words, interviews and record sleeves (as well as the regional accent of much of Morrissey's singing).[11] The band's Irish provenance was, then, less pronounced than that of their second-generation Irish contemporaries, such as Kevin Rowland or Shane MacGowan. In stark contrast to such exteriorised invocations of ethnicity, The Smiths would arguably dramatise (in oblique and abstracted ways) certain second-generation sentiments, not least via the trope of ambivalence in their address to both origins and 'home'. With this in mind, the band's work might be seen as less an effacement of Irish ethnicity than as constitutive of a complex Irish-English musical 'route'. As Marr explains, the band became more – not less – aware of their Irishness during The Smiths' career. 'The Irish thing', he says, 'we became more conscious of as we went on.'[12]

Accounts of the second-generation Irish suggest that identities amongst this group are marked less by an affiliation with either England or Ireland than by an ambivalence towards both the host society and the ethnic 'home'. Rather than taking a clear-cut subject position on either side of a neatly forged (Irish-English) binary, then, many second-generation people have expressed 'in-betweenness' or uncertainty.[13] Several Irish-English creative figures have also located themselves in this way; for instance, the London-Irish playwright, Martin McDonagh, has explained:

> I always felt somewhere kind of in-between [Irish and English] …
> I felt half-and-half and neither, which is good … I'm happy having
> a foot in both camps. I'm not into any kind of definition, any kind
> of -ism, politically, socially, religiously, all that stuff. It's not that I
> don't think about those things, but I've come to a place where the
> ambiguities are more interesting than choosing a strict path and following it.[14]

Interestingly, Morrissey and Marr – as the epigraphs that preface this chapter attest – have expressed very similar views. Thus, Morrissey suggests that he is 'stuck in the midst of the Irish-British divide', stressing his dislike of 'any isms towards either country'.[15]

In the light of such suggestions of 'in-betweenness', it is striking that the work of The Smiths, rather than seeking to assuage such dilemmas by asserting an excessive ethnicity (in the manner of, say, The Pogues) or striving to pass as 'native' (which Morrissey briefly did in his early solo career),[16] offered instead an evocation of this ambivalence itself, with the group invoking a marked uncertainty towards notions of origins and 'home'. As well as being 'fiercely ambivalent' (as Johnny Marr has put it), The Smiths were markedly dissident, not least with regard to hegemonic Englishness.[17] Their expressly marginal standpoint (the band positioned themselves 'on the outside')[18] pertained, of course, to a range of factors (not least region and class) that can arguably inflect (as well as augment) ethnicity. Indeed, while The Pogues and Dexys sought to address certain Irish-in-England issues, The Smiths were concerned with a more broadly conceived set of radical positions that coalesced in opposition to the right-wing nationalism of the Thatcher regime. Thus, the band aligned themselves with anti-monarchism, Britain's striking miners, and Ken Livingstone's Greater London Council (the sort of constituencies, in other words, that Thatcher saw as the 'enemy within').[19] Eschewing an overt address to Irishness qua Irishness, then, The Smiths engaged a more elusive subjectivity, issuing a radical critique of England from a displaced perspective rather than asserting ethnic difference. Regardless of how self-conscious (or not) this was, the ensuing absence of an openly Irish subject position would afford the group – in the political and pop-cultural context of Eighties Britain – a more effective stage for their dissident project.

My discussion of The Smiths will not contrive, then, to tease out an essential Irishness at the core of the band's efforts, not least because popular music has been shaped, as Tony Mitchell explains, by a 'constant flow of appropriations in which origins ... are often difficult, if not impossible, to trace'.[20] In this context, popular song in England has been 'saturated', as A.L. Lloyd observed, with 'Irish melodic influences' since at least the eighteenth century.[21] Notwithstanding such points, certain critics have – on occasion – claimed to detect in The Smiths quintessentially Irish qualities. John Waters, for instance, has argued that the band's 'dark introspection, tragic narcissism, ironic world-view and swirling tunefulness fashioned a profound, existential connection with those of us born [in mid-twentieth-century Ireland], a connection which it is impossible to explain in other than mystical terms'.[22] The tacit objective of such accounts is to counter the assumption that The Smiths were unambiguously English with the claim that they were – in fact – quintessentially Irish. Each of these views is born of a highly reductive conception of nationality/ethnicity, and this chapter contests both by locating The Smiths as a certain *second-generation* venture that eschewed the constrictions of both Irish essentialism and English assimilation. In doing this, the chapter explores specific themes in the band's œuvre, including ambivalence, unease and elusiveness. Before presenting this account, I will outline the particular context from which The Smiths emerged.

'It's time the tale were (re)told': a short biography of The Smiths

The Smiths came together in Manchester in May 1982 when John Maher, an eighteen-year-old musician, made contact with Steven Morrissey (who was then twenty-two) with a view to forming a song-writing partnership (with Morrissey as lyricist/vocalist and Maher as guitarist/composer). After early collaborations between the pair proved fruitful, Maher (who elected, after the group's formation, to switch to 'Marr') drafted in a rhythm section, recruiting as bass player an old school friend and musical partner, Andy Rourke (aged eighteen), after enlisting Mike Joyce (nineteen) as the group's drummer. The group played their first live show in October 1982, and later signed to the independent label, Rough Trade, with whom they remained until their disbandment in August 1987. Throughout The Smiths' career, Morrissey and Marr were the key musicians and writers, and attention is accordingly focused on them in this chapter.[23]

Morrissey's parents, who were both from Dublin, settled in the Hulme and Moss Side districts of Manchester in the mid-1950s, where Morrissey (born 1959) was raised in an extended Irish family of uncles, aunts and grandparents all living on the same street.[24] The singer has explained that he 'grew up in a strong Irish community', adding: 'We were quite happy to ghettoise ourselves as the Irish community in Manchester, the Irish stuck rigidly together and there'd always be a relation living two doors down, around the back or up the passage.'[25] This Irish dimension 'steeped', as Morrissey puts it, 'into everything [he] knew growing up'. He recalls that he 'was very aware of being Irish', noting 'we were quite separate from the … kids around us – we were different to them'.[26] This awareness of Irish difference was underlined by trips to Ireland (a place that Morrissey found 'immensely attractive'), as well as by his experience of anti-Irish prejudice, not least being addressed as 'Paddy' when it served as a 'bitter and malevolent slur'.[27]

Perhaps it is no surprise that the youngster felt a distinct sense of 'un-belonging' in 1970s Manchester: 'with so much Irishness around us', Morrissey says, he 'never really felt' Mancunian.[28] This sense of separa-tion was augmented by his attendance of Catholic schools in Hulme and Stretford, where many of Morrissey's teachers were Irish.[29] (Despite the assimilationist ethos of Catholic schools in England, their Irish Catholic teaching staff often imbued pupils with what Terry Eagleton has called a 'sense of being askew to the major consensus'.[30]) The singer had what he calls a 'severe Catholic upbringing', not only through his 'very repressive' schools but also via the 'vividly Catholic' environs of his immigrant Irish – and 'absurdly Catholic' – family.[31] Unlike the other Smiths, though, he would not serve as an altar boy, seeing the Church as a 'detrimental influence' on his life, and viewing Catholicism as 'morbid', 'severe' and restrictive.[32] Indeed, this appears to have tem-pered his feelings towards Ireland, which he occasionally bemoaned as 'the most repressed country in the world'.[33]

Whether or not this view of Irish repression pertained to the singer's (ambivalent) sexuality, it is clear that the teenage Morrissey was seen to be at variance with the normative codes of Irish immigrant life, a point noted by his second-generation peer group, who recall:

> We were first [*sic*] generation Irish, all from strong Catholic back-grounds, all in culture shock. We knew the macho world of Irish pubs. Most of our fathers worked in the building trade. You were told all the time that you were *men*. You've got this fellow [Morrissey] wander-ing around with you and he seems feminine. It was a bit bewildering. When somebody didn't act the accepted norm, it set them apart.[34]

Eschewing this 'macho world of Irish pubs' (with which Morrissey's father, a hospital porter, was not unfamiliar),[35] Morrissey instead became interested, under the tutelage of his librarian mother, in Irish writing. While his mother would afford him access, through her own interests, to 'masses of books on Irish politics and Irish history',[36] it was a specifi-cally (Irish) literary interest that Morrissey acquired from his mother. 'She instilled Oscar Wilde into me', he later explained, noting that this process had begun before he reached adolescence.[37] (The role played by Morrissey's mother is worth reflecting on here, as it was often Irish women who assumed the role of encouraging Irish cultural interests amongst the second generation, a task that was not straightforward in the 1970s, when, as Jim Mac Laughlin explains, the 'wish to make ... children relate positively to their roots' was rendered difficult by the Troubles.[38])

The young Morrissey certainly made a positive identification with Irish writing, and came to reflect that 'most of the people I ever cared about in literature came from Ireland'.[39] His special area of interest was undoubtedly that of Wilde: 'I've read everything he wrote and everything written about him and I still find him totally awe-inspiring', the singer explained.[40] Despite his lack of academic success (Morrissey left Stretford Technical School with three O levels), his literary interests had the effect, as Simpson suggests, of marginalising Morrissey – within his working-class Irish milieu – as 'a mummy's boy and a bookworm'.[41] Thus, if the singer felt somewhat alienated from the host culture, he was also at odds with certain aspects of his Irish milieu (unlike his sister, for instance, he eschewed the social rituals of the local Irish club).[42] In this context, Morrissey explains that the experience of growing up second-generation Irish was, for him, 'confusing'.[43] Similar comments have been made by John Lydon (who felt 'confused' about his Irish family, and 'where [he] came from'),[44] and Morrissey would (like other second-generation Irish figures) seek a symbolic 'home' in 1970s punk, sending letters and reviews to the music press, writing a book on The New York Dolls, and performing as vocalist/lyricist for The Nosebleeds (*c.* 1978).[45] Despite his obvious attraction to punk, however, the youngster felt ill at ease – as an inchoate singer – with punk's aesthetic frame (which he says was too 'aggressive' for his 'inhibited' style).[46] If punk was too pugnacious for the young Morrissey, the more ponderous forms of pop were, he says, too 'folksy' and 'gentle' for his tastes. Thus, while he wished to sing and write song lyrics, he felt distanced from the available styles. 'I couldn't quite see where I could possibly fit into music', recalls Morrissey of this pre-Smiths period. 'Where did I belong? Which soil could I grow from? That was the question', he explains.[47]

Johnny Marr's parents left their home in Athy, County Kildare, in the early 1960s before settling amongst an extended Irish family on two adjacent streets in Ardwick, a working-class district of Manchester.[48] Marr (born 1963) has explained that he was raised in a 'young Irish community', and was 'surrounded' during his formative years 'by Irish culture', stressing that 'it does rub off'.[49] This aspect of Marr's upbringing was enhanced by frequent trips to Ireland (where he spent several months of each year), as well as by his experience of anti-Irish prejudice, with the youngster becoming 'accustomed to being branded an "Irish pig" at school and on the terraced streets of his native Ardwick': 'I was called "Irish pig" all the time, even by a couple of teachers … There was a certain sensitivity to being Irish. I was pretty sensitive to it.'[50] Marr recalls having 'to put up with an awful lot of snide remarks and false media reports about the Irish in England', and adds, 'I certainly did feel very different from the rest of my friends.'[51] Being of Irish descent was, then, a constitutive part of Marr's subjectivity:

> There was without a doubt a sense of that being part of your identity. There was no way that you could ignore it, either from an internal point of view – like within your household – or an external point of view from the messages you were getting from the people outside of it. We subjectively were aware that our [English] friends had a different kind of experience and a different kind of lifestyle than us.[52]

Consequently, the young Marr, like his future co-song-writer, felt somewhat at odds with the host milieu. 'Just like Morrissey will tell you, growing up in an Irish family in Manchester in the 1970s you did feel at a bit of a remove.'[53]

While the major source of employment amongst the Maher family was in manual labour and construction, the guitarist's parents also organised local music events, and his extended family regularly performed Irish songs at social gatherings in the Maher household.[54] There was, he says, 'a lot of melancholy in the music, which I was really drawn to', pointing in particular to 'melodic Irish ballads, like "Black Velvet Band", which I used to love'.[55] If the musical practices of the Maher family offered a forum in which to express Irish difference, they might consequently be seen as a form of ethnic boundary-maintenance. As Marella Buckley explains, the domestic space of Irish migrants often marked 'a boundary of difference inside which … cultural practices which refer[ed] to the country of origin [could] be maintained and shielded from the alien environment of the street'.[56] In the case of the Irish in England, it was usually music – notes Martin Stokes – that supplied the means through which this was achieved.[57]

Maher family music events were not confined to Irish styles, however, for they comprised a broad range of forms, including folk and country as well as pop and rock.[58] Marr recalls hearing accordions and penny whistles, as well as records by the Everly Brothers and Irish showbands such as Big Tom and The Mainliners, suggesting that his parents were 'caught in between' the 'old music' and the emerging 'pop music'.[59] These musical events, then, did not serve only as an arena of ethnic difference, for their eclecticism equipped Marr with a broad taste for music per se, affording the youngster a means, to borrow from Stokes, of 'constructing trajectories' as much as 'boundaries', thus 'transcending the limitations' of ethnic specificity.[60] This point is underlined by the fact that Marr's family were – unlike those of, say, MacGowan – 'very happy' to be in England, and brought him up, he explains, 'to be suspicious of people who', in his words, 'do the "old country blarney" thing',[61] a term that denotes the more regressive aspects of Irish migrant life. Indeed, Marr has expressed an aversion to the more 'kitsch' forms of Irish culture (he recalls that his 'first ever exposure to music came from seeing not very good Irish showbands play in Manchester'),[62] and it seems that he, like Noel Gallagher, felt somewhat 'stifled' by the 'traditional' Irish scene,[63] instead conceiving of musical literacy as – to borrow from John Shepherd – a 'medium' for 'the expansion of individual and cultural horizons'.[64] Reflecting on this point, Marr suggests that his upbringing was marked by a certain 'schizophrenia', a term that has been used by second-generation Irish people to denote ambivalence or duality.[65] 'I had this schizophrenic kind of upbringing', the guitarist recalls, citing his family's 'overt pro-Mancunian sensibility' and his own 'awareness of all the advantages and opportunities of being brought up in [England]', whilst noting that this was offset by the 'super-Irish environment' in which he was raised, which 'you couldn't escape even if you tried … plus I was there [in Ireland] a few months [every] year.'[66] (Marr explains that he missed 'chunks of school' whilst on trips to Kildare with his 'homesick' parents.[67]) Thus, while Marr viewed England and English culture as 'this incredible opportunity and adventure', he was at the same time 'steeped in' and 'swimming in' Irish life. He recalls the ethnic iconography with which he was 'constantly surrounded' – including harps, shamrocks and ornaments inscribed with 'Éire', as well as Irish tricolours and Sacred Heart images – and describes his early environs as 'super-Catholic' and 'super-Irish'.[68] It is clear, then, that while Marr would learn – from his parents – to be 'very pro-Manchester' and to 'appreciate the opportunities we were being given in Manchester', he was simultaneously immersed in Irish culture, not least via his parents' home, with its 'strong Irish Catholic symbols'.[69] Marr's affective investment in Manchester was consequently offset, he suggests, by an 'appreciation of Irish culture, music and iconography'.[70] In this context, Marr notes the repulsion that he felt towards British nationalism, stressing that he 'never felt an affinity' with the Union Jack. 'I've always hated that flag', he says, seeing it as 'a sign of aggression towards immigrants', including the Irish. At the same time, though, Marr saw little value in the 'hokey, bullshit Irish romanticism' expressed by sections of his migrant milieu. The young Marr thus accrued a certain ambivalence, seeing himself as '[not] quite the definite article'.[71] (He tellingly views his Irish-English peer group as a 'floating generation': 'we are on our own', he suggests.[72]) In this regard, there is a striking parallel between Marr and U2 guitarist The Edge, who was raised in Dublin by British (Welsh Protestant) parents. 'I've always felt something of an outsider in Ireland', The Edge explains.

> Growing up as a kid, I always felt that I didn't quite belong here, for
> one reason or another. Nor do I belong anywhere else. I guess I've
> grown accustomed to being just slightly displaced – not in any heavy
> way, but I have this sense of being just slightly different. And in a
> weird way, that's why I got into music, maybe in an attempt to resolve
> that to some extent.[73]

Whether or not music is able to 'resolve' such displacement, Marr says
that his migrant upbringing had 'a lot to do with [him] being a musician', and he was certainly encouraged (not to say expected) to engage
in musical practices from a very young age.[74] During the weekly music
events that were staged at his parents' house, Marr's father (who sang and
played the accordion) taught his son the harmonica (an instrument that
Marr deployed throughout The Smiths' career).[75] Such tuition continued
on trips to Kildare, where a youngish uncle taught Marr to play Irish
ballads and popular songs.[76] His interest in the guitar was first sparked,
however, by an Irish rock musician: 'the man who changed my musical
life was Rory Gallagher', explains Marr. 'I picked up a guitar because of
him. I used to love the sound of his name.'[77] Marr's first electric guitar
was, moreover, a Rory Gallagher-style Stratocaster copy, and he would
subsequently track Gallagher's live shows with 'hawkish vigilance'.[78]
At the same time, Marr acquired an interest in certain folk guitarists,
including Martin Carthy, an English musician (of Irish descent) whose
'novel approach to the acoustic-guitar accompaniment of traditional
songs owed much to the Irish virtuoso *uilleann*-piper Séamus Ennis,
whose playing Carthy tried to translate into guitar techniques'.[79] Marr
also followed a few Irish folk ensembles, such as The Bothy Band and
early Clannad.[80]

Despite his keen musical interests, Marr received no formal training, and fared little better than Morrissey in his school examinations,
leaving his 'seriously Catholic' secondary school with few qualifications.[81] However, during this period Marr had assembled a group (with
future Smiths bass player Andy Rourke) called The Paris Valentinos
(*c.* 1977–79), who performed cover versions of songs by Rory Gallagher
and Thin Lizzy (acts viewed as 'the success-stories of Irish guitar playing' at that time).[82] Interestingly, Marr and Rourke also played guitars
at Sunday folk Masses in exchange for the use of a Catholic club to
rehearse their various rock projects.[83] After leaving school, Marr continued to be involved (usually alongside Rourke) with rock ensembles,
most notably White Dice (*c.* 1979–81), before experimenting with
dance/funk styles in The Freak Party (*c.* 1981–82) during the period
immediately prior to The Smiths.[84]

Andy Rourke (born 1964) was raised by an Irish-descended father (whose family was from Cork) in Ashton-upon-Mersey (and later Sharston) after his English mother had separated from Rourke's father (a self-employed businessman) and left the family home. Rourke explains: 'we were quite a traditional Irish Catholic family rather than an English one'.[85] Attending the same Catholic secondary school as Marr, Rourke – like the guitarist – left at sixteen with few qualifications. He subsequently found work in a timber yard whilst engaging (usually with Marr) in various rock, pop and funk projects.[86] Mike Joyce (born 1963), meanwhile, had grown up in Fallowfield, with his father from Shrule, County Galway, and his mother from County Kildare. He recalls visits to Ireland with his family, as well as the 'solidarity' of the community in which he was raised.[87] In common with the other Smiths, Joyce left his Catholic secondary school at sixteen, and (with the exception of a few flute lessons) had no formal musical training. Nevertheless, he went on to experience moderate success with a local punk group The Hoax (*c*. 1978–81), before joining a Northern Irish (though Manchester-based) punk act called Victim (*c*. 1981–82).[88]

Although it was an 'amazing coincidence', says Marr, that he assembled, in The Smiths, a band of second-generation Irish Catholics, he suggests that their Irish ethnicity was a crucial point of group commonality about which the band were highly conscious. 'We talked about it a lot', Marr explains,[89] noting that the group 'always had a very special sort of Irish connection'.[90] This point is confirmed by Joyce, who says 'We had an absolute affinity because of our Irishness', laying stress on the group's shared background in migrant families.[91] Thus, whilst Irish parentage was not, in Goddard's terms, 'strictly prerequisite' for Smiths membership, it certainly 'played its part in establishing The Smiths' inter-group chemistry.'[92] Indeed, the Irish aspect was so intrinsic to the group's dynamic that it did not, at least for Joyce, require expression. 'It was just *there*', the drummer recalls – 'We didn't need to express that.'[93] For Marr, though, this second-generation Irish context would serve to inform, in various ways, the band's work and persona.[94]

Evocations of Irishness

In early Smiths interviews, Morrissey made it clear that he and his colleagues were of Irish descent, noting that 'with having Irish parents as everyone in the group has, we're all deeply embedded there [in Ireland]'.[95] Marr also drew attention to this point, explaining: 'All The Smiths come from a very similar background. We all have Irish-Catholic families', adding that he had been raised in 'a typical traditional Irish musical family'.[96] Such points were underlined by the group's extensive Irish concert tours. The Smiths' first major show outside England was a (previously undocumented) concert at Dublin's Trinity College, and the band played another sixteen shows in Ireland in just twenty-two months, a period in which that country's best-known group – U2 – performed at home just once.[97] These tours took in not only the major cities but also small towns such as Waterford, Dundalk and Letterkenny, despite the band being advised against visiting such non-metropolitan locales.[98] The itinerary of the Irish tours was conceived by Morrissey, who made reference to the group's Irishness from the stage, most notably by switching the opening lines of 'Still Ill' (1983) to '*Ireland* is mine' from the usual 'England'.[99]

The time that The Smiths spent in Ireland did not go unnoticed by English fans, who carped at the band's habit of 'vanishing to Ireland all the time'.[100] Meanwhile, critics seemed bemused by the band's wish to entertain 'the Micks', as *Melody Maker* put it.[101] The Irish tours were, however, quite significant for the band, particularly Marr, who explains that The Smiths' time in Ireland 'ignited this thing that was inside [him]' and 'reconnected' him with his upbringing. 'When I went to Ireland', he recalls, 'I was like, "Oh yeah ... this thing I've got inside of me is actually pretty unique and quite important to me, and *useful*", and I kind of put a little spotlight on it and magnified it ... I was sort of celebrating it.'[102] This 'spotlight' was most vivid, Marr explains, on the song 'Please, Please, Please, Let Me Get What I Want' (1984), which was originally called 'The Irish Waltz', and which listeners claim is redolent of 'some long-forgotten Irish folk song', with its striking mandolin solo serving to heighten the song's 'emphatically Irish air'.[103] Marr had composed the tune whilst reflecting on his early migrant milieu, and the matrix message that follows the track – on the vinyl run-off groove of *Hatful of Hollow* (1984) – features the word 'Eire', an overt acknowledgment of Marr's (and, by extension, the band's) Irish provenance.[104] (It is interesting to note, in this regard, that The Smiths commenced many of their Irish shows with a version of 'Please, Please, Please ...' despite its being an 'unlikely set opener', as Goddard suggests.[105]) Morrissey would engage in similar gestures, not least by wearing a Claddagh ring, a popular symbol of Irish ethnicity that has been worn by figures such as Shane MacGowan, Elvis Costello and Noel Gallagher.[106] If such signals were not sufficiently clear, then a string of alleged phone calls to the UK media by Morrissey's father in which he insisted on the singer's Irishness served to spell out the group's ethnicity.[107]

The band's Catholicity was, if anything, more overt. Thus, Morrissey posed with rosary beads – and occasionally halos and stigmata – whilst discussing his Catholic upbringing and education, attracting, in the process, the epithet 'Pope of Pop' (which was of a piece with his self-confirmed celibacy, abstinence and expressly 'clean' image).[108] Morrissey would also sing about a specific Catholic church (the Holy Name) in Manchester (which members of The Smiths had attended), albeit in the slightly veiled scenario of 'Vicar In A Tutu' (1986) (in which the parish priest appears as an Anglican).[109] The singer also associated himself with radical Catholic figures, such as Joan of Arc and Guy Fawkes, and when probed about his Catholicism would often refer directly to Ireland, suggesting that – for him – these two issues were entwined.[110] Indeed, certain critics would conflate the singer's Irishness with his Catholicism: 'Does the Irish ancestry make for a religious Morrissey?', asked one UK interviewer in 1983.[111]

The Irish aspects of the group did not go unnoticed by their fans. Certain second-generation listeners would confirm that The Smiths' Irish provenance was a key part of their appeal. Noel Gallagher recalls his first reaction to The Smiths in terms of a shared Irishness, putting his appreciation of Morrissey down to 'the fact we're both Anglo-Irish', whilst making comparable points about Marr: 'I came from an Irish background and so did this geezer Johnny Marr and it would be like, "There's another thing I can relate to".'[112] In a similar vein, the journalist Terry Christian suggests that his interest in The Smiths was enhanced by the fact that he had 'the same Irish Catholic background' as the group members.[113] The former Suede guitarist Bernard Butler (who is also second-generation Irish) goes even further, observing a 'huge Irish influence' in The Smiths.[114]

Contributors to 1980s fanzines such as *Smiths Indeed* located Morrissey in the context of certain 'Anglo-Irish writers', seeing his lyrics as an instance of 'Anglo-Irish culture'.[115] This perspective would persist long after the group's demise, not only amongst Irish fans – who cite 'specific Irish resonances' in The Smiths' work – but also amongst Latino fans in the US, who place special emphasis on the group's ethnicity.[116] Observers have explained that The Smiths' popularity in this context is based on perceived 'parallels between the Latino community in the US and the experience of being Irish in England', with Latino fans noting – in the band – an 'outsider mentality' that they view as a feature of migrancy.[117]

An awareness of the band's Irishness was less evident, however, in the British music press. This is not to say that this aspect of the band was completely overlooked, for it *was* noted on occasion during The Smiths' career – thus, one of the band's first music press interviews explained:

'Like the other Smiths [Morrissey] was born in Manchester of Irish parents and his voice is an intimate mixture of Anglo-Irish ancestry.'[118] Meanwhile, one of the band's final press encounters highlighted their singer's 'Irish manner'.[119] Elsewhere, fellow musicians, such as Mark E. Smith of The Fall, would inform music journalists that Morrissey was a 'Paddy'.[120]

Locating The Smiths' aesthetic: between eclecticism and authenticity

Marr has claimed that The Smiths' Irish provenance had 'a huge influence' on the group, adding that it 'absolutely informed' his own writing and playing.[121] There were certainly traces in the band's work of styles associated with Irish migrants, most notably country and folk.[122] Indeed, the 'all-engulfing sound of folk-rock' was, for Julian Stringer, 'everywhere apparent' in The Smiths, an aspect of their œuvre that was only enhanced by Marr's 'folk' guitar tunings, and use of the mandolin, most famously on 'Please, Please, Please …'.[123] It is, nevertheless, worth noting that Marr – the group's sole composer and arranger – was 'harmonically and melodically' not attracted to Irish music, and found overt expressions of Irishness somewhat off-putting.[124] Rather than engaging with an audibly Irish style, then, The Smiths embarked on an innovative venture in the realm of 'independent' guitar-based rock, pursuing what Stringer calls a 'pluralist approach' to musical styles.[125] This included the 'neo-folk' of 1960s US west-coast bands like The Byrds ('This Charming Man'), British folk-revival artists such as Bert Jansch and Martin Carthy ('Back To The Old House', 'Reel Around The Fountain'), 1950s rock and roll ('Nowhere Fast', 'Shakespeare's Sister'), 1960s rhythm and blues ('I Want The One I Can't Have'), 1970s funk ('Barbarism Begins At Home'), and the fusing of standard rock patterns with jazz ('Heaven Knows I'm Miserable Now') and high-life ('Ask') inflections.[126]

Throughout The Smiths' work, Marr displayed a distinctively 'clean' and 'bright' guitar sound, heavily laden with 'chorus' and reverb, and characterised by multi-layered textures of guitar overdubs.[127] In terms of his playing style, Marr sought to perform both lead and rhythm parts simultaneously; so rather than simply strumming a succession of power chords, he tended towards the plucking of individual strings.[128] However, while Marr's style was typically marked by high-register phrasing ('This Charming Man', 'Heaven Knows I'm Miserable Now', 'Ask'), he performed very few conventional solos (a trait that underscored The Smiths' rebuttal of rock machismo).[129]

Marr's guitar – which was usually tuned a couple of semitones higher than concert pitch[130] – was accompanied by Rourke's (conventionally tuned) bass, which tended towards independent melodic lines (most pronounced in tracks like 'This Charming Man', 'Rusholme Ruffians' and 'Barbarism Begins At Home'). In turn, Joyce adhered to a standard rock beat,[131] although the drummer explains that his style also functioned as a counterpoint to Rourke's bass parts, yielding a unique attribute of the group's sound. 'I'd always be going against what Andy would be playing', Joyce recalls, suggesting that this 'made The Smiths sound different [to] other groups'.[132]

An even more prominent aspect of The Smiths' sound was, of course, the singer's voice, which evinced the 'studied ordinariness' – lacking in 'resonance' and 'range' – that Allan F. Moore observes in other indie singers, with a middle-register 'spoken-sung' delivery imbuing much of Morrissey's work.[133] Such an 'untrained' style of vocal served, as Stan Hawkins notes, to legitimise Morrissey's singing as 'authentic' and 'natural'.[134] In this context, Simon Reynolds discerns a quasi-'folky' singing style in The Smiths' songs.[135] Perhaps the most salient aspect of Morrissey's vocal, though, was its straining, in Stringer's terms, 'for "correct" [and] clear English diction', a relatively unusual practice for English rock vocalists.[136] Despite the 'twangs of Irish ancestry' that certain listeners heard in the singer's work, the emotive connotations of Morrissey's vocal had little in common with other second-generation Irish singers (such as Lydon, Rowland or MacGowan), with Morrissey delivering the bulk of his song words in a calm and restrained manner.[137] His singing was often adorned, however, by a number of – in Stringer's terms – 'indulgent or excessive traits that [were] redundant to the job of simply getting the words across'. These included 'a specific form of attack and delay, whereby lines are sung with a quick or drawn-out emphasis, then held [and] sustained through melisma', 'a constant use of irony, both through tone and phrasing', and 'the use of wild falsetto'.[138] There was also, notes Hawkins, a great deal of 'vocal straining', invoking 'a sense of increased emotional intensity'.[139] Such non-linguistic features were tempered by what Nadine Hubbs calls a lack of 'melodic motion' in the singer's style, with 'the static quality of his melodies' bestowing a 'declamatory emphasis' on his 'distinctive' words.[140]

Adopting a self-consciously literary persona, Morrissey talked at length about his bookish pursuits, seeing song lyrics as a quasi-literary form that he would later call a 'new poetry'.[141] The singer's words would often draw, moreover, on specific literary sources, especially Oscar Wilde and the (Salford-Irish) playwright Shelagh Delaney;[142] thus, when Morrissey explained that 'at least 50 per cent' of his reason for

Photograph: Peter Ashworth

writing could be 'blamed on Shelagh Delaney', it was clear that the remaining percentage was assigned to Wilde.[143] These writers would suffuse The Smiths' œuvre via references in song lyrics, interviews and ancillary media.[144] While Rowland and MacGowan aligned themselves with Brendan Behan, then, Morrissey invoked a different Irish literary source, citing Wilde (and Delaney) habitually, whilst accessorising with Wilde's work and wearing T-shirts featuring the Irish writer. 'It's like carrying your rosary around with you', he explained of this attachment to Wilde.[145] In Smiths tour programmes, Morrissey listed Wilde as his 'favourite person', and posters of Wilde and Delaney appeared on Salford streets in The Smiths' final video, while Delaney – who was honoured (albeit in Anglicized form) in the song 'Sheila Take A Bow' (1987) – featured on the sleeve of Smiths records.[146] The association with Wilde, though, was undoubtedly most significant, as evidenced by the fact that the latter's Paris tombstone became, in the 1980s, a sort of graffiti board for Smiths song lyrics.[147]

Despite such studied (and self-conscious) literary associations, The

Smiths would effect a conflation of Morrissey, the singer, with the songs' narrating speaker (or 'I'). As Hubbs explains, Smiths song words were characterised by Morrissey's 'singular first-person perspective', a point that was underlined by the singer's claim that Smiths songs were about his 'own life', with the lyrics being drawn from 'direct experience' and 'autobiography'.[148] While such conflations of lived experience and creative expression should not be taken at face value, the point to note is that this was a key effect of The Smiths' persona. Thus, the band's songs were viewed as a sort of expression of Morrissey's personal life. The dominant themes of this work would be seen as 'despair' and 'alienation' – as well as 'self-mockery and deprecation' – with fans claiming that Smiths songs 'preyed upon the theme of belonging/not belonging'.[149]

A major part of the band's persona was their sartorial style, which, as Zoe Williams points out, 'was far more complex and controversial than the standard indie uniform of grubby black items and ill-hewn hair'.[150] During the period in which Rowland had fashioned Dexys as 'raggle-taggle' gypsies, and MacGowan had contrived The Pogues' 'Paddy chic' scheme, Morrissey assembled himself as a different type of outsider ('standing up', as Marr explained, 'for the gawk'), wearing oversized shirts together with beads and broaches, and National Health Service spectacles and hearing aids (describing the latter as 'disability chic').[151] The singer would also decorate himself with flowers – especially daffodils and gladioli (in homage to Wilde) – whilst making an ungainly attempt at dancing (a spectacle that, for Stringer, conveyed 'neurosis').[152] Such flamboyance would deviate starkly from the sombre hues of post-punk English dress codes, whilst simultaneously eschewing the showy apparel of the 1980s pop mainstream, yielding instead what Sean O'Hagan calls a 'resolute ordinariness'.[153] In early interviews with 'style' journals such as *The Face*, Marr advised readers to reject the ethos of 'cool', whilst Morrissey encouraged fans to 'display their weaknesses'.[154] Such comments were underscored by the latter's emaciated physique, with the (abstinent and vegetarian) singer serving, for Joe Brooker, as a sort of pop-cultural 'hunger-striker'.[155]

Alongside such oppositional aspects, however, the band took on the styles of an 'authentic' (and rather 'retro') rock aesthetic, with an attire of denim, suede and turtlenecks accompanying Marr's suite of classic rock guitars (such as Rickenbacker, Gibson and Gretsch).[156] This stress on 'authenticity' was also evoked in the group's name, which, from their perspective, offered a neo-realist retort to the extravagantly titled synth-pop acts of the early 1980s (such as Orchestral Manœuvres in the Dark).[157] In this context, 'The Smiths' sounded, for Morrissey, 'down to earth'.[158]

Photograph: Tom Sheehan

The Smiths' antipathy to synthesized sound was not registered solely through nomenclature. In fact, for Morrissey The Smiths' sound was a tacit refusal of synth style; thus, he proclaimed in interviews that The Smiths offered an 'argument against' the 'non-human feel' of contemporary pop.[159] Mainstream popular music in the early 1980s was, as Moore observes, 'flowing not with guitars, but with synthesizers', and in this context, 'the work of committed *guitar*-based performers' was, in Middleton's terms, 'taken to signify commitment to the "classic" values of rock tradition'.[160] Such values were based not only in 'authenticity' but also in the attendant ideas of honesty and sincerity, which were openly addressed – and clearly endorsed – by The Smiths.[161] Morrissey would typically insist, for instance, that 'everything we say and do, we mean', describing The Smiths' work as 'real music played by real people', 'with real heart and soul'.[162] This was a point with which Marr clearly agreed: 'we really mean what we say', he explained, suggesting: 'We don't put on any act, we don't adopt a persona that says, "We are The Smiths." *We just are*. This is *us*, there's no great mystique.'[163] While MacGowan and Rowland staged certain forms of *ethnic* authenticity, then, The Smiths invoked a different sort of pop-cultural authenticity – one that Stringer has termed 'the realist aesthetic of rock ideology'.[164]

As well as serving as a shot across the bows of 1980s pop culture, The Smiths might also be seen as a response to the roots rock that, for Moore, corresponded with synth-pop, especially if we locate – as

Moore does – The Pogues in this context.[165] The timing of The Smiths'
first live show is quite striking in this regard, as it coincided with The
Pogues' first live event (both groups performed their debut concert on
4 October 1982).[166] In this context, the curiously coincident – and yet
highly divergent – paths of The Smiths and The Pogues served to illustrate the distinction in popular music between, on the one hand, an
'historical authenticity', based largely on ethnicity and "roots"', and, on
the other hand, a 'personal authenticity' built on 'self-expression'.[167]

Speaking for The Smiths: introspective Irishness/abstracted ethnicity

The divergence outlined above points to an especially crucial aspect of
the differing Smiths/Pogues projects, for while MacGowan's band fashioned an upfront display of collective Irish difference (yielding a form of
catharsis as well as a symbolic sense of community), The Smiths appeared
to register (in rather more oblique ways) certain second-generation sentiments at the level of the *personal* (staging the Irish/English quandary
as an interiorised and isolated – as well as a highly abstracted – experience). Thus, if the band's approach to sexuality offered, as Simpson
notes, 'an exploration of *interior* androgyny' (in contrast to the 'exterior
androgyny of glam rock'),[168] then their address to Irishness might be
seen as a type of interiorised (and abstracted) ethnicity (in contrast to
the exterior ethnicity of The Pogues). The Smiths were, as Marr explains,
'way more introvert' than The Pogues, and were more concerned, he suggests, with 'melancholic isolation' and 'the ethos of exclusion'.[169] With
this in mind, it might be argued that while MacGowan sought refuge
in the pub (in 'Streams Of Whiskey') and Rowland retreated to a curative Irish coast (in 'Knowledge Of Beauty'), The Smiths recoiled from
Thatcher's Britain to stage a sort of 'resistance through withdrawal', as
Reynolds put it, with an isolated and interiorised self becoming the de
facto site of abdication.[170] Morrissey and Marr appear to have dealt with
their upbringings through what Marr calls 'an absolutely *massive* capacity for introspection': 'I always kept it to myself', the guitarist reflects.[171]
Morrissey, similarly, would address his Irishness 'quietly' and 'in [his]
heart', as the singer puts it, rather than 'hanging from the balcony singing Gaelic sea-shanties'.[172]

The highly personalised perspective outlined here perhaps explains
why the work of The Smiths, from the viewpoint of the more overtly
Irish Pogues (who are tacitly invoked in the above quote), represented
only 'Morrissey' rather than any discrete social group.[173] This point is

confirmed by Len Brown, who notes that, at a time of deep social cleavages, The Smiths' singer 'insisted on being individual ... a card-carrying member of nothing but the cult of his own personality'.[174] Against the backdrop of Morrissey's Irish milieu, then – which he felt lacked 'self-expression' and 'individuality' – the singer would see 'insularity' (and therefore withdrawal) as 'very productive'.[175] Meanwhile, from a specifically *musical* perspective – and despite the 'trace' of 'community' that has been heard in Marr's 'allusions to country, rockabilly, the blues, folk and skiffle'[176] – The Smiths' guitarist explains that Irish traditional sounds evoked, for him, the sort of music from which he was 'trying to escape' (implying his own search for self-expression).[177] Marr adds, in this context, that he often sought to invoke, in The Smiths' music, the *mood* of his early Irish milieu, but in a highly subjective and personal way that eschewed any collectivist style (a point I explore later).[178]

What this individuated ethos afforded The Smiths, of course, was a means by which to resonate with *other* socially marginal groups – hence the claim (made by many Smiths fans) that the band 'appealed to people who saw themselves as misfits', with Morrissey acting as 'an icon' for 'minorities in general'.[179] This amalgam of 'outsiders' would, moreover, respond to The Smiths in distinctly individuated ways, with Smiths fandom offering, for Karl Maton, 'a highly individualist form of subcultural membership' in which fans assumed a 'one-to-one relationship with Morrissey', who was seen to address 'everybody *individually*'. Being a fan of The Smiths offered the band's audience, then, 'a source of collective identity but of a highly individualist kind', with the fans' 'feelings of identification with Morrissey' failing to translate into 'feelings of identification with other fans'. Thus, while followers of the group were 'able to enjoy the sense of solidarity' offered by Smiths fandom, they nevertheless maintained a sense of themselves as 'individuals and different' rather than as a 'social community', with the crucial line of demarcation (more commonly found around the subculture) being 'drawn around the individual rather than the group'.[180] If MacGowan sang for the (second-generation Irish) collective, then, Morrissey sang both of and for the (more generically displaced) individual, with the collective solidarity facilitated by The Pogues contrasting with the 'personalised sense of belonging' offered by The Smiths.[181] Thus, while The Smiths' work appealed to a broader constituency, it did so in a more exclusivist way (via the band's subcultural kudos and their singer's remote persona), offering a very different experience to The Pogues, whose ethnic specificity was (paradoxically) more inclusive. This is a point with which Marr agrees: he contrasts the 'inclusive party' of The Pogues with the 'expression of exclusivity' staged by The Smiths.[182]

While this sense of exclusivity was not drawn upon demographic lines – the band appealed to diverse listeners – The Smiths' 'outsider' resonance was often felt to be delimited around issues of 'race', especially after Morrissey had made some troubling comments about black music in 1986, prompting claims that the singer was racist.[183] Such claims were dismissed by the band: Morrissey declared that his views had been distorted ('how can I hate black music? 55% of all my records are by black artists', he explained), and launched a legal action ('We're suing the *Melody Maker*, and they tell us they can't find the tapes').[184] Marr was less measured. 'We're not in the habit of issuing personal threats', he said, 'but that was such a vicious slur-job that we'll kick the shit out of him [the critic who had made the claims]. Violence is disgusting but racism's worse and we don't deal with it.'[185] Such comments were underlined by other gestures in The Smiths' work, not least their 1984 concert – with the reggae group Misty in Roots – for the multiculturalist GLC, their support for Artists Against Apartheid (and refusal to retail work in South Africa), their stated interest in black music (while Morrissey endorsed Motown, Marr acknowledged the influence of 'the more traditional aspects of black music'), and their invocation of black styles (critics heard 'an essential black element' in Rourke's bass, a 'sublime African feel' in Marr's guitar, and a 'Blues aesthetic' in Morrissey's lyrics).[186] It is also worth noting, in this context, that The Smiths' audience included certain black and Asian listeners, some of who identified with the band's sense of 'outsiderness'.[187] Nabeel Zuberi recalls that The Smiths' 'sense of not completely belonging to a landscape' had 'a resonance for [him] as a fan in the 1980s'.[188]

Certain observers would later allude to Morrissey's Irishness in an attempt to offset the accusation of racism. Simpson, for instance, suggests that 'to be northern, working class and Irish' – like Morrissey – was 'the next best worst thing to being a nigger', adding that the singer was 'a product of immigration'.[189] The point to note, however, is that Morrissey appeared less as an Irish 'outsider' than as – in Bracewell's terms – an 'outsider beyond the outsiders', a view that was evinced in 1980s fanzines such as *Smiths Indeed*, in which the singer was described as the 'Jimmy Porter/James Dean/Oscar Wilde [i.e. archetypal outsider] of the Eighties', with a fan base of 'genuine outsider types'.[190]

With its appeal to an assortment of 'outsiders', The Smiths' œuvre had something in common with earlier migrant song cultures, not least those of Irish migrants in Victorian Manchester, which often conveyed, as Phil Eva explains, a sense of 'emotional and psychic displacement' that resonated beyond the city's Irish districts, appealing to a 'pervasive sense of social and cultural dislocation'. Such songs would, then, project 'a metaphor for a general sense of alienation', and 'chimed' with a variegated 'sense' of 'dislocation'. Thus, while certain forms of exile song performed 'an assertion of [ethnic] difference, of the distinct and separate identity of the Irish in a foreign and hostile land', another strand would stage 'a sense of displacement that was shared with English listeners'.[191] If the former served as a sort of precedent for The Pogues, then the latter might be seen as analogous to The Smiths, whose work came to 'articulate' (in the sense outlined in the previous chapter) with an abstract marginality over an exclusive ethnicity. (The band refused to be 'regimented', said Morrissey, towards 'a certain sect of people'.[192]) Despite the Irish inflections that were observed in The Smiths by certain fans (as outlined above), it is clear that the band would not resonate – in the manner of, say, The Pogues – with an Irish ethnicity in England. (Thus, Terry Christian's claim that The Smiths were 'more Irish than the Pogues' was based on genetic – not aesthetic – grounds.[193]) This lack of an overt Irish resonance was underscored by the band's name, whose 'peculiarly English connotations gave the lie', as Rogan explains, to their 'full-blooded Irish extraction'.[194] This 'extraction' was further obscured by Maher's adoption of 'Marr' shortly after The Smiths' formation. Whilst this change was born, in part, of a wish to distinguish himself from another Mancunian musician (Buzzcocks drummer, John Maher), it also pertained to the mispronunciation of his name in England: 'the English could never pronounce my surname properly', explains Marr; 'it would come out as Meyer or something like that. So to make it easier, I just used the phonetic spelling.'[195] In this respect, Marr was simply adhering to a long-standing custom amongst musicians of migrant descent, many of whom have assumed stage names.[196] Nevertheless, even if Marr's name change was prompted by pragmatic concerns – rather than a wish to 'pass' – it arguably had the effect of concealing his (and thus the group's) Irishness.

The band's failure to 'articulate' with an Irish ethnicity also pertained, however, to issues of style. Notwithstanding their eschewal of 'ethnic' sounds, the particular sort of 'authentic', self-expressive rock on which The Smiths drew has rarely been concerned with ethnic issues, not least because such issues have not been easy to adopt in a genre shaped – as Rolston notes – by 'more transitory' and 'less articulate' concerns.[197] It is also worth noting that the creative work of the Irish in England has often shown little interest in staging what Eamonn Hughes calls a 'located' ethnic 'community' that 'sees itself as Irish-British and which requires cultural articulation'.[198] The literary work of the Irish in Britain has, instead, been more concerned with individual figures (over collective formations), who inhabit less a 'world of open aggression' that must be 'openly confronted and dealt with' than a locale 'in which the continuously jarring effects of living in ... a culture like and yet unlike one's own have to be internalised'. As Hughes points out, then, this strand of Irish creative expression signals less 'an aggressively defensive stance against blatant attack' than a 'feeling of being continuously off-balance'. With such expressive forms evoking the effects of migration at the level of individual consciousness, Hughes suggests that any address to Irish migrant culture should take into account not only the 'public stance of being Irish-in-Britain' but also 'the private consciousness; the feeling that one lives in an out-of-kilter world'. In this context, Hughes suggests that the experience of being Irish in Britain has most often been registered 'at the level of the idea of that most private of spaces, "home"', with the 'contemporary fiction of Irish-Britain' being nothing less than 'obsessed' with ideas of 'home'. Alongside this concern, a great deal of 'Irish-in-Britain writing' has, says Hughes, been marked by the tropes of paradox, inversion, contradiction and irony over and above any 'Irish' concerns. And while it has been claimed that these are features of 'some supposed Irish mentality', it makes more sense, as Hughes points out, 'to say that these features arise from, or are at least reinforced by, the experience of being Irish-in-Britain'.[199] The cultural endeavours outlined here by Hughes provide a striking analogy for the work of The Smiths, which evoked ideas of home, return, belonging and origins in highly personalised ways that were marked, notably, by ambivalence.

Songs of ambivalence and uncertainty

Accounts of the second-generation Irish have laid stress on the ambivalence that is 'contained in [the] everyday lives' of this generation, highlighting the 'ambivalent status' that 'places them at the meeting point of two cultural, social and political worlds', and noting that a major source of this condition is 'the job of assimilating conflicting demands on their allegiances to both English and Irish cultures'.[200] This issue of ambivalence has also been evoked in second-generation Irish creative work. In an account of Irish-English literary texts, for example, Aidan Arrowsmith notes that ambivalence and uncertainty – as well as indeterminacy and confusion – have imbued this body of work. Indeed, the theme that is most prevalent in second-generation Irish literary work is what Arrowsmith calls 'the sheer confusion of identity', with a 'disorientating and contradictory relationship to any sense of identity' effecting the 'figuration of ... confused identity through the indeterminacy or absence of "home"'.[201] Ethnographies also observe the 'troubled relationship' of the second-generation Irish with 'the meaning of "home"'.[202]

This theme has also been discerned in the work of second-generation Irish rock musicians. Jon Savage, for instance, suggests that an 'ambivalence towards their roots is present in the work of both the Smiths and Oasis', pointing, in particular, to an 'aspirant will to succeed, to move on up and out, to go further than their parents were allowed to go, allied to a fierce pride and anger about their background'.[203] Similarly, Rogan notes – in The Smiths – a 'peculiar sense of longing … which betrayed the ambivalence of first-generation immigrant sons caught between present and past'.[204] Elsewhere, a certain 'homing desire' – an outlook associated with the displaced subject[205] – was observed in The Smiths' work, with Reynolds hearing in the band a 'yearning … to belong somewhere', or a 'pining for a home'.[206] Such comments provide a useful point of departure from which to assess The Smiths' work, as their address to 'home' and origins was marked by such uncertainty. In the sparsely arranged, slow-paced lament of 'Back To The Old House' (1983), for example, Morrissey's plaintive first-person speaker repeatedly insists, throughout the opening bars: 'I would rather not go/ back to the old house', before alluding, in the higher register of the bridge, to the 'too many bad memories there'.[207] This rebuttal of 'home' sits incongruously, however, with the song's harmonic mode, as Marr's delicately picked acoustic guitar pursues a 'folksy' style more commonly associated with a yearning or desire for home (what Moore calls, in a different context, the 'backward glance').[208] The quietly contrapuntal relationship that this sets up between the song lyrics and their musical setting is momentarily resolved, however, in the song's final verse, when Morrissey – with no discernible shift in register, tone or phrasing – emits a lyrical volte-face, disclosing a hitherto unspoken wish for 'return': 'I would *love* to go/ back to the old house/ but I never will'. If this contrary gesture – with its nod towards the futility of such yearning – conjures ambivalence rather than closure, this is only underscored by Marr's unresolved coda, which restores the song's opening section only to fade on an 'open' major seventh chord, suggesting melancholy.[209] As the track fades out, meanwhile, the guitarist gently hammers on the note (D from C#) that would at least supply harmonic (in the absence of thematic) resolution, in a teasing musical gesture that simply lingers unresolved.

The openly incongruous urges evinced in such songs were underlined by the band's public comments on their background and upbringing. Thus, in music press interviews Morrissey would explain, 'It was really easy to lose my past, because I was so determined. I wanted to move on and forget', before going on to describe the 'roots of the group' as something 'you can't really get away from', a point with which Marr concurred: 'I don't think it's a matter of rising above it [the group's background]', the guitarist explained. 'To lose the thread of it would be quite dangerous. It's part of our lives. We can't lose it. I don't want to not be associated with it.'[210] A similar dynamic has been observed in second-generation Irish life writing, which has staged Irish-English subjectivity in what Liam Harte calls 'dialogical and contrapuntal terms', offering an 'ongoing conversation between warring selves' (a characteristic that seems of a piece with the musician Kate Bush's claim that she felt 'torn *between*' the Irish and English aspects of her sense of self).[211] Such sentiments arguably imbue The Smiths' œuvre, particularly their songs that conjure journeying and relocation – themes that are, of course, at the hub of migrancy. Although the second generation are not, strictly speaking, migrants in the sense of having physically moved from one place to another, the 'psychological journey of migration', as Bobby Gilmore has explained with regard to the Irish in England, 'is far longer than the geographical one', and does not simply end with the migrating generation.[212] Thus, the displacement felt by Irish migrants has, as Tony Murray explains, been 'very strong for their offspring also', with the effect that the latter faced their own 'ruptured sense of cultural belonging', and often remained, note Malone and Dooley, 'psychologically [and] emotionally ... *mobile*'.[213] What this ongoing condition of migrancy has entailed for the second generation, then, is, as Gray explains, a certain 'state of being "in-between"' – not least 'between here and there' – as well as the attendant 'experience of living in [one] place' with strong 'memories of somewhere else'.[214]

This sense of spatial 'in-betweenness' (of being pulled 'This way and that way, and this way and that way', as Morrissey sings on 'Stretch Out And Wait' (1985)) is evinced in songs such as 'Is It Really So Strange?' (1986), which supplies a first-person account of a ceaseless geographical journey between a putative destination and an original point of departure.[215] The opening lines of each verse thus signal the particular (and spatially contrary) direction in which the song's speaker is headed. In the course of the song, then, the coordinates of 'here' and 'there' are gradually conflated, until the subject (who feels increasingly 'confused') openly refutes, in the closing bars, the very notion of 'return' to a home-like space ('And I realised, I realised/ That I could never/ I could never, never go back home again/ No'). The only stable conclusion that the song's speaker is able to reach on this confusing journey, then, is a stuttering acceptance of the fact that 'home' is a place that cannot be restored (in other words, that there is no available *place* like 'home').[216] If the sombre certainty of this lyrical finale is somewhat tempered by the tune's upbeat tenor (invoked by the singer's comic asides and Marr's jaunty guitar slides), it finds an even more conspicuous counterpoint in the song's clear-cut closure on (what is called) its 'home triad' – the 'chord on the key-note of a song' – in this case, a ringing 'open' major in E, underscored by a punctuating 'crash' cymbal.[217] As Sheila Whiteley has explained, such chords have 'strong connotations of home-centredness',[218] and thus render the song's refusal of 'home' – in the final verse – somewhat incongruous.

A similar quandary takes shape in 'London' (1986).[219] Here, Marr's unusually repetitive guitar riff on a single low-register note ('bottom' E tuned to F#) works, with Joyce's snare-drum shuffle, to evoke the rail journey related by Morrissey's narrating subject.[220] Stressing the anxiety of a home-leaving addressee, the theme of uncertainty is invoked by the recurrent lyrical hook ('Do you think you've made/ the right decision this time?') that marks the end of each verse, as well as – crucially – the singer's coda. This theme is embellished, moreover, by Morrissey's serial groans (and the guitar's incessant stuttering), yet is also tempered – throughout the song's course – by the sheer exuberance of the band's fast pace, connoting the visceral joys of departure, a point that, in turn, is evoked by the speaker's noting of the 'Jealousy in the eyes/ Of the ones who had to stay behind' – a 'grieving' family unit whose cloying domesticity is matched by the flattened, compacted sound of Marr's unusually 'dry' guitar. The implied desire to leave is subsequently rendered uncertain, however, by the track's solemn and cyclical coda, in which Marr's ceaseless succession of minor chords refutes (in the absence of thematic resolution) any possible harmonic closure. An accelerated shift in tempo during the final bars only serves to exacerbate this, effecting a frustratingly circular denouement that matches the melodic contours of Morrissey's vocal, which sets, for Hubbs, 'its own narrow confines and paces back and forth within them … retracing its own path'.[221] Unable to resolve its own conflicting urges, the song is forced to fade. Thus, while the musical scale, with its 'intervals, progressions and modulations', is 'capable', as Gerry Smyth explains, 'of creating impressions of home [and] travel', songs such as 'London' display a reluctance towards the key that constitutes their 'home',[222] rendering the narrating-subject's journey always unfinished or incomplete.

The ambivalence evinced in such songs – which convey a sense of living between different spaces, with no satisfactory conclusion – was something about which Marr was highly conscious. 'That feeling of ambivalence is [there] without doubt', he explains, suggesting that this was born, at least for him, of certain aspects of his early migrant milieu, which he feels informed his musical character.[223] In this context, Marr points to the mixture of vibrancy and melancholia that marked the musical culture in which he was raised, and notes a dynamic tension that he felt between, on the one hand, an excitement about being in England and the sense of adventure that this entailed, whilst, on the other hand, feeling a certain yearning for an (absent) Ireland that was evoked in innumerable ways in his early migrant milieu.[224] Reflecting on the mood of the songs outlined above, Marr points to 'a feeling of my mentality being about this pro-opportunity thing and excitement [about being in England], but your heart actually saying something different [about Ireland]' – hence the sense of ambivalence (and mixture of vibrancy and melancholy) that, he says, characterised The Smiths' work.[225] 'I'm glad that the music did that', Marr notes, 'because otherwise I'd have just gone through life not voicing that side of myself.'[226] If music supplied Marr with a means through which to 'voice' such ambivalence, this was a quality he felt he shared with Morrissey. Referring to the sense of excitement that he says informed The Smiths' work, Marr explains that

> balanced with this [excitement] was this sensibility that has always been tuned to melancholia – which wasn't that difficult because me and Morrissey had that disposition in us. It was a strange thing: we were ecstatic about what was happening to us and we had the melancholy.[227]

Elaborating on this point, Marr suggests that this was an 'Irish thing', a 'weird schizophrenic disposition' (by which he appears to mean ambivalence), noting: 'the two of us were harnessing that melancholy and putting it into our music'.[228]

'When you walk without ease': elusive outsiders

Notwithstanding Marr's comments, it is clear that the songs that have been addressed thus far have invoked the theme of ambivalence in quite abstract terms, evading any specific Irish context in which this might be staged. However, as Arrowsmith has explained, engagements with Irishness in second-generation Irish creative work often bear the traces of other discourses (such as region and class), and, thus, if some of The Smiths' songs cited above are ostensibly concerned with, say, the absence of a former physical home or travel between a north–south English divide, the sentiments engaged in such songs can nevertheless serve as an index of the band's broader stance on issues of origins and 'home' (whether in terms of Irishness or, for instance, northernness).[229] Moreover, The Smiths would occasionally make clear that certain songs had been shaped by this Irish-in-England context. Morrissey, for instance, would explain that his song lyrics were informed by the marginality he had experienced as a Manchester-Irish youth.[230] The opening lines of 'Never Had No One Ever' (1986) (a track that has been seen as the band's 'defining' song) are striking in this regard.[231] Prompted by the drum kit's awkwardly accented preface (and curiously languid pace), Morrissey's vocal – 'When you walk without ease/ On these/ streets where you were raised' – is marked by 'the kind of "blue" or "dirty" notes' that he usually 'studiously avoids'.[232] If this connotes anxiety, the lyrical theme of unease is compounded by Marr's cyclical sequence of minor seventh chords, set in taut 12/8 time.[233] The guitarist would explain that this music was conceived whilst reflecting on his early Irish milieu, adding that the band's work at the time was 'strongly rooted in our sense of being on the outside'.[234] Morrissey made similar points about the source of his lyrical theme: 'It was the frustration I felt at the age of 20', he recalled, 'when I still didn't feel easy walking around the streets on which I'd been born, where all my family had lived – they're originally from Ireland but had been here since the Fifties'. Expounding on this point, the singer confessed, 'It was a constant confusion to me why I never really felt "This is my patch. This is my home. I know these people. I can do what I like, because this is mine." It never was. I could never walk easily.'[235]

Morrissey's 'placing' of his song words in terms of this specific experience calls to mind the comments of other Irish-English creative figures, such as Brian Keaney, a second-generation Irish writer who grew up in England at the same time as the singer. Keaney explained in 1985 – the year in which The Smiths composed 'Never Had No One Ever' – that his semi-autobiographical short stories were an attempt to address 'what it feels like to be growing up slightly at odds with your surroundings', noting that 'as a boy I felt not entirely *at ease* with either my Irish parents or my English companions. I think this is something that a lot of children of immigrants feel.'[236] This sense of being displaced – a prominent feature, as Hughes points out, of Irish creative expression in England – arguably imbued The Smiths' œuvre. It might be seen in the falsetto shriek ('I'm just a country-mile behind/ the world') in the frenetic, thrashed-out coda of 'Miserable Lie' (1983), and it seems to inform the speaker's envy in 'These Things Take Time' (1983) of someone who knows 'where [they] came from' and knows 'where [they] belong' (suggesting the subject's lack of such qualities).[237] In this context, Morrissey would later reflect that his songs' speaker did not 'belong' in England.[238]

On occasion, though, the songs' persona sought to seize territorial space, not least via the title of 'A Rush And A Push And The Land Is Ours' (1987) – which was sourced from the Irish-nationalist poems of Oscar Wilde's mother – as well as through the speaker's insistence (in the opening lines of 'Still Ill') that 'England is *mine*', which might be seen to offset the expression of 'unease' addressed above.[239] Ultimately, though, the songs' protagonist only feels at 'home' in the state of melancholia, with the singer mournfully casting himself as 'sorrow's native son' in the song words of 'Pretty Girls Make Graves' (1984).[240]

There is a crucial semantic difference, of course, between sorrow and melancholy, a point to which The Smiths were alert. As Marr explains, both he and Morrissey 'recognised the beauty of melancholia'. He says they 'talked about it, often. About the difference between depression and melancholia. About how depression was just useless, but melancholia was a real emotion and a real place, a creative place that dealt in images and music and creative aspects of the self.' On this point, Marr concludes: 'I think me and Morrissey were coming from the same place', describing that 'place' as 'Expressive melancholia'.[241] From Morrissey's perspective, The Smiths' expression of 'negative' feelings was, by virtue of them being expressed, a 'positive' endeavour, a point redolent of Adorno's view that 'thought achieves happiness in the expression of unhappiness', as well as Murray's claim that the blues often served to 'get rid of' the very condition they sought to express.[242] In this sense, then, The Smiths seemed to stage a certain catharsis for the 'melancholia' outlined above. But from whence did this melancholy come?

Marr offers a clue to its possible source when he suggests that the music that he wrote for The Smiths often sought to evoke the mood of his early Irish migrant milieu. Rather than seeking to activate identifiably Irish sounds, then, Marr self-consciously invoked the ambience of Irish immigrant life (as a sort of psychological state), which he describes, in close detail, as 'very intense' and 'fairly dark', with people 'drinking pretty heavily and swearing and being quite aggressive', alongside an 'overt Catholicism' – as well as music marked by 'melancholy' and 'yearning' – creating what he calls a 'gothic intensity' that had a 'sort of intrigue' for him. Recalling the regular musical parties that took place in his parents' house, Marr explains that 'as the night wore on, invariably the music got sadder and that time was a really magical time for me because the music got really interesting', noting that such music conveyed an 'other-worldly' or 'spook'-like quality.[243] For Marr, then, the 'melodies from those sad Irish tunes' – as well as what he calls the more 'morbid' aspects of Irish migrant life – 'definitely went into [him] and The Smiths'. Thus, he relates that in the process of writing music for The Smiths, he would often reflect on his migrant Irish upbringing, sensing that it offered a creative source.

> As I started to write more and more music, and then go to Ireland [with The Smiths], I was like, 'Hang on a minute, there's a thing that I do here, an aspect that is coming from that place that I had as a kid that is pretty fucking powerful and that is a part of what I'm about', so I drew from it, and I wanted to acknowledge it.[244]

It was this 'emotional aspect' of his upbringing, then, that Marr says he sought to 'evoke' in The Smiths' work. 'There are certain things in The Smiths' music', he suggests, 'that nail that emotional place and that evocative time for me.' He says that 'The best example of it is "Please, Please, Please, Let Me Get What I Want", which is very much a case of me missing my home when I was living in London [in 1984] and almost kind of writing this sort of musical letter to my mother.' It is interesting, in this respect, that the song was originally called 'The Irish Waltz', and that in it Marr expressed his own homesickness by echoing the sound and mood of his early Irish milieu, and particularly the songs of 'yearning' that his parents had enjoyed in England.[245]

In addition to 'Please, Please, Please ...', Marr cites – as part of this evocation of an Irish migrant ambience – the 'gothic' waltz-time coda of 'That Joke Isn't Funny Anymore', as well as

> musically the entire message from 'Last Night I Dreamt That Somebody Loved Me', just because it's gothic, almost quasi-religious really, dark, quite provincial. For some reason it doesn't sound like a London band – Blur or The Kinks wouldn't have been able to do it, I don't think. And I don't think it's entirely English either, it's definitely got a kind of Celtic aspect to it, but it's not Scottish either ... You throw in my background and my sensibility and that's where you get that tune from.[246]

Whether or not the song evinced such a 'Celtic aspect', it is clear that Marr's work was informed by a wish to capture this 'emotional place',[247] and the mood of his co-song-writer's lyrics would – in turn – be born, the singer suggests, of Marr's melodies (to which Morrissey would add his song words).[248] In this context, the singer was keenly alert to the mood of Marr's music, which, says Morrissey, 'combined sorrow and happiness': 'even the jovial tunes that he produced ... had a tinge of terrible sadness', notes the singer, adding that this 'really drew' him to Marr's work.[249]

It is perhaps also worth noting, at this juncture, the time signatures of certain Smiths songs, particularly those in 3/4 or 6/8 times (which are arguably more common to Irish folk than indie rock). 'That definitely comes from my background', suggests Marr, citing songs such as 'Stretch Out And Wait', 'I Know It's Over', 'Please, Please, Please ...', 'That Joke Isn't Funny Anymore' and 'Meat Is Murder' (which, he says, is 'musically like the really woozy end of a party'). 'That goes directly to my childhood', he observes, noting that 'it all kind of comes from one song: "Black Velvet Band"'. He says, 'I fucking loved that song when I was a little kid.' However, while this creative sourcing of an Irish migrant ambience was, for Marr, quite productive, it was also rather demanding, and he occasionally had to withdraw. 'I had to get away from that for a while', he explains; 'it was just too heavy. It was too emotional for me to deal with.'[250]

The Smiths' engagement with origins was thus marked in part by melancholy, and this perhaps confirms, to some degree, the view of the band as 'miserablist'.[251] However, there was also a wish, in the group's œuvre, to mock the importance of origins – hence the speaker's citation in 'Stretch Out And Wait' of the 'Eskimo blood in [his] veins', or the protagonist's 'discovery', in 'The Queen Is Dead' (1986), that he's the 'eighteenth pale descendant/ of some old queen or other'.[252] This playful address to ancestry was played out elsewhere, however, as a masking of personal origins – hence Morrissey's deadpan declaration at the start of 'How Soon Is Now?' (1984) that imparts a flicker of self-revelation ('I am the son and the heir') but only so as to quickly obfuscate ('of nothing ... in particular').[253] Such gestures clearly resonated with the singer's public comments at this time. During a concert tour of Scotland, for instance, Morrissey dealt with questions about his 'Celtic blood' with conspicuous reticence (and not a little humour): 'No, no, no', he avowed, 'I've got no blood anymore', concluding, 'no blood ... all drained'.[254] Meanwhile, in another exchange the singer was exceptionally reticent when answering an enquiry about his middle name, uttering 'Patrick' in what the interviewer described as a 'barely audible' manner. 'What use does one make of a middle name?' the singer scoffed, whilst dismissing the designation in its (Irish-associated) variant form of 'Paddy'.[255] The vexation displayed here perhaps pertained to the low social status of 'Paddy' during Morrissey's formative years, but such sentiments were also suggestive of what Hubbs calls the singer's 'complex and elusive subjectivity'.[256] As Hubbs notes, Morrissey's persona in this sense bore a resemblance to that of Oscar Wilde,[257] whom The Smiths would invoke in various ways. The band's best-known citation of Wilde – in the song 'Cemetry [*sic*] Gates' (1986)[258] – arguably points to their position on Irish–English affairs. In the opening verse of this song (whose morbid locale is at odds with Marr's upbeat 'high-life' flourishes and Joyce's buoyant drumming), the speaker signals his allegiance with the Irish author: 'Keats and Yeats are on your side', he relates to an addressee, 'While Wilde is on mine'. This gesture is revisited, moreover, in the final moments of the song, when Morrissey's speaker concludes: 'Keats and Yeats are on your side/ *but you lose/* because Wilde is on mine', instancing a closure underscored by Marr's return, in the coda, to the song's sanguine prelude. Reflecting on this identification with Wilde, certain critics, such as Len Brown, have claimed that Wilde's Irish nationalism would 'naturally' have 'appealed' to Morrissey.[259] It is, however, more complex than this, for the singer – in this song – eschews authors associated with England (Keats) *and* Ireland (Yeats), affiliating himself instead with a figure (Wilde) who has occupied ambiguous terrain between these national frames. Wilde's nationality was, says Eagleton, 'unstable' and 'Janus-faced', and the writer became 'adept', notes Jerusha McCormack, 'at living on both sides of the [Anglo-Irish] hyphen'; 'Given a choice between being English or Irish, then, Wilde chose both'.[260] (If Wilde's sexuality also played a part in Morrissey's identification with the writer, then the singer's view of his own orientation as 'in the middle somewhere, straddling' might serve as an analogy of his standpoint on Irish–English affairs.[261]) Such sentiments were arguably evident in The Smiths' public comments on social boundaries. Thus, while Morrissey would occasionally make reference to the band's Irish provenance, he would also make clear his wish 'to produce music that transcends boundaries', explaining that the 'main blemish' on English life was 'the absolute segregation which seems to appear on every level, with everything and everybody'.[262] These are significant remarks from someone raised in an immigrant enclave, for rather than asserting ethnic difference, or expressing an assimilative wish, such signals conveyed a negation of the notion of boundaries per se. This standpoint was also evoked in the group's song words, such as the plaintive lament that prefaced 'Miserable Lie', one of the group's first songs, in which Morrissey offered – over a gentle guitar arpeggio and slow-paced descending bass – a sombre expression of sorrow at a failed transgressive bond: 'So, goodbye/ please stay with your own kind/ and I'll stay with mine'.

This theme of boundary-crossing was also evinced at the group's live shows, where a pre-recorded tape of 'March Of The Capulets' (from Prokofiev's *Romeo and Juliet*, a dramatic evocation of transgression) announced the band's arrival onstage, and where audience members were granted access – at the concerts' buoyant finales – to the stage, thus dissolving the (literal and symbolic) division between the musicians and their fans.[263] This feature of The Smiths' live shows was evidently quite important to the group, who felt – according to their tour manager – that a lack of stage 'invaders' meant that their performance had been weak, even – as he explains – 'if their playing had been excellent'.[264] With such points in mind, it would seem that while The Smiths were often marked by melancholic introspection (not least with regard to 'home' and origins), they at the same time appeared to stage, through an evocation of transgression, more enabling sentiments.

Beyond the tropes of ambivalence and unease, then, the group engaged a more productive take on marginality. Many migrant-descended creative figures have, as John McLeod has explained, made 'a virtue from necessity' by suggesting that the 'displaced position' associated with migration is 'an entirely valuable one', with the marginalised subject being in a conceivably 'better position than others to realise that all systems of knowledge, all views of the world, are never totalising, whole or pure, but incomplete, muddled and hybrid'. Thus, while the experience of displacement 'may well evoke the pain' and 'loss' of 'not being firmly rooted in a secure place', it can also furnish 'a world of immense possibility with the realisation that new knowledges and ways of seeing can be constructed'.[265] This migrant perspective has also been pursued by many second-generation Irish musicians, such as John Lydon and Cáit O'Riordan.[266] In this context, O'Riordan maintains that 'it's a privilege to be an immigrant's kid in a colonial nation', because the experience can afford what she calls 'an outsider perspective' that 'makes you look at *both* sides'.[267] A similar position is outlined by the writer John O'Callaghan, who notes that to be 'brought up as an Irish Catholic in England is to be nurtured as a schizophrenic', before pointing to the potential benefits of this experience: 'You are born outside furrows of thought that some pure natives never see over.' For O'Callaghan, then, 'It is worth *risking the schizophrenia* to be reared without blinkers.'[268]

A similar 'schizophrenia' was, of course, also cited by Marr, who sees this as a sensibility for which he is 'super grateful'.[269] Morrissey, meanwhile, has explained that being 'stuck' in an 'Irish–British divide' is 'not a bad place to be',[270] stressing the creative benefits of an 'outsider' view: 'When you're detached and sealed off", the singer observed, 'you have a very clear view of what's going on. You can stand back and you can look and you can assess.'[271] In a similar vein, Irish-descended writers, such as Hilary Mantel, have explained that their upbringings enabled them to 'realise that there was this thing called "Englishness", but it wasn't necessarily what you possessed. It was located somewhere else'.[272] Many second-generation Irish figures have expressed a congruent view, elaborating on their sense of 'separateness' from 'mainstream Englishness'.[273] With this in mind, it is worth noting that The Smiths – who were not shy of making statements on Anglo-Irish tensions ('I certainly don't think that in England there's any desire, politically, to make life any easier in Belfast', claimed Morrissey)[274] – eschewed the politics of Irish particularity for a critique of hegemonic Englishness, offering gestures of affiliation with a range of marginal positions that coalesced against the nationalist conservatism of the Thatcher regime. These included Ken Livingstone's GLC, Britain's striking miners, and 'Red Wedge', a left-wing platform that sought to mobilise young British people.[275] Elsewhere, the group aligned themselves with the causes of animal rights and feminism.[276] It was, however, Thatcherism and the monarchy that became the locus of The Smiths' critique of Englishness.

Irish descent/English dissent

In the immediate aftermath of Thatcher's accession to power in 1979, the rock critic Bill Graham observed that a certain second-generation Irish musician, John Lydon – whom he viewed as an 'outsider' formed by an Irish upbringing – would act against this 'proprietoress [*sic*] of "English" culture'. In a remark that could have served as an apposite index of Morrissey, Graham said that Lydon '*won't be one of Margaret's pupils*'.[277] The Smiths' animus towards Thatcher was unveiled in a 1984 interview, in which Morrissey declaimed that the 'entire history of Margaret Thatcher' had been 'one of violence and oppression and horror', insisting that people 'must *not* lie back and cry about it', before effectively calling for her assassination: 'She's only one person, and she can be destroyed. I just pray that there is a Sirhan Sirhan somewhere. It's the only remedy for this country at the moment.'[278] While such comments were somewhat histrionic, they were also quite prescient, for later that year Thatcher became the target of an attack (by the IRA at Brighton's Grand Hotel) that 'came within an ace' of killing the prime minister.[279] The bomb attack, which took the lives of five people and injured thirty others, was followed by a chilling message from the IRA: 'Today we were unlucky, but remember, we have only to be lucky once. You will have to be lucky always.'[280] The attack was met with widespread anger and condemnation, including calls to 'Hang the IRA bombers', a plea endorsed by Lord Denning, who claimed that those responsible 'could be hanged for high treason'. 'They are just as guilty as Guy Fawkes was 380 years ago', explained Denning shortly after the attack.[281] In this fraught atmosphere, blame for the bomb was quickly (and erroneously) apportioned to second-generation Irish people: the British press claimed that the bombers were 'English-born volunteers, second and third generations from Irish families living here', and noted that the '*apparent Englishness* of the unit – four or five strong – could have allowed them to visit the Grand Hotel in Brighton, where they planted the bomb, over the year'.[282]

Despite the fact that the attack – an expressly seditious act – had been linked to the second-generation Irish, Morrissey was quick to issue his own public response, praising the IRA for being 'accurate in selecting their targets', whilst stressing his 'sorrow' that Thatcher had 'escaped unscathed'.[283] Amidst the pervasive sense of shock and fury, then, Morrissey made it clear that he was 'relatively happy' about the attack.[284] In this context, Len Brown suggests that, 'As an Irish Mancunian, with the deaths of the IRA hunger strikers in painful recent memory, it was perhaps inevitable that Morrissey would express disappointment that Thatcher did not die [in the IRA attack]'.[285] While it is true that the hunger strike engaged the interests of many second-generation Irish people – and encouraged some to pursue political and (even) para-military action[286] – it was certainly not inevitable that the singer would express his views so forcibly in public. Indeed, whilst Morrissey's public comments – with their 'obvious myth- and money-making potential' – should be approached, as Hubbs suggests, somewhat sceptically,[287] it is unlikely that even the most desperate of record-company publicists would have desired Morrissey's response to the bomb. Letters of complaint quickly appeared in the British music press, attacking the singer for aligning himself with 'extreme fascists', and denouncing his remarks as 'perverted' and 'malicious', whilst suggesting that his support of the bomb 'should not be tolerated' or allowed to 'soil the pages' of the press, who were seen as 'sick' for simply printing his words.[288] Meanwhile, the local press in Manchester chastised the singer's 'shocking views', which they claimed were an 'outrage'.[289] Even The Smiths' management (who generally did not comment on the group's views) confessed that they were 'not altogether happy' with Morrissey's words.[290]

The furore caused by the singer's comments was only compounded by the group's (immediate) commitment to a ten-day Irish tour that included shows in Northern Ireland. In this context, even pro-IRA news-sheets – not noted for their restraint – warned that Morrissey's statements 'would be somewhat dangerous at any time but, coming before a tour of Ireland which includes both Coleraine University and the Ulster Hall in Belfast, they might be judged somewhat more than foolhardy'.[291] The singer's remarks thus aroused concern amongst The Smiths' camp, especially after the band were handed a copy of *An Phoblacht* (an Irish-republican paper) by what Marr calls an 'IRA-affiliated' individual in Manchester:

> The guy who was living below Mike Joyce was a member of ... [an] IRA-affiliated organisation and – the week [Morrissey's] statements came out – he introduced himself to Mike and he posted [*An Phoblacht*] through Mike's door, and suddenly that week it had a pop page, and guess who was on it? We [The Smiths] were very useful [to Irish nationalists]. It's all in a small way, but that week there was a pop page and we were it.[292]

An Phoblacht – whose pages were usually taken up with political/military news – praised Morrissey for his Brighton-bomb comments (which it reprinted in full), whilst stressing The Smiths' Irish provenance: 'with names like that who could doubt their antecedents?' The paper – not known for its interest in rock – also praised The Smiths' 'anti-establishment' ethos and concern for the 'dispossessed', before offering a ringing endorsement: The Smiths, proclaimed *An Phoblacht*, were 'very good indeed'.[293]

As the band embarked on their Irish tour, they were 'worried', their tour manager explained, 'about more extreme attitudes' because they had – in his words – 'affiliated themselves with the IRA'.[294] The situation was, however, somewhat more complex, as the band received what Marr has called 'threats from both sides', with Loyalist paramilitaries advising them to stay away whilst republicans insisted that they could not 'pull out'. As Marr explains:

> There was a very deliberate threat. The Irish government contacted our agent and said 'okay, these guys [The Smiths] have to come now, but the only way we're going to let you do it is if you take one of our security guys (who were part of whatever the Irish SAS is), and he's going to smooth things out between one faction and the other faction, and you have to absolutely do what this guy says'. When we got outside one of those towns we had to sit and wait on the bus while he got in a car and had a 'meet'. The IRA wanted to get up and make some speeches before we went on, which obviously angered the other side. The IRA wanted to address our audience and use our gig as a platform. And when we went across the border [into the North] we were told we had to have our heads down, we had to get down. After those shows we had the sniffer dogs on the bus, we had sniffer dogs under the stage, it was fucking scary.[295]

Marr's concerns were not without foundation: in the mid-1970s an Irish pop act had been attacked – after a show in Northern Ireland – by Loyalist paramilitaries, who shot and killed three of the musicians, leaving another critically injured.[296] The attack, as the press observed at the time, was 'the first time that musicians [had] been chosen as a target for violence', and the carnage made it clear that rock bands were now, as Smyth notes, 'as likely as anyone else to be identified in the restrictive religious and/or political terms that defined the Troubles'.[297] There is little doubt as to how The Smiths were viewed in this context. Marr explains that before one of the shows, The Smiths were forced 'to wait while some guy went out and made a [pro-IRA] speech'.[298] This only exacerbated the Loyalist threat, and the group had to rearrange certain plans as a precautionary measure.[299] When the tour culminated at Belfast's Ulster Hall, there was, says Rogan, a palpable 'tension in the air' due to the 'concern with security.'[300]

Despite such difficulties, The Smiths renewed their attack on the British prime minister, electing to call their third album 'Margaret on the Guillotine', a title they were forced to discard before the record's release.[301] While the reason for this change of plan is unclear, Jo Slee has explained that when a track called 'Margaret On The Guillotine' appeared on Morrissey's first solo album, the question of the singer's 'clandestine affiliation with a radical terrorist organisation [presumably the IRA] was raised with the Manchester police', prompting a Special Branch visit to his home for a recorded interview.[302] With regard to the album title, rather than retracting from their dissident task, The Smiths simply switched targets, renaming the record *The Queen is Dead*, a title that, for Morrissey, served as a 'very obvious reference' to '*drowning* the monarchy'[303] (the song of the same name depicts 'her very Lowness with her head in a sling'). Such virulent anti-monarchism – which was by no means customary in Britain's pop milieu[304] – was a major aspect of the group's persona. 'I despise royalty', declared Morrissey in interviews, condemning the royal family as 'fascist' (thus invoking John Lydon's 'God Save The Queen' lyric, in which the monarchy was renounced as a 'fascist regime').[305] Expounding on this point, the singer observed that the 'very idea of the monarchy and the Queen of England is being reinforced and made to seem more useful than it really is', stressing his dislike of the royals in curiously Irish terms: 'We don't believe in leprechauns', he said, 'so why should we believe in the Queen?'[306] This sentiment had also been broached in the group's song words, not least the comic second verse of 'Nowhere Fast' (1985) ('I'd like to drop my trousers to the Queen'), but reached its expressive apogee on 'The Queen Is Dead', The Smiths' 'consciously intended … sequel' to the Sex Pistols' 'God Save The Queen', a track that served as an 'anti-national anthem' during the monarch's silver-jubilee celebrations in 1977.[307] The latter song offered, notes Savage, 'the only serious anti-Jubilee protest, the only

rallying call for those who didn't agree with the Jubilee because they didn't like the Queen, either because like John Lydon, they were Irish, or … because they resented being steamrollered … by a view of England which had not the remotest bearing on their everyday experience.'[308] The link between the two songs was observed by contemporary critics, who explained that in 'The Queen Is Dead' The Smiths had 'served notice on "England's dreaming"', an obvious allusion to Lydon's earlier lyric (which had announced, 'There is no future/ In England's dreaming')'.[309] Despite being viewed as a 'fantasy of regicide' (the song, for Brooker, 'dreams of violence against the monarch'),[310] Morrissey's lyrics were born of more arch concerns than simple anti-monarchism – hence his description of the track as a 'general observation on the state of the nation'.[311] This point is confirmed by Goddard, who discerns in the song 'a howl of near-Swiftian disgust at Thatcher's decaying Britain'.[312] Zuberi, similarly, sees it as an assault on 'the official version of England and English history' that was 'hyped by Margaret Thatcher'.[313] The song sets its sights on the royals, then, as the supreme 'symbol of the "national family"',[314] with the head of state serving (like 'Elizabeth' in Dexys' 'The Waltz') as an index of England. 'The Queen Is Dead' can thus be read, suggests Goddard, as a 'rejection of England itself'.[315] Considering this point in light of Laing's proposal that 'the political effects of a musical utterance are first and foremost a factor within the particular politics and balance of forces *within* music'[316] allows us to map the enactment – in the song's opening moments – of a critique of Englishness.

The track begins with a sampled excerpt of 'Take Me Back To Dear Old Blighty', a patriotic British services' tune from the First World War invoking the desire – amongst troops stationed abroad – for their national home.[317] Thus, the term 'Blighty' (which emerged during British rule in India) would signify, for Brophy and Partridge, 'England, in the sense of home', evoking a 'paradise' or 'never-never land' as well as all things 'homelike' and 'ideal'.[318] 'Blighty' was, then, notes DeGroot, not merely 'a place' but also 'an idea' and 'a set of warm-heated, cozy emotions'.[319] Perhaps because of this charged resonance, 'Take Me Back To Dear Old Blighty' would endure beyond the First World War (when it was written) to be revived during the Second World War, an event that has loomed large in the imaginary of post-war Englishness,[320] but which has lacked a subjective significance for second-generation Irish youths such as Marr. Thus, the events that came – in national memory – to be revered as Britain's 'finest hour', and which helped shape the consciousness of those born in its aftermath ('Tales of heroism by the brave pilots of Spitfires and Hurricanes were important to my postwar childhood', notes Paul Gilroy),[321] held little meaning for Marr. 'The Second World

War meant fuck all to me', he explains, stressing its lack of resonance for his sense of self (rather than any lack of respect for the war effort), and noting that while his English peers enjoyed an attachment to this event (not least via family ties), it was, by contrast, 'a complete non-chapter in [his] background', and 'played absolutely no part in [his] story' (other than increasing his sense of difference).[322]

Whilst British war narratives held no attraction for Marr, neither did the subtext of 'Take Me Back To Dear Old Blighty': the guitar player's 'disenchantment with the myth of "Blighty"' was 'utterly entrenched', relates Dave Simpson.[323] In marked contrast, the song words with which Morrissey followed the excerpt of the song in 'The Queen Is Dead' offered a viewpoint with which Marr fully identified. Thus, whilst Marr often failed to relate to Morrissey's lyrics, 'The Queen Is Dead' was a song with which he not only identified but one he admired both 'poetically and politically'. Marr explains that 'Lyrically it's probably my favourite Smiths track.'[324] With this in mind, it is worth noting that the song – which bids 'farewell' to England's 'cheerless marshes' – offsets the cheery sentiments of ' Take Me Back To Dear Old Blighty' with a de-idealised Albion, depicting, for Zuberi, 'a grim, urban landscape' that 'offers no hope of finding a home' or 'a place to belong'.[325] It is, however, at the musical level of the track that the sabotage of 'Take Me Back To Dear Old Blighty' in 'The Queen Is Dead' is most strikingly staged, for as the extract of 'Dear Old Blighty' starts to fade, its antiquated mood – underscored by the haughty inflection of the sampled singer, Dame Cicely Courtneidge (who had sung for the troops in the Second World War)[326] – segues into the sinister sound of Marr's unsettling 'feedback' and Joyce's rapidly-struck drum pattern. This in turn converges with ominously 'swelling' cymbals (and an incongruous 'wah-wah' effect) before Marr's 'slashing and thrashing, abrasive guitar' sets off 'the hardest, most spacious rock' in The Smiths' canon.[327] In this respect, the track serves as an instance of 'code-switching', juxtaposing jingoistic music-hall ('Take Me Back To Dear Old Blighty') with militant proto-punk (Marr's introduction was informed by the MC5).[328]

In an account of migrant songs in the post-war US, Slobin points to 'a clear-cut example of sharp, stark codeswitching' that serves as a useful parallel for 'The Queen Is Dead'. Recounting a 'Jewish-American comedy number of the late 1940s' that 'begins with … a perfectly standard recitation of Longfellow's hoary all-American poem "The Midnight Ride of Paul Revere"', Slobin relates that the 'diction and dialect' are 'standard, slightly pompous American English'. Suddenly, however, 'the nationalistic reverie is broken by a brief silence' and what Slobin calls a 'highly dramatic codeswitch' – in this case, signalled by 'a band playing

an Eastern European Jewish dance tune'.[329] While the aforementioned
Smiths track does not switch to an ethnic idiom in the manner outlined
by Slobin, the song's satiric citation of an English military tune – and
subsequent shift to 'the most explosive music the band ever played'[330]
– emits a critique of Englishness that has been seen, by certain critics,
as the moment in The Smiths' work when 'the group's Irish rebel roots
show through most defiantly'.[331] The song was certainly viewed, in its
initial reception, as an attack on hegemonic Englishness, 'provoking',
as Slee explains, 'a flourish of quasi-nationalistic consternation', with
people 'heckling the placard [that bore the song's title] with which
Morrissey opened the live shows', and tabloid newspapers complaining that the group had 'showered abuse at the royals' in this allegedly
'sick' song.[332] Meanwhile, British MPs denounced the song as 'utterly
sick' and 'offensive', and asked the Thatcher government to 'crack down'
accordingly.[333] Even the leaders of the Salford Lads' Club – the location
that appeared as a backdrop to the band on *The Queen is Dead* sleeve –
felt compelled to comment, condemning The Smiths' anti-monarchist
stance, and publicly disassociating themselves from the group.[334] More
seriously, perhaps, the band faced attacks from far-right groups at some
live shows, at least one of which was terminated when the group were
assailed with maliciously thrown objects during their performance of
this track.[335] 'I saw Morrissey walking off and he had blood all over
him', explained Marr. 'I was pretty scared; I finished the song and got
off.'[336] Such incidents recall John Lydon's experience of violent assaults
at the time of 'God Save The Queen'.[337] The hostility of such reactions
was somewhat misplaced, however, as these songs were hardly sectarian
expressions of anti-English sentiment. As Lydon has explained: 'You
don't write "God Save The Queen" because you hate the English race,
you write it because you love them and you're fed up with them being
mistreated.'[338] In a similar vein, Morrissey would stress (shortly after The
Smiths' demise), 'There are very few aspects of Englishness I actually
hate', insisting instead that he could 'see the narrowness, and love[d] to
sing about it'.[339] What such assertions point to is a strand of second-
generation music-making that has offered, most strikingly, a critique
of Englishness from a marginal standpoint, over an overt assertion of
ethnic difference. This sentiment is not without precedent, moreover,
for as Eva points out in his account of Irish street singers in Victorian
Manchester, the nostalgic expression of 'the exile theme' among 'first
and second generation Irish listeners' always sat alongside a separate
urge to project the migrant's 'bitter attack on England's rulers'.[340] The
sensibilities of this latter trend prefigured the concerns of The Smiths
nearly a century and a half later, affording an 'attack' on Englishness

that was arguably rendered more effective by its absence of an Irish speaking position.

'I keep mine hidden': the importance of being 'un-Irish'

The dissident gesture staged by The Smiths was arguably more tricky to classify, control or contain than that offered by, say, The Pogues, for if MacGowan had – like Morrissey – offered upfront support for an IRA attack, it would likely have been seen as a somewhat hackneyed (and thus less effectual) 'mad Paddy' response. It is interesting to note, in this regard, that MacGowan was keen to distance The Pogues from IRA violence, and when he did tackle such issues head on, faced a de facto media ban.[341] In stark contrast to Morrissey, then, MacGowan was deeply reticent about addressing Irish political concerns. 'It is not worth the agro', explained The Pogues in 1985: 'We get grief just because we play Irish songs!' From MacGowan's perspective, the British press and public had been quick to conflate Irish ethnicity and the IRA; the singer explained, 'They think that because you do "Paddy On The Railways" that you're an active service unit!'[342] Also at this time, Kevin Rowland began to feel that his address to Irish issues on *Don't Stand Me Down* (1985) had been 'too much of a statement', with the singer withdrawing certain songs to avoid any implied equation, in the public realm, of Irishness and the IRA.[343]

In such a fraught context, what The Smiths' eschewal of an openly Irish speaking position in effect afforded them was a means by which to assail certain aspects of Englishness (Thatcherism, the monarchy, military jingles) without being dismissed (or disparaged) as 'plastic Paddies'.[344] As Savage has explained, pop's address to identity politics is most effectively staged 'not by specifics or slogans, but by hints and inferences loose enough for the imagination to leap in and resonate'. The public's 'tolerance of divergence', he says, 'only goes so far', and 'usually evaporates when things get a bit real', as evinced by certain 'queer' musicians (such as the 1980s synth group Soft Cell), who Savage claims 'paid the price of flaunting their divergence'.[345] Similar points have been made about Irish-descended musicians, some of whom faced 'negative consequences', relates Rolston, when they 'broke from the herd',[346] a point evidenced by the response to The Pogues' song, 'Birmingham Six' (1988).[347]

Fifteen years earlier, Britain's most celebrated musicians, John Lennon and Paul McCartney, had faced widespread criticism for their engagements with Irish affairs. Whilst as Beatles they had not concealed their Irish origins (both musicians were third-generation Irish),[348] in the period after the group's demise they took an overt stance on Irish issues. Thus, Lennon issued two (highly polemical) songs – 'Sunday Bloody Sunday' and 'The Luck Of The Irish' (1972) – in response to the early Troubles, invoking his Irishness in interviews, and announcing that 'if it's a choice between the IRA and the British Army, I'm with the IRA'.[349] Meanwhile, McCartney released his own Troubles-themed song, 'Give Ireland Back To The Irish' (1972), whilst alluding to his early Liverpool-Irish habitus.[350] Whether or not such gestures were ill conceived or ill informed,[351] they were evidently not popular: the response to Lennon's work was 'so negative', notes Jon Weiner, that a single of 'The Luck Of The Irish' was withdrawn, and his claims to Irishness were ridiculed ('Liverpool Irish, what's *that*?', asked Kate Millet).[352] Fans were also critical of the singer's Irish 'turn', and chastised the former Beatle as a 'poorly informed', 'instant authority on the Irish problem'.[353] McCartney's intervention met a similar fate: EMI initially refused to distribute his 'Irish' single on the grounds that it was 'too inflammatory', and the released song met with poor reviews (it was, said critics, 'somewhat crass') and a media ban.[354] The single was also attacked by certain fans, who were 'shocked and angry' at its message, which they claimed was 'disgraceful' and 'monstrous'.[355] The record did, however, have its defenders, not least a young Shane MacGowan, who would explain – in the period during which he wrote 'Birmingham Six' – that McCartney was 'from an Irish family', and thus 'had a right to make that statement'.[356]

Whether or not one requires such a 'right' in order to engage with Irish issues, it is clear that The Smiths were aware of this context: the young Morrissey had argued with second-generation Irish classmates about McCartney's single, and his own comments on the Troubles – via the Brighton bomb – provoked similar reactions.[357] The point to note, though, is that The Smiths' eschewal of such overt Irish signalling enabled them to enact certain forms of dissent at which more openly Irish figures would have baulked. Thus, Morrissey's father – who appeared at a Smiths show in Dublin shortly after the singer's comments on the IRA bomb – expressed his 'shock' at his son's remarks, before adding, tellingly, 'He says things I wouldn't dare say.'[358] If the 'apparent Englishness' of the assumed Brighton bombers had enabled them to access Thatcher's hotel residence, so The Smiths' evasion of an upfront Irish subject position afforded them a useful platform for their 'outsider' views. Regardless of how (self-) conscious this was, it seems, once again, redolent of Wilde, who – for Morrissey – 'mocked British society and British nobility' in a 'clever' and imaginative way.[359] Indeed, critics such as Bracewell note that Wilde and Morrissey, 'both Anglo-Irishmen', acted as 'England's underground analysts at either end of the century'.[360] Of course, these figures were 'Anglo-Irish' in very different ways (the term conflates those born in England of Irish Catholic descent with those born in Ireland of English Protestant descent), and whilst the Ascendancy – and their expressive culture – are an acknowledged part of the archipelagic interface,[361] their Irish-English obverse are often overlooked in this context. With this in mind, it might be useful to view The Smiths as a second-generation Irish musical 'route'. As theorists of migration, such as Avtar Brah, have argued, post-war diaspora settlements – whether 'African-Caribbean, Irish, Asian [or] Jewish' – have reshaped England's cultural fabric, with such migrations intersecting 'with the entity constructed as "Englishness"', and 'thoroughly re-inscribing it in the process'.[362] If migrant Irish forms have (like those of other migrant groups) reconfigured England's cultural fabric, then the work of The Smiths (alongside that of Lydon, MacGowan and Rowland) might be seen as a second-generation Irish thread in English popular music. With this in mind, Savage has observed that 'little' in English pop has 'match[ed] the wit and gleeful, lacerating revenge of the Sex Pistols' "God Save The Queen", Dexys Midnight Runners' "Dance Stance" [and] the Smiths' "The Queen Is Dead"'.[363] Rather than disregarding the Irishness of The Smiths on the grounds of their lack of fidelity to an 'authentic' Irish aesthetic, or contriving to square their work with essentialist concepts of ethnic song, what Savage's point illumines is a strand of second-generation Irish music-making that has not been constrained by either Irish essentialism or English assimilation. Recognition of this point offers a means by which to map the diverse musical 'routes' traversed by the second-generation Irish, highlighting their variegated expressive styles, and illuminating the intricacies of their address to the often complex dialectic between 'where you're at' and 'where you're from'.[364]

Coda:

From the Margins to the Centre

This book has addressed the diverse 'routes' pursued by second-generation Irish musicians, exploring three high-profile projects in the 1980s. Its account of Rowland, MacGowan and Morrissey/Marr illumines the different means by which Irishness was engaged by Irish-descended figures in the popular-cultural sphere, stressing the significance of this issue for second-generation music-makers. While Rowland sought to mediate between Irish and English cultures, staging an intervention against certain silences and misconceptions about the Irish in Britain, MacGowan served to express the lived experience of *being* both Irish *and* English, forging an irreducibly *London*-Irish style, and evoking the traditional/ ethnic and contemporary/urban aspects of second-generation life in equal measure. At the same time, Morrissey and Marr evinced an ambivalence and uncertainty towards notions of 'home' and origins (a sensibility that resonates with many second-generation Irish people) while staging a dissident critique of England. Informing all of these projects, it would seem, was a wish to claim space for, and to give voice to, a certain 'outsider' view. In this context, Morrissey says that the satisfaction he felt in The Smiths came from 'standing in front of people and *forcing* them to accept you, or take your life on board'.[1] In a similar vein, both MacGowan and Rowland sought – in different ways – to stage definite 'outsider' views. In this respect, the musicians surveyed in this book underline pop's potential to act as 'a voice and a face for the dispossessed',[2] reminding us that pop can bring 'visibility and partial social inclusion', as Jon Savage puts it, to 'previously outcast social groups'.[3]

The Irish-English 'routes' observed in this book can also illuminate what, for Simon Frith, is 'most interesting about music' – that is, 'its blurring of insider/outsider boundaries'.[4] Thus, the migrant Irish slip, through a certain musical sphere, into the stream of English culture, confusing – in the process – centre/margin distinctions. Reflecting on this point, Kevin Rowland suggests that the most 'significant thing' about the second-generation Irish is their place at the forefront of *British* culture, as evinced through their role in British pop.[5] Such transitions (from fringes to hub) can be fruitful and dynamic, re-energising the host culture whilst enabling the migrant group. In this context, England has not acted simply as 'perfidious Albion' (as it has in Irish-nationalist discourses),[6] for it has furnished both possibility *and* prejudice, and has thus helped to facilitate (as well as constrain) second-generation Irish creative pursuits. If this generation accrued – from their upbringing – certain tastes and sensibilities associated with the migrant group, then these would come to interface with (and perhaps be enlivened by) the frames and styles of the host culture.

While the musicians surveyed here often saw Irish ethnicity as a wellspring for their work, they equally saw in England 'opportunity and adventure' – as Marr would put it – and pursued the national popular culture with aspirational desire whilst being alert (and also subjected) to anti-Irish prejudice.[7] Thus, the musicians observe that while their work was often born of an Irish context, it simultaneously drew on strands of the host culture (and other sources), suggesting that we might think of music as – in Mark Slobin's terms – 'coming from many places'.[8] In this context, Rowland says that while he sought to engage with Irish styles and themes, he did not wish to do *just* an Irish thing', pointing to the 'massive influence' of England and its urban cultures, which he says he was 'shaped' by and in turn 'embraced'.[9] Even MacGowan – the most overtly 'Irish' of the musicians addressed here – was keen to stress the English aspects of The Pogues' œuvre. Leaving aside his *London*-Irish persona (and metropolitan imaginary), the singer would occasionally claim that The Pogues were a 'London band' that played 'Irish music'.[10] Moreover, MacGowan's colleagues would observe in his lyrics not only the afflictions of the outsider but also an affection for England.[11] Such affection has also been expressed by Morrissey, who, despite seeing England as a place of constraint ('it hammers people down and it pulls you back and it prevents you'), has evinced an attachment to the place, often in overblown ways.[12] While this investment in England (which emerged shortly after The Smiths' demise) was first expressed rather quaintly ('I'm the only person I know who can take a day-trip to Carlisle and get emotional about what he sees', he explained in 1987),[13] it would accrue more troubling tones. In an interview in 2007, for instance, Morrissey bemoaned the changes that he claimed had been wrought by immigration, complaining that 'anybody can have access to England and join in'.[14] Such gestures, which had echoes of the singer's flirtation with far-right discourses in the 1990s, were at odds with his own back-ground, and served, said one critic, as an 'abandonment of everything that made The Smiths a band for outsiders', especially as Morrissey had aligned himself – through his lyrics – with 'the underdog, the victim and those in the minority'.[15] It is not uncommon, however, for the offspring of immigrants to engage in acts of (over)identification with the host culture.[16] Indeed, it is worth noting that certain second-generation Irish people have been drawn to extreme forms of nationalism (both Irish and English) as a means of assuaging the ambivalence of being in-between. In this context, Kevin Day – a second-generation Irish comedian who grew up in 1970s London – explains that his own 'flirtation with the far right' in the 1970s was 'very much part of looking for an identity and was a reaction against the Irish thing'.[17] This was followed, moreover, by a retreat into Irish nationalism through Day's attendance of Irish clubs (where he would 'stand for the national anthem') and studying of the Irish language.[18] Eventually, Day would conclude that his identity was a 'London' one (which comprised aspects of both cultures) rather than one based on (either) nationality.[19]

Morrissey's onstage claim in 2004 that he was 'ten parts Crumlin and ten parts Old Trafford' suggests a similar accommodation.[20] Prior to this, though, the singer had (in the early 1990s) waved a Union flag onstage, and later brandished an Irish tricolour.[21] Such retreats into nationalist discourse have also been evinced by MacGowan, who has withdrawn – in the post-Pogues period – into an expressly Irish-nationalist space, asserting a de-Anglicized Irishness ('I am completely Irish', he explained in 2000) and distancing himself from England (which he came to see as 'stinking' and 'miserable').[22] This wish to disavow (and disengage from) England points to an evasion of the in-between, and stresses the gap between MacGowan's post-Pogues persona (with its retreat into what Paul Gilroy has called, in a different context, the 'dubious comfort' of ethnic purity[23]) and that which he assumed in The Pogues (which was expressly hybrid, diasporic and *English*-based).

When MacGowan was asked to reflect, in 2006, on the prevalence of second-generation Irish musicians in British popular music, he suggested that this was an effect of a sort of Irish ethnic genius.[24] MacGowan's work with The Pogues, though, was (like that of the other musicians surveyed here) born of an expressly *inter*-cultural dynamic, and it is perhaps worth acknowledging – with this in mind – the role that the host culture played in second-generation Irish music-making. Most obviously, its urban centres gave this generation (whose parents hailed from largely rural backgrounds[25]) access to a vast popular-musical apparatus (from music media and record stores to musical instrument outlets, rehearsal rooms, performance spaces, music management and record labels) as well as the opportunity to mix and perform with diverse (non-Irish) musicians in metropolitan settings that comprised, for Rehan Hyder, a 'vibrant and transformative potential' through their 'dynamic processes of inter-cultural exchange'.[26] Through such processes, the second generation were able to engage music as a means – to borrow from Stokes – of 'constructing trajectories rather than boundaries', thus 'transcending the limitations' of Irish ethnicity.[27]

The inter-cultural exchange cited above was partly facilitated by the specific musical culture in which the second generation were raised. In this context, Marr recalls the 'amazing musical community' that was engendered by the Irish in post-war Manchester, with its network of Irish clubs, such as the Ard Rí and Carousel, whose social events would extend, Marr says, into the private sphere of migrant's homes.[28] Thus, the guitarist explains (of his parents and extended Irish family): 'They'd be playing these songs on record players and on instruments in the houses and then they'd be going out and seeing the bands play the songs on a Friday and Saturday.'[29] Rowland makes a similar point, recalling his attendance of Irish clubs in the west Midlands, and reflecting that when his parents returned from social events with friends and family, they would sing Irish songs in the Rowland home.[30] In this regard, the migrant culture in which the second generation were raised was, from Marr's perspective, more 'musically rich' and 'intense' than that of his English peers:

> My mates' parents listened to music on a Sunday morning and they were listening to Glen Campbell or Johnny Mathis or whoever was the sort of 70s MOR thing of the day, but my folks *every night* were listening to [country, pop and Irish music]. It was just done to the nth degree, it meant more to them. They did it like they did their religion. They did their music like they did their religion.[31]

For Marr, then, this migrant culture played a crucial role in the musicality of the second generation. 'I'm the product of it', he explains. Elaborating on this point, Marr relates that he 'knew loads about music that no one else knew, because of [his] parents', and notes the scene's strong participatory ethos, in which the second generation were, he explains, *expected* to perform (whether through singing, musicianship or dance). In this context, Marr recalls:

> I was talked to like I was a musician when I was about five. I think because they saw that I had some musical capability (I used to be able to play the harmonica in time, and keep the tune and everything). But they just talked to me like I was an adult. (Adopts Irish accent): 'Oh, come on now John, give us a tune, come on now.' You were expected to deliver a tune.[32]

This milieu thus supplied the second generation with a certain symbolic capital, as well as, it seems, transferable skills, all of which have been seen as an aid to their engagement with popular music. In a rare and brief speculation on this point, Miranda Sawyer would suggest, in 2009, that

> There's something about the romance and musicality of an Irish background, not to mention being made to sing at family events, that combines with a first-generation English work ethic to make a brilliant pop star.[33]

Notwithstanding such ideas of the 'romantic' and 'brilliant', the notion of a second-generation work ethic is certainly one that is invoked in the musicians' accounts.[34] If a migrant Irish upbringing has furnished this quality, then it also engendered, for Cáit O'Riordan, a certain outlook. Stressing the apparent benefits of being an 'immigrant's kid' in England, she explains:

> it gives you an outsider perspective, which will get you through the rest of your life, even if you have to get over bumpy bits where you can turn very extreme, violent and have angry thoughts. If you get through the other side, you're left with the outsider's perspective, which always makes you look at *both* sides, and not even at both sides, at all seven or eight different sides to everything. I think if you grow up monocultural, then you're [restricted] … whereas if you're the immigrant's kid/second generation, it's a blessing, whatever if feels like when you're growing up, if you can just get out the other side, and you don't turn it against yourself and you don't turn it against anybody else, it makes you a better person.[35]

Whether or not this is true, it is a view that has been expressed by many second-generation Irish people.[36] Thus, while the achievements of the second generation might be seen to have emerged in spite of the host culture (which was often anti-Irish in orientation), it would seem that the socio-cultural configuration of England in the post-war decades helped to bring about the musical projects surveyed in this book. Such projects were undoubtedly shaped by an Irish–English interface: the interventionist ethos of Dexys, the hybrid aspects of The Pogues and the ambivalent signals of The Smiths all pertained in part to this Irish-in-England context. Such inter-cultural exchanges in the field of music have been rightly valorised.[37] However, this should not obscure the inherent power dynamic that has informed host/migrant relations, and which accrues a non-reciprocal charge in which the centre makes of the margins for its own (economic and cultural) ends whilst offering scant acknowledgement (or appreciation) of the minority group. There is also a crucial distinction, of course, between cultural visibility (via the presence of migrant figures on the popular-musical stage) and structural equality (that is, the material experience of migrant people in the host country) – something to which I return below. The point to note for the moment is that the more fruitful effects of the Irish–English exchange have not always been perceived as a migrant input to national life, and thus the role of England's Irish has – quite often – been overlooked. Central to this book, therefore, has been a wish to challenge the invisibility of the second-generation Irish in accounts of popular music. It has also sought to highlight the complexity and diversity of second-generation Irish subjectivities, and to detail the productive and diverse ways in which this generation has reconfigured popular culture in England. Much of the imperative for this project came from my own experiences growing up in an Irish Catholic family in the north of England in the 1970s and 1980s. In this sense, the book is informed by a wish to confound some of the simplistic assumptions about Irishness that gained prevalence in British culture,[38] and to reconceive the role of Irish migrants, which has been seen as quite peripheral and problematic.

In the period immediately prior to the post-war influx of Irish migrants that brought about the musicians surveyed in this book, the English social commentator J.B. Priestley made a note – in his celebrated *English Journey* – of the effects that Irish migrants had had on English life.[39] In his account, which stressed the cultural gains of immigration and warned of anti-immigrant prejudice (endorsing an 'open house' England against the insularity he observed in English life),[40] Priestley unveiled his views on the Irish–English interface: 'A great many speeches have been made and books written on the subject of what England has done to Ireland', Priestley acknowledged, noting that he 'should be interested to hear a speech and read a book or two on the subject of what Ireland has done to England.'[41] What Priestley had in mind was not the contribution made by Irish migrants (so strikingly evinced by Irish labour in England) but, rather, the 'ignorance and dirt and drunkenness and disease' that he saw as the sum total of Irish influence on England.[42] Such views, in fairness to Priestley, had long been evident in English social histories, not least the work of Friedrich Engels, whose account of the English working class comprised a distinctly unflattering view of Irish migrants, who he considered a 'degrading influence' on life in England.[43] In this context, Engels was keen to point out the vast numbers of second-generation Irish who, having grown up amidst 'Irish filth', were seen as potential infectors of the indigenous populace:

> For when, in almost every great city, a fifth or a quarter of the workers are Irish, or children of Irish parents, who have grown up among Irish filth, no one can wonder if the life, habits, intelligence, moral status – in short, the whole character of the working class, assimilates a great part of the Irish characteristics.[44]

In a similar vein, E.P. Thompson's account of working-class life notes the 'tens of thousands ... born in Britain of Irish parentage' before paying the migrant Irish a backhanded compliment: the main influence of the Irish on English life was, says Thompson, their infusion of the indigenous populace with a 'rebellious disposition' and a recourse to 'physical force'.[45]

The view of Irish immigration as a potential peril was still evident – albeit in less explicit form – in the late twentieth century, when the popular press depicted Irish migrants as (amongst other things) professional benefit scroungers (and therefore a drain on the state's scarce resources), a point that was only compounded by tabloid claims that Irish migrants had sourced British welfare funds to finance IRA actions (a contention that seemed to conflate a vast range of stereotypes, from 'feckless' to 'deceitful' and 'terrorist').[46] As the preceding chapters have shown, such views of the migrant Irish became prominent in the 1970s and 1980s, but continued well into the 1990s. In the following extract, for example, the *Daily Mail* reported, in the mid-Nineties, the allegedly fraudulent pursuits of Britain's immigrant groups: 'First into the field, *needless to say*, were the Irish, who flock across the Irish Sea in great numbers to exploit Britain's welfare state, which they regard as a kind of *patriotic duty*.'[47] With such views enjoying public prevalence, the achievements of the migrant Irish – and particularly the second generation – were obscured and overlooked. There were, of course, sporadic attempts to correct such immigrant 'myths'. As I explained in the prologue, one such effort was made by the Commission for Racial Equality, which – shortly after the *Daily Mail* claim cited above – launched a high-profile effort to correct certain myths about the effects of immigration by detailing the long-standing contribution made to British life by migrants of all backgrounds. In this context, the CRE noted that

> No one today would deny ... the incalculable value of Irish labour going back a very long time... Yet, in their own day, the activities of these migrants went unnoticed as achievements, and were, by and large, either taken for granted, or belittled and reviled.[48]

Despite this overt acknowledgement of Irish migrants, when the CRE
came to detail the *contribution* of migrant groups, the second-generation
Irish (unlike the British-born descendants of other migrant groups) were
wholly absent. (So, while the Irish were acknowledged in terms of their
existence, their *contribution* was rendered invisible.) Perhaps the most
remarkable omission, here, was in the section on popular music, where
the authors failed to register a single Irish-descended musician despite
the vital role played by such musicians in post-war British pop.[49] Other
such projects – including those devised by Irish community groups to
highlight the 'positive contribution' of the Irish in Britain – have focused
on quite narrow areas, such as construction and nursing,[50] which, though
indubitably important, are not the sole fields of Irish activity.

In light of such omissions and oversights, the account offered in this
book of second-generation creativity at the hub of British cultural life
can, perhaps, serve as something of a corrective. This is not to supply
succour to chauvinistic claims of Irish 'greatness', although this view
has occasionally been nurtured – and also dismissed – by the musicians
addressed here (both MacGowan and Rowland would go through a
phase of thinking that 'everything Irish is great').[51] Instead, the narrative
contained in this book might have a more useful effect, for as Sabina
Sharkey explains,

> Where they [the Irish in Britain] have no profile … both their needs
> and their contribution to the community can be ignored. Their agency
> can be discredited and their statements about the needs of vulner-
> able sections of their community such as the elderly, homeless or the
> mentally ill can be decried on the basis that there is no research to
> support any claims of special needs.[52]

While there are now a number of valuable studies to support such claims
of disadvantage and discrimination,[53] this book can, I hope, form part of
a corresponding endeavour to demonstrate the 'agency' and 'contribution'
of Irish migrants in England.

This book also has, I think, a capacity to resonate beyond the specific interests and concerns of the Irish ethnic group. Most obviously,
it serves to demonstrate the complex processes of cultural negotiation
that characterise *any* inter-ethnic context, highlighting the means by
which creative figures of migrant descent seek to make sense of their
in-betweenness (as both a wellspring *and* a burden). The book might
also have some significance for a Britain that has, in the present century, invoked other 'enemies within', often in ways that have echoed
the experience of the Irish earlier on. Thus, the 'suspect community'

status that the Irish once had to endure has, in the post-2000 period, been conferred onto other ethnic groups, some of whom have been viewed as 'the new Irish'.[54] In this context, a member of The Pogues would suggest, in 2006, that being Irish in Eighties Britain was 'a bit like being a young Muslim now'.[55] The account of Irish ethnicity that has unfolded in this book might, then, have a potential significance for the effort to conceive of a genuinely multi-ethnic Britain, for, as Avtar Brah has explained, in such a trans-cultural context 'where several diasporas intersect – African, Jewish, Irish, South Asian, and so on – it becomes necessary to examine how these groups are similarly or differently constructed vis-à-vis one another'.[56] As I explained in the prologue, second-generation Irish musicians have conventionally been framed in a notionally homogeneous (white) Englishness, against which more identifiably immigrant-descended rock and pop musicians have been positioned and differentiated, and from which such musicians have – at key moments (such as Britpop) – been excluded.

It is perhaps not surprising that some musicians of African-Caribbean and South Asian descent have expressed concerns about the racial connotations of Britpop. For Aniruddha Das of Asian Dub Foundation, Britpop was 'an attempt to reassert a sort of mythical whiteness', and was thus 'implicitly racist'.[57] Similar criticisms of Britpop have also been made by musicians of Irish descent, not least Johnny Marr, who expressed his 'despair' at the 'nationalism' of Britpop whilst invoking his Irishness,[58] and noting his antipathy towards the Union flag, the principal signifier of Britpop, which he saw as 'a sign of aggression towards immigrants', including the Irish.[59] However, despite musicians of Irish descent – such as Marr – having articulated an aversion to Britpop, they were nevertheless appropriated as key Britpop figures,[60] and were therefore quite crucial in its construction of a 'mythical whiteness'. Accordingly, if Britpop was indeed implicitly racist, then this was arguably due not only to its exclusion of musicians of African-Caribbean and South Asian descent but also its symmetrical *inclusion* of second-generation Irish musicians. In other words, Britpop's incorporation of the offspring of Irish migrants suggests that its principles of exclusion were determined less by the historical fact of having an immigrant background than by a quiescent conflation of race and nation. This convergence of race and nation has, of course, not been restricted to discourses about popular music. In fact, for Bronwen Walter, such '[e]xclusionary ideas about "race" lie at the heart of British national identity'. As Walter explains:

> The term 'immigrants' has a racialised meaning which makes it synonymous with black skin colour … Shared whiteness is thus a

central reason for Irish inclusion. The power of racialised exclusion on grounds of skin colour would be seriously weakened if ... divisions in the white population were exposed.[61]

Walter's point here unveils the assumptions that underpin ideas of 'ethnic' difference (and thus the origins of the absence of an Irish dimension in accounts of British popular music). However, it also raises crucial questions about Britpop's assertion of a 'mythical whiteness', for an acknowledgement of Irish ethnicity in England could, by drawing attention to the immigrant-descended heterogeneity of the ostensibly homogeneous 'white English' category, make visible the racialising logic that informed Britpop's mechanisms of inclusion.

Such an assertion of second-generation Irish difference could, then, provide a useful strategy for the deconstruction of monolithic identity cat-egories such as 'white English', demonstrating the immigrant-descended heterogeneity that makes up such ostensibly homogeneous groupings. This could, in turn, allow us to map Irish migration in a multi-ethnic context, a point to which the second generation have been cognisant. John Lydon, for instance, has explained that he 'grew up [with] Irish immigrant parents in a heavy Jamaican, Irish, Greek, Turkish multi-mixture race called Arsenal/Finsbury Park ... We had to grow up and muck in together. It was a melting pot.'[62] Similar perspectives have been offered by MacGowan and Rowland,[63] as well as other second-generation figures, such as the Birmingham-Irish 'Jo-Jo', whose views on multi-ethnicity surfaced in an ethnographic account of black–white relations in the late 1980s: 'Balsall Heath is the centre of the melting-pot, man, 'cos all I ever see when I go out is half-Arab, half-Pakistani, half-Jamaican ... half-Irish, I know 'cos I am [half-Irish]'.[64]

If such points serve to fracture 'white ethnicity' in England, then this impulse has, since the late 1990s, been nurtured by a noticeable shift regarding the recognition of Irishness. As I explained in the prologue, the British music press has tended to elide the ethnicity of second-generation Irish musicians. However, this tendency would undergo certain modifications at the turn of the twenty-first century. In the summer of 2000, Britain's best-selling rock magazine, *Q*, ran a special theme issue – replete with glossy Union-flag cover – entitled 'The 100 Greatest British Albums'. In an apparent attempt to quell simplistic celebrations of a racially exclusive Britishness, the issue included an ethnically sensitive editorial essay, entitled 'One nation under a groove'. Moreover, a large-type pull-out quote from the article used to illustrate the text emphasised that 'Britain's multi-ethnic mix and links with the Commonwealth have contributed to a potent shebeen of home-grown music'. In the actual text itself, however, this assertion was punctuated with a parenthetical recognition of Irish ethnicity that read: 'Britain's multi-ethnic mix (wherein the immigrant Irish have proved most crucial, from The Beatles to Oasis) …'[65] Clearly, this acknowledgement marks a striking deviation from previous journalistic accounts, for rather than being omitted (or at best Anglicized), the Irish are in this instance privileged as the 'most crucial' ethnic group. While the significance of this assertion may be somewhat diminished by its parenthetical status (not to mention its omission from the truncated pull-out quote), it nevertheless served to prise open the narrow parameters of the prevailing critical paradigm, particularly as this special issue had shown – throughout its articles – an uncommon sensitivity towards Irish ethnicity in England. In a brief account of The Pogues, the journal explained:

> Being white of skin and Western European of culture, Britain's Irish are the invisible immigrants. Young Irish men in English bars need their culture however. Shane MacGowan articulated the aspirations and disappointments of the London Irish, fuelled by drink and despair.[66]

Notwithstanding the mobilisation, here, of an essentialist model of Irishness, this approach to MacGowan's work was markedly different to the magazine's treatment of the singer's ethnicity the previous year (when it bemoaned his 'half-baked Irishness').[67] Elsewhere, the issue noted 'the rebel-song tradition of the north London Irish community that created Johnny Rotten'.[68] More surprising still was the account of The Beatles' *Revolver* (1966), the record that *Q* had selected as the greatest British album of all time: here, the group were described as 'third or fourth generation Irish-English'.[69] Although this special treatment was not extended to all Irish-descended musicians (The Smiths were once again elided in this context), *Q*'s tentative turn towards an Irish dimension was echoed in contemporary scholarly work, albeit in marginal ways. Thus, a 1997 article on Englishness and popular music comprised an important endnote that acknowledged the ethnicity of second-generation Irish musicians, suggesting that

> some of the most allegedly 'English' of voices have had their roots elsewhere. In punk Johnny Rotten was of Irish descent, and Oasis – often portrayed as both 'English' and part of 'Britpop' – are led by the Gallagher brothers, who are also of Irish descent.[70]

If Irish ethnicity, in this article, was obliged a brief endnote, then in other work at this time it made the transition from endnote to main text (albeit parenthetically). Thus, a discussion of Britpop in 1999 noted that 'the narrow nationalism of the term "Britpop" hardly needs comment (though the Irish roots of the two brothers, Noel and Liam Gallagher, at the centre of Oasis, make the[ir] relationship ... to the phenomenon quite complex)'.[71] Such acknowledgements (as bracketed and brief as they were) implied an important shift in terms of the recognition of Irish ethnicity, and this point would be taken further – and conceived more broadly – in the high-profile report, published in 2000, on *The Future of Multi-ethnic Britain*. This project – led by Bhikhu Parekh – was highly sentient of Irish ethnicity, showing an awareness of Irish migrants and an understanding of their experience.[72] Describing the Irish as Britain's 'insider-outsiders', the report saw the position of the Irish in Britain as 'uniquely relevant to the nature of its multi-ethnic society'.[73] While the report has been viewed as a repudiation of the racial connotations of Britishness,[74] it might also be seen, in the context of the issues raised in this book, as a corrective to similarly conventionalised assumptions – in both the popular and scholarly realms – about the second-generation Irish in England. The conceivable paradigm shift that this might engender could perhaps facilitate a fuller understanding of the complex and diverse contours that constitute Britain's multi-ethnic margins, offering a means to trace the intricate inter-ethnic threads traversing this 'diaspora space',[75] and illuminating the complex cultural filaments that make up its rich national fabric.

Notes & References

'Dwellers on the Threshold': A Prologue to the Book

1 Address by Donogh O'Malley, minister for health, to the National University of Ireland Club, Grosvenor House, London, on St Patrick's Day, 1966. NAI DT 96/6/437, p. 5.
2 Kevin Rowland, interview with the author, Brick Lane, London, 18 Sept. 2007.
3 Address by Michael D. Higgins to the Economy of the Arts conference, Temple Bar, Dublin, Dec. 1994.
4 Simon Frith, 'Music and identity', in Stuart Hall and Paul du Gay (eds.), *Questions of Cultural Identity* (London: Sage, 1996), p. 122.
5 Stuart Maconie et al., 'The 100 greatest British albums ever!', *Q*, June 2000, pp. 83–4.
6 See Sean Campbell, 'Popular music-making amongst the Irish diaspora in England', in Barra Boydell and Harry White (eds.), *Encyclopedia of Music in Ireland* (Dublin: University College Dublin Press, forthcoming).
7 For a discussion of this point, see Sean Campbell, 'Sounding out the margins: Ethnicity and popular music in British cultural studies', in Gerry Smyth and Glenda Norquay (eds.), *Across the Margins: Cultural Identities and Change in the Atlantic Archipelago* (Manchester: Manchester University Press, 2002), pp. 117–36; Sean Campbell, 'Ethnicity and cultural criticism: Evocations and elisions of Irishness in the British music press', *Celtic Cultural Studies: An Interdisciplinary Online Journal*, no. 1, 'Music and Identity' (2007).
8 The term 'second-generation Irish' is used in this book to refer to the immediate descendants of Irish-born immigrants. The book focuses on the English-born offspring of Irish Catholic immigrants from the Irish Republic. My emphasis on this particular section of the second generation is an attempt to be historically specific rather than politically exclusive.
9 Such was the prominence of the second-generation Irish musician at this time that it even received fictional dramatisation in the popular media. Most striking in this regard was Trevor Griffiths' *Oi for England*, which was broadcast on the ITV network in 1982, and gained widespread public attention. See Mike Poole and John Wyver, *Powerplays: Trevor Griffiths in Television* (London: British Film Institute, 1984), pp. 169–79; Stuart Cosgrove, 'Refusing consent: The "Oi for England" project', *Screen*, vol. 24, no. 1 (Jan.–Feb. 1983), pp. 92–6. This teleplay centred on a Manchester-Irish singer called Finn, whose ethnicity served as a major theme, not least for his (nationalistic) English band-mates. Accounts of the play relate that it 'invests Finn, the apparent guiding spirit and genuine talent in the band, with an aura of difference from his compatriots. Resistant to any racism in the group's songs or choice of venues, his Irish background becomes the subject of much comment on his loyalties. That emphasis on Finn's Irishness sets up the closing scene, in which he smashes the group's instruments in disgust, under the

humanising influence of an Irish folk song' (Neil Nehring, *Flowers in the Dustbin: Culture, Anarchy, and Postwar England* (Ann Arbor: University of Michigan Press, 1993), pp. 323–4). Although, as critics would note, this final scene 'seems to pose more questions about the relevance of Finn's Irish parentage and allegiance than the action can possibly accommodate' (Edward Braun, 'Introduction', *Trevor Griffiths: Collected Plays for Television* (London: Faber and Faber, 1988), p. 29), it nonetheless highlights the centrality of this issue in the play, a point that was registered by Britain's rock media, who observed Finn's 'Irish extraction' in their accounts of the play (see, for example, Paul Tickell, 'Reds, white and blue: The politics of colour', *New Musical Express* (henceforth, *NME*), 17 Apr. 1982, p. 25). A less serious rendition of this figure appeared a few years later in the popular TV comedy series *Only Fools and Horses*, in the form of a fictionalised singer called Mickey Maguire, whose angry persona (he is nicknamed 'Mental Mickey') evoked John Lydon (BBC 1, 14 Mar. 1985). The singer's origins were underlined when he performed at an Irish social club (the 'Paddies' Moulin Rouge', as it is described in the show) before an appearance on *Top of the Pops*. Like *Oi for England*, then, this episode seemed to point to an implied association between Irish ethnicity and English rock.

10   See Campbell, 'Popular music-making'.

11   See, for example, Bill Rolston, '"This is not a rebel song": The Irish conflict and popular music', *Race and Class*, vol. 42, no. 3 (2001), p. 53; Barra Ó Cinnéide, *Riverdance: The Phenomenon* (Dublin: Blackhall Publishing, 2002), pp. 195–6.

12   See Carol Clerk, *Pogue Mahone: The Story of The Pogues* (London: Omnibus Press, 2006), p. 90; *The Story of ... Fairytale of New York*, BBC 3, 19 Dec. 2005; Julian Vignoles, 'What is Irish popular music?', *The Crane Bag*, vol. 8, no. 2 (1984), p. 72.

13   Rowland, interview with the author.

14   Lydon was widely considered to be the principal icon of English punk. See, for example, Julie Burchill and Tony Parsons, *'The Boy Looked at Johnny': The Obituary of Rock'n'Roll* (London: Pluto, 1978), p. 78; Charles Shaar Murray, 'We didn't know it was loaded ...', *NME*, 9 July 1977, pp. 28–9.

15   For an account of post-punk, see Simon Reynolds, *Rip It Up and Start Again: Post-Punk, 1978–84* (London: Faber and Faber, 2005).

16   This notion of 'routes' is drawn from Paul Gilroy's work on diasporic popular music, in which he points to the validity and inexorability of hybrid, transcultural forms that exceed the narrow frames of a fixed – and supposedly 'authentic' – ethnic music, and thus confound 'any simplistic ... understanding of the relationship ... between folk cultural authenticity and pop cultural betrayal' (Paul Gilroy, *The Black Atlantic: Modernity and Double Consciousness* (London: Verso, 1993), p. 99). Although Gilroy is primarily concerned with cultures of the 'black Atlantic', the theoretical frames that his work proffers can be usefully deployed in studies of other – differently located – migrant groups.

17   The preponderance of male musicians – which is in part an effect of popular music practice – is offset by the attention given to Cáit O'Riordan, who is cited throughout the book, and plays a major role in the chapter on The Pogues.

18   *Second Generation*, RTÉ Radio 1, Jan.–Feb. 2003. Such invocations of in-betweenness should not, as Rehan Hyder explains, be seen as 'the articulation of

any kind of "identity confusion"'; instead, they point to 'the inadequacies of dis-courses of race and ethnicity which fail to provide a suitably complex vocabulary able to express the elaborate processes at work in the negotiation of self-identifi-cation' (Rehan Hyder, *Brimful of Asia: Negotiating Ethnicity on the UK Music Scene* (Aldershot: Ashgate, 2004), p. 166).

19 Cáit O'Riordan, interview with the author, Dublin, 24 Nov. 2005; Johnny Marr, interview with the author, Night and Day café, Manchester, 4 Dec. 2006; Rowland, interview with the author.

20 Morrissey declined to participate in an interview for this book. Newspapers and magazines were sourced at the British Library Newspaper Library at Colindale, and at Cambridge University Library.

21 For an elaboration of such approaches, see, for example, Sheila Whiteley (ed.), *Sexing the Groove: Popular Music and Gender* (London: Routledge, 1997); Sara Cohen, *Decline, Renewal and the City in Popular Music Culture: Beyond The Beatles* (Aldershot: Ashgate, 2007); Nathan Wiseman-Trowse, *Performing Class in British Popular Music* (Basingstoke: Palgrave, 2008).

22 The Smiths, in particular, have been viewed in terms of gender and sexuality. See, for example, Nadine Hubbs, 'Music of the "fourth gender": Morrissey and the sexual politics of melodic contour', in Thomas Foster, Carol Siegel and Ellen E. Berry (eds.), *Bodies of Writing: Bodies in Performance* (New York: New York University Press, 1996), pp. 266–96. The Pogues, meanwhile, have tended to be seen in terms of a general – rather than a specifically second-generation – Irishness. For scholarly accounts of The Pogues, see Kieran Keohane, 'Unifying the fragmented imaginary of the young immigrant: Making a home in the post modern with The Pogues', *Irish Review*, vol. 9, no. 1 (1990), pp. 71–9; Noel McLaughlin and Martin McLoone, 'Hybridity and national musics: The case of Irish rock music', *Popular Music*, vol. 19, no. 2 (2000), pp. 190–2; Joe Cleary, *Outrageous Fortune: Capital and Culture in Modern Ireland* (Dublin: Field Day Publications, 2006), pp. 200–26. There are currently no scholarly – and few 'serious' journalistic – accounts of Dexys Midnight Runners. See John Aizlewood, 'Thankfully not living in Yorkshire it doesn't apply', in Aizlewood (ed.), *Love is the Drug* (London: Penguin, 1994), pp. 21–37; Kevin Pearce, *Something Beginning with O* (London: Heavenly, 1993), pp. 39–47.

23 There are a number of very useful accounts of national identity and British popular music. See, for example, Andy Bennett, '"Village greens and terraced streets": Britpop and representations of "Britishness"', *Young: Nordic Journal of Youth Research*, vol. 5, no. 4 (Nov. 1997), pp. 20–33; Martin Cloonan, 'What do they know of England? "Englishness" and popular music in the mid-1990s', in Tarja Hautamaki and Helmi Jarviluoma (eds.), *Music on Show: Issues of Performance* (Tampere: University of Tampere, 1998), pp. 66–72; David Hesmondhalgh, 'British popular music and national identity', in David Morley and Kevin Robins (eds.), *British Cultural Studies: Geography, Nationality and Identity* (Oxford: Oxford University Press, 2001), pp. 273–86; Nabeel Zuberi, *Sounds English: Transnational Popular Music* (Urbana and Chicago: University of Illinois Press, 2001). These accounts have – with the exception of Zuberi – overlooked the ethnicity of sec-ond-generation Irish musicians.

24 For an account of Britpop, see Zuberi, *Sounds English*, pp. 64–72.

25 Cited in Roy Shuker, *Key Concepts in Popular Music* (London: Routledge, 1998), p. 36.

26 See, for instance, David Bennun, Paul Lester, Taylor Parkes, Dave Simpson and Ian Watson, 'Britpop', *Melody Maker*, 22 July 1995, pp. 29–33; Andy Richardson, 'The battle of Britpop', *NME*, 12 Aug. 1995, pp. 28–30.

27 Robert Yates, 'Looking back in anger', *Observer*, 'Review' section, 7 Mar. 1999, p. 3; David Halliwell and Ste Mack, 'The Johnny Marr interview', *The Official Oasis Magazine*, no. 1 (winter 1996), no pagination. The individual members of Oasis had had varying degrees of involvement with Irish music in Manchester before the group formed in the early 1990s. See Paul Gallagher and Terry Christian, *Brothers: From Childhood to Oasis – The Real Story* (London: Virgin, 1996), p. 131; Paolo Hewitt, *Getting High: The Adventures of Oasis* (London: Boxtree, 1997), pp. 67, 69–70, 141; Chris Hutton and Richard Kurt, *Don't Look Back in Anger: Growing Up With Oasis* (London: Simon & Schuster, 1997), p. 165.

28 Steve Sutherland, 'See! Hear! Now!', *NME*, 20 Sept. 1997, p. 40. If Oasis were to some extent complicit in this process, then this was best evinced through their identification with Britpop's principal signifier, the Union flag. However, it is worth noting that the 'swirl' Union-flag graphic that adorned official Oasis paraphernalia originated from an early demo tape sleeve that featured, according to Johnny Marr, 'the Union Jack going down the toilet' (Halliwell and Mack, 'The Johnny Marr interview', *The Official Oasis Magazine*, no. 1 (winter 1996), no pagination). In August 1996, Oasis played what was then the biggest ever concert in British rock history. See Johnny Cigarettes, 'Five go mad for it', *NME*, 17 Aug. 1996, p. 35.

29 Bennun et al., 'Britpop', *Melody Maker*, 22 July 1995, pp. 29–33; Jon Wilde, 'Listening to England', *Livewire*, Feb./Mar. 1995, pp. 14–19.

30 Gallagher cited in Eugene Masterson, *The Word on the Street: The Unsanctioned Story of Oasis* (Edinburgh: Mainstream, 1996), p. 56. This gesture was underpinned by the band's authorised biography, which made frequent reference to their Irishness. See Hewitt, *Getting High*. For an account of this book, see Sean Campbell, 'Review of Paolo Hewitt, *Getting High*', *Popular Music*, vol. 18, no. 1 (1999), pp. 158–60.

31 Bennun et al., 'Britpop', *Melody Maker*, 22 July 1995, pp. 32–3; Dave Simpson, 'Why two's company', *Guardian*, 13 July 1996, p. 30.

32 John Lydon, *Rotten: No Irish, No Blacks, No Dogs* (London: Hodder & Stoughton, 1994), pp. 13–14, 249, 274.

33 'Questionnaire', *Q*, Jan. 1995, p. 322. For an account of Morrissey's engagement with Englishness in his early solo career, see Zuberi, *Sounds English*, pp. 17–20.

34 See, for example, Sutherland, 'See! Hear! Now!', *NME*, 20 Sept. 1997, p. 40; Wilde, 'Listening to England', *Livewire*, Feb./Mar. 1995, pp. 14–19; Tony Parsons, 'A divine spark in the British soul', *Daily Mirror*, 17 May 1999, p. 9; Michael Bracewell, *England is Mine: Pop Life in Albion from Wilde to Goldie* (London: HarperCollins, 1997). For an exception to this view, see Jon Savage, 'Rough emeralds', *Guardian*, second section, 17 Mar. 1995, p. 11.

35 A version of this paper was published as part of the conference proceedings. See Cloonan, 'What do they know of England?', pp. 66–72.

36 The Commission for Racial Equality, *Roots of the Future: Ethnic Diversity in the Making of Britain* (London: CRE, 1996), p. 39. For an account of this book, see

Sean Campbell, '"Race of angels": The critical reception of second-generation Irish musicians', *Irish Studies Review*, vol. 6, no. 2 (1998), pp. 165–74.

37   Commission for Racial Equality, *Roots of the Future*, pp. 75, 121. For an account of Oasis, see Sean Campbell, '"What's the story?": Rock biography, musical "routes" and the second-generation Irish in England', *Irish Studies Review*, vol. 12, no. 1 (2004), pp. 63–75.

38   It is worth noting here that many second-generation Irish people in England are not white. The ethnic diversity of the second-generation Irish has been most visibly demonstrated by the inclusion of many footballers of both Irish *and* African-Caribbean descent in the Republic of Ireland football team, most notably Chris Hughton, Terry Phelan and Phil Babb.

39   Liam Ryan, 'Irish emigration to Britain since World War II', in Richard Kearney (ed.), *Migrations: The Irish at Home and Abroad* (Dublin: Wolfhound Press, 1990), p. 60.

40   John Rex, 'Immigrants and British labour: The sociological context', in Kenneth Lunn (ed.), *Hosts, Immigrants and Minorities: Historical Responses to Newcomers in British Society, 1870–1914* (Folkestone: Dawson, 1980), p. 26.

41   Patrick J. Bracken, Liam Greenslade, Barney Griffin and Marcelino Smyth, 'Mental health and ethnicity: An Irish dimension', *British Journal of Psychiatry*, vol. 172 (1998), p. 103; 'The 1980s', *Irish Post*, 5 Jan. 1980, p. 4; Seeromanie Harding and Rasaratnam Balarajan, 'Patterns of mortality in second generation Irish living in England and Wales: Longitudinal study', *British Medical Journal*, vol. 312, no. 7043 (1 June 1996), p. 1392. In the mid-twentieth-century decades, around one million Irish-born migrants arrived and settled in Britain (Enda Delaney, *The Irish in Post-War Britain* (Oxford: Oxford University Press, 2007), pp. 2, 13). The vast bulk of these were working-class Catholics from rural parts of the Republic. They settled in largely urban areas, and found work in low-skilled professions, having been educated – for the most part – to only primary level. Such migrants saw English life as a short-term sojourn in a 'strange' and 'foreign' place, and viewed the experience of migration as a 'deeply traumatic moment' (Delaney, *The Irish in Post-War Britain*, pp. 8, 32, 63, 124, 128). This point did not go unnoticed by their offspring: 'My father's grief for Ireland was fierce', notes the second-generation Irish writer Nikki Walsh, 'and I grew up with a distinct sense of loss' (Nikki Walsh, 'The house that Dad built', *The Dubliner*, June 2008, p. 34). Such grief was often assuaged by the widely held dream of 'return', and by the 'constant movement' of such migrants – and their English-born children – 'back and forth across the Irish Sea' (Delaney, *The Irish in Post-War Britain*, pp. 39, 67).

42   See John McCaughey, 'Mixed-up kids!', *Irish Post*, 23 Dec. 1970, p. 5. The school in question was St William of York. For Lydon's attendance of this school, see Lydon, *Rotten*, p. 31. In early interviews with the music press, Lydon described the school's governors as an 'Irish mafia' (Charles Shaar Murray, 'John, Paul, Steve and Sidney: The social rehabilitation of the Sex Pistols', *NME*, 6 Aug. 1977, p. 26).

43   McCaughey, 'Mixed-up kids!', *Irish Post*, 23 Dec. 1970, p. 5.

44   Philip Ullah, 'Second-generation Irish youth: Identity and ethnicity', *New Community*, vol. 12, no. 2 (summer 1985), pp. 310, 312.

45   Harding and Balarajan, 'Patterns of mortality', pp. 1389, 1392. This was a longitudinal study (followed up from 1971 to 1989) by the Office of Population

Censuses and Surveys (now the Office for National Statistics) of 3,075 men and 3,233 women aged 15 and over in 1971. The study's conclusions were reported in the mainstream press. See, for example, Cal McCrystal, 'Emigration "poses huge danger to Irish health"', *Observer*, 9 June 1996, p. 3; Owen Bowcott, 'Concern over health of Irish immigrants', *Guardian*, 9 Feb. 1998, p. 2.

46 Bracken et al., 'Mental health and ethnicity', p. 103.

47 Harding and Balarajan, 'Patterns of mortality', p. 1392. For an account of migrant health research, see David Kelleher, 'A defence of the use of the terms "ethnicity" and "culture"', in David Kelleher and Sheila Hillier (eds.), *Researching Cultural Differences in Health* (London: Routledge, 1996), pp. 69–90.

48 See, for example, Mary J. Hickman, Sarah Morgan and Bronwen Walter, *Second-Generation Irish People in Britain: A Demographic, Socio-Economic and Health Profile* (London: Irish Studies Centre, University of North London, 2001).

49 Michael P. Hornsby-Smith and Angela Dale, 'The assimilation of Irish immigrants in England', *British Journal of Sociology*, vol. 39, no. 4 (1988), pp. 519–44.

50 Ibid. p. 521, emphasis added.

51 Ibid. p. 530, emphasis added. Most strikingly, the daughters of immigrants from the Irish Republic exceeded the English control sample by two to one for 'higher qualifications' (one or more A levels or above, including teaching and nursing qualifications). Meanwhile, for 'intermediate qualifications' (any qualifications below A level), the sons of immigrants from the Irish Republic exceeded the English control sample by almost ten per cent. This particular research was based on a sample of 243 male and 245 female children of immigrants from the Republic of Ireland, and an English control sample of 559 men and 584 women. The authors used the General Household Survey for 1979 and 1980 carried out by the Office of Population Censuses and Surveys (now the Office for National Statistics). See ibid. pp. 527–30.

52 Hornsby-Smith and Dale, 'The assimilation of Irish immigrants in England'.

53 The post-war wave of immigrants from the Republic arrived in England 'with low levels of educational qualifications' (Hornsby-Smith and Dale, 'The assimilation of Irish immigrants in England', p. 534). For instance, '82 per cent of Irish-born British residents in 1961 had left school at 15 or earlier' (Bernard Canavan, 'Story-tellers and writers: Irish identity in emigrant labourers' autobiographies, 1870–1970', in Patrick O'Sullivan (ed.), *The Irish World Wide: The Creative Migrant* (Leicester: Leicester University Press, 1992), p. 169). For discussions of the health patterns of the first-generation Irish, see Harding and Balarajan, 'Patterns of mortality', and Bracken et al., 'Mental health and ethnicity'.

54 John Haskey, 'Mortality among second generation Irish in England and Wales', *British Medical Journal*, vol. 312, no. 7043 (1 June 1996), pp. 1373–4, emphases added.

55 See, for example, Harding and Balarajan, 'Patterns of mortality'; Joanne Abbotts, Rory Williams and Graeme Ford, 'Morbidity and Irish Catholic descent in Britain: Relating health disadvantage to socio-economic position', *Social Science & Medicine*, vol. 52, no. 7 (2001), pp. 999–1005; Mary Hickman and Bronwen Walter, *Discrimination and the Irish Community in Britain* (London: Commission for Racial Equality, 1997); Kenneth Mullen, Rory Williams and Kate Hunt, 'Irish descent, religion, and alcohol and tobacco use', *Addiction*, vol. 91, no. 2 (1996),

pp. 243–54; Joyce O'Connor, *The Young Drinkers: A Cross-National Study of Social and Cultural Influences* (London: Tavistock Publications, 1978); Ullah, 'Second-generation Irish youth'; Mary J. Hickman, *Religion, Class and Identity: The State, the Catholic Church and the Education of the Irish in Britain* (Aldershot: Avebury, 1995); Paul Michael Garrett, *Social Work and Irish People in Britain: Historical and Contemporary Responses to Irish Children and Families* (Bristol: The Policy Press, 2004). Moreover, even in instances where the second generation are not the principal point of discussion, they are often invoked as a 'problem'. Thus, Roy Foster has implied that the development of Irish studies in Britain has been constrained by a wish to 'massage the *susceptibilities* of a second generation emigrant [*sic*] community' (Peter Gray, 'Our man at Oxford', *History Ireland*, vol. 1, no. 3 (autumn 1993), p. 12, emphasis added).

56 For rare exceptions, see Aidan Arrowsmith, 'Plastic Paddy: Negotiating identity in second generation Irish-English writing', *Irish Studies Review*, vol. 8, no. 1 (Apr. 2000), pp. 35–44; Liam Harte, 'Migrancy, performativity and autobiographical identity', *Irish Studies Review*, vol. 14, no. 2 (May 2006), pp. 225–38.

57 In this way, the migrant group can be seen to reshape the very culture into which they are assumed to assimilate. For an elaboration of this point, see George Lipsitz, *Dangerous Crossroads: Popular Music, Postmodernism and the Poetics of Place* (London: Verso, 1994), p. 126.

58 See, for example, Norah Casey (ed.), 'You Say: The forum for the Irish in Britain', *Irish Post*, 13 Feb. 1999, p. 14. See also *Irish Post*, 25 June 1977, p. 6; *Irish Post*, 9 July 1977, p. 6; *Irish Post*, 23 July 1977, p. 6.

59 Mary Kells, 'Ethnic identity amongst young middle class Irish migrants in London', Occasional Papers Series, no. 6 (London: University of North London Press, 1995), p. 15.

60 For a discussion of this phenomenon, see Gerry Smyth, 'Who's the greenest of them all? Irishness and popular music', *Irish Studies Review*, vol. 1, no. 2 (1992), pp. 3–5.

61 Marcus Free, 'Tales from the fifth green field: The psychodynamics of migration, masculinity and national identity amongst Republic of Ireland soccer supporters in England', *Sport in Society*, vol. 10, no. 3 (May 2007), pp. 476–94. See also Marcus Free, '"Angels" with drunken faces? Travelling Republic of Ireland supporters and the construction of Irish migrant identity in England', in Adam Brown (ed.), *Fanatics! Power, Identity and Fandom in Football* (London: Routledge, 1998), pp. 219–32.

62 Free, 'Tales from the fifth green field', p. 482.

63 Free, '"Angels" with drunken faces?', p. 224.

64 See, for example, Bronwen Walter, '"Shamrocks growing out of their mouths": Language and the racialisation of the Irish in Britain', in Anne J. Kershen (ed.), *Language, Labour and Migration* (Aldershot: Ashgate, 2000), p. 68; John Healy, *The Grass Arena: An Autobiography* (London: Faber and Faber, 1988), p. 10; Brian Dooley, *Choosing the Green? Second Generation Irish and the Cause of Ireland* (Belfast: Beyond the Pale, 2004), p. 111; Bernard O'Mahoney, *Soldier of the Queen* (Dingle: Brandon, 2000), p. 31; Mary Lennon, Marie McAdam and Joanne O'Brien, *Across the Water: Irish Women's Lives in Britain* (London: Virago, 1988), p. 222; Phil McNeill, 'A man out of time', *The Hit*, 21 Sept. 1985, p. 14; Lydon, *Rotten*, pp. 13, 274; Free, 'Tales from the fifth green field', p. 480.

65　The most successful Irish football squad to date (which reached the quarter-finals of the World Cup in Italy in 1990) included twelve players born outside of Ireland. Gerry Peyton, Chris Morris, Chris Hughton, Mick McCarthy, Andy Townsend, Tony Galvin, John Aldridge and Tony Cascarino were all born in England. David O'Leary and Paul McGrath, though raised in Ireland, were also born in England. Ray Houghton was born in Scotland, and Kevin Sheedy in Wales. Michael Holmes has suggested that 'the football team's success has contributed to a far greater awareness and appreciation of the Irish diaspora' (Holmes, 'Symbols of national identity and sport: The case of the Irish football team', *Irish Political Studies*, vol. 9 (1994), p. 58).

66　David Morley and Kevin Robins, 'No place like *heimat*: Images of home(land) in European culture', in Erica Carter, James Donald and Judith Squires (eds.), *Space and Place: Theories of Identity and Location* (London: Lawrence & Wishart, 1993), p. 27.

67　D. O'Brien, cited in Judy Chance, 'The Irish in London: An exploration of ethnic boundary maintenance', in Peter Jackson (ed.), *Race and Racism: Essays in Social Geography* (London: Allen & Unwin, 1987), p. 154.

68　Ibid.

69　Bernard McGrath, 'Angst of the Irish in Britain', *Irish Post*, 24 Apr. 1999, p. 13.

70　'The 1980s', *Irish Post*, 5 Jan. 1980, p. 4, emphases added.

71　Breda Gray, 'Curious hybridities: Transnational negotiations of migrancy through generation', *Irish Studies Review*, vol. 14, no. 2 (May 2006), p. 212, emphases added.

72　Bronwen Walter, 'Invisible Irishness: Second-generation identities in Britain', *Association of European Migration Institutions Journal*, vol. 2 (2004), p. 187.

73　This is not to suggest that the discursive construction of such differences has been restricted to this Celticist moment, but instead to emphasise that this was an especially prominent instance of such constructions. For an account of Celticist binary divisions, see Seamus Deane, *Celtic Revivals: Essays in Modern Irish Literature, 1880–1980* (London: Faber and Faber, 1985), pp. 17–27. For a broader historical address to constructions of Irishness in Britain, see Lewis Perry Curtis Jr., *Apes and Angels: The Irishman in Victorian Caricature* (Newton Abbot: David and Charles, 1971); Liz Curtis, *Nothing But the Same Old Story: The Roots of Anti-Irish Racism* (London: Information on Ireland, 1984); Hickman, *Religion, Class, and Identity*. For an account of the particular post-war context in which second-generation Irish identity-formation processes have been shaped, see Steven Fielding, *Class and Ethnicity: Irish Catholics in England, 1880–1939* (Buckingham: Open University Press, 1993), pp. 127–33; Hickman, *Religion, Class, and Identity*, pp. 203–49; Bronwen Walter, *Outsiders Inside: Whiteness, Place and Irish Women* (London: Routledge, 2001), pp. 162–93.

74　McCaughey, 'Mixed-up kids!', *Irish Post*, 23 Dec. 1970, p. 5. In an ethnographic survey of the second generation in the 1980s, the majority of respondents saw themselves as 'half English, half Irish' (Ullah, 'Second-generation Irish youth', p. 312).

75　Mary J. Hickman, Sarah Morgan, Bronwen Walter and Joseph Bradley, 'The limitations of whiteness and the boundaries of Englishness: Second-generation Irish identifications and positionings in multiethnic Britain', *Ethnicities*, vol. 5, no. 2 (2005), p. 178, emphases added.

Chapter 1: *'Here is a Protest': Intervention and Recovery in Dexys Midnight Runners*

1   *Young Guns Go For It*, BBC 2, 13 Sept. 2000.
2   Sean O'Hagan, 'Tangled up in blue', *NME*, 7 Sept. 1985, p. 31. 'The Waltz', *Don't Stand Me Down* (Mercury, 1985). I do not wish to reduce the band's work to this Anglo-Irish issue, but to suggest that it was a major aspect of their œuvre. The band went on to release one further single, 'Because Of You' (Mercury, 1986), after *Don't Stand Me Down*, but the album is generally viewed as the end of Dexys' career.
3   'Dance Stance' (EMI/Oddball Productions, 1979). Rowland laid stress on the song's interventionist gesture in numerous interviews. See, for example, Phil Sutcliffe, 'The dexedrine gang', *Sounds*, 19 Jan. 1980, p. 13; Gavin Martin, 'Overnight bag sensations', *NME*, 14 June 1980, p. 29; Dermot Stokes, 'Dexys Midnight Runners', *Hot Press*, 14–28 Aug. 1980, p. 18; Jim Green, 'Dexys Midnight Runners', *Trouser Press*, Nov. 1980, p. 8. For examples of the 'thick Paddy' stereotype in popular discourses, see Curtis, *Nothing But the Same Old Story*.
4   See, for example, Aizlewood, 'Thankfully not living in Yorkshire', pp. 21–37; Pearce, *Something Beginning with O*, pp. 39–47.
5   For an account of Rowland's career, see Richard White, *Dexys Midnight Runners: Young Soul Rebels* (London: Omnibus Press, 2005).
6   'Dance Stance' was released in November 1979, while the first Pogues single, 'Dark Streets Of London' (Pogue Mahone, 1984), was not issued until May 1984. For details of the release dates, see White, *Dexys Midnight Runners*, p. 205, and Ann Scanlon, *The Pogues: The Lost Decade* (London: Omnibus Press, 1988), p. 128.
7   Pete Williams, the band's original bass player, sees Rowland as Dexys' 'major driving force' (*Dexys Midnight Runners: It Was Like This* (ILC DVD, 2004)). Similarly, Chris Roberts views Rowland as 'the energy at the centre' of the band (Chris Roberts, 'Stairway to Kevin', *Melody Maker*, 9 Apr. 1988, p. 28). As if to underline this point, Dexys were renamed 'Kevin Rowland and Dexys Midnight Runners' in the period 1982–83.
8   See McNeill, 'A man out of time', *The Hit*, 21 Sept. 1985, p. 14; Dexys Midnight Runners, *Coming to Town* tour programme, 1985; Gordon Thomson, 'My team', *Observer Sport Monthly*, 2 Nov. 2003, p. 62; Stokes, 'Dexys Midnight Runners', *Hot Press*, 14–28 Aug. 1980, p. 18; 'Kevin Rowland: The early years', *Keep on Running*, no. 6 (Jan. 1997), no pagination; Kevin Rowland, 'Profile', *Record Mirror*, 17 July 1982, p. 11; Rowland, interview with the author; Simon Price, 'A dark knight of the soul', *Independent*, 'Friday Review' section, 5 Apr. 2002, p. 15.
9   Kevin Rowland, 'Kevin Rowland replies to Julie Burchill', *The Face*, Sept. 1983, p. 62; Paolo Hewitt, 'Keeping up', *Melody Maker*, 7 Aug. 1982, p. 20; Thomson, 'My team', *Observer Sport Monthly*, 2 Nov. 2003, p. 62; Liam Mackey, 'The leader of the band', *Hot Press*, 8–23 Oct. 1982, p. 18.
10 Hickman, *Religion, Class and Identity*, p. 200.
11 Diane Cross, 'Status quo? Great!', *Record Mirror*, 30 Nov. 1985, p. 55; Rowland, interview with the author.
12 Rowland, interview with the author.
13 Kevin Courtney, 'Midnight run', *Irish Times*, 'The Ticket' section, 13 Nov. 2003,

p. 6. Terry Eagleton recalls an analogous encounter with nationalist songs from his own childhood: 'sitting with my mother on a crowded Salford bus, I piped up with the first lines of "Kevin Barry" ... My mother told me sharply to be quiet, and I was aware that I had blundered unwittingly on something secret and shameful, some illicit crime of origin' (Eagleton, 'A different sense of who I was', *Irish Reporter*, no. 13 (1994), p. 14).

14   Rowland, interview with the author.

15   Ibid.; Stokes, 'Dexys Midnight Runners', *Hot Press*, 14–28 Aug. 1980, p. 18.

16   Hickman et al., 'The limitations of whiteness', p. 169.

17   Barry McIlheney, 'Burning the midnight oil', *Melody Maker*, 2 Nov. 1985, p. 19; McNeill, 'A man out of time', *The Hit*, 21 Sept. 1985, pp. 12, 14; Cross, 'Status quo? Great!', *Record Mirror*, 30 Nov. 1985, p. 55.

18   Martin, 'Overnight bag sensations', *NME*, 14 June 1980, p. 29; Rowland, 'Profile', *Record Mirror*, 17 July 1982, p. 11. Rowland would later discuss his song-writing in terms of manual labour: '... it's like a bricklayer laying bricks', he explained, 'you just use all the skill and care that you can and try to be the best at your trade' (Gavin Martin, 'A folk hero of the 80s: The Kevin Rowland interview', *NME*, 3 July 1982, p. 53).

19   Hewitt, 'Keeping up', *Melody Maker*, 7 Aug. 1982, p. 21; Martin, 'A folk hero of the 80s', *NME*, 3 July 1982, p. 24; Jon Wilde, 'My story: Kevin Rowland', *Dazed and Confused*, June 1999, p. 5. Martin Stokes notes the 'Country and Irish' sub-genre that has been popular with the Irish in Britain (Stokes, 'Introduction: Ethnicity, identity and music', in Stokes (ed.), *Ethnicity, Identity and Music: The Musical Construction of Place* (Oxford: Berg, 1994), p. 3). See also Sarah Hughes, 'Surgical spirit', *Observer*, *Observer* Music Monthly section, 20 Nov. 2005, p. 11.

20   Rowland, interview with the author. See also *Alexei on Dexys*, BBC Radio 2, 14 Feb. 2004; Hewitt, 'Keeping up', *Melody Maker*, 7 Aug. 1982, p. 21.

21   Courtney, 'Midnight run', *Irish Times*, 'The Ticket' section, 13 Nov. 2003, p. 6. See also Mackey, 'The leader of the band', *Hot Press*, 8–23 Oct. 1982, p. 17.

22   Rowland, interview with the author.

23   Ibid.

24   Ibid.

25   Ibid.

26   Ibid.

27   White, *Dexys Midnight Runners*, pp. 9–10; Romhany, 'Dexys: Let's get this straight from the start', *Jamming!*, no. 14 (1983), p. 6. For an account of English punk, see Jon Savage, *England's Dreaming: Sex Pistols and Punk Rock* (London: Faber and Faber, 1991).

28   White, *Dexys Midnight Runners*, pp. 10–11.

29   Rowland, interview with the author.

30   Martin, 'Overnight bag sensations', *NME*, 14 June 1980, p. 29. For an account of The Killjoys, see Frances Lass, 'Would you let these people drink in your bar?', *Sounds*, 21 Jan. 1978, p. 26; *Punk in London* (Wolfgang Büld, Germany, 1978).

31   For an account of this process, see Dick Hebdige, *Subculture: The Meaning of Style* (London: Methuen, 1979), and Savage, *England's Dreaming*.

32   See Roy Carr, 'Dexys: Funky butt fassst!', *NME*, 12 Jan. 1980, p. 16; Mike Stand, 'Hearts full of soul', *The Face*, May 1980, pp. 41–3; Kevin Archer, 'Hello goodbye',

Mojo, July 2009, p. 154; John Reed, 'A tale of two Kevins', *Record Collector,* July 2009, p. 26; Sutcliffe, 'The dexedrine gang', *Sounds,* 19 Jan. 1980, p. 13; *Alexei on Dexys,* BBC Radio 2, 14 Feb. 2004.

33 Sutcliffe, 'The dexedrine gang', *Sounds,* 19 Jan. 1980, p. 13. For Rowland's position on alcohol and recreational drug use, see ibid. p. 13; Derek Johnson, 'Dexys' passion runs dry', *NME,* 14 Mar. 1981, p. 3.

34 Carr, 'Dexys', *NME,* 12 Jan. 1980, p. 16.

35 Green, 'Dexys Midnight Runners', *Trouser Press,* Nov. 1980, p. 8.

36 Reynolds, *Rip It Up and Start Again,* p. 289.

37 Pete Williams cited in *Young Guns Go For It,* BBC 2, 13 Sept. 2000.

38 Reynolds, *Rip It Up and Start Again,* pp. 293–4.

39 Keith Cameron, 'Kevin, Kevin and Kevin go large!', *NME,* 7 Oct. 2000, p. 24.

40 White, *Dexys Midnight Runners,* p. 51; John Aizlewood, 'Bullish', *Q,* Aug. 1996, p. 135. Chairmen of the Board were a Motown-influenced act in the early 1970s (see Phil Hardy and Dave Laing, *The Faber Companion to 20th-century Popular Music* (London: Faber and Faber, 1995, revised edn.), p. 158). Rowland has confirmed that General Johnson was an influence on his singing (see Jim Irvin, 'Regrets? I've had a few', *Mojo,* Sept. 2000, p. 37).

41 Reynolds, *Rip It Up and Start Again,* p. 293; White, *Dexys Midnight Runners,* p. 51.

42 For a discussion of punk and regional accents, see Dave Laing, *One Chord Wonders: Power and Meaning in Punk Rock* (Milton Keynes: Open University Press, 1985), pp. 57–8; Simon Frith, *Music for Pleasure: Essays in the Sociology of Pop* (Cambridge: Polity Press, 1988), p. 127.

43 Aizlewood, 'Bullish', *Q,* Aug. 1996, p. 135.

44 See 'Young soul rebels play Old Vic', *NME,* 31 Oct. 1981, p. 3.

45 Martin, 'Overnight bag sensations', *NME,* 14 June 1980, pp. 28–29.

46 Reynolds, *Rip It Up and Start Again,* p. 293.

47 See Tony Fletcher, 'The wild-hearted outsider: A profile of Kevin Rowland', *Jamming!,* Oct. 1985, p. 20; Stand, 'Hearts full of soul', *The Face,* May 1980, p. 41; Gill Pringle, 'Dexys Midnight Runners', *Record Mirror,* 16 Aug. 1980, p. 30.

48 See, for example, *NME,* 26 July 1980, p. 9; *NME,* 16 Aug. 1980, p. 8; *NME,* 7 Mar. 1981, p. 37.

49 See Aizlewood, 'Bullish', *Q,* Aug. 1996, p. 135; Pearce, *Something Beginning with O,* p. 39; Roberts, 'Stairway to Kevin', *Melody Maker,* 9 Apr. 1988, p. 30; Wilde, 'My story: Kevin Rowland', *Dazed and Confused,* June 1999, p. 5.

50 Johnny Rogan, 'Dexys Midnight Runners', *Record Collector,* Sept. 2000, p. 62; Johnson, 'Dexys' passion runs dry', *NME,* 14 Mar. 1981, p. 3. See also Sutcliffe, 'The dexedrine gang', *Sounds,* 19 Jan. 1980, p. 13; Wilde, 'My story: Kevin Rowland', *Dazed and Confused,* June 1999, pp. 5–6; David Hutcheon, '10 questions for Kevin Rowland', *Mojo,* Oct. 2003, p. 42.

51 For a brief account of Rowland's fasting, see Aizlewood, 'Thankfully not living in Yorkshire', p. 21; Rowland, 'Profile', *Record Mirror,* 17 July 1982, p. 11. For references to the band's renowned tea consumption, see Martin, 'Overnight bag sensations', *NME,* 14 June 1980, pp. 28–9; Stand, 'Hearts full of soul', *The Face,* May 1980, p. 42; Sutcliffe, 'The dexedrine gang', *Sounds,* 19 Jan. 1980, p. 12; Pearce, *Something Beginning with O,* p. 40.

52 *Live in Concert,* BBC Radio 1, 16 Mar. 1983.

53   See Romhany, 'Dexys', *Jamming!*, no. 14 (1983), p. 6; Martin, 'Overnight bag sensations', *NME*, 14 June 1980, p. 29. For the band's use of Italian colours, see the video clip and sleeve art for 'There, There, My Dear' (EMI/Late Night Feelings, 1980). Rowland would later discuss this 'Italian' look (Martin, 'A folk hero of the 80s', *NME*, 3 July 1982, p. 26), and acknowledge its cinematic origins (Phil McNeill, 'Let's get this straight from the start', *The Hit*, 28 Sept. 1985, p. 28; *Young Guns Go For It*, BBC 2, 13 Sept. 2000; *Alexei on Dexys*, BBC Radio 2, 14 Feb. 2004). The singer evidently felt that *Mean Streets* invoked Catholic themes (Rowland, 'Kevin Rowland replies to Julie Burchill', *The Face*, Sept. 1983, p. 63), and *On the Waterfront* features a Catholic priest and characters with Irish names (such as Molloy, Dugan and Doyle). For examples of Rowland's 'Carlo Rolan' persona, see the sleeve art of 'Dance Stance', as well as Carr, 'Dexys', *NME*, 12 Jan. 1980, p. 16; Romhany, 'Dexys', *Jamming!*, no. 14 (1983), p. 6; Aizlewood, 'Bullish', *Q*, Aug. 1996, p. 135. The singer had originally wanted to name himself 'Giorgio Kilkenny' (evoking both Irish and Italian ethnicity) but had been persuaded otherwise. Rowland notes that his dark skin often led to confusion about his ethnicity. 'Because I'm dark, darker than, say, the rest of my family, I've often been taken for different races. Occasionally Irish, but sometimes anything but Irish' (Rowland, interview with the author).

54   Cameron, 'Kevin, Kevin and Kevin go large!', *NME*, 7 Oct. 2000, p. 25; Martin, 'A folk hero of the 80s', *NME*, 3 July 1982, p. 26. As Enda Delaney explains, the image of the 'navvy' – as 'a hard-working and heavy-drinking "rough" and unpredictable character, prone to violence, who refused to settle in any one place' – was 'one of the most enduring in collective memory', and 'dominated perceptions as the ubiquitous "Paddy" or "Mick"' (Delaney, *The Irish in Post-War Britain*, p. 114). For an account of the 'navvy', see Ultan Cowley, *The Men Who Built Britain: A History of the Irish Navvy* (Dublin: Wolfhound Press, 2001).

55   See Sutcliffe, 'The dexedrine gang', *Sounds*, 19 Jan. 1980, p. 13; Martin, 'Overnight bag sensations', *NME*, 14 June 1980, p. 29; Stokes, 'Dexys Midnight Runners', *Hot Press*, 14–28 Aug. 1980, p. 18; Green, 'Dexys Midnight Runners', *Trouser Press*, Nov. 1980, p. 8; Lesley White, 'Fact and fiction', *The Face*, Sept. 1982, p. 34; McNeill, 'A man out of time', *The Hit*, 21 Sept. 1985, p. 14.

56   Anthony J. Chapman, Jean R. Smith and Hugh C. Foot, 'Language, humour and intergroup relations', in Howard Giles (ed.), *Language, Ethnicity and Intergroup Relations* (London: Academic Press, 1977), p. 147. For an account of the 'Irish joke', see Patrick O'Sullivan, 'The Irish joke', in Patrick O'Sullivan (ed.), *The Creative Migrant. The Irish World Wide Series: History, Heritage, Identity. vol. 3* (London: Leicester University Press, 1994), pp. 57–82. As L.P. Curtis explains, anti-Irish prejudice has been 'one of the largest secular trends in English cultural history' (Curtis Jr., *Apes and Angels*, p. 27).

57   Rowland, interview with the author. See also *Alexei on Dexys*, BBC Radio 2, 14 Feb. 2004; Edmund Leach, 'The official Irish jokesters', *New Society*, 'The Books People Buy' section, 20/27 Dec. 1979, pp. vii–ix.

58   Rowland, interview with the author; Shane MacGowan, interview with the author, Royal Garden Hotel, Kensington, 18 Dec. 2006. See also *Alexei on Dexys*, BBC Radio 2, 14 Feb. 2004.

59   It is perhaps worth mentioning that the IRA denied responsibility for this bomb

attack. See Breda Gray, 'From "ethnicity" to "diaspora": 1980s emigration and "multicultural" London', in Andy Bielenberg (ed.), *The Irish Diaspora* (London: Longman, 2000), p. 84.

60   Robert Kee, *Trial and Error: The Maguires, the Guildford Pub Bombings and British Justice* (London: Penguin, 1989, 2nd edn.), p. 50.

61   Kaja Irene Ziesler, 'The Irish in Birmingham, 1830–1970' (unpublished Ph.D. thesis, University of Birmingham, 1989), p. 341.

62   Cited in B.J. Whelan and J.G. Hughes, *EEC Study of Housing Conditions of Migrant Workers: Irish Contribution – A Survey of Returned and Intending Emigrants in Ireland* (Dublin: ESRI, 1976), pp. 43–4.

63   John Gabriel, *Racism, Culture, Markets* (London: Routledge, 1994), p. 85.

64   See, for example, Free, 'Tales from the fifth green field', p. 480.

65   *Second Generation* (RTÉ Radio 1, 13 Jan. 2003). For an account of St Patrick's Day in Britain, see Mike Cronin and Daryl Adair, *The Wearing of the Green: A History of Saint Patrick's Day* (London: Routledge, 2002), pp. 195–9.

66   Sutcliffe, 'The dexedrine gang', *Sounds*, 19 Jan. 1980, p. 13; White, 'Fact and fiction', *The Face*, Sept. 1982, p. 34.

67   Rowland, interview with the author. See also Charles Shaar Murray, 'Tom Jones/ Hammersmith', *NME*, 16 Mar. 1974, p. 43.

68   Aizlewood, 'Bullish', *Q*, Aug. 1996, p. 135.

69   Dick Hebdige notes the 'left-libertarian multiculturalism' of the British music press at this time (see Hebdige, 'Digging for Britain: An excavation in seven parts', in *The British Edge* (Boston: Institute of Contemporary Arts, 1987), p. 44). For an account of politics and the popular music press, see John Street, *Rebel Rock: The Politics of Popular Music* (London: Basil Blackwell, 1986), pp. 83–8.

70   See Alan Lewis, 'Singles', *Sounds*, 7 May 1977, p. 24. For *Sounds*' anti-racism special issue, see Phil Sutcliffe, Caroline Coon, Vivien Goldman, Jon Savage, Pete Silverton, 'It can't happen here', *Sounds*, 25 Mar. 1978, pp. 25–33. For examples of anti-Irish humour, see 'Irish skateboard', *Sounds*, 19 Nov. 1977, p. 55; Sandy Robertson, 'Do you sincerely want to be rich?', *Sounds*, 17 Dec. 1977, p. 17; 'Rat again (like we did last week)', *Sounds*, 8 July 1978, p. 10; Robin Katz, 'Hear the one about a group of Irish superstars …?', *Sounds*, 19 Mar. 1977, p. 28.

71   Leach, 'The official Irish jokesters', *New Society*, 'The Books People Buy' section, 20/27 Dec. 1979, p. vii. Such 'jokes' were a noted source of aggravation for Irish people in Britain. See 'Farewell the Seventies', *Irish Post*, 5 Jan. 1980, p. 1.

72   Leach, 'The official Irish jokesters', *New Society*, 'The Books People Buy' section, 20/27 Dec. 1979, p. viii. Leach maintained that the 'ethnic element' in such jokes was 'latently racist' (p. ix).

73   Curtis, *Nothing But the Same Old Story*, p. 94.

74   Christopher Bagley and Gajendra K. Verma, 'Inter-ethnic attitudes and behaviour in British multi-racial schools', in Gajendra K. Verma and Christopher Bagley (eds.), *Race and Education Across Cultures* (London: Heinemann, 1975), pp. 248–51. See also Michael Stanton, 'Pupils' views of national groups', *Journal of Moral Education*, vol. 1, no. 2 (Feb. 1972), pp. 147–51.

75   See Chris Arnot, 'Marie Gillespie: A good sense of humour', *Guardian*, 'Education' section, 7 Nov. 2006, p. 11; Fleur Britten, 'Siobhan again', *Sunday Times*, 22 Nov. 2009, p. 2.

76 Rowland, interview with the author.

77 Ibid.

78 Martin, 'Overnight bag sensations', *NME*, 14 June 1980, p. 29.

79 White, *Dexys Midnight Runners*, p. 50.

80 Sabina Sharkey, 'A view of the present state of Irish Studies', in Susan Bassnett (ed.), *Studying British Cultures: An Introduction* (London: Routledge, 1997), p. 118.

81 MacGowan, interview with the author.

82 Reynolds, *Rip It Up and Start Again*, p. 296.

83 Sutcliffe, 'The dexedrine gang', *Sounds*, 19 Jan. 1980, p. 13.

84 Green, 'Dexys Midnight Runners', *Trouser Press*, Nov. 1980, p. 8; Stokes, 'Dexys Midnight Runners', *Hot Press*, 14–28 Aug. 1980, p. 18. Later on, Rowland explained: 'What I was saying [in 'Dance Stance'] was that I was having to listen to stupid people in [England] telling me that the Irish are stupid' (McNeill, 'A man out of time', *The Hit*, 21 Sept. 1985, p. 14).

85 White, *Dexys Midnight Runners*, p. 49. See, for example, the Dexys adverts in *NME*, 19 Jan. 1980, p. 18; 26 Jan. 1980, p. 45; 2 Feb. 1980, p. 4; 16 Feb. 1980, p. 20; 15 Mar. 1980, p. 42; 5 Apr. 1980, p. 23; *Sounds*, 22 Mar. 1980; p. 33; *Hot Press*, 17–31 July 1980, p. 11.

86 Stand, 'Hearts full of soul', *The Face*, May 1980, p. 43.

87 The song had originally been written as 'Burn It Down', to which it was later re-titled when it reappeared (in re-recorded form) as the opening track on Dexys' debut album, *Searching for the Young Soul Rebels* (EMI/Late Night Feelings, 1980). 'I suppose it meant "burn down that prejudice"', explains Rowland of the alternate title, noting that it was borrowed from an earlier song of the same name by Roger Chapman (Rowland, interview with the author).

88 White, *Dexys Midnight Runners*, pp. 54, 205.

89 For an account of Two Tone, see Dick Hebdige, *Cut 'n' Mix: Culture, Identity and Caribbean Music* (London: Comedia, 1987), pp. 106–14.

90 Reynolds, *Rip It Up and Start Again*, p. 289. For a discussion of Two Tone and anti-racism, see *Two Tone Britain*, Channel 4, 29 Nov. 2004.

91 Richard Eddington, *Sent From Coventry: The Chequered Past of Two Tone* (London: Independent Music Press, 2004), pp. 112–15; Reynolds, *Rip It Up and Start Again*, p. 289.

92 Simon Frith, 'The Specials/The Selecter/Dexys Midnight Runners', *Melody Maker*, 8 Dec. 1979, p. 36. For Dexys' relationship with Two Tone, see George Marshall, *The Two Tone Story* (Glasgow: Zoot, 1990), p. 30; Rogan, 'Dexys Midnight Runners', *Record Collector*, Sept. 2000, p. 61. The group failed to sign to Two Tone. 'We didn't want to become part of anyone else's movement', explained Rowland. 'We'd rather be our own movement' (Carr, 'Dexys', *NME*, 12 Jan. 1980, p. 16).

93 Johnny Rogan, 'Dexys Midnight Runners, *Searching for the Young Soul Rebels*', *Mojo*, Sept. 2000, p. 112. For details of the release of 'Dance Stance', see White, *Dexys Midnight Runners*, p. 49.

94 Pete Saunders cited in White, *Dexys Midnight Runners*, p. 49.

95 Eddington, *Sent From Coventry*, p. 119.

96 See White, *Dexys Midnight Runners*, p. 50.

97 Stokes, 'Dexys Midnight Runners', *Hot Press*, 14–28 Aug. 1980, p. 18.

98   Ibid., original emphasis. For an account of the word 'Paki', see Nabeel Zuberi, '"The last truly British people you will ever know": Skinheads, Pakis and Morrissey', in Henry Jenkins, Tara McPherson and Jane Shattuc (eds.), *Hop on Pop: The Politics and Pleasures of Popular Culture* (Durham: Duke University Press, 2002), p. 542.

99   See Hickman et al., 'The limitations of whiteness', p. 175.

100   O'Riordan, interview with the author.

101   Rowland, interview with the author.

102   Ibid.

103   Ibid.

104   Aizlewood, 'Thankfully not living in Yorkshire', p. 24.

105   Dave Simpson, 'The kindness of strangers', *Guardian*, 'Film and Music' section, 24 Aug. 2007, p. 10. It is interesting to note that the release of 'Dance Stance' coincided with the announcement of the Sense of Ireland festival, a major cultural initiative in 1980 that sought to 'demonstrate in Britain the depth and strength of Ireland's heritage and contemporary culture', and make 'a significant contribution to improving understanding and relations between the peoples of these islands' ('A Sense of Ireland', *Irish Post*, 17 Nov. 1979, p. 9). It was also hoped that this event would attract significant numbers of second-generation Irish, to whom it could offer 'answers to intellectual and identity questions which, consciously or unconsciously, are prevalent' ('Ireland now', *Irish Post*, 26 Jan. 1980, p. 4).

106   See, for example, Julie Burchill, 'Julie Burchill', *The Face*, Mar. 1983, p. 68; Julie Burchill, 'Greeneland revisited', *The Face*, Aug. 1983, pp. 62–65.

107   Lindsay Shapero, 'Red devil', *Time Out*, 17–23 May 1984, p. 27. The expression of noxious comments has been a key aspect of Burchill's work. Nevertheless, it is significant that such a high-profile journalist has, on several occasions, attacked the Irish in this way.

108   Burchill, 'Julie Burchill', *The Face*, Mar. 1983, p. 68. For an account of Ireland's neutrality during the Second World War, see Clare Wills, *That Neutral Island: A Cultural History of Ireland During the Second World War* (London: Faber and Faber, 2007).

109   Burchill, 'Greeneland revisited', *The Face*, Aug. 1983, p. 64. For a more informed account of the 'dirty protest', see Allen Feldman, *Formations of Violence: The Narrative of the Body and Political Terror in Northern Ireland* (Chicago: University of Chicago Press, 1991), pp. 147–217. Brendan O'Leary observes that the IRA of this period were generally not 'pious believers' in Catholicism, and were 'less overtly and traditionally Catholic' than previous generations of volunteers. See O'Leary, 'Mission accomplished? Looking back at the IRA', *Field Day Review*, no. 1 (Dublin: Field Day Publications, 2005), p. 226.

110   Burchill, 'Greeneland revisited', *The Face*, Aug. 1983, p. 64. The Catholic Church had excommunicated members of the IRA before the post-1969 Troubles, and continued to condemn IRA actions in the following period. The Provisional IRA would, in turn, ignore Church advice, whether from bishops or the Pope. If excommunications did not continue in the post-1969 period, this was partly informed by the fact that they had previously been counterproductive. For a discussion of this point, see Marianne Elliott, *The Catholics of Ulster: A History* (London: Allen Lane, 2000), pp. 471–2; O'Leary, 'Mission accomplished?', pp. 221, 226.

111   Rowland, interview with the author.

112 Rowland, 'Kevin Rowland replies to Julie Burchill', *The Face*, Sept. 1983, p. 63. Rowland's letter would, in turn, prompt ill-tempered reactions from Burchill and her then partner, Tony Parsons. See Julie Burchill, 'Thermometer 3', *The Face*, Oct. 1983, p. 47; Tony Parsons, 'Letters', *The Face*, Oct. 1983, p. 78.

113 See, for example, Kevin Rowland, 'A day full of Dexys', *Melody Maker*, 21 Nov. 1981, p. 29; Colin Irwin, 'The other side of midnight', *Melody Maker*, 3 July 1982, p. 18; Pearce, *Something Beginning with O*, p. 43.

114 Rowland cited in *Young Guns Go For It*, BBC 2, 13 Sept. 2000.

115 Dave McCullough, 'The return of Kevin Rowland', *Sounds*, 24 July 1982, p. 27.

116 Both tracks appear on *Too-Rye-Ay* (Mercury, 1982).

117 White, *Dexys Midnight Runners*, p. 112; Martin, 'A folk hero of the 80s', *NME*, 3 July 1982, p. 26. Rowland confirmed, at the time, that Catholicism had informed his song lyrics (see Mackey, 'The leader of the band', *Hot Press*, 8–23 Oct. 1982, p. 18).

118 For an account of Irish stereotypes in British popular culture, see Curtis, *Nothing But the Same Old Story*.

119 McIlheney, 'Burning the midnight oil', *Melody Maker*, 2 Nov. 1985, p. 19.

120 Rowland, interview with the author.

121 See, for example, J.M. Flood, *Ireland: Its Saints and Scholars* (Dublin: Talbot Press, 1917).

122 Dexys Midnight Runners, 'Geno', *Sounds*, 22 Mar. 1980, p. 33. Behan, an Irish playwright and novelist, was born in Dublin in 1923 and died in 1964. He was publicly associated with Irish republicanism, and had a reputation for heavy drinking. For an account of Behan's life, see Ulick O'Connor, *Brendan Behan* (London: Hamish Hamilton, 1970).

123 See Rowland, 'Profile', *Record Mirror*, 17 July 1982, p. 11. 'Reminisce Part One' appeared on the B-side of the re-released 'Celtic Soul Brothers' single (Mercury, 1983). The song lyrics for this track seem to have been informed by a visit that Rowland made to Dublin in 1980 (see Stokes, 'Dexys Midnight Runners', *Hot Press*, 14–28 Aug. 1980, p. 18).

124 See David Quantick, 'The quare fellow', *NME*, 24 Mar. 1984, p. 52.

125 See Victoria Mary Clarke and Shane MacGowan, *A Drink with Shane MacGowan* (London: Sidgwick & Jackson, 2001), p. 215.

126 Stuart Cosgrove and Sean O'Hagan, 'Gael force: Two nations under a groove – an A to Z of partisan pop', *NME*, 2 May 1987, p. 30.

127 See Aizlewood, 'Thankfully not living in Yorkshire', p. 21; Johnson, 'Dexys' passion runs dry', *NME*, 14 Mar. 1981, p. 3; Rowland, 'Profile', *Record Mirror*, 17 July 1982, p. 11.

128 Behan's best-known work, *Borstal Boy* (London: Hutchinson, 1958), details the writer's experience in England.

129 Niall Cunningham, 'Celebrate all that makes us distinct', *Irish Post*, 3 June 2000, p. 12.

130 Kathy Burke, 'Kathy comes home', *Observer*, 'Review' section, 1 Feb. 2004, p. 5.

131 Rowland, interview with the author.

132 Ibid.; Kevin Rowland, 'Inside track', *Uncut*, Oct. 2000, p. 100.

133 *Saturday Live*, BBC Radio 4, 21 Apr. 2007. Although most journalists have assumed that the photo was taken when the British army arrived in Belfast in

1969 (see Aizlewood, 'Thankfully not living in Yorkshire', p. 23; Gavin Martin, 'Anarchic in the UK', *Uncut,* Oct. 2000, p. 100), O'Shaughnessy recalls that it was shot during internment in 1971.

134 *Saturday Live,* BBC Radio 4, 21 Apr. 2007; Aizlewood, 'Thankfully not living in Yorkshire', p. 23.

135 Brah suggests that 'at the heart of the notion of diaspora is the image of a journey' (Brah, *Cartographies of Diaspora: Contesting Identities* (London: Routledge, 1996), p. 182).

136 See *Searching for the Young Soul Rebels,* 'There, There, My Dear', 'Keep It Part Two (Inferiority Part One)' (EMI/Late Night Feelings, 1980); *Too-Rye-Ay,* 'Jackie Wilson Said' (Mercury, 1982); 'This Is What She's Like' (Mercury, 1985); *Intense Emotion Review* tour programme (1980). For press adverts, see *NME,* 5 Apr. 1980, p. 23. For an evocation of this theme in the work of second-generation Irish visual artists, see Marion Urch, *The Long Road* (Kent Institute of Art & Design, 1991).

137 For the video of 'Geno', see *Searching for the Young Soul Rebels* (EMI CD, 2000). For the videos of 'Celtic Soul Brothers' (1982) and 'Come On Eileen' (1982), see *Too-Rye-Ay* (Mercury CD, 2000). For the video of 'Knowledge Of Beauty' (1985) (re-titled as 'My National Pride'), see *Don't Stand Me Down: The Director's Cut* (EMI CD, 2002).

138 See White, *Dexys Midnight Runners,* p. 123.

139 For a theoretical elaboration of this point, see Morley and Robins, 'No place like *heimat*', pp. 3–31.

140 Rowland, interview with the author.

141 Ibid.

142 Delaney, *The Irish in Post-War Britain,* p. 170. For an account of London's Irish social clubs, see Catherine Dunne, *An Unconsidered People: The Irish in London* (Dublin: New Island, 2003).

143 See White, *Dexys Midnight Runners,* p. 61.

144 Rowland, interview with the author. For a schedule of contemporaneous events at the National Ballroom, see *Irish Post,* 2 Aug. 1980, p. 19; *Irish Post,* 9 Aug. 1980, p. 19. Although it later became known as a rock venue, and hosted shows by The Pogues and The Smiths (Danny Kelly, 'Triumph of the swill', *NME,* 20/27 Dec. 1986, p. 49; Johnny Rogan, *Morrissey and Marr: The Severed Alliance* (London: Omnibus Press, 1992), p. 332), Dexys were the first mainstream music act to play at the National Ballroom. See also White, *Dexys Midnight Runners,* p. 81.

145 See *Irish Post,* 26 July 1980, p. 19; Paulo Hewitt, 'Cheapo, Dexys!', *Melody Maker,* 16 Aug. 1980, p. 16; 'Tour news', *Melody Maker,* 26 July 1980, p. 4.

146 Dexys Midnight Runners, *Intense Emotion Review.*

147 Rowland, interview with the author.

148 Ibid.

149 Ibid.; Hewitt, 'Cheapo, Dexys!', *Melody Maker,* 16 Aug. 1980, p. 16.

150 Rowland, interview with the author.

151 Ibid.

152 Ibid.

153 Ibid.

154 Reynolds, *Rip It Up and Start Again,* p. 296.

155 Dexys Midnight Runners, *Intense Emotion Review.*

156 Rowland, interview with the author.

157 Ibid.

158 Ibid.

159 Ibid. The short-lived second line-up of Dexys that emerged in 1981 (and which is often seen as Dexys Mark II) failed to record an album or perform a major tour, and, thus, the subsequent (and more productive and successful) incarnation that emerged in 1982 is a more significant second phase (for an account of this period, see White, *Dexys Midnight Runners*, pp. 82–109).

160 Rowland, interview with the author.

161 'Celtic Soul Brothers' (Mercury, 1982). Whilst marking a clear change of direction, this title also implied continuity with Dexys' past, recalling the 'Young Soul Rebels' of their debut album.

162 See Irwin, 'The other side of midnight', *Melody Maker*, 3 July 1982, p. 18; Sunie, 'Singles', *Record Mirror*, 13 Mar. 1982, p. 14; Phil McNeill, 'Gift from a flower to a garden', *NME*, 31 July 1982, p. 27. Critics observed that the band's new instrumentation (of '[f]iddles, tenor banjo and vamping piano') was 'more normally associated with Irish traditional dance music' (Dermot Stokes, 'Singles', *Hot Press*, 30 July–12 Aug. 1982, p. 20).

163 Allan F. Moore, *Rock: The Primary Text. Developing a Musicology of Rock* (Buckingham: Open University Press, 1993), pp. 146–53.

164 For an account of synth-pop, see Moore, *Rock: The Primary Text*, pp. 133–6.

165 See Vivien Goldman, 'WOMAD', *NME*, 24 July 1982, pp. 18–21; Moore, *Rock: The Primary Text*, p. 150.

166 See 'UK singles', *NME*, 7 Nov. 1981, p. 2; 'UK Singles', *NME*, 20 Nov. 1982, p. 2.

167 See *The Great Hunger: The Life and Songs of Shane MacGowan*, BBC 2, 4 Oct. 1997.

168 Gary Hurr, 'The Dexys soul-ution', *Record Mirror*, 19 June 1982, p. 9; Dave McCullough, 'Morrison at midnight', *Sounds*, 24 July 1982, p. 30. Elsewhere, the project was seen as a 'warm and welcome antidote to the overdressed refrigeration of the dominant synth bands' (Dermot Stokes, '82 45s', *Hot Press*, 16 Dec. 1982, p. 15). It is also worth noting here the influence of Rowland's former collaborator, Kevin Archer, who had played the singer a demo tape (in late 1981) of some of his own songs, which featured a piano with violins. This combination of instruments evidently played a part in Rowland's formulation of the *Too-Rye-Ay* sound. 'I was influenced by his sound, I put that into the mix', the singer explains, noting: 'I was more influenced than I should've been by that combination of instruments' (Rowland, interview with the author). In this context, the singer made belated financial and public gestures towards his former band-mate. See Phil Sutcliffe, 'This is my confession', *Q*, Aug. 1993, p. 30; Cameron, 'Kevin, Kevin and Kevin go large!', *NME*, 7 Oct. 2000, p. 25.

169 Adrian Thrills, 'In search of the passion patrol', *NME*, 24 Sept. 1983, p. 28.

170 Ibid. p. 13, original emphasis. For an account of 'Celtic' music, see Martin Stokes and Philip V. Bohlman (eds.), *Celtic Modern: Music at the Global Fringe* (Lanham, MD: Scarecrow Press, 2003).

171 Van Morrison, *Beautiful Vision* (Mercury, 1982). For a contemporary review of the album, see Paul Du Noyer, 'Van still the man', *NME*, 6 Mar. 1982, p. 33.

172 Rowland, interview with the author.

173 Ibid. See Van Morrison, 'You Don't Pull No Punches, But You Don't Push The River', *Veedon Fleece* (Warner Brothers, 1974).

174 Rowland, interview with the author.

175 Although this song, which was included on the *Beautiful Vision* album, was not released until February 1982 (the month in which Dexys recorded 'Celtic Soul Brothers'), Rowland seems to have had access to an advance copy of the album through his record label, to which Morrison was also signed (Rowland, interview with the author).

176 Ibid.

177 Marr, interview with the author. This seems to have been especially true of the band's new attire, which coincided with an increasing interest in 'primitivist' styles. See Claire Wilcox, *Vivienne Westwood* (London: V&A Publications, 2004), pp. 17, 57–61.

178 See Paul Gilroy, *'There Ain't No Black in the Union Jack': The Cultural Politics of Race and Nation* (London: Hutchinson, 1987), pp. 51–9, 72–113. The unrest of 1981 received a significant amount of attention in the music press. See, for example, Paul Du Noyer, 'The burning of Southall', *NME*, 11 July 1981, p. 3; Ray Lowry and Chris Salewicz, 'Anarchy in the UK: The reality', *NME*, 18 July 1981, pp. 4–5.

179 Greil Marcus, 'Elvis Costello explains himself', *Rolling Stone*, 2 Sept. 1982, p. 15.

180 For a discussion of this context, see Tim Pat Coogan, *The IRA* (London: HarperCollins, 2000, revised edn.), pp. 486–501, 513–14.

181 Terence Morris, 'The divisions that will welcome a Pope', *Guardian*, 28 May 1982, p. 15. See also Terry Eagleton, *The Gatekeeper: A Memoir* (London: Allen Lane, 2001), p. 11.

182 'The Pope amid the ferment', *Guardian*, 28 May 1982, p. 14.

183 Martin McLoone, *Irish Film: The Emergence of a Contemporary Cinema* (London: British Film Institute, 2000), p. 60. For the cartoon in question, see Jak, 'The Irish: The ultimate in psychopathic horror', *Standard*, 29 Oct. 1982, p. 6. See *'The Sun says'*, *The Sun*, 26 May 1982, p. 6.

184 *Young Guns Go For It*, BBC 2, 13 Sept. 2000.

185 See *The Great Hunger: The Life and Songs of Shane MacGowan*, BBC 2, 4 Oct. 1997; Scanlon, *The Pogues*, p. 8.

186 Rowland, interview with the author.

187 Rolston, '"This is not a rebel song"', p. 53. Van Morrison would make a similar point about London in the 1960s: 'if you were Irish', he explained, 'you were fucked. You were just Paddy. Even if you were a rock star!' (Victoria Clarke, 'The hardest thinking man in showbiz', *Q*, Aug. 1993, p. 64).

188 'Celtic Soul Brothers' was originally released in March 1982, when its failure to enter the top 40 'left the group crestfallen' (White, *Dexys Midnight Runners*, pp. 118, 206).

189 See White, 'Fact and fiction', *The Face*, Sept. 1982, p. 34; McCullough, 'The return of Kevin Rowland', *Sounds*, 24 July 1982, p. 26. Rowland explained: 'I don't think "Too-Rye-Aye" [*sic*] is *that* traditional Irish music influenced! It's not folk music' (McCullough, 'The return of Kevin Rowland', *Sounds*, 24 July 1982, p. 26).

190 See McCullough, 'The return of Kevin Rowland', *Sounds*, 24 July 1982, p. 26.

191 Martin, 'A folk hero of the 80s', *NME*, 3 July 1982, p. 26; White, 'Fact and fiction',

The Face, Sept. 1982, p. 34; Jim Green, 'This man believes', *Trouser Press*, May 1983, p. 28.

192   This appeared in the sleeve notes of the original 1982 release.

193   Mark Ellen, 'Midnight express', *Smash Hits*, 22 July–4 Aug. 1982, p. 40.

194   Price, 'A dark knight of the soul', *Independent*, 'Friday Review' section, 5 Apr. 2002, p. 15; Rowland, interview with the author. For a contemporaneous ethnography of the second-generation Irish, see Ullah, 'Second-generation Irish youth', pp. 310–20.

195   McNeill, 'A man out of time', *The Hit*, 21 Sept. 1985, p. 14. See also the sleeve notes for the first reissue of *Don't Stand Me Down* (Creation CD, 1996).

196   Rowland, interview with the author.

197   McCullough, 'The return of Kevin Rowland', *Sounds*, 24 July 1982, p. 27. See, for example, *The Tube*, Channel 4, 18 Mar. 1983. The band's performance had been recorded (but not broadcast) for an earlier edition of the show in December 1982. As part of its minority remit, Channel 4 took a special interest in Irish affairs, paying 'particular attention to the interests of the Irish community in Britain' (Stephen Lambert, *Channel Four: Television with a Difference?* (London: British Film Institute, 1982), p. 145).

198   Rowland, interview with the author.

199   See Hewitt, 'Keeping up', *Melody Maker*, 7 Aug. 1982, p. 21; Romhany, 'Dexys', *Jamming!*, no. 14 (1983), p. 6.

200   For an account of Celticism, see Deane, *Celtic Revivals*, pp. 17–27. I do not wish to suggest that Dexys' 'Celtic' persona was self-consciously derived from Celticist discourses – rather, that it seemed indebted to them.

201   See Terence Brown, *Ireland's Literature: Selected Essays* (Dublin: Lilliput Press, 1988), p. 7; Martin Stokes and Philip V. Bohlman, 'Introduction', in Stokes and Bohlman, *Celtic Modern*, p. 1.

202   This sensibility had perhaps been foreshadowed by the title of an earlier Dexys' B-side, an instrumental called '… And Yes, We Must Remain The Wild Hearted Outsiders' ('Liars A To E' (Mercury, 1981)). For an account of popular 'street singing' and the Irish in nineteenth-century Britain, see Phil Eva, 'Home sweet home? The "culture of exile" in mid-Victorian popular song', *Popular Music*, vol. 16, no. 2 (1997), pp. 145–9.

203   Gavin Martin, 'Mahone ranger's handbook', *NME*, 13 Aug. 1983, p. 22.

204   O'Riordan, interview with the author.

205   See Don Watson (ed.), 'Gasbag', *NME*, 3 Sept. 1983, p. 42.

206   This assignation appears in the sleeve notes of the original 1982 release of 'Celtic Soul Brothers'. In a similar vein, Steve Shaw was renamed Brennan and Mick Gallick became Giorgio Kilkenny. See White, *Dexys Midnight Runners*, pp. 108, 115–16.

207   Ian O'Doherty, *Shane MacGowan: Last of the Celtic Soul Rebels* (Dublin: Blackwater Press, 1994), pp. 72–3.

208   Mike Nicholls, 'Fiddler's dream', *Record Mirror*, 31 July 1982, p. 21. Other critics discerned 'evidence' of 'a sort of ponderous humour at play' (see Sunie, 'Singles', *Record Mirror*, 13 Mar. 1982, p. 14). For an account of 'authenticity' in popular music, see Kier Keightley, 'Reconsidering rock', in Simon Frith, Will Straw and John Street (eds.), *The Cambridge Companion to Pop and Rock* (Cambridge: Cambridge University Press, 2001), pp. 131–9.

209   Rowland, interview with the author.

210   Hewitt, 'Keeping up', *Melody Maker*, 7 Aug. 1982, p. 21; *Alexei on Dexys*, BBC Radio 2, 14 Feb. 2004.

211   McCullough, 'The return of Kevin Rowland', *Sounds*, 24 July 1982, p. 26; Hewitt, 'Keeping up', *Melody Maker*, 7 Aug. 1982, p. 21. 'Come On Eileen' became the best-selling single of 1982, reaching no. 1 in the UK and later the US (Fletcher, 'The wild-hearted outsider', *Jamming!*, Oct. 1985, p. 21).

212   Hewitt, 'Keeping up', *Melody Maker*, 7 Aug. 1982, p. 21; McCullough, 'The return of Kevin Rowland', *Sounds*, 24 July 1982, p. 26.

213   Max Bell, 'Kevin Rowland', *SFX*, 12–24 Aug. 1982, emphases added.

214   Wilde, 'My story: Kevin Rowland', *Dazed and Confused*, June 1999, p. 6.

215   *Alexei on Dexys*, BBC Radio 2, 14 Feb. 2004; 'Anderson's people', *Irish Post*, 2 Oct. 1982, p. 20; Rowland, 'Profile', *Record Mirror*, 17 July 1982, p. 11. Although it would seem that 'Eileen McClusky' was a fictionalised name, the song was nevertheless based on Rowland's encounter with an actual girl (Rowland, interview with the author).

216   'Come On Eileen' (Old Gold, 1989).

217   Martin, 'A folk hero of the 80s', *NME*, 3 July 1982, p. 53. Previously, the singer had explained that the 'fundamental idea' of Dexys was '*change-change-change*' (Stokes, 'Dexys Midnight Runners', *Hot Press*, 14–28 Aug. 1980, p. 19), and critics have noted that 'constant reinvention' was the band's 'raison d'être' (Alexis Petridis, 'Electro-pop? New folk, you mean', *Guardian*, 'Film and Music' section, 22 Feb. 2008, p. 14). Rowland has made clear his desire to distance himself from his stage persona, noting that throughout his work with Dexys he liked to 'put on a show' (adding that this was informed by his fondness for Irish showbands, which he had seen in both Ireland and England, and which – he points out – often had brass sections). In this context, the singer was keen to maintain a distinction between his 'actual' and 'stage' selves, and often wished that he had performed under a stage name. 'One thing I did think it would do was give me a distance between what I was doing and myself. I could see that having a separate name, like a character, would separate me from it. I thought that was actually quite a good idea. So that I wouldn't feel it necessarily, if anything negative happened. I could separate it and leave it there and come home and be me' (Rowland, interview with the author).

218   These profiles appeared in the sleeve notes of the single's 1983 re-release.

219   See Dexys Midnight Runners, *The Bridge* (Spectrum Video, 1983), which features the band's performance at London's Shaftesbury Theatre in October 1982. For Dexys' preference for old-fashioned theatres, see 'Young soul rebels play Old Vic', *NME*, 31 Oct. 1981, p. 3; 'Cap'n Kevin on the bridge', *NME*, 11 Sept. 1982, p. 3; Aizlewood, 'Bullish', *Q*, Aug. 1996, p. 135. For an account of the *Too-Rye-Ay* live show, see Jim Shelley, 'Kevin Rowland and Dexys Midnight Runners', *Smash Hits*, 14–27 Oct. 1982, p. 53.

220   'Young soul rebels play Old Vic', *NME*, 31 Oct. 1981, p. 3.

221   These quotes are taken from Richard White, Cáit O'Riordan, Phil McNeil and Paul Speare, respectively. See White, *Dexys Midnight Runners*, p. 118; O'Riordan, interview with the author; McNeill, 'Gift from a flower to a garden', *NME*, 31 July 1982, p. 27; Speare cited in White, *Dexys Midnight Runners*, p. 117. See also Sunie, 'Singles', *Record Mirror*, 13 Mar. 1982, p. 14.

222   See White, *Dexys Midnight Runners*, p. 131; Colin Irwin, 'Stand and deliver', *Melody Maker*, 7 Sept. 1985, p. 32; Shelley, 'Kevin Rowland and Dexys Midnight Runners', *Smash Hits*, 14–27 Oct. 1982, p. 53; MacGowan cited in Scanlon, *The Pogues*, p. 9.

223   Marr, interview with the author.

224   Martin, 'Mahone ranger's handbook', *NME*, 13 Aug. 1983, p. 22.

225   Colin Irwin, 'A parcel of rogues', *Southern Rag*, 1 Oct.–31 Dec. 1982, p. 11; Irwin, 'The other side of midnight', *Melody Maker*, 3 July 1982, p. 18.

226   Rowland, interview with the author.

227   Green, 'This man believes', *Trouser Press*, May 1983, p. 28.

228   'Anderson's people', *Irish Post*, 2 Oct. 1982, p. 20; Reynolds, *Rip It Up and Start Again*, p. 302. Rowland has explained that he 'really wanted', at this time, to have 'mainstream success' (Wilde, 'My story: Kevin Rowland', *Dazed and Confused*, June 1999, p. 6), and noted – during the *Too-Rye-Ay* tour – the 'real cross-section' of the band's new audience (Mackey, 'The leader of the band', *Hot Press*, 8–23 Oct. 1982, p. 16). For an example of the *Too-Rye-Ay* live shows, see Dexys Midnight Runners, *The Bridge* (Spectrum Video, 1983).

229   Mackey, 'The leader of the band', *Hot Press*, 8–23 Oct. 1982, pp. 16–17.

230   Richard Middleton, *Studying Popular Music* (Milton Keynes: Open University Press, 1990), p. 9. For examples of Pogues gigs, see *The Great Hunger: The Life and Songs of Shane MacGowan*, BBC 2, 4 Oct. 1997; *The Pogues: Completely Pogued* (Start Video, 1988).

231   Rowland, interview with the author.

232   Ibid.

233   See Paul Evers, 'Dexys Midnight Runners', *Oor*, 17 Nov. 1982, p. 29; Dexys Midnight Runners, *The Bridge* (Spectrum Video, 1983).

234   For a brief discussion of this point, see Smyth, 'Who's the greenest of them all?', p. 5.

235   Bell, 'Kevin Rowland', *SFX*, 12–24 Aug. 1982.

236   Although the song was performed (as 'Burn It Down') at the band's first *Too-Rye-Ay* show (a BBC radio concert in Newcastle in June 1982), it is absent from all other known set-lists from that tour (see White, *Dexys Midnight Runners*, pp. 212–15). In fairness to Rowland, the vast bulk of rock musicians have, as Rolston explains, found it difficult to deal with Irish politics within the confines of pop's generic frame. See Rolston, '"This is not a rebel song"', p. 64.

237   Rowland, interview with the author.

238   Ibid.

239   For a brief elaboration of this binary, see Gerry Smyth, 'The isle is full of noises: Music in contemporary Ireland', *Irish Studies Review*, vol. 12, no. 1 (Apr. 2004), pp. 4–5.

240   Harry White, *The Keeper's Recital: Music and Cultural History in Ireland, 1770–1970* (Cork: Cork University Press, 1998), pp. 43–4. The Moore song was evidently a particular favourite of Rowland's mother (see Mackey, 'The leader of the band', *Hot Press*, 8–23 Oct. 1982, p. 17).

241   Leith Davis, 'Irish bards and English consumers: Thomas Moore's "Irish Melodies" and the colonized nation', *Ariel: A Review of International English Literature*, vol. 24, no. 2 (Apr. 1993), pp. 7, 15.

242 See Martin, 'Mahone ranger's handbook', *NME*, 13 Aug. 1983, p. 22.

243 Liner notes, *Too-Rye-Ay* deluxe edn. (Mercury CD, 2007).

244 Rowland, interview with the author.

245 Liner notes, *Too-Rye-Ay* deluxe edn.

246 Rowland, interview with the author.

247 See McCullough, 'The return of Kevin Rowland', *Sounds*, 24 July 1982, p. 27; Nat Shapiro, *An Encyclopedia of Quotations About Music* (Newton Abbot: David & Charles, 1978), p. 263.

248 For Rowland's account of the Doonican reference, see Neil Warburton, 'It Was August 1997 ...', *Keep on Running*, no. 9 (Oct. 1997), no pagination. The band performed 'Kathleen Mavourneen' on their 1985 concert tour and on a televised set for *The Tube*, Channel 4, 11 Oct. 1985. See White, *Dexys Midnight Runners*, pp. 173, 215. This song was eventually released as the B-side of their final single, 'Because Of You'. Like the Moore song cited above, 'Kathleen Mavourneen' was a favourite of Rowland's mother (see Mackey, 'The leader of the band', *Hot Press*, 8–23 Oct. 1982, p. 17).

249 See, for example, Martin, 'Mahone ranger's handbook', *NME*, 13 Aug. 1983, p. 22; O'Riordan, interview with the author.

250 McNeill, 'A man out of time', *The Hit*, 21 Sept. 1985, p. 14.

251 Mackey, 'The leader of the band', *Hot Press*, 8–23 Oct. 1982, p. 17.

252 See Eva, 'Home sweet home?', p. 135.

253 Price, 'A dark knight of the soul', *Independent*, 'Friday Review' section, 5 Apr. 2002, p. 15; Rowland cited in White, *Dexys Midnight Runners*, p. 131.

254 Davis, 'Irish bards and English consumers', pp. 16–17, 23.

255 Gray, 'From "ethnicity" to "diaspora"', p. 71. Such was the extent of Livingstone's affiliation with the Irish community – and particularly with Irish Catholics – that he became the alleged target of an assassination plot by Loyalist paramilitaries (see Keith Dovkants, 'My plot to assassinate Ken Livingstone on the Tube', *Evening Standard*, 1 Nov. 2006, pp. 10–11).

256 'Jak cartoon "typical of the gutter press"', *Irish Post*, 4 Dec. 1982, p. 9; Ray Burke, 'GLC seeks assurance on Irish voting rights', *Irish Post*, 4 Dec. 1982, p. 9.

257 Rowland has confirmed that it was Livingstone's address to Irish issues that led to the reference in the song. 'Again, it's wanting to tell English people about Ireland', he suggests (Rowland, interview with the author).

258 I take this term 'suspect community' from Paddy Hillyard. See Hillyard, *Suspect Community: People's Experience of the Prevention of Terrorism Acts in Britain* (London: Pluto Press, 1993).

259 As Catherine Dunne has explained, The Crown (which is located in the Cricklewood district of London) was a focal point for Irish labourers seeking work. See Dunne, *An Unconsidered People*, p. 11. Such was the extent of The Crown's association with the immigrant Irish that The Pogues would later host press interviews there. See, for example, Robert Elms, 'Pogue in the eye', *The Face*, Mar. 1985, pp. 30–32, 35.

260 Rowland, interview with the author.

261 Ibid.; Rowland, 'Profile', *Record Mirror*, 17 July 1982, p. 11.

262 Rowland, interview with the author.

263 Chris Roberts, 'Grand stand', *Uncut*, May 2002, p. 76. 'I wanted to get back to

something more meaningful, deeper', Rowland explains (Rowland, interview with the author).

264   Roberts, 'Grand stand', *Uncut*, May 2002, p. 76.

265   Seamus Heaney, *Finders Keepers: Selected Prose, 1971–2001* (London: Faber and Faber, 2002), p. 368. For a discussion of this period, see Coogan, *The IRA*, pp. 514–16.

266   Dermot Stokes, 'The long run', *Hot Press*, 10 Oct. 1985, p. 23.

267   Irwin, 'Stand and deliver', *Melody Maker*, 7 Sept. 1985, p. 32; Price, 'A dark knight of the soul', *Independent*, 'Friday Review' section, 5 Apr. 2002, p. 15. See Roberts, 'Grand stand', *Uncut*, May 2002, p. 76.

268   Rowland, interview with the author. Kevin Kelly, *The Longest War: Northern Ireland and the IRA* (Dingle: Brandon, 1982); Eamonn McCann, *War and an Irish Town* (Harmondsworth: Penguin, 1974). As Ullah explains, The Wolfe Tones' 'emotive accounts of the historical struggle for Irish freedom' have been 'very popular with the second generation Irish' (Ullah, 'Rhetoric and ideology in social identification: The case of second generation Irish youths', *Discourse and Society*, vol. 1, no. 2 (1990), p. 179). Interestingly, Noel and Liam Gallagher (of Oasis) would later express their fondness for this band. See Hewitt, *Getting High*, p. 15; *Right Here, Right Now*, BBC 1, 20 Aug. 1997.

269   Rowland, interview with the author.

270   Ibid.

271   Ibid. The singer says that he felt 'very bad' that the planned concert did not take place.

272   The singer's painstaking efforts in this regard meant that *DSMD* far exceeded the album's original budget and scheduled release dates. See White, *Dexys Midnight Runners*, pp. 147–70. In this context, critics claimed that it was 'one of the most expensive albums ever recorded' (Fletcher, 'The wild-hearted outsider', *Jamming!*, Oct. 1985, p. 21).

273   David Hutcheon, 'Rides up with wear', *Mojo*, May 2002, p. 118; Roberts, 'Grand stand', *Uncut*, May 2002, p. 76; Daryl Easlea, 'Don't stand me down', *Record Collector*, Apr. 2002, p. 51. It is worth noting, though, that the album was not restricted to Irish themes. 'I wasn't doing an all-out Irish thing with *Don't Stand Me Down*', the singer explains. 'It was never my intention to do an all-out Irish thing … although there's a lot of that in there' (Rowland, interview with the author).

274   McNeill, 'A man out of time', *The Hit*, 21 Sept. 1985, p. 14; Cross, 'Status quo? Great!', *Record Mirror*, 30 Nov. 1985, p. 55.

275   McNeill, 'A man out of time', *The Hit*, 21 Sept. 1985, p. 14.

276   See, for example, McIlheney, 'Burning the midnight oil', *Melody Maker*, 2 Nov. 1985, pp. 18–19, 45. Such questioning did not catch Rowland unawares. 'I did anticipate that: "Who are you, to say you're Irish?" And that's what came up, really' (Rowland, interview with the author).

277   McIlheney, 'Burning the midnight oil', *Melody Maker*, 2 Nov. 1985, p. 19. Rowland's comment here offers an ironic inversion of the quote famously attributed to the Duke of Wellington, who disassociated himself from his Irish birthplace by suggesting: 'A man is not a horse because he happens to have been born in a stable' (cited in Henry Gerald Hope, untitled, *Notes and Queries*, s7–ix (Jan.–June 1890),

p. 336). Rowland explains that his father had passed this expression on to him when he was a child (Rowland, interview with the author).

278 'Desperately seeking attention', *Record Mirror*, 21 Dec. 1985, p. 39.

279 See Roberts, 'Stairway to Kevin', *Melody Maker*, 9 Apr. 1988, p. 30; Wilde, 'My story: Kevin Rowland', *Dazed and Confused*, June 1999, p. 5; Aizlewood, 'Bullish', *Q*, Aug. 1996, p. 135; Pearce, *Something Beginning with O*, p. 39.

280 McNeill, 'Let's get this straight from the start', *The Hit*, 28 Sept. 1985, p. 28.

281 See, for example, Johnny Rogan, 'Don't Stand Me Down', *Record Collector*, Apr. 2002, p. 58; Irwin, 'Stand and deliver', *Melody Maker*, 7 Sept. 1985, p. 32; McNeill, 'Let's get this straight from the start', *The Hit*, 28 Sept. 1985, p. 28.

282 *Coming to Town* tour programme (1985). For an account of the 'respectable' modes of Irishness that were evinced in the migrant Irish community, see Meg Maguire, 'Missing links: Working-class women of Irish descent', in Pat Mahony and Christine Zmroczek (eds.), *Class Matters: 'Working-Class' Women's Perspectives On Social Class* (London: Taylor & Francis, 1997), p. 93.

283 Joe Boyd, *White Bicycles: Making Music in the 1960s* (London: Serpent's Tail, 2005), p. 125.

284 See, for example, Irwin, 'Stand and deliver', *Melody Maker*, 7 Sept. 1985, p. 32; O'Hagan, 'Tangled up in blue', *NME*, 7 Sept. 1985, p. 31.

285 Roberts, 'Grand stand', *Uncut*, May 2002, p. 76.

286 Rowland, interview with the author.

287 See Rowland's liner notes, *Don't Stand Me Down* (Creation CD, 1996). Since this 1996 reissue, all pressings of the CD have listed the track as 'My National Pride'.

288 Easlea, 'Don't Stand Me Down', *Record Collector*, Apr. 2002, p. 51.

289 See Brian Dooley, 'Your name could put you in jail', *New Statesman*, 4 Oct. 2004, p. 17.

290 Hutcheon, 'Rides up with wear', *Mojo*, May 2002, p. 118.

291 McIlheney, 'Burning the midnight oil', *Melody Maker*, 2 Nov. 1985, p. 19.

292 Chris Roberts, 'The Midnight's hour', *Sounds*, 12 Oct. 1985, p. 9.

293 Harry Sedgwick, 'Dexys Midnight Runners: *Don't Stand Me Down*', *Jamming!*, Oct. 1985, p. 50.

294 Price, 'A dark knight of the soul', *Independent*, 'Friday Review' section, 5 Apr. 2002 p. 15.

295 McIlheney, 'Burning the midnight oil', *Melody Maker*, 2 Nov. 1985, p. 19; 'One Of Those Things', *Don't Stand Me Down*.

296 Roberts, 'The Midnight's hour', *Sounds*, 12 Oct. 1985, p. 9. 'You mentioned Ireland and they fucking hated it', recalls Rowland of his conversations with left-wing activists (Rowland, interview with the author). As Tom Hayden explains, 'the New Left … generally excluded Northern Ireland from its menu of progressive causes' (Hayden, *Irish on the Inside: In Search of the Soul of Irish America* (London: Verso, 2001), p. 111).

297 McNeill, 'A man out of time', *The Hit*, 21 Sept. 1985, p. 14. The singer would later explain that he had been 'going through a phase of feeling totally misplaced' when he wrote the song (see Rowland's liner notes, *Don't Stand Me Down* (1996)).

298 Stokes, 'The long run', *Hot Press*, 10 Oct. 1985, p. 23, original emphasis.

299 White, *Dexys Midnight Runners*, p. 166.

300 This term 'magical recovery' is borrowed from early accounts of youth subcultures. See, for example, Phil Cohen, 'Subcultural conflict in a working class community', *Working Papers in Cultural Studies*, no. 2 (1972), University of Birmingham, pp. 5–51; John Clarke, 'The skinheads and the magical recovery of community', in Stuart Hall and Tony Jefferson (eds.), *Resistance Through Rituals: Youth Subcultures in Post-war Britain* (London: Hutchinson, 1976), pp. 99–102.

301 See, for example, Maguire, 'Missing links', p. 95.

302 *The Quiet Man* (John Ford, USA, 1952). For an account of the film's significance for the Irish diaspora, see Luke Gibbons, *The Quiet Man* (Cork: Cork University Press, 2002). As Martin McLoone explains, the Irish west has functioned, in popular culture, as 'a kind of ideal regenerative environment for the troubled and worried mind of modernity' (McLoone, *Film, Media and Popular Culture in Ireland: Cityscapes, Landscapes, Soundscapes* (Dublin: Irish Academic Press, 2008), p. 79).

303 The video, which was shot on 35mm film, is included on *Don't Stand Me Down: The Director's Cut*. See Easlea, 'Don't Stand Me Down', *Record Collector*, Apr. 2002, p. 54.

304 White, *Dexys Midnight Runners*, p. 166.

305 Easlea, 'Don't Stand Me Down', *Record Collector*, Apr. 2002, p. 55.

306 Sedgwick, 'Dexys Midnight Runners', *Jamming!*, Oct. 1985, p. 50.

307 White, *Dexys Midnight Runners*, p. 166.

308 Walter et al. suggest that many second-generation Irish people have embarked on 'a personal quest in adulthood' to achieve 'a public dimension' to their Irishness, and have 'strengthened their sense of a shared national heritage' through this 'search process'. See Bronwen Walter, Sarah Morgan, Mary J. Hickman and Joseph Bradley, 'Family stories, public silence: Irish identity construction amongst the second-generation Irish in England', *Scottish Geographical Journal*, vol. 118, no. 3 (2002), pp. 201, 214.

309 John Mulvey, 'The third coming', *Uncut*, May 2002, p. 100.

310 Hutcheon, 'Rides up with wear', *Mojo*, May 2002, p. 118.

311 Stokes, 'Dexys Midnight Runners', *Hot Press*, 14–28 Aug. 1980, p. 18. Rowland rebukes a 'dumb patriot' in the song lyrics of 'There, There, My Dear' (1980) and 'Old' (1982). Meanwhile, in the *Intense Emotion Review* tour programme, he lists 'patriotism' as his personal 'dislike'.

312 McIlheney, 'Burning the midnight oil', *Melody Maker*, 2 Nov. 1985, p. 19.

313 Rowland, interview with the author.

314 Mary E. Malone and John P. Dooley, '"Dwelling in displacement": Meanings of "community" and *sense* of community for two generations of Irish people living in north-west London', *Community, Work and Family*, vol. 9, no. 1 (Feb. 2006), pp. 15–16, 22, 26.

315 Rowland, interview with the author, original emphasis.

316 See *Intense Emotion Review* tour programme.

317 Rowland, interview with the author.

318 See, for example, Free, 'Tales from the fifth green field', pp. 478, 481.

319 Lydon, *Rotten*, p. 27.

320 See Rowland's liner notes, *Don't Stand Me Down* (1996).

321 Rowland, interview with the author.

322 Bhikhu Parekh, *The Future of Multi-ethnic Britain* (London: Profile Books, 2000), p. 24.
323 White, *Dexys Midnight Runners*, p. 168.
324 For a discussion of this point, see Mary J. Hickman, 'The religio-ethnic identities of teenagers of Irish descent', in Michael P. Hornsby-Smith (ed.), *Catholics in England, 1950–2000: Historical and Sociological Perspectives* (London: Cassell, 1999), p. 185.
325 Rowland, interview with the author.
326 Rowland's liner notes, *Don't Stand Me Down* (1996).
327 Warburton, 'It Was August 1997 ...', *Keep on Running*, no. 9 (Oct. 1997).
328 McIlheney, 'Burning the midnight oil', *Melody Maker*, 2 Nov. 1985, p. 19. In this context, Rowland would claim that his refusal to 'align' himself with a specific political position on Ireland was born of a pragmatic wish to not alienate fans that simply liked his music whilst evading those only interested in his politics (see ibid.).
329 For a range of contemporary responses to the album, see O'Hagan, 'Tangled up in blue', *NME*, 7 Sept. 1985, p. 31; Chris Heath, 'Albums', *Smash Hits*, 11–24 Sept. 1985, p. 77; Irwin, 'Stand and deliver', *Melody Maker*, 7 Sept. 1985, p. 21; Chris Roberts, 'Stand and deliver', *Sounds*, 7 Sept. 1985, p. 31; Sedgwick, 'Dexys Midnight Runners', *Jamming!*, Oct. 1985, p. 50; Robert Elms, 'Death to dull rock', *The Face*, Nov. 1985, p. 101. For accounts of the low attendance at the band's 1985 live shows, see Tom Morton, 'Dexys Midnight Runners', *Melody Maker*, 9 Nov. 1985, p. 20; White, *Dexys Midnight Runners*, p. 173; *Alexei on Dexys*, BBC Radio 2, 14 Feb. 2004.
330 Hutcheon, 'Rides up with wear', *Mojo*, May 2002, p. 118.
331 Mulvey, 'The third coming', *Uncut*, May 2002, p. 100.

Chapter 2: *The Importance of Being (London) Irish: Hybridity, Essentialism and The Pogues*

1 McCann cited in *The Great Hunger: The Life and Songs of Shane MacGowan*, BBC 2, 4 Oct. 1997.
2 Liz Hoggard, 'Playboy of the West End world', *Independent*, magazine, 15 June 2002, p. 10.
3 Nuala O'Connor, *Bringing It All Back Home: The Influence of Irish Music* (London: BBC Books, 1991), p. 159.
4 Bill Graham, 'Get your yeah yeahs out!', *Hot Press*, 15 Dec. 1988, p. 23, emphasis added.
5 T. Price, 'From Beethoven to The Pogues', *Irish Post*, 16 Nov. 1985, p. 6. See also Neil Ferguson, 'Ain't that a Shane', *Philadelphia Weekly*, 14–20 Mar. 2007, p. 36.
6 Josh Kun, *Audiotopia: Music, Race, and America* (Berkeley: University of California Press, 2005), p. 23, original emphasis.
7 See, for example, Mary J. Hickman, 'Hybrid and hyphenated', *Catalyst: Debating Race, Identity, Citizenship and Culture* (London: Commission for Racial Equality, 2007); Ullah, 'Second-generation Irish youth', pp. 310–20.
8 See, for example, *The Pogues: Completely Pogued* (Start Video, 1988); Glenn O'Brien,

'Pogues gallery', *Spin*, June 1986, p. 53; Alastair Sutherland, 'The Pogues: Féach amach!', *Graffiti*, vol. 4, no. 9 (1988), p. 32.

9   Sean O'Hagan relates this critique in O'Hagan, 'Wild rovers' return', *NME*, 21 Mar. 1987, p. 24.

10 For scholarly accounts of The Pogues, see Keohane, 'Unifying the fragmented imaginary of the young immigrant', pp. 71–9; McLaughlin and McLoone, 'Hybridity and national musics', pp. 190–2; Cleary, *Outrageous Fortune*, pp. 200–26.

11 For the erroneous suggestion that MacGowan was born in Ireland, see Tony Clayton-Lea and Richie Taylor, *Irish Rock: Where It's Come From, Where It's At, Where It's Going* (Dublin: Gill & Macmillan, 1992), p. 118; Malcolm Rogers, 'The 100 most influential Irish people', *Irish Post*, 22 Aug. 1998, p. 33; *The Great Hunger: The Life and Songs of Shane MacGowan*, BBC 2, 4 Oct. 1997. For the correct account of MacGowan's birthplace, see Scanlon, *The Pogues*, p. 10; O'Doherty, *Shane MacGowan*, p. 10; Johnny Rogan, 'Rebel yell', *Irish Post*, 'The Craic!' section, 26 Sept. 1998, p. 6.

12 Rogan, 'Rebel yell', *Irish Post*, 'The Craic!' section, 26 Sept. 1998, p. 6.

13 MacGowan, interview with the author. See also Scanlon, *The Pogues*, p. 10. It is perhaps worth noting that MacGowan would later see himself (in the post-Pogues period) as first rather than second-generation Irish, hence his assertion – in 2006 – that he 'didn't grow up Irish in London', but 'grew up Irish in Ireland ... a lot of the time' (MacGowan, interview with the author). However, while his early years in Ireland were no doubt formative, the singer's English birthplace, education and accent served to locate him as second generation, and this was how he presented himself, and how his band-mates saw him, during The Pogues' career (see, for example, Molly McAnailly-Burke, 'Pogue lore', *Hot Press*, 30 Jan. 1986, p. 10; *The Pogues: Completely Pogued* (Start Video, 1988); Clerk, *Pogue Mahone*, p. 49). There might be grounds for locating MacGowan in what certain theorists have called the '1.5 generation', which refers to people who have migrated in their childhood or early teens. See, for example, Andrew Janes, 'The 1.5 generation', *The New Zealand Listener*, 17–23 July 2004, pp. 20–3.

14 Therese MacGowan cited in *The Great Hunger: The Life and Songs of Shane MacGowan*, BBC 2, 4 Oct. 1997.

15 Ibid.

16 Ibid.

17 Ibid.

18 See Joe Merrick, *London Irish Punk: Life and Music ... Shane MacGowan* (London: Omnibus Press, 2001), pp. 7–8; *If I Should Fall from Grace: The Shane MacGowan Story* (Sarah Share, Ireland, 2001); *The Great Hunger: The Life and Songs of Shane MacGowan*, BBC 2, 4 Oct. 1997.

19 *If I Should Fall from Grace: The Shane MacGowan Story* (Sarah Share, Ireland, 2001).

20 Clarke and MacGowan, *A Drink with Shane MacGowan*, p. 292.

21 Merrick, *London Irish Punk*, p. 7.

22 *The Great Hunger: The Life and Songs of Shane MacGowan*, BBC 2, 4 Oct. 1997; Clerk, *Pogue Mahone*, p. 15.

23 Scanlon, *The Pogues*, p. 10.

24 Martin Townsend, 'The secret life of a Pogue', *The Hit*, 21 Sept. 1985, p. 25.

25　MacGowan, interview with the author.

26　For an account of such identity politics, see Ullah, 'Second-generation Irish youth', pp. 310–20.

27　Clarke and MacGowan, *A Drink with Shane MacGowan*, p. 51. 'There were a few London-Irish', MacGowan would later explain, 'who were not proud to be Irish, and who would not play for Ireland, who wouldn't have an Irish passport' (MacGowan, interview with the author).

28　Don Watson, 'A Pogue in the eye with a sharp stick', *NME*, 27 Apr. 1985, p. 34.

29　MacGowan, interview with the author. See also Mat Snow, 'The sweet smell of success', *NME*, 22 Mar. 1986, p. 20; Townsend, 'The secret life of a Pogue', *The Hit*, 21 Sept. 1985, p. 24; Scanlon, *The Pogues*, p. 10; Merrick, *London Irish Punk*, p. 13; Ann Scanlon, 'Celtic soul rebels', *Mojo*, Sept. 2004, p. 78.

30　Clarke and MacGowan, *A Drink with Shane MacGowan*, p. 77; *If I Should Fall from Grace: The Shane MacGowan Story* (Sarah Share, Ireland, 2001); Scanlon, 'Celtic soul rebels', *Mojo*, Sept. 2004, p. 78.

31　Merrick, *London Irish Punk*, pp. 13–14; Dave Simpson, 'Old habits die hard', *Guardian*, 'Friday Review' section, 26 Nov. 2004, p. 8.

32　Clerk, *The Pogues*, p. 2. See also Scanlon, 'Celtic soul rebels', *Mojo*, Sept. 2004, p. 79.

33　*If I Should Fall from Grace: The Shane MacGowan Story* (Sarah Share, Ireland, 2001).

34　MacGowan, interview with the author. See also Clarke and MacGowan, *A Drink with Shane MacGowan*, p. 192; Bill Graham, 'New wave a Paddy plot?', *Hot Press*, 23 June 1977, pp. 13–14; Jon Savage, *The England's Dreaming Tapes* (London: Faber and Faber, 2009), p. 311.

35　Allan Jones, 'Rotten!', *Melody Maker*, 4 June 1977, p. 52. See also John Blake, 'Rock's swastika revolution', *London Evening News*, 7 May 1977, p. 11.

36　See Murray, 'John, Paul, Steve and Sidney', *NME*, 6 Aug. 1977, p. 23; David Widgery, *Beating Time: Riot 'n Race 'n Rock 'n Roll* (London: Chatto & Windus, 1986), p. 64.

37　Savage, *England's Dreaming*, p. 12; Bill Graham, 'The hard stuff', *Hot Press*, 21 Sept. 1984, p. 11. Savage points out that English punk was made up of a 'cluster of minorities', attracting a wide variety of social outsiders, or 'misfits from all classes' (Savage, *England's Dreaming*, p. 12).

38　O'Hagan, cited in *The Great Hunger: The Life and Songs of Shane MacGowan*, BBC 2, 4 Oct. 1997; Clerk, *Pogue Mahone*, p. 2.

39　MacGowan's highly visible presence in English punk was registered in numerous contemporary accounts, not least when he appeared as an anonymous cover star for the music paper *Sounds* (see 'Images of the new wave', *Sounds*, 2 Apr. 1977, p. 1). Previously, photographs of the singer at a punk concert had appeared in the *NME* (see Miles, 'Cannibalism at Clash gig', *NME*, 6 Nov. 1976, p. 43), and he was later described as a 'well-known face' on the punk scene (Dave McCullough, 'Death to art rock!', *Sounds*, 19 May 1979, p. 16). See also the celebrated film, *Punk Rock Movie* (Don Letts, UK, 1978). For MacGowan's editorship of *Bondage*, see Savage, *England's Dreaming*, p. 281.

40　For visual evidence of the Union Jack shirt, see *If I Should Fall from Grace: The Shane MacGowan Story* (Sarah Share, Ireland, 2001); Adrian Boot and Chris

Salewicz, *Punk: The Illustrated History of a Music Revolution* (London: Penguin Studio, 1996), p. 10.

41 See, for example, Boot and Salewicz, *Punk*, p. 6. See also Mark Blake (ed.), *Punk: The Whole Story* (London: Dorling Kindersley, 2006), p. 163. The band's sleeve designer, Jamie Reid, suggests that this reworking of the flag was 'an attempt to make the point about the declining empire' (Blake, *Punk*, p. 163).

42 Lydon, *Rotten*, p. 99.

43 Clarke and MacGowan, *A Drink with Shane MacGowan*, pp. 150–1.

44 MacGowan's pseudonym was frequently cited in the press at the time. See, for example, Adrian Thrills, 'Ears of a clown', *NME*, 27 Oct. 1979, p. 23; Adam Sweeting, 'The Nips', *NME*, 22 Mar. 1980, p. 54.

45 Laing, *One Chord Wonders*, p. 50.

46 Savage, *England's Dreaming*, pp. 192–3.

47 See, for example, Lydon, *Rotten*, p. 225.

48 Clerk, *Pogue Mahone*, p. 1; Dee O'Mahony, cited in Clerk, *Pogue Mahone*, p. 11.

49 Clerk, *Pogue Mahone*, p. 3.

50 Ibid. p. 11.

51 Stephen Gordon, 'Raw rags at midnite', *NME*, 17 June 1978, p. 52; Thrills, 'Ears of a clown', *NME*, 27 Oct. 1979, p. 23.

52 See Townsend, 'The secret life of a Pogue', *The Hit*, 21 Sept. 1985, p. 24; Scanlon, *The Pogues*, p. 13; Clerk, *Pogue Mahone*, pp. 9, 54.

53 McAnailly-Burke, 'Pogue lore', *Hot Press*, 30 Jan. 1986, p. 10. See 'Nipped in the bud', *Sounds*, 8 Mar. 1980, p. 2; Townsend, 'The secret life of a Pogue', *The Hit*, 21 Sept. 1985, p. 24. For an account of roots rock and synth-pop, see Moore, *Rock: The Primary Text*, pp. 133–6, 146–53. For MacGowan's critique of synth-pop, see Thrills, 'Ears of a clown', *NME*, 27 Oct. 1979, p. 23.

54 Scanlon, *The Pogues*, p. 14; Clerk, *Pogue Mahone*, p. 45.

55 Andy Hurt, 'A whip round with the Pogues', *Sounds*, 17 Aug. 1985, p. 18; *The Great Hunger: The Life and Songs of Shane MacGowan*, BBC 2, 4 Oct. 1997.

56 *The Great Hunger: The Life and Songs of Shane MacGowan*, BBC 2, 4 Oct. 1997.

57 Colin Irwin, 'The thorn birds', *Melody Maker*, 6 Oct. 1984, p. 36.

58 Clerk, *Pogue Mahone*, p. 88.

59 See Mark Cordery, 'Shamrock it', *Record Mirror*, 27 Oct. 1984, p. 10; Clerk, *Pogue Mahone*, pp. 88–9. The 'Streams Of Whiskey' video later appeared on *Poguevision* (Warners Video, 1998).

60 Clarke and MacGowan, *A Drink with Shane MacGowan*, p. 213; Rose Rouse, 'Brutabilly', *Sounds*, 24 Mar. 1984, p. 12.

61 Sean Campbell and Gerry Smyth, *Beautiful Day: Forty Years of Irish Rock* (Dublin: Atrium Press, 2005), p. 97.

62 Clerk, *Pogue Mahone*, pp. xii, 52; As Joe Cleary explains, the *céilí*-based styles on which the group drew were viewed as 'tacky or an affront to sophisticated good taste' (Cleary, *Outrageous Fortune*, p. 207).

63 See, for example, *The Pogues: Completely Pogued* (Start Video, 1988).

64 McAnailly-Burke, 'Pogue lore', *Hot Press*, 30 Jan. 1986, p. 10.

65 For an account of anti-Irish prejudice in the early 1980s, see Curtis, *Nothing But the Same Old Story*.

66 Spider Stacy in *The Story of … Fairytale of New York*, BBC 3, 19 Dec. 2005. Jem

Finer explains: 'To be Irish in those days was quite difficult in London, probably a bit like being a young Muslim now' (Clerk, *Pogue Mahone*, p. 90).

67   See *If I Should Fall from Grace: The Shane MacGowan Story* (Sarah Share, Ireland, 2001).

68   Clerk, *Pogue Mahone*, p. 11, original emphasis.

69   Spider Stacy cited in Scanlon, 'Celtic soul rebels', *Mojo*, Sept. 2004, p. 79.

70   See *If I Should Fall from Grace: The Shane MacGowan Story* (Sarah Share, Ireland, 2001); John Le Page, 'Pogue mahone', *The Face*, Oct. 1983, p. 9. On another occasion, members of the National Front sought to disrupt one of the group's concerts by releasing tear gas into the audience (Clerk, *Pogue Mahone*, p. 160).

71   Clerk, *Pogue Mahone*, pp. 101–2.

72   MacGowan, interview with the author. See also Elms, 'Pogue in the eye', *The Face*, Mar. 1985, p. 31; Clarke and MacGowan, *A Drink with Shane MacGowan*, p. 213.

73   MacGowan, interview with the author; MacGowan cited in *The Pogues: Completely Pogued* (Start Video, 1988).

74   Scanlon, 'Celtic soul rebels', *Mojo*, Sept. 2004, p. 79.

75   See Clarke and MacGowan, *A Drink with Shane MacGowan*, pp. 192–3.

76   MacGowan, interview with the author.

77   Scanlon, *The Pogues*, pp. 8–9. The Lydons were raised in a council flat close to Finsbury Park station. See Savage, *England's Dreaming*, p. 115.

78   For an account of The Pogues' formation and line-up changes, see Clerk, *Pogue Mahone*.

79   See Molly Mac Anailly Burke, 'Cool Cait', *Sunday Independent*, 31 Jan. 1988, p. 14; Clarke and MacGowan, *A Drink with Shane MacGowan*, p. 202.

80   O'Riordan, interview with the author; Mac Anailly Burke, 'Cool Cait', *Sunday Independent*, 31 Jan. 1988, p. 14. The Troops Out Movement sought the withdrawal of Britain's armed forces from Northern Ireland.

81   See Clerk, *Pogue Mahone*.

82   Ibid, p. 58, emphasis added; Scanlon, *The Pogues*, p. 9. The band appear to have sourced their name from James Joyce's *Ulysses* (1922), in which the phrase 'pogue mahone' is uttered by Buck Mulligan during an exchange with Stephen Dedalus. See James Joyce, *Ulysses* (London: Penguin, 1986), p. 169.

83   See Scanlon, *The Pogues*, pp. 24, 30; Gavin Martin, 'Pogue mahone', *NME*, 15 Jan. 1983, p. 36; Martin, 'Mahone ranger's handbook', *NME*, 13 Aug. 1983, p. 22.

84   Scanlon, *The Pogues*, p. 30. Certain fans of the group would suggest that The Pogues performed 'traditional songs' in an 'alternative' manner. See, for instance, Maurice McCrohan, 'From Beethoven to The Pogues', *Irish Post*, 16 Nov. 1985, p. 6.

85   By the time of The Pogues' first live show, 'Come On Eileen' had sold over one million copies in Britain alone. See British Market Research Bureau, 'Top 75 singles', *Music and Video Week*, 2 Oct. 1982, p. 13. The single remained at the top of the UK chart for four weeks in August and September, while its host album, *Too-Rye-Ay*, enjoyed three weeks at no. 1. See White, *Dexys Midnight Runners*, pp. 130–1.

86   O'Riordan, interview with the author.

87   MacGowan, interview with the author.

88   Martin, 'Mahone ranger's handbook', *NME*, 13 Aug. 1983, p. 22; Scanlon, *The*

Pogues, p. 9. Clerk notes that there was a 'world of difference' between The Pogues and Dexys (Clerk, *Pogue Mahone*, p. 70).

89   See, for example, *If I Should Fall from Grace: The Shane MacGowan Story* (Sarah Share, Ireland, 2001); Barry McIlheney, 'Celtic swingers', *Melody Maker*, 27 Oct. 1984, p. 25; O'Riordan, interview with the author; Scanlon, *The Pogues*, pp. 23–4, 30; Antonella Black, 'Me no pop eye', *Sounds*, 6 Apr. 1985, p. 26; Graham, 'Get your yeah yeahs out!', *Hot Press*, 15 Dec. 1988, p. 23; Rouse, 'Brutabilly', *Sounds*, 24 Mar. 1984, p. 12; Clerk, *Pogue Mahone*, pp. 81–2, 109. For an account of traditional music in London's Irish pubs in the pre-Pogues era, see Michael Foley, 'Awareness and interest in music that is Irish', *Irish Times*, 4 Aug. 1977, p. 10.

90   Scanlon, 'Celtic soul rebels', *Mojo*, Sept. 2004, p. 80.

91   Moore, *Rock: The Primary Text*, p. 147.

92   Cleary, *Outrageous Fortune*, p. 205.

93   Ibid. pp. 205–8.

94   See Grainne Ni Scanlain, 'A reflection of reality', *Irish Post*, 21 Dec. 1985, p. 22; Black, 'Me no pop eye', *Sounds*, 6 Apr. 1985, p. 26. For other accounts of the influence of these singers on MacGowan's vocal style, see Shane MacGowan, 'Heroes', *Melody Maker*, 18 Oct. 1986, p. 29; Clarke and MacGowan, *A Drink with Shane MacGowan*, pp. 169, 281; Helen Terry, 'Singles', *Melody Maker*, 27 Oct. 1984, p. 26.

95   'It's impossible to sing an Irish song, to put feel and emotion into it, without going into some kind of Irish accent', MacGowan explained, adding: 'You can't sing Verdi in an English accent. You have to sing it in an Italian accent' (Carol Clerk, 'Sore heads and fairy tails', *Melody Maker*, 28 Nov. 1987, p. 15).

96   Jack Barron, 'Band of unholy joy', *Sounds*, 13 Dec. 1986, p. 26. For MacGowan's discussion of 'Paddy chic' and Behan, see Clarke and MacGowan, *A Drink with Shane MacGowan*, pp. 168, 213. The Pogues also performed a rendition of Behan's song, 'The Auld Triangle', on their debut album, *Red Roses For Me* (Stiff, 1984), and cited Behan in the song lyrics of various tracks. See, for example, 'Streams Of Whiskey' (*Red Roses For Me*); 'Thousands Are Sailing' (*If I Should Fall from Grace With God*, Pogue Mahone, 1988). MacGowan also eulogised Behan in interviews. See MacGowan, 'Heroes', *Melody Maker*, 18 Oct. 1986, p. 29.

97   Clarke and MacGowan, *A Drink with Shane MacGowan*, p. 168.

98   For examples of this sartorial trend amongst post-war Irish immigrants, see *The Irishman* (Philip Donnellan, UK, 1964).

99   See, for example, Scanlon, 'Celtic soul rebels', *Mojo*, Sept. 2004, p. 76. Tartan had been a prominent aspect of English punk attire. See, for example, Blake, *Punk*, p. 85.

100   Cleary, *Outrageous Fortune*, p. 206. These forms were also a strike against the overt artifice of the prevailing popular music.

101   See Mark J. Prendergast, *Irish Rock: Roots, Personalities, Directions* (Dublin: O'Brien Press, 1987), p. 112.

102   Ferguson, 'Ain't that a Shane', *Philadelphia Weekly*, 14–20 Mar. 2007, p. 36.

103   Clarke and MacGowan, *A Drink with Shane MacGowan*, p. 223. For other accounts of the fans' display of Irishness, see Kelly, 'Triumph of the swill', *NME*, 20/27 Dec. 1986, p. 49; O'Hagan, 'Wild rovers' return', *NME*, 21 Mar. 1987, p. 25; Scanlon, *The Pogues*, pp. 54, 65, 115.

104 Clerk, *Pogue Mahone*, p. 102. Brennan notes that many punks and folk fans expressed an aversion to The Pogues' new aesthetic, with both constituencies objecting to the alleged pollution of their preferred style (ibid. p. 102).

105 O'Connor, *Bringing It All Back Home*, p. 159.

106 Sutherland, 'The Pogues', *Graffiti*, vol. 4, no. 9 (1988), p. 31. The band enjoyed support from Britain's 'alternative' scene, as well as from the international folk and world music circuit, with appearances at the Cambridge, Vienna and WOMAD festivals. See Scanlon, *The Pogues*, pp. 65, 70.

107 Frith, 'Music and identity', p. 123.

108 John Waters, *Race of Angels: The Genesis of U2* (London: Fourth Estate, 1994), p. 193.

109 Scanlon, *The Pogues*, p. 65. For similar points about the band's audience, see Andrea Miller, 'Everything's gone green!', *NME*, 28 Sept. 1985, p. 56.

110 Chevron, e-mail to the author, 30 May 2006. Such was the extent of the group's association with the second-generation Irish that MacGowan felt compelled to announce that their audience was not made up solely of this constituency. See, for example, Hurt, 'A whip round with the Pogues', *Sounds*, 17 Aug. 1985, p. 18.

111 For a brief discussion of this point, see Smyth, 'Who's the greenest of them all?', p. 5. For the claim that The Pogues had excluded certain fans, see the letter cited in Sean O'Hagan (ed.), 'Utensil', *NME*, 17 Jan. 1987, p. 42.

112 MacGowan, interview with the author.

113 Phil Udell, 'The Radiators at Oxegen: Video interview', *hotpress.com*. http://www.hotpress.com/oxegen/2743930.html; Simpson, 'Old habits die hard', *Guardian*, 'Friday Review' section, 26 Nov. 2004, p. 9; O'Riordan, interview with the author.

114 Chevron cited in Matthew Magee, 'Pogues pogo on', *Sunday Tribune*, 'Artlife' section, 19 May 2002, p. 5; Chevron cited in Clerk, *Pogue Mahone*, p. 92; Chevron, e-mail to the author.

115 O'Hagan, 'Wild rovers' return', *NME*, 21 Mar. 1987, p. 24.

116 McLaughlin and McLoone, 'Hybridity and national musics', p. 191.

117 This notion of 'articulation', which has been developed (in a musical context) by Richard Middleton, is elaborated upon below. See Middleton, *Studying Popular Music*, pp. 8–11.

118 Frith, 'Music and identity', pp. 109, 124, emphases added.

119 *If I Should Fall from Grace: The Shane MacGowan Story* (Sarah Share, Ireland, 2001); Merrick, *London Irish Punk*, p. 60, emphases added.

120 Clarke and MacGowan, *A Drink with Shane MacGowan*, p. 223.

121 Barron, 'Band of unholy joy', *Sounds*, 13 Dec. 1986, p. 26. The band were also seen as a 'touchstone' for the second-generation Irish, offering 'a link between that home there and this home here' (Pete Silverton, 'When Irish eyes are bloodshot', *Mail on Sunday*, 'You' magazine, 13 Mar. 1988, p. 76).

122 Udell, 'The Radiators at Oxegen: Video interview', *hotpress.com*. http://www.hotpress.com/oxegen/2743930.html. The soccer analogy employed by O'Riordan was remarkably apposite in light of the high degree of Irish-related sports paraphernalia that adorned the group's live shows. See, for example, O'Hagan, 'Wild rovers' return', *NME*, 21 Mar. 1987, p. 25; Scanlon, *The Pogues*, pp. 54, 65, 115.

123 O'Riordan, interview with the author, original emphases. MacGowan suggests that

The Pogues' experience was also a catharsis for him: 'through song-writing I got the chance to expel all that negative energy in a positive way instead of squandering it in violence or actions of hatred' (Victoria Clarke, 'The Pogues: The sweet smell of excess', *Melody Maker*, 1 June 1991, p. 43).

124 Ranken cited in O'Hagan, 'Wild rovers' return', *NME*, 21 Mar. 1987, p. 25.

125 Watson, 'A Pogue in the eye with a sharp stick', *NME*, 27 Apr. 1985, p. 34.

126 See Kelly, 'Triumph of the swill', *NME*, 20/27 Dec. 1986, p. 49; Miller, 'Everything's gone green!', *NME*, 28 Sept. 1985, p. 56. In this context, Frank Murray, the group's former manager, explained that The Pogues' live audience 'were really part of the show', an aspect that emerged quite 'naturally' due to the band being 'very connected' to their audience (Clerk, *Pogue Mahone*, p. 145).

127 Eamonn McCann, 'Celtic soul brotherhood', *Hot Press*, 28 Jan. 1988, p. 18, emphasis added.

128 McCrohan, 'From Beethoven to The Pogues', *Irish Post*, 16 Nov. 1985, p. 6.

129 Middleton, *Studying Popular Music*, p. 9. For a further elaboration of 'articulation', see Ernesto Laclau and Chantal Mouffe, *Hegemony and Socialist Strategy: Towards a Radical Democratic Politics* (London: Verso, 1985), pp. 93–148.

130 See 'Music', *Time Out*, 15–21 Mar. 1984, p. 51; Scanlon, *The Pogues*, pp. 35, 41, 78; Elms, 'Pogue in the eye', *The Face*, Mar. 1985, pp. 30–5.

131 Clerk, *Pogue Mahone*, p. 224. For examples of the band's involvement with St Patrick's Day, see O'Hagan, 'Wild rovers' return', *NME*, 21 Mar. 1987, p. 25; Paul Lester, 'The Pogues: The last gang in town', *Melody Maker*, 25 Mar. 1989, p. 8; Clerk, *Pogue Mahone*, p. 224. For an account of St Patrick's Day in Britain, see Cronin and Adair, *The Wearing of the Green*, pp. 195–9. For a discussion of Irish theme pubs in 1990s Britain, see Mark McGovern, 'The "craic" market: Irish theme bars and the commodification of Irishness in contemporary Britain', *Irish Journal of Sociology*, vol. 11, no. 2 (2002), pp. 77–98.

132 Ronan McGreevy, 'Award shows Pogues' glory days are gone', *Irish Post*, 4 Feb. 2006, p. 16.

133 Bill Black, 'Serious drinking', *Sounds*, 12 Oct. 1984, p. 22. For MacGowan's use of the term 'subculture' to refer to the migrant Irish, see Hurt, 'A whip round with the Pogues', *Sounds*, 17 Aug. 1985, p. 18. Significantly, this term, like that of 'London Irish', would soon be taken up by the music press. See, for example, O'Hagan, 'Wild rovers' return', *NME*, 21 Mar. 1987, p. 24; Elms, 'Pogue in the eye', *The Face*, Mar. 1985, p. 32.

134 Merrick, *London Irish Punk*, p. 60; O'Riordan, interview with the author.

135 Hurt, 'A whip round with the Pogues', *Sounds*, 17 Aug. 1985, p. 18, emphasis added. There were obvious commercial incentives for making such a point, although, as mentioned above, MacGowan was correct to suggest that The Pogues' music was not the sole preserve of Irish migrants.

136 O'Riordan, interview with the author; Hoggard, 'Playboy of the West End world', *Independent*, magazine, 15 June 2002, p. 10.

137 Graham, 'The hard stuff', *Hot Press*, 21 Sept. 1984, p. 11.

138 Silverton, 'When Irish eyes are bloodshot', *Mail on Sunday*, 'You' magazine, 13 Mar. 1988, p. 76.

139 Rose Rouse, 'Pogue-o-schtick', *Sounds*, 6 Oct. 1984, p. 38, emphases added.

140 See Elms, 'Pogue in the eye', *The Face*, Mar. 1985, pp. 30–1.

141 Stud Brothers, 'Sham rock', *Melody Maker*, 21/28 Dec. 1985, p. 22, emphases added.

142 Ibid.

143 'Music', *Time Out*, 16–22 Feb. 1984, p. 47; 'Music', *Time Out*, 23–29 Feb. 1984, p. 49; 'Music', *Time Out*, 9–15 Feb. 1984, p. 47; 'Music', *Time Out*, 8–14 Mar. 1984, p. 56; 'Music', *Time Out*, 15–21 Mar. 1984, p. 51; 'Music', *Time Out*, 29 Mar.–4 Apr. 1984, p. 58. For a brief account of *Time Out* (and its progressive self-image), see David Smith, '*Time Out* at 40', *Observer*, 10 Aug. 2008, p. 21.

144 Terry, 'Singles', *Melody Maker*, 27 Oct. 1984, p. 26.

145 See the letters in Penny Reel (ed.), 'Gasbag', *NME*, 25 May 1985, p. 78.

146 See the letters in O'Hagan (ed.), 'Utensil', *NME*, 17 Jan. 1987, p. 42.

147 McIlheney, 'Celtic swingers', *Melody Maker*, 27 Oct. 1984, p. 25. The singer was evidently attacked (on account of his identification with Irishness) on a number of occasions (see Clerk, *Pogue Mahone*, p. 98).

148 For a discussion of this point, see Andy Strickland, 'Pogue mania!', *Record Mirror*, 21 Sept. 1985, p. 52.

149 This critique was cited by Frank Murray on the *BP Fallon Orchestra*, RTÉ Radio 2, 21 Sept. 1985.

150 King cited in Clayton-Lea and Taylor, *Irish Rock*, p. 46. For King's interest in hybrid styles, see the RTÉ/BBC television series *Bringing It All Back Home* (Hummingbird Productions, 1991).

151 Patrick Humphries, 'Phil the folker', *Folk Roots*, Nov. 1985, p. 30.

152 McAnailly-Burke, 'Pogue lore', *Hot Press*, 30 Jan. 1986, p. 11. The Pogues were later embraced by parts of the traditional scene, not least The Dubliners, whose collaboration with The Pogues, 'The Irish Rover' (Stiff, 1987), became a UK hit.

153 Joe Breen, 'Getting the lash', *Irish Times*, 23 Aug. 1985, p. 10, emphasis added. For an account of 'authenticity', see Keightley, 'Reconsidering rock', pp. 131–9.

154 Nick Kelly, 'The spirit is willing', *Hot Press*, 19 Oct. 1984, p. 19; Molly McAnailly-Burke, 'Pogues' gallery', *Hot Press*, 5 July 1985, p. 35.

155 See the *BP Fallon Orchestra*, RTÉ Radio 2, 21 Sept. 1985. This was an edited broadcast of a 'roundtable' event originally recorded on 5 Sept. 1985 (thanks to Philip Chevron and John Foyle for locating a recording of this event).

156 Michael Cunningham, '*BP Fallon Orchestra*', *Irish Times*, 21 Sept. 1985, p. 13.

157 John Foyle, 'BP Fallon/RTÉ interview 1985', http://www.pogues.com/forum/viewtopic.php?f=24&t=9639

158 'Whistle test', *Irish Times*, 4 June 1985, p. 17.

159 *BP Fallon Orchestra*, RTÉ Radio 2, 21 Sept. 1985, emphasis added.

160 See Bronwen Walter, 'Voices in other ears: "accents" and identities of the first- and second-generation Irish in England', in Guido Rings and Anne Ife (eds.), *Neo-colonial Mentalities in Contemporary Europe? Language and Discourse in the Construction of Identities* (Cambridge: Cambridge Scholars Press, 2008), pp. 174–82.

161 See Dooley, *Choosing the Green?*, p. 8.

162 Maude Casey, *Over the Water* (London: Livewire, 1987), p. 70.

163 Ibid. p. 99.

164 John Walsh, *The Falling Angels* (London: HarperCollins, 1999), p. 14.

165 Lydon, *Rotten*, p. 13.

166 Ibid. p. 274.

167   Lindsay Shapero, 'New riders of the purple sage', *Time Out*, 22–28 Mar. 1984, p. 55. MacGowan's point was confirmed by observers, not least Ronnie Drew of The Dubliners, who heard in The Pogues an 'emigrant's memory of what Irish music is like' (Declan Lynch, 'A Dubliner and the quare 'oul times', *Hot Press*, New Year special 1987, p. 33).

168   *BP Fallon Orchestra*, RTÉ Radio 2, 21 Sept. 1985.

169   Ibid.

170   Stuart Hall, 'Encoding/decoding', in Stuart Hall, Dorothy Hobson, Andrew Lowe and Stuart Willis (eds.), *Culture, Media, Language: Working Papers in Cultural Studies, 1972–79* (London: Hutchinson, 1980), p. 131.

171   Walter, '"Shamrocks growing out of their mouths"', p. 68.

172   Free, '"Angels" with drunken faces?', p. 224; Dooley, *Choosing the Green?*, p. 111; O'Mahoney, *Soldier of the Queen*, p. 31.

173   Healy, *The Grass Arena*, pp. 10–11.

174   McNeill, 'A man out of time', *The Hit*, 21 Sept. 1985, p. 14.

175   O'Riordan, interview with the author.

176   Colin Irwin, 'Pursuing poguemahone', *Southern Rag*, 1 Apr.–30 June 1984, p. 24; MacGowan, interview with the author.

177   Philip Chevron, 'BP Fallon/RTÉ interview 1985', http://www.pogues.com/forum/viewtopic.php?f=24&t=9639

178   O'Riordan, interview with the author, original emphases.

179   *BP Fallon Orchestra*, RTÉ Radio 2, 21 Sept. 1985.

180   Ibid.

181   Barbara Bradby, '"Imagining Ireland" conference, Dublin, Oct. 30th-31st 1993', *Popular Music*, vol. 13, no. 1 (1994), p. 109. For an account of such 'misunderstanding', see Hall, 'Encoding/decoding', p. 131.

182   *BP Fallon Orchestra*, RTÉ Radio 2, 21 Sept. 1985. Brian Dooley suggests that an Irish passport was 'the ultimate validation' of the second generation's claims to Irishness (Dooley, *Choosing the Green?*, p. vii).

183   McIlheney, 'Burning the midnight oil', *Melody Maker*, 2 Nov. 1985, p. 19.

184   Joe Ambrose, e-mail to the author, 12 Mar. 2009.

185   Malcolm Rogers, 'Tommy made it', *Irish Post*, 'The Craic!' section, 1 May 1999, pp. 6–7.

186   Chevron, e-mail to the author.

187   P.J. Boyle, 'The Pogues an insult to Irish music', *Irish Post*, 26 Oct. 1985, p. 10, emphasis added.

188   Price, 'From Beethoven to The Pogues', *Irish Post*, 16 Nov. 1985, p. 6. Elvis Costello – an occasional producer of The Pogues – underlined this view, suggesting that the group had 'saved folk [music] from the folkies' (Neil McCormick, 'Elvis unmasked', *Hot Press*, 23 Feb. 1989, p. 26).

189   Hebdige, *Subculture*, p. 97.

190   'Shane McGowan [*sic*] diaries', *Melody Maker*, 10 Dec. 1988, p. 7.

191   Stuart Maconie, 'Pungent spice', *Q*, Aug. 1999, p. 100, emphases added.

192   See Miller, 'Everything's gone green!', *NME*, 28 Sept. 1985, p. 56; Donald McRae, 'Blithe spirits', *NME*, 21/28 Dec. 1985, p. 73; Ron Rom, 'Rum runaway', *Sounds*, 29 Mar. 1986, p. 28.

193   See Paul Gilroy, '"It ain't where you're from, it's where you're at": The dialectics of diasporic identification', *Third Text*, vol. 5, no. 13 (1991), pp. 3–16.

194   Ann Scanlon, 'The rogues of Tralee', *Sounds*, 28 Nov. 1987, p. 22.

195   Elms, 'Pogue in the eye', *The Face*, Mar. 1985, p. 35, original emphasis. See also *South of Watford*, London Weekend Television, 30 Mar. 1984.

196   McLaughlin and McLoone, 'Hybridity and national musics', p. 191. This evocation of diaspora was evident in other Pogues record sleeves, notably the portrait of John F. Kennedy on *Red Roses for Me*, and the excess baggage that appears on *If I Should Fall from Grace with God*.

197   Martin, 'Mahone ranger's handbook', *NME*, 13 Aug. 1983, p. 22, emphasis added.

198   See O'Brien, 'Pogues gallery', *Spin*, June 1986, p. 53; *The Pogues: Completely Pogued* (Start Video, 1988); Sutherland, 'The Pogues', *Graffiti*, vol. 4, no. 9 (1988), p. 32. MacGowan's band-mates would confirm that, during the group's early period, they 'never really thought of him as Irish', seeing him instead as 'London-Irish' (Clerk, *Pogue Mahone*, p. 49).

199   The band's songbook, for Dorian Lynskey, was 'full of people leaving' (Lynskey, 'Readers recommend goodbye songs', *Guardian*, 'Film and Music' section, 11 Apr. 2008, p. 4). 'The Leaving Of Liverpool' and 'The Wild Rover' were originally released on the 12-inch single of 'Sally MacLennane' (Stiff, 1985). 'Poor Paddy' and 'Kitty' featured on the group's debut album, *Red Roses for Me*. 'Muirchin Dirkin' was included on the 12-inch single of 'A Pair Of Brown Eyes' (Stiff, 1985). 'The Parting Glass' appeared on the 12-inch single of 'Dirty Old Town' (Stiff, 1985).

200   Chevron cited in *If I Should Fall from Grace: The Shane MacGowan Story* (Sarah Share, Ireland, 2001). Emphasising that 'there are two Irelands' – 'the people who live on the island' and 'the people who went away or who are second generation' – Chevron suggests that the latter 'very often' provide 'a different point of view on the culture and what it is to be "Irish"' (ibid.).

201   Martina Sheehan, 'On the road: The Pogues', *Time Out Chicago*, 1–7 Mar. 2007, p. 133.

202   Marr, interview with the author.

203   Elms, 'Pogue in the eye', *The Face*, Mar. 1985, p. 32.

204   Clerk, *Pogue Mahone*, p. 90; 'Dark Streets Of London' (Stiff, 1984).

205   Brah, *Cartographies of Diaspora*, pp. 208–10. For an account of the ways in which music can transform social space, see Stokes, 'Introduction', pp. 1–27.

206   R.F. Foster, *Paddy and Mr Punch: Connections in Irish and English History* (London: Allen Lane, 1993), p. xiii.

207   See Kerby Miller, *Emigrants and Exiles: Ireland and the Irish Exodus to North America* (New York: Oxford University Press, 1985), p. 522.

208   Fintan O'Toole, 'Nowhere man', *Irish Times*, 'Weekend' section, 26 Apr. 1997, p. 1.

209   Clerk, *Pogue Mahone*, p. 156.

210   'Transmetropolitan' (*Red Roses for Me*).

211   This tendency is evident in songs like 'The Mountains Of Mourne' (Percy French, 1896) and 'Galway Bay' (Arthur Colahan, 1947).

212   McLaughlin and McLoone, 'Hybridity and national musics', p. 191.

213   MacGowan, interview with the author.

214   Joyce, *Ulysses*, p. 121.

215   For a discussion of this point, see James Clifford, 'Diasporas', *Cultural Anthropology*, vol. 9, no. 3 (1994), pp. 302–38.

216 See ibid.

217 Delaney, *The Irish in Post-War Britain*, pp. 16, 64. For an account of second-generation Irish return migration, see Sara Hanafin, 'The idea of Ireland as "home": Place, identity and second generation return migration', conference of the British Association of Irish Studies, University of Liverpool, 15 Sept. 2007.

218 See Liam Greenslade, Maggie Pearson and Moss Madden, 'A good man's fault: Alcohol and Irish people at home and abroad', *Alcohol and Alcoholism*, vol. 30, no. 4 (1995), p. 411.

219 Malone and Dooley, '"Dwelling in displacement"', pp. 11–28.

220 Martin, 'Mahone ranger's handbook', *NME*, 13 Aug. 1983, p. 22; Prendergast, *Irish Rock*, p. 109. 'The Body Of An American', *Poguetry in Motion* (Stiff, 1986). 'The Body Of An American' appeared to include an allusion to John Ford's *The Quiet Man* (the pop-cultural ur-text of Irish diaspora nostalgia), making reference to a fight with 'the champ in Pittsburgh', thus recalling the vocation and location of Sean Thornton, the titular character in Ford's film.

221 O'Hagan, 'Wild rovers' return', *NME*, 21 Mar. 1987, p. 24; Gavin Martin, 'Once upon a time in the west', *NME*, 2 Jan. 1988, p. 31; Terry Staunton, 'It's the Shane old song', *NME*, 2 Dec. 1989, p. 51. 'The Broad Majestic Shannon' appeared on *If I Should Fall from Grace with God*.

222 Scanlon, 'The rogues of Tralee', *Sounds*, 28 Nov. 1987, p. 22; Scanlon, *The Pogues*, p. 95.

223 Albert Murray, *Stomping the Blues* (London: Quartet Books, 1978), p. 54.

224 This gesture arguably goes to the heart of The Pogues' position on 'traditional' culture. MacGowan saw The Pogues as both at variance with and indebted to traditional Irish folk. 'We can't be traditional because we don't stick to just what was handed down', he averred, 'but we can't be against tradition because we were built on a tradition' (Ni Scanlain, 'A reflection of reality', *Irish Post*, 21 Dec. 1985, p. 22). Chevron confirms that The Pogues 'saw the merit of writing both within and against the tradition' (Clerk, *Pogue Mahone*, p. 92).

225 As Breda Gray explains, the GLC in the early 1980s 'led the way in developing "multicultural" policy and service provision and in fostering "ethnic" cultural activities' (Gray, 'From "ethnicity" to "diaspora"', p. 70). Brixton is an area of London historically associated with African-Caribbean people.

226 MacGowan, interview with the author. This point is confirmed by MacGowan's band-mates, who claim that Pogues songs were shaped as much by the 'multiculturalism of London' as they were by concerns with Irishness, a point previously made by Bill Graham, who described the London invoked by The Pogues as 'cosmopolitan', stressing its commonality with left-wing multiculturalism. In a similar vein, Chevron would explain that The Pogues addressed not only a second-generation Irish perspective, but also 'a cosmopolitan one formed by migrants to London' more generally (see Hunt cited in Clerk, *Pogue Mahone*, p. 91; Graham, 'Get your yeah yeahs out!', *Hot Press*, 15 Dec. 1988, p. 22; Chevron, e-mail to the author).

227 Watson, 'A Pogue in the eye with a sharp stick', *NME*, 27 Apr. 1985, p. 34; Ni Scanlain, 'A reflection of reality', *Irish Post*, 21 Dec. 1985, p. 22.

228 Price, 'From Beethoven to The Pogues', *Irish Post*, 16 Nov. 1985, p. 6; Ni Scanlain, 'A reflection of reality', *Irish Post*, 21 Dec. 1985, p. 22.

229 'London Girl' and 'A Rainy Night In Soho' served as the opening tracks on *Poguetry in Motion*. 'Lullaby Of London' appeared on *If I Should Fall from Grace with God*. Though included in an anthology of MacGowan's song lyrics, 'NW3' was only ever performed live by The Pogues. See Shane MacGowan, *Poguetry: The Lyrics of Shane MacGowan* (London: Faber and Faber, 1989), p. 73. 'London, You're A Lady', 'Boat Train' and 'White City' featured on *Peace and Love* (WEA CD, 1989). 'Sea Shanty' appeared on *Red Roses for Me*, while 'The Sick Bed Of Cuchulainn' and 'The Old Main Drag' served as the opening tracks on *Rum, Sodomy and the Lash* (Stiff, 1985).

230 Mary Louise Pratt, *Imperial Eyes: Travel Writing and Transculturation* (London: Routledge, 1992), p. 7. Although Pratt primarily uses the term to address encounters between the colonised and the coloniser, I have extended it here to include relations between migrants of different backgrounds.

231 For a brief discussion of this point, see Frith, 'Music and identity', p. 125.

232 'A Pistol For Paddy Garcia' appeared on the B-side of 'Dirty Old Town'. 'Fiesta', 'Metropolis' and 'Turkish Song Of The Damned' were included on *If I Should Fall from Grace with God*.

233 Michael Dwyer, 'Mac the mouth', *Sunday Tribune*, 'People' section, 2 Aug. 1987, p. 1.

234 Bill Graham, 'State of grace', *Hot Press*, 28 Jan. 1988, p. 23.

235 As Luke Gibbons has explained, one potential means by which to negotiate the condition of diaspora is 'to make provision, not just for vertical mobility from the periphery to the centre, but for "lateral" journeys along the margins which short-circuit the colonial divide' (Gibbons, 'Unapproved roads: Postcolonialism and Irish identity', in Trisha Ziff (ed.), *Distant Relations: Chicano/Irish/Mexican Art and Critical Writing* (New York: Smart Art Press, 1995), p. 67). The Pogues' invocation of a multi-ethnic London appears to serve as an illustration of this point.

236 O'Brien, 'Pogues gallery', *Spin*, June 1986, p. 53.

237 Magee, 'Pogues pogo on', *Sunday Tribune*, 'Artlife' section, 19 May 2002, p. 5.

238 *The Great Hunger: The Life and Songs of Shane MacGowan*, BBC 2, 4 Oct. 1997.

239 Sean O'Hagan, 'It's all in the bollocks …', *NME*, 9 July 1988, p. 20.

240 Clerk, *Pogue Mahone*, p. 291. 'Birmingham Six' appears on *If I Should Fall from Grace with God*.

241 Hillyard, *Suspect Community*, p. 13. The successful renewal of the Act meant that the British government had effectively 'defied a ruling of the European Court of Human Rights which [had] declared it illegal' ('UK commentary: The Guildford Four: English justice and the Irish community: An interview with Gareth Peirce', *Race and Class*, vol. 31, no. 3 (1990), p. 85). Indeed, lawyers such as Gareth Peirce explained that 'almost every aspect' of Britain's 'treatment of Irish detainees' was 'in breach of international human rights law' ('UK commentary', p. 83). For an account of the Birmingham and Guildford cases, see Chris Mullin, *Error of Judgement: The Truth about the Birmingham Bombings* (London: Chatto & Windus, 1986), and Robert Kee, *Trial and Error: The Maguires, the Guildford Pub Bombings and British Justice* (London: Penguin, 1989, 2nd edn.).

242 Hillyard, *Suspect Community*, p. 5.

243 Vincent Maguire, aged seventeen, was sentenced to five years' imprisonment, while his younger brother Patrick, who was only thirteen at the time of the bombings,

was sentenced to four years in youth custody. For an account of the cases of the Guildford Four and the Maguire Seven, see Kee, *Trial and Error*. For a broader account of the Prevention of Terrorism Act's effect on the second-generation Irish, see Dooley, *Choosing the Green?*, pp. 116–19.

244 Dooley, *Choosing the Green?*, p. 106.

245 Tom Barclay, *Memoirs and Medleys: The Autobiography of a Bottle Washer* (Leicester: Edgar Backus, 1934), p. 23. Barclay, who was raised by Irish parents in nineteenth-century England, recalls being 'hounded and harassed' by the 'Sassenach kids': '"Hurroo Mick!", "Ye Awrish Paddywack", "bad luck to the ships that brought ye over!" These were the salutes from the happy English child: We were battered, threatened, elbowed, pressed back to the door of our kennel amid boos and jeers and showers of small missiles.' In response to such events, Barclay 'began to feel' that 'things Irish' should be 'put away' (ibid. pp. 5, 23–4). For an account of Barclay's text, see Sean Campbell, 'Beyond "Plastic Paddy": A re-examination of the second-generation Irish in England', *Immigrants and Minorities*, vol. 18, nos. 2 & 3 (1999), pp. 267–70.

246 Clerk, 'Sore heads and fairy tails', *Melody Maker*, 28 Nov. 1987, p. 15. MacGowan notes that his family experienced verbal abuse from British security forces when travelling between Britain and Ireland (MacGowan, interview with the author).

247 Clerk, *Pogue Mahone*, p. 291.

248 Annette Gartland, 'Terrorist ban hits pop song', *Observer*, 20 Nov. 1988, p. 4. The IBA was a 'government-established body' that regulated commercial media and 'formally owned the transmission network' (Greg Philo, 'Television, politics and the rise of the new right', in Greg Philo (ed.), *Glasgow Media Group Reader, Volume 2: Industry, Economy, War and Politics* (London: Routledge, 1995), p. 222).

249 Bill Graham, 'Pogues off the air', *Hot Press*, 15 Dec. 1988, p. 7.

250 See David Miller, 'The media and Northern Ireland: Censorship, information management and the broadcasting ban', in Philo (ed.), *Glasgow Media Group Reader*, p. 48; 'Pogues fall from grace with government', *NME*, 19 Nov. 1988, p. 3.

251 Miller, 'The media and Northern Ireland', p. 57.

252 Irwin, 'Pursuing poguemahone', *Southern Rag*, 1 Apr.–30 June 1984, p. 23; David Quantick and Sean O'Hagan, 'For a few ciders more', *NME*, 11 Aug. 1984, p. 11; Watson, 'A Pogue in the eye with a sharp stick', *NME*, 27 Apr. 1985, p. 34. Before 'Birmingham Six' had been released, The Pogues were keen to stress its lack of 'anti-English' sentiment. See, for instance, Colin Irwin, 'Pogueology', *Folk Roots*, Aug. 1987, p. 35.

253 Clerk, 'Sore heads and fairy tails', *Melody Maker*, 28 Nov. 1987, p. 15.

254 See Clerk, *Pogue Mahone*, p. 249; Barry McIlheney, 'All I want for Christmas is my two front teeth', *Melody Maker*, 21/28 Dec. 1985, p. 15. For an account of the Lambeg and the *bodhrán*, see Fintan Vallely (ed.), *The Companion to Irish Traditional Music* (Cork: Cork University Press, 1999), pp. 29–32, 210.

255 McIlheney, 'All I want for Christmas is my two front teeth', *Melody Maker*, 21/28 Dec. 1985, p. 15.

256 See Kelly, 'Triumph of the swill', *NME*, 20/27 Dec. 1986, p. 49. For similar accounts, see Miller, 'Everything's gone green!', *NME*, 28 Sept. 1985, p. 56; Barron, 'Band of unholy joy', *Sounds*, 13 Dec. 1986, p. 26; O'Hagan, 'Wild rovers'

return', *NME*, 21 Mar. 1987, p. 25; Scanlon, *The Pogues*, pp. 54, 65, 115; Clarke and MacGowan, *A Drink with Shane MacGowan*, p. 223. For an account of Glasgow Celtic, see Joseph M. Bradley (ed.), *Celtic Minded: Essays on Religion, Politics, Society, Identity ... and Football* (Glendaruel: Argyll Publishing, 2004).

257   McCann, 'Celtic soul brotherhood', *Hot Press*, 28 Jan. 1988, p. 17.

258   Townsend, 'The secret life of a Pogue', *The Hit*, 21 Sept. 1985, p. 24.

259   Dwyer, 'Mac the mouth', *Sunday Tribune*, 'People' section, 2 Aug. 1987, p. 1.

260   See the letter cited in O'Hagan (ed.), 'Utensil', *NME*, 17 Jan. 1987, p. 42.

261   McCann, 'Celtic soul brotherhood', *Hot Press*, 28 Jan. 1988, p. 17.

262   Ibid.

263   For a brief discussion of this point, see Smyth, 'Who's the greenest of them all?', pp. 3–5.

264   Barron, 'Band of unholy joy', *Sounds*, 13 Dec. 1986, p. 26; O'Hagan, 'Wild rovers' return', *NME*, 21 Mar. 1987, p. 25.

265   MacGowan cited in *The Pogues: Completely Pogued* (Start Video, 1988). The most 'bigoted' comment that MacGowan appears to have made during the Pogues period was an ostensibly light-hearted aside with a Northern Irish journalist, in which the singer expressed surprise that his interviewer was not a Catholic. 'You a Prod?', MacGowan enquired, before uttering 'C---', and adding: 'I'm only kidding' (McIlheney, 'All I want for Christmas is my two front teeth', *Melody Maker*, 21/28 Dec. 1985, p. 15).

266   Barron, 'Band of unholy joy', *Sounds*, 13 Dec. 1986, p. 26.

267   Prendergast, *Irish Rock*, p. 109.

268   Other musical fusion projects have met a similar fate. In this context, Paul Gilroy notes that US rap, 'a form which flaunts and glories in its own malleability as well as its transnational character', came to be viewed as 'an expression of some authentic Afro-American essence' (Gilroy, '"It ain't where you're from"', p. 6).

269   Clerk, *Pogue Mahone*, p. 11.

270   O'Riordan, interview with the author. For MacGowan's endorsement of a united Ireland, see Elms, 'Pogue in the eye', *The Face*, Mar. 1985, p. 32. The most forthright comment that MacGowan made on the Troubles during the Pogues period was his claim that 'Armed people are legitimate targets.' 'If you're carrying a gun, if you're prepared to shoot somebody, you've got to be prepared to die yourself', he observed (Clerk, 'Sore heads and fairy tails', *Melody Maker*, 28 Nov. 1987, p. 15).

271   Clerk, *Pogue Mahone*, p. 143. In the post-Pogues period, however, MacGowan would retreat to a far more nationalist position, suggesting that The Pogues had indeed supported militant nationalism. 'We were an IRA support team', he explained in 2006 (MacGowan, interview with the author). This, however, is at odds with the accounts of other band members (see Clerk, *Pogue Mahone*, p. 143).

272   McIlheney, 'Celtic swingers', *Melody Maker*, 27 Oct. 1984, p. 25; O'Riordan, interview with the author. Chevron describes the band's politics as progressive liberal-left, a point borne out by their support for organisations such as the GLC, the Nicaraguan Solidarity Campaign and Artists Against Apartheid (Chevron, e-mail to the author; Scanlon, *The Pogues*, pp. 60, 65, 68, 104; Clerk, *Pogue Mahone*, pp. 170–1).

273   Clerk, *Pogue Mahone*, p. 150.

274   Finer cited in ibid. p. 90.

275   O'Hagan, 'It's all in the bollocks …', *NME*, 9 July 1988, p. 20; Dorian Lynskey, 'Songs about London', *Guardian*, 'Film and Music' section, 7 July 2006, p. 4.

276   McAnailly-Burke, 'Pogue lore', *Hot Press*, 30 Jan. 1986, p. 11.

277   Smyth, 'Who's the greenest of them all?', p. 5.

278   See, for example, Steve Redhead, *The End of the Century Party: Youth and Pop Towards 2000* (Manchester: Manchester University Press, 1990), p. 14.

279   Liam Fay, 'I drink therefore I am', *Hot Press*, 10 Aug. 1989, p. 31. See also Sutherland, 'The Pogues', *Graffiti*, vol. 4, no. 9 (1988), p. 30.

280   *The Great Hunger: The Life and Songs of Shane MacGowan*, BBC 2, 4 Oct. 1997.

281   Ni Scanlain, 'A reflection of reality', *Irish Post*, 21 Dec. 1985, p. 22. For an account of the band's first photo shoot, see *The Story of … Fairytale of New York*, BBC 3, 19 Dec. 2005. For examples of alcohol-related objects in Pogues photo shoots, see the cover image of *Melody Maker*, 27 Oct. 1984; Irwin, 'The thorn birds', *Melody Maker*, 6 Oct. 1984, p. 36; Townsend, 'The secret life of a Pogue', *The Hit*, 21 Sept. 1985, p. 25; Price, 'From Beethoven to The Pogues', *Irish Post*, 16 Nov. 1985, p. 6.

282   See O'Hagan, 'It's all in the bollocks …', *NME*, 9 July 1988, p. 20; Barron, 'Band of unholy joy', *Sounds*, 13 Dec. 1986, p. 26; McRae, 'Blithe spirits', *NME*, 21/28 Dec. 1985, p. 73; Sutherland, 'The Pogues', *Graffiti*, vol. 4, no. 9 (1988), p. 31. For images of the band imbibing onstage, see 'Naval lark', *Sounds*, 10 Aug. 1985, p. 10; McRae, 'Blithe spirits', *NME*, 21/28 Dec. 1985, p. 73; Push, 'Collecting the empties', *Melody Maker*, 28 Nov. 1987, p. 23.

283   Smyth, 'Who's the greenest of them all?', p. 5; Clerk, 'Sore heads and fairy tails', *Melody Maker*, 28 Nov. 1987, p. 14.

284   Clerk, *Pogue Mahone*, pp. 114, 296. Hunt confirms that the band's drinking 'damaged people quite a bit' (Clerk, *Pogue Mahone*, p. 297).

285   O'Riordan, interview with the author. See also Clarke and MacGowan, *A Drink with Shane MacGowan*, p. 223; *If I Should Fall from Grace: The Shane MacGowan Story* (Sarah Share, Ireland, 2001). Certain band members could occasionally be seen vomiting during concerts (see Adrian Thrills, 'L'Uomo Pogue', *NME*, 4 Jan. 1986, p. 8; Sean O'Hagan, 'In the heat of the night', *NME*, 2 July 1988, p. 30).

286   MacGowan has described the band's live audience as 'boozy' (see *The Great Hunger: The Life and Songs of Shane MacGowan*, BBC 2, 4 Oct. 1997), a point that is confirmed by many observers (see, for example, Hurt, 'A whip round with the Pogues', *Sounds*, 17 Aug. 1985, p. 19; Clerk, *Pogue Mahone*, p. 114). For references to audience members passing drinks to the band, see O'Hagan, 'In the heat of the night', *NME*, 2 July 1988, p. 53; Clerk, *Pogue Mahone*, p. 202. Photographs of MacGowan accepting drinks from the audience were occasionally published in the music press. See, for example, Dee Pilgrim, 'Nightshift', *Sounds*, 10 Aug. 1985, p. 39.

287   McIlheney, 'All I want for Christmas is my two front teeth', *Melody Maker*, 21/28 Dec. 1985, p. 15.

288   'Tour news', *Melody Maker*, 8 Dec. 1984, p. 21.

289   Clerk, *Pogue Mahone*, p. 118.

290   McIlheney, 'Celtic swingers', *Melody Maker*, 27 Oct. 1984, p. 33; McIlheney, 'All I want for Christmas is my two front teeth', *Melody Maker*, 21/28 Dec. 1985, p. 15.

291   Fay, 'I drink therefore I am', *Hot Press*, 10 Aug. 1989, p. 31.

292   Watson, 'A Pogue in the eye with a sharp stick', *NME*, 27 Apr. 1985, p. 24.

293   Black, 'Me no pop eye', *Sounds*, 6 Apr. 1985, p. 26; *The Pogues: Completely Pogued*
      (Start Video, 1988). Elsewhere, MacGowan claimed that heavy drinking 'makes
      reality more acute' (Clarke, 'The Pogues: The sweet smell of excess', *Melody Maker*,
      1 June 1991, p. 42).
294   Cordery, 'Shamrock it', *Record Mirror*, 27 Oct. 1984, p. 10.
295   Ni Scanlain, 'A reflection of reality', *Irish Post*, 21 Dec. 1985, p. 22.
296   McIlheney, 'Celtic swingers', *Melody Maker*, 27 Oct. 1984, p. 25. 'There is drinking
      in lots of the songs because there is drinking in life', MacGowan explained, adding:
      'I spend a lot of time drinking' (Clarke, 'The Pogues: The sweet smell of excess',
      Melody Maker, 1 June 1991, p. 42).
297   'Waxie's Dargle' was included on *Red Roses for Me*, while 'Whiskey, You're The
      Devil' appeared on the B-side of 'A Pair Of Brown Eyes'. 'I'm A Man You Don't
      Meet Every Day' featured on *Rum, Sodomy and the Lash*.
298   'Repeal Of The Licensing Laws' appeared on the B-side of 'Boys From The County
      Hell' (Stiff, 1984).
299   This song was 'London Girl'.
300   O'Hagan and Quantick, 'For a few ciders more', *NME*, 11 Aug. 1984, p. 11.
301   Clerk, *Pogue Mahone*, p. 59. MacGowan has explained that Stan Brennan, the
      group's first manager, felt that the song's overt alcohol theme would adversely affect
      potential radio play. See Clarke and MacGowan, *A Drink with Shane MacGowan*,
      p. 214.
302   Jim Sullivan, 'Pogues throw more in the mix', *Boston Globe*, 3 Oct. 1989, p. 27.
303   MacGowan cited in Martin, 'Mahone ranger's handbook', *NME*, 13 Aug. 1983,
      p. 22; Clerk, *Pogue Mahone*, p. 89.
304   Dorian Lynskey, 'Songs about drinking', *Guardian*, 'Film and Music' section, 16
      Dec. 2005, p. 5.
305   Clerk, *Pogue Mahone*, p. 89.
306   Delaney, *The Irish in Post-War Britain*, p. 173; Ryan, 'Irish emigration to Britain
      since World War II', p. 56.
307   Walter, '"Shamrocks growing out of their mouths"', p. 67; Hickman et al., 'The
      limitations of whiteness', p. 170. For a discussion of the pub as an 'ethnic space'
      for the Irish in Britain, see McGovern, 'The "craic" market', pp. 90–3.
308   See O'Connor, *The Young Drinkers*; Greenslade et al., 'A good man's fault',
      pp. 407–17; J.H. Foster, 'The Irish alcohol misuser in England: Ill served by
      research and policy? Some suggestions for future research opportunities', *Drugs:
      Education, Prevention and Policy*, vol. 10, no. 1 (2003), pp. 57–63.
309   Smyth, 'Who's the greenest of them all?', p. 5; Keohane, 'Unifying the fragmented
      imaginary', p. 76; Clerk, *Pogue Mahone*, p. 114. 'Boys From The County Hell'
      appeared on *Red Roses for Me*.
310   See 'Music', *Time Out*, 24–30 May 1984, p. 58; Dave Walters, 'Albums', *Time Out*,
      4–10 Oct. 1984, p. 79; Sutherland, 'The Pogues', *Graffiti*, vol. 4, no. 9 (1988), p. 30.
      For other examples of the media's focus on this drink theme, see O'Hagan and
      Quantick, 'For a few ciders more', *NME*, 11 Aug. 1984, p. 11; Cordery, 'Shamrock
      it', *Record Mirror*, 27 Oct. 1984, p. 10; Fay, 'I drink therefore I am', *Hot Press*, 10
      Aug. 1989, p. 31.
311   Elms, 'Pogue in the eye', *The Face*, Mar. 1985 pp. 32, 35.
312   Fay, 'I drink therefore I am', *Hot Press*, 10 Aug. 1989, pp. 30–1.

313 'The booze brothers', *Q*, May 1988; 'A fair intake of ale in New York', *Record Mirror*, 19 Dec. 1987; O'Hagan and Quantick, 'For a few ciders more', *NME*, 11 Aug. 1984, p. 11; Fay, 'I drink therefore I am', *Hot Press*, 10 Aug. 1989, p. 30.

314 Dermot Stokes, 'Kiss of life', *Hot Press*, 16 Nov. 1984, p. 25.

315 Hurt, 'A whip round with the Pogues', *Sounds*, 17 Aug. 1985, p. 18.

316 Ibid. p. 19; Fay, 'I drink therefore I am', *Hot Press*, 10 Aug. 1989, p. 31. James Fearnley explains: 'It became really wearisome that journalists' and the public's perception of The Pogues should centre so firmly on drink. Yeah, we did drink a lot, but I don't think any more than anybody else did. It was always the first question out of a journalist's mouth.' Ranken agrees: 'It did piss us off. I can't say that it wasn't founded on fact, because it was, but it was annoying. I mean, we did have this quite rowdy audience right from the start who were interested in having a few jars, and we never discouraged them.' 'It might have had something to do with people's perceptions of us as an Irish band' (Clerk, *Pogue Mahone*, pp. 142, 186).

317 See, for example, Neil Taylor, 'Singles', *NME*, 14 Dec. 1985, p. 19; Adrian Deevoy, 'Married to the Murphia', *Q*, Sept. 1989, p. 46.

318 Fay, 'I drink therefore I am', *Hot Press*, 10 Aug. 1989, p. 31.

319 O'Riordan, interview with the author. 'People hear what they want to hear', she suggests, 'and if they want to think all Paddies are drunken buffoons, they could hear the most beautiful poetry in the world and still think "Oh, he's obviously had a few."'

320 Clerk, *Pogue Mahone*, p. 114.

321 As Jon Savage has explained, innovative forms of popular culture tend to be filtered through processes of reduction once they encounter 'the mass market and mass media'. In such processes, 'simplicity', for Savage, is 'imposed on complex phenomena' (Savage, *England's Dreaming*, p. 278).

322 MacColl cited in *The Pogues: Completely Pogued* (Start Video, 1988).

323 Stuart Bailie, 'The first thing people think ...', *Record Mirror*, 29 Dec. 1987, p. 41; Granuaille, 'Asses to asses', *Zigzag*, Dec. 1985, p. 24.

324 Bailie, 'The first thing people think ...', *Record Mirror*, 29 Dec. 1987, p. 41.

325 O'Riordan, interview with the author; Clerk, *Pogue Mahone*, p. 97.

326 Clerk, *Pogue Mahone*, pp. 103–4; Sutherland, 'The Pogues', *Graffiti*, vol. 4, no. 9 (1988), p. 30.

327 Graham, 'The hard stuff', *Hot Press*, 21 Sept. 1984, p. 11.

328 Clerk, *Pogue Mahone*, p. 104.

329 Deevoy, 'Married to the Murphia', *Q*, Sept. 1989, p. 47.

330 See, for example, *The Great Hunger: The Life and Songs of Shane MacGowan*, BBC 2, 4 Oct. 1997; *If I Should Fall from Grace: The Shane MacGowan Story* (Sarah Share, Ireland, 2001). Whilst MacGowan would concede that The Pogues were 'real alchies [alcoholics]', he added that this had 'nothing to do with what we do as a group'. See Ni Scanlain, 'A reflection of reality', *Irish Post*, 21 Dec. 1985, p. 22.

331 John Nagle, '"Everybody is Irish on St. Paddy's Day": Ambivalence and alterity at London's St. Patrick's Day 2002', *Identities: Global Studies in Culture and Power*, vol. 12, no. 4 (Oct.–Dec. 2005), p. 567.

332 See, for example, Free, '"Angels" with drunken faces?', p. 231.

333 Ibid.

334 Terry Eagleton, *Heathcliff and the Great Hunger: Studies in Irish Culture* (London: Verso, 1995), p. 1.

335 Frantz Fanon, *Black Skin, White Masks*, trans. Charles Lam Markmann (London: MacGibbon & Kee, 1968), p. 115. While Fanon's comment was made in a very different (French-Martiniquan) context, his point can be applied to other – differently located – migrant groups. As Sonia Kruks points out, Fanon's comment – which she suggests was an 'authentic response to racism' – was based on a 'demand to be recognised in one's difference' (Kruks, 'Fanon, Sartre and identity politics', in Lewis R. Gordon, T. Denean Sharpley-Whiting and Renée T. White (eds.), *Fanon: A Critical Reader* (Oxford: Blackwell, 1996), p. 129).

336 McAnailly-Burke, 'Pogue lore', *Hot Press*, 30 Jan. 1986, p. 10.

337 Stokes, 'Kiss of life', *Hot Press*, 16 Nov. 1984, p. 25.

338 See, for example, Stephen Haseler, *The English Tribe: Identity, Nation and Europe* (Basingstoke: Macmillan, 1996), p. 104.

339 See, for example, Stuart Hall, 'What is this "black" in black popular culture?', in Gina Dent (ed.), *Black Popular Culture* (Seattle: Bay Press, 1992), pp. 21–33; Hyder, *Brimful of Asia*.

340 Nagle, '"Everybody is Irish on St. Paddy's Day"', p. 572.

341 Kruks, 'Fanon, Sartre and identity politics', p. 130. The work of The Pogues might, then, be understood as a form of strategic essentialism, a term used by the post-colonial theorist Gayatri Chakravorty Spivak to denote certain short-term, context-specific tactics that are (self-consciously) deployed by minority group members to assert a group identity (for specific reasons), and which are only effective as long as they remain unfixed as essential characteristics in the eyes of the dominant group. See Stephen Morton, *Gayatri Chakraorty Spivak* (London: Routledge, 2003), p. 75.

342 For an account of 'interpellation', see Louis Althusser, *Lenin and Philosophy and Other Essays*, trans. Ben Brewster (London: New Left Books, 1971), pp. 160–5.

343 See Gerry Smyth, *Noisy Island: A Short History of Irish Popular Music* (Cork: Cork University Press, 2005), p. 75; Smyth, 'Who's the greenest of them all?', p. 5.

344 McLaughlin and McLoone, 'Hybridity and national musics', p. 191.

345 Cleary, *Outrageous Fortune*, p. 203.

346 Smyth, 'Who's the greenest of them all?', pp. 4–5.

347 Clerk, *Pogue Mahone*, p. 141.

348 Ibid. p. 151.

349 Ibid. pp. 309, 322–3, 335–8, 340, 356.

350 Zane/Dave Jennings, 'A gig too fleadh', *Melody Maker*, 8 June 1991, p. 26.

351 Scanlon, 'Celtic soul rebels', *Mojo*, Sept. 2004, p. 82.

Chapter 3: *'Oscillate Wildly': Ambivalence, Elusiveness and The Smiths*

1 Brian Boyd, 'Paddy Englishman', *Irish Times*, 'Arts' section, 20 Nov. 1999, p. 5.

2 http://www.jmarr.com ('Q&A', Mar. 2001).

3 Catherine Ellis, *Aboriginal Music: Education for Living* (St Lucia: University of Queensland Press, 1985), p. 15, emphases added.

4 For an account of this show, see Róisín Dwyer, 'Saint Patrick', *Hot Press*, 26 Jan. 2005, p. 67.

5 For an account of the group's reception, see Sean Campbell, '"Race of angels": The

critical reception of second-generation Irish musicians', *Irish Studies Review*, vol. 6, no. 2 (1998), pp. 165–74.

6   Bracewell, *England is Mine*, pp. 219, 223. This thesis was perhaps nourished by Morrissey's engagement with issues of Englishness in his solo career.

7   Mark Sinker, 'Look back in anguish', *NME*, 2 Jan. 1988, p. 14.

8   Donald McRae, 'The Smiths' Anti-Apartheid benefit', *NME*, 3 Jan. 1987, p. 28; Gavin Martin, 'Angst', *NME*, 26 Sept. 1987, p. 58. See also Len Brown, 'Morrissey', *Guardian*, 'Review' section, 30 Dec. 1988, p. 22, and Nick Kent's comments on the *South Bank Show*, ITV, 18 Oct. 1987.

9   Boyd, 'Paddy Englishman', *Irish Times*, 'Arts' section, 20 Nov. 1999, p. 5.

10 For an account of The Smiths' musical styles, see Simon Goddard, *The Smiths: Songs That Saved Your Life* (London: Reynolds & Hearn, 2004, 2nd edn.).

11 For lyrical citations of English places, see 'Miserable Lie', 'Suffer Little Children' (*The Smiths*, Rough Trade, 1984), 'The Headmaster Ritual', 'Rusholme Ruffians', 'What She Said' (*Meat is Murder*, Rough Trade, 1985), 'Panic' (Rough Trade, 1986), 'Is It Really So Strange?', 'London' (*Louder Than Bombs*, Sire, 1987). For an example of Morrissey's citation of English towns in Smiths interviews, see Simon Garfield, 'This charming man', *Time Out*, 7–13 Mar. 1985, p. 19; Gary Leboff, 'Goodbye cruel world', *Melody Maker*, 26 Sept. 1987, p. 27. Several record sleeves, including 'Heaven Knows I'm Miserable Now' (Rough Trade, 1984), 'Barbarism Begins At Home' (Rough Trade, 1985), *The Queen is Dead* (Rough Trade, 1986) and *Strangeways, Here We Come* (Rough Trade, 1987), evoke distinctively English locales.

12 Marr, interview with the author.

13 See, for example, Ullah, 'Second-generation Irish youth', pp. 317–19; Aidan Arrowsmith, 'Writing "home": Nation, identity and Irish emigration to England' (unpublished Ph.D. thesis, University of Staffordshire, 1998), pp. 214, 219–21, 236–7.

14 O'Toole, 'Nowhere man', *Irish Times*, 'Weekend' section, 26 Apr. 1997, p. 1.

15 Paul Nolan, 'I've something to get off my chest', *Hot Press*, 2 July 2008, p. 41.

16 In the early 1990s, the singer flirted with the iconography of British nationalism. Interestingly, this project seems to have been launched in Dublin, where the singer appeared wearing a Union Jack badge in the shape of Britain. See Kevin Cummins, *The Smiths and Beyond* (London: Vision On, 2002), no pagination. For an account of this period in Morrissey's career, see Zuberi, *Sounds English*, pp. 17–20.

17 Marr, interview with the author.

18 *Earsay*, Channel 4, 7 July 1984 (I refer to the unedited forty-five-minute interview, not all of which was included in the original broadcast). See also Marr, interview with the author.

19 See, for example, Julian Haviland, 'Attack on "enemy within"', *The Times*, 20 July 1984, p. 1; David Edgar, 'Bitter harvest', in James Curran (ed.), *The Future of the Left* (Cambridge: Polity Press, 1984), p. 40. For evidence of the band's affiliations, see Rogan, *Morrissey and Marr*, pp. 248–9, 313, 320. Observing the group's 'anti-establishment' stance, Joe Brooker notes that The Smiths were 'keener to fill the dock with the powerful than to draw fine distinctions between them' (Brooker, 'Has the world changed or have I changed? The Smiths and the challenge of

Thatcherism', in Sean Campbell and Colin Coulter (eds.), *Why Pamper Life's Complexities? Essays on The Smiths* (Manchester: Manchester University Press, forthcoming).

20 Tony Mitchell, *Popular Music and Local Identity: Rock, Pop and Rap in Europe and Oceania* (London: Leicester University Press, 1996), p. 8.

21 Phil Eva, citing A.L. Lloyd, in Eva, 'Home sweet home?', p. 132.

22 John Waters, 'Those charming men', *Irish Times*, 'Weekend' section, 25 Apr. 1992, p. 3. Even Shane MacGowan, who expressed his dislike of The Smiths in the 1980s (see MacGowan, 'Singles', *Melody Maker*, 6 July 1985, p. 26), later claimed that Irish ethnicity was evident in their œuvre (MacGowan, interview with the author).

23 See Rogan, *Morrissey and Marr*, pp. 149, 162–3, 169, 233, 275–86.

24 Johnny Rogan, *The Smiths: The Visual Documentary* (London: Omnibus Press, 1994), pp. 10–15.

25 Boyd, 'Paddy Englishman', *Irish Times*, 'Arts' section, 20 Nov. 1999, p. 5. This suggestion of 'ghettoisation' is confirmed by Anne Higgins, who states that Irish Catholics in mid-twentieth-century Manchester were 'under a kind of sense of siege' (see Lennon, McAdam and O'Brien, *Across the Water*, p. 146).

26 Boyd, 'Paddy Englishman', *Irish Times*, 'Arts' section, 20 Nov. 1999, p. 5.

27 Neil McCormick, 'All men have secrets', *Hot Press*, 4 May 1984, p. 18; Boyd, 'Paddy Englishman', *Irish Times*, 'Arts' section, 20 Nov. 1999, p. 5.

28 Boyd, 'Paddy Englishman', *Irish Times*, 'Arts' section, 20 Nov. 1999, p. 5. See also Frank Owen, 'Home thoughts from abroad', *Melody Maker*, 27 Sept. 1986, p. 16; Brian Boyd, 'Johnny take a bow', *Irish Times*, 'The Ticket' section, 31 Aug. 2007, p. 9.

29 See Boyd, 'Paddy Englishman', *Irish Times*, 'Arts' section, 20 Nov. 1999, p. 5; McCormick, 'All men have secrets', *Hot Press*, 4 May 1984, p. 18; Danny Kelly, 'The further thoughts of Chairman Mo', *NME*, 8 June 1985, p. 28; Rogan, *Morrissey and Marr*, pp. 39–83.

30 Patrick O'Connor and Seán Daffy, 'On the importance of not-being earnest: A dialogue with Terry Eagleton', *Irish Studies Review*, vol. 16, no. 1 (Feb. 2008), p. 63. See also Eagleton, 'A different sense of who I was', p. 15. For an account of the assimilationist ethos of Catholic schools in England, see Hickman, *Religion, Class and Identity*.

31 McCormick, 'All men have secrets', *Hot Press*, 4 May 1984, p. 18; *Earsay*, Channel 4, 7 July 1984; Kelly, 'The further thoughts of Chairman Mo', *NME*, 8 June 1985, pp. 24, 28.

32 Richard Purden, 'Keeping up with The Smiths', *Irish Post*, 1 Sept. 2007, p. 17; McCormick, 'All men have secrets', *Hot Press*, 4 May 1984, p. 18; Kelly, 'The further thoughts of Chairman Mo', *NME*, 8 June 1985, p. 28; *Earsay*, Channel 4, 7 July 1984.

33 *Earsay*, Channel 4, 7 July 1984. See also McCormick, 'All men have secrets', *Hot Press*, 4 May 1984, p. 18.

34 Mike Moore cited in Rogan, *Morrissey and Marr*, p. 69, original emphasis. As Mairtin Mac an Ghaill explains, Irish-nationalist culture has often comprised a form of sexual politics that has 'specific implications for the construction of young masculinities' (Mac an Ghaill, 'What about the lads? – Emigrants, immigrants,

ethnics and transnationals in late 1990s diaspora', in Ronat Lentin (ed.), *Emerging Irish Identities: Proceedings of a Seminar Held in Trinity College Dublin, 27 November 1999* (Dublin: Trinity College, Dublin, 2000), p. 52.

35   See *Earsay*, Channel 4, 7 July 1984; Rogan, *Morrissey and Marr*, pp. 35–6.

36   Peter Murphy, 'The unbearable lightness of being Morrissey', *Hot Press*, 8 Apr. 2009, p. 39.

37   Elissa Van Poznak, 'Morrissey: *The Face* interview', *The Face*, July 1984, p. 32; *Earsay*, Channel 4, 7 July 1984. See also Rogan, *Morrissey and Marr*, p. 71; David Fricke, 'Keeping up with The Smiths', *Rolling Stone*, 9 Oct. 1986, pp. 32–3.

38   Jim Mac Laughlin, 'The new vanishing Irish: Social characteristics of "new wave" Irish emigration', in Mac Laughlin (ed.), *Location and Dislocation in Contemporary Irish Society: Emigration and Irish Identities* (Cork: Cork University Press, 1997), p. 155. See also Sharon Lambert, *Irish Women in Lancashire, 1922–1960: Their Story* (University of Lancaster: Centre for North-west Regional Studies, 2001), p. 43; Delaney, *The Irish in Post-War Britain*, p. 208.

39   McCormick, 'All men have secrets', *Hot Press*, 4 May 1984, p. 18.

40   Ibid. Other Irish-descended musicians have embarked on similar excursions into Irish literature. Elvis Costello, for instance, has explained, 'I read all the Irish writers by the time I was 13 or 14', putting this down to 'some sort of teenage cultural identity crisis where [he] suddenly felt it absolutely necessary [to] read all of Seán O'Casey's plays' (Bill Graham, 'The king and I', *Hot Press*, 27 Mar. 1986, p. 22).

41   Mark Simpson, *Saint Morrissey* (London: SAF, 2004), p. 164; *Earsay*, Channel 4, 7 July 1984; Rogan, *Morrissey and Marr*, p. 83.

42   Terry Christian, 'The Smiths forever', unpublished article for the *Daily Mail* (May 2004). See also Terry Christian, 'The outsiders will have their day', *The Times*, 12 Feb. 2010, p. 6.

43   Keith Cameron, 'Who's the daddy?', *Mojo*, June 2004, p. 79.

44   Lydon, *Rotten*, p. 14.

45   See Rogan, *Morrissey and Marr*, pp. 74, 82, 96–7, 101–2, 105, 108, 158.

46   *Front Row*, BBC Radio 4, 18 Feb. 2009.

47   Ibid.

48   See Rogan, *Morrissey and Marr*, pp. 112–14; Talking Music, *The Interview: The Smiths* (Speek CD, 1998); Marr, interview with the author.

49   Simon Goddard, 'Crowning glory', *Uncut*, Jan. 2006, p. 52; www.jmarr.com, 'Q&A' (Mar. 2001).

50   Stephen Dalton, 'Getting away with it', *Uncut*, Apr. 1999, p. 52; Barry McIlheney, 'The thoughts of Chairman Marr', *Melody Maker*, 3 Aug. 1985, p. 33; Rogan, *Morrissey and Marr*, p. 114; Talking Music, *The Interview: The Smiths* (Speek CD, 1998); Marr, interview with the author. 'I certainly wasn't going to be ashamed about it [being of Irish descent]', Marr explains, suggesting that his experience of anti-Irish prejudice made him 'steely' (ibid.).

51   Brian Boyd, 'Johnny, We Never Knew You', *Irish Times*, 'Arts' section, 8 May 1999, p. 6. Marr explains that he was 'made to feel different', especially through 'the racism and prejudice that [he] had to deal with all the time' (Marr, interview with the author).

52   Marr, interview with the author.

53   Boyd, 'Johnny take a bow', *Irish Times*, 'The Ticket' section, 31 Aug. 2007, p. 9.

54 McIlheney, 'The thoughts of Chairman Marr', *Melody Maker*, 3 Aug. 1985, p. 33;
    Rogan, *Morrissey and Marr*, p. 114; Talking Music, *The Interview: The Smiths*
    (Speek CD, 1998).

55 Goddard, 'Crowning glory', *Uncut*, Jan. 2006, p. 52.

56 Marella Buckley, 'Sitting on your politics: The Irish among the British and the
    women among the Irish', in Mac Laughlin, *Location and Dislocation*, pp. 110–11.

57 See Stokes, 'Introduction', p. 3.

58 McIlheney, 'The thoughts of Chairman Marr', *Melody Maker*, 3 Aug. 1985, p. 33;
    Joe Gore, 'Johnny Marr', *Guitar Player*, Jan. 1990, p. 71; Dalton, 'Getting away
    with it', *Uncut*, Apr. 1999, p. 52; Talking Music, *The Interview: The Smiths* (Speek
    CD, 1998); Marr, interview with the author.

59 Marr, interview with the author.

60 Stokes, 'Introduction', p. 4.

61 www.jmarr.com, 'Q&A' (Mar. 2001).

62 Boyd, 'Johnny, we never knew you', *Irish Times*, 'Arts' section, 8 May 1999, p. 6.

63 Gallagher and Christian, *Brothers*, p. 68.

64 John Shepherd, 'Music as cultural text', in John Paynter, Tim Howell, Richard
    Orton and Peter Seymour (eds.), *Companion to Contemporary Musical Thought*,
    vol. 1 (London: Routledge, 1992), p. 147.

65 Marr, interview with the author. See also Kevin O'Connor, *The Irish in Britain*
    (Dublin: Torc Books, 1974), pp. 146–7.

66 Marr, interview with the author.

67 Stuart Clarke, public interview with Johnny Marr, Trinity College, Dublin, 2 Oct.
    2007. I am grateful to Paul Nolan of *Hot Press* for providing a transcript of this
    interview.

68 Marr, interview with the author.

69 Richard Purden, 'Mancunian Marr is still proud of his Irish roots', *Irish Post*,
    'Rí-Rá' section, 7 July 2007, p. 3.

70 Marr cited in Kevin Cummins, *Manchester: Looking for the Light through the
    Pouring Rain* (London: Faber and Faber, 2009), p. 147.

71 Marr, interview with the author.

72 Purden, 'Mancunian Marr is still proud of his Irish roots', *Irish Post*, 'Rí-Rá' section,
    7 July 2007, p. 3. In his post-Smiths career, Marr composed a song called 'The
    InBetweens', which he suggests was informed by this context (Marr, interview
    with the author). See Johnny Marr and the Healers, *Boomslang* (New Voodoo
    Limited, 2003).

73 The Edge, cited in Waters, *Race of Angels*, p. 289. The guitarist was born in London
    to Welsh parents, who moved to Dublin when he was one. See Eamon Dunphy,
    The Unforgettable Fire: The Story of U2 (London: Viking, 1987), p. 57.

74 www.jmarr.com, 'Q&A', no. 4 (2000) (http://jmarr.com/qanda4.html); Martin
    Roach, *The Right to Imagination & Madness: An Essential Collection of Candid
    Interviews with Top UK Alternative Songwriters* (London: Independent Music
    Press, 1994), p. 310; Marr, interview with the author.

75 Gore, 'Johnny Marr', *Guitar Player*, Jan. 1990, p. 71. Marr's harmonica can be heard
    in the opening bars of the group's debut single, as well as in the fading coda of
    their final album. See 'Hand In Glove' (Rough Trade, 1983), and 'I Won't Share
    You' (*Strangeways, Here We Come*).

76   Gore, 'Johnny Marr', *Guitar Player*, Jan. 1990, p. 71. McIlheney, 'The thoughts of Chairman Marr', *Melody Maker*, 3 Aug. 1985, p. 33; Rogan, *Morrissey and Marr*, p. 114.

77   Boyd, 'Johnny take a bow', *Irish Times*, 'The Ticket' section, 31 Aug. 2007, p. 8.

78   Rogan, *Morrissey and Marr*, p. 117.

79   Hardy and Laing, *The Faber Companion to 20th-century Popular Music*, p. 153. See also McIlheney, 'The thoughts of Chairman Marr', *Melody Maker*, 3 Aug. 1985, p. 33; Carol McDaid, 'He chopped up a piano with Dylan', *Observer*, 'Review' section, 20 May 2001, p. 14.

80   Clarke, public interview with Johnny Marr, Trinity College, Dublin, 2 Oct. 2007.

81   Ibid.; Rogan, *Morrissey and Marr*, pp. 114, 121, 123.

82   The Edge cited in Waters, *Race of Angels*, p. 237; Rogan, *Morrissey and Marr*, pp. 118–19; Rogan, *The Smiths*, pp. 22–3.

83   Rogan, *Morrissey and Marr*, pp. 120, 124.

84   Ibid. p. 123–30.

85   Purden, 'Keeping up with The Smiths', *Irish Post*, 1 Sept. 2007, p. 17; Rogan, *Morrissey and Marr*, pp. 114, 124.

86   Rogan, *Morrissey and Marr*, pp. 114, 124.

87   Purden, 'Keeping up with The Smiths', *Irish Post*, 1 Sept. 2007, p. 17; Rogan, *Morrissey and Marr*, pp. 144–5.

88   Rogan, *Morrissey and Marr*, pp. 145–9.

89   Marr, interview with the author. See also Andrew Male, 'Get the message', *Q/Mojo Classic: Morrissey and the Story of Manchester* (2006), p. 79.

90   Clarke, public interview with Johnny Marr, Trinity College, Dublin, 2 Oct. 2007.

91   Purden, 'Keeping up with The Smiths', *Irish Post*, 1 Sept. 2007, p. 17.

92   Goddard, *The Smiths*, p. 25.

93   Purden, 'Keeping up with The Smiths', *Irish Post*, 1 Sept. 2007, p. 17, emphasis added.

94   Male, 'Get the message', *Q/Mojo Classic: Morrissey and the Story of Manchester* (2006), p. 79; Marr, interview with the author.

95   Frank Worrall, 'The cradle snatchers', *Melody Maker*, 3 Sept. 1983, p. 27; McCormick, 'All men have secrets', *Hot Press*, 4 May 1984, p. 19. Interestingly, when Morrissey interviewed the actress Pat Phoenix for a British magazine, he was keen to enquire about her 'affinity' with Ireland. See Morrissey, 'Never turn your back on mother earth', *Blitz*, May 1985, p. 28.

96   Nick Adams, 'Johnny too bad', *No. 1*, 25 Aug. 1984, p. 32; McIlheney, 'The thoughts of Chairman Marr', *Melody Maker*, 3 Aug. 1985, p. 33. See also Cary Darling, 'Marr needs guitars', *BAM: Bay Area Music Magazine*, 3 July 1987, p. 18.

97   Clarke, public interview with Johnny Marr, Trinity College, Dublin, 2 Oct. 2007. See also John McKenna, 'The Smiths: These charming men', *Hot Press*, 27 Jan.–9 Feb. 1984, p. 16; Dave Fanning, 'The Smiths at the SFX', *Irish Times*, 23 May 1984, p. 10. For details of The Smiths' Irish tours, see Rogan, *Morrissey and Marr*, pp. 316–29. For details of U2's only formal Irish show in this period, see Dunphy, *The Unforgettable Fire*, p. 252.

98   Marr, interview with the author. See also 'Smiths go to Ireland', *Melody Maker*, 13 Oct. 1984, p. 3. 'I remember The Smiths going to places like Letterkenny and

Coleraine', Morrissey later recalled, noting that 'the crowds were fantastic'. He also explained that The Smiths 'were never able to play Derry', implying that the band had wished to perform in that city (Boyd, 'Paddy Englishman', *Irish Times*, 'Arts' section, 20 Nov. 1999, p. 5).

99   Marr, interview with the author; Goddard, *The Smiths*, p. 58. 'Still Ill' was originally broadcast as part of a radio session for the *John Peel Show* (BBC Radio 1, 21 Sept. 1983), and was later released on the band's debut album, *The Smiths*.

100   See Steve Sutherland (ed.), 'Backlash', *Melody Maker*, 24 Nov. 1984, p. 26.

101   'Talk, talk, talk', *Melody Maker*, 24 Nov. 1984, p. 6.

102   Marr, interview with the author, original emphasis.

103   Ibid.; Marr, 'It's our most enduring record', *Uncut*, Mar. 2007, p. 48; Steve Lowe et al., 'Now my chart is full', *Q/Mojo Special Edition: The Smiths and Morrissey* (2004), p. 134; Goddard, *The Smiths*, p. 106.

104   www.jmarr.com, 'Q&A', no. 4. *Hatful of Hollow* (Rough Trade, 1984). Significantly, the matrix message that appeared in the vinyl run-off groove at the end of the group's next album, *Meat is Murder*, read: 'Doing the Wythenshawe Waltz', a reference to the geographical locale and prevailing musical style of Marr's early years.

105   Goddard, *The Smiths*, p. 107. The band had previously never opened their set with this song, and subsequently did so only once. See Rogan, *Morrissey and Marr*, pp. 313–33.

106   For examples of the Claddagh ring, see The Smiths, 'Bigmouth Strikes Again', *Smash Hits*, 4–17 June 1986, p. 60; *Smash Hits*, 'Morrissey', *Smash Hits*, 3–16 Jan. 1985, p. 48; Mark Frith (ed.), *The Best of* Smash Hits*: The 80s* (London: Sphere, 2006), p. 59; Jo Slee, *Peepholism: Into the Art of Morrissey* (London: Sidgwick & Jackson, 1994), title pages. See also *NME*, 2 May 1987, p. 1; Elvis Costello, *Almost Blue* (F-Beat, 1981), and Oasis, *(What's the Story) Morning Glory?* (Creation, 1994).

107   See Andrew O'Hagan, 'Cartwheels over broken glass', *London Review of Books*, 4 Mar. 2004, p. 19.

108   Kelly, 'The further thoughts of Chairman Mo', *NME*, 8 June 1985, p. 24. See *NME*, 8 June 1985, p. 1.

109   In this respect the song is reminiscent of Aretha Franklin's version of 'Eleanor Rigby' (Rhino, 1970), in which 'Father Mackenzie' was Protestantised as 'Pastor'. Mike Joyce had made his First Holy Communion at the Holy Name church (see http://www.mikejoyce.com/start.html ('Smiths photographs II')).

110   For the reference to Joan of Arc, see 'Bigmouth Strikes Again' (Rough Trade, 1986). The matrix message on the vinyl run-off groove of *Strangeways, Here We Come* read: 'Guy Fawkes was a genius'. In a 1984 television interview, Morrissey – when asked about his Catholicism – turned attention to Ireland (see *Earsay*, Channel 4, 7 July 1984).

111   'The Smiths: Message understood', *Rorschach Testing*, Dec. 1983, p. 16.

112   Simon Goddard and Paul Lester (eds.), 'The *Uncut* 100', *Uncut*, Sept. 2005, p. 75; Paul Lester, 'Titanic!', *Uncut*, Mar. 2000, p. 62.

113   Terry Christian, *My Word* (London: Orion, 2007), p. 106.

114   Kit Aitken, 'String driven thing', *Uncut*, Dec. 1999, p. 84. Butler has described himself as 'second-generation Irish'. See John Mulvey, 'Rogue man star', *NME*, 10 Jan. 1998, p. 43.

115 Susan Corrigan, 'What's to be done with her?', *Smiths Indeed*, no. 10 (winter 1988), no pagination.

116 For an account of the band's popularity in Ireland, see Eoin Devereux, 'Being wild(e) about Morrissey: Fandom and identity', in Mary Corcoran and Michel Peillon (eds.), *Uncertain Ireland* (Dublin: Institute of Public Administration, 2006), pp. 235–45; Joe Breen, 'Staking their claim', *Irish Times*, 22 Feb. 1985, p. 12. For a discussion of Smiths fandom amongst Latinos in southern California, see Jennifer Torres, 'Morrissey has strong bond with Latinos', *Stockton Record*, 'LENS' section, 27 Apr. 2007, p. 1.

117 Wallie Mason cited in Torres, 'Morrissey has strong bond with Latinos', *Stockton Record*, 'LENS' section, 27 Apr. 2007, p. 1; fan cited in Jason A. Heidemann, 'The Morrissey the merrier', *Time Out Chicago*, 10–16 May 2007, p. 96.

118 Worrall, 'The cradle snatchers', *Melody Maker*, 3 Sept. 1983, p. 26.

119 Paul du Noyer, 'Oh, such drama!', *Q*, Aug. 1987, p. 58.

120 See Sean O'Hagan and James Brown, 'The Three Horsemen of the Apocalypse', *NME*, 25 Feb. 1989, p. 14.

121 Marr, interview with the author.

122 See, for example, 'Girl Afraid' (*Hatful of Hollow*) and 'Shakespeare's Sister' (Rough Trade, 1985). Marr wrote the music for the latter 'after listening intently to some Johnny Cash albums' (Nick Kent, 'Isolation', *Q/Mojo Classic: Morrissey and the Story of Manchester* (2006), p. 62). Country music has often been popular amongst the Irish in England (Stokes, 'Introduction', p. 3), with Cash being a particular favourite amongst this constituency (Sarah Hughes, 'Surgical spirit', *Observer*, *Observer* Music Monthly section, 20 Nov. 2005, p. 11).

123 Julian Stringer, 'The Smiths: Repressed (but remarkably dressed)', *Popular Music*, vol. 11, no. 1 (1992), p. 19. For a brief discussion of Marr's application of folk tunings, see Gore, 'Johnny Marr', *Guitar Player*, Jan. 1990, p. 72. For details of the use of 'folk' guitar tunings in Irish traditional music, see Vallely, *The Companion to Irish Traditional Music*, pp. 161–2.

124 Marr, interview with the author.

125 Stringer, 'The Smiths', p. 19. For an account of 'independent' music, see David Hesmondhalgh, 'Indie: The institutional politics and aesthetics of a popular music genre', *Cultural Studies*, vol. 13, no. 1 (1999), pp. 34–61.

126 Marr has acknowledged these sources. See, for example, McIlheney, 'The thoughts of Chairman Marr', *Melody Maker*, 3 Aug. 1985, p. 33; Gore, 'Johnny Marr', *Guitar Player*, Jan. 1990, pp. 72–3; *Granada Reports*, Granada Television, 21 Feb. 1985. 'This Charming Man' (Rough Trade, 1983), 'Back To The Old House', 'Reel Around The Fountain' (*Hatful of Hollow*), 'Nowhere Fast', 'I Want The One I Can't Have', 'Barbarism Begins At Home' (*Meat is Murder*), 'Ask' (Rough Trade, 1986).

127 See Gore, 'Johnny Marr', *Guitar Player*, Jan. 1990, pp. 68–74; *Top Ten Guitar Heroes*, Channel 4, 24 Mar. 2001.

128 Marr has discussed and demonstrated this point. See, for example, *Granada Reports*, Granada Television, 21 Feb. 1985.

129 See Andrew Mueller, 'Johnny Marr', *Melody Maker*, 30 Sept. 1989, p. 8. For an account of masculinity in 1970s rock, see Simon Frith and Angela McRobbie, 'Rock and sexuality', *Screen Education*, no. 29 (winter 1978/79), pp. 5–8.

130 See Gore, 'Johnny Marr', *Guitar Player*, Jan. 1990, p. 73.

131   Moore, *Rock: The Primary Text*, p. 36.

132   Rogan, *Morrissey and Marr*, p. 155.

133   Moore, *Rock: The Primary Text*, p. 133. As Moore has explained: 'Register and range describe simply the relative height and the spread of the pitches used in a song' (ibid. p. 43).

134   Stan Hawkins, *Settling the Pop Score: Pop Texts and Identity Politics* (Aldershot: Ashgate, 2002), p. 86.

135   Simon Reynolds, 'Whatever happened to Britpop?', *salon.com*, http://www.salon.com/ent/music/review/2007/12/08/britbox/

136   Stringer, 'The Smiths', p. 19. As Laing points out, prior to the late 1970s, 'British accents in British rock music had been in a small minority' (Laing, *One Chord Wonders*, p. 26).

137   John Aizlewood et al., '100 greatest singers and their 1000 greatest songs', *Q*, Apr. 2007, p. 78. This notion of 'emotive connotations' is taken from Gino Stefani, and refers, as Richard Middleton explains, to 'the agreed affective implications of musical events'. Thus, 'punk is associated with aggression', while 'singer-songwriters' are equated 'with confessional intimacy' (Middleton, *Studying Popular Music*, p. 232). Morrissey's vocal style appeared to gravitate towards the latter.

138   Stringer, 'The Smiths', pp. 19–20.

139   Hawkins, *Settling the Pop Score*, p. 87.

140   Hubbs, 'Music of the "fourth gender"', pp. 272–3. As Laing has explained, 'by excluding the musicality of singing, the possible contamination of the lyric message by the aesthetic pleasures offered by melody, harmony, pitch and so on, is avoided' (Laing, *One Chord Wonders*, p. 54).

141   See, for example, *Earsay*, Channel 4, 7 July 1984; *South Bank Show*, ITV, 18 Oct. 1987; Barney Hoskyns, 'The Smiths: These disarming men', *NME*, 4 Feb. 1984, p. 13. For Morrissey's use of the term 'new poetry', see *Front Row*, BBC Radio 4, 18 Feb. 2009.

142   For an inventory of references to both Wilde and Delaney in Morrissey's song lyrics, see Goddard, *The Smiths*. Terry Eagleton sees Delaney as evidence of the 'Irish émigré influence' on Salford (see Eagleton, *The Gatekeeper*, p. 54).

143   Ian Pye, 'Some mothers do 'ave 'em', *NME*, 7 June 1986, p. 30.

144   See McCormick, 'All men have secrets', *Hot Press*, 4 May 1984, p. 19; Van Poznak, 'Morrissey: *The Face* interview', *The Face*, July 1984, p. 32; Fricke, 'Keeping up with The Smiths', *Rolling Stone*, 9 Oct. 1986, pp. 32–3; Ian Birch, 'The Morrissey collection', *Smash Hits*, 21 June–4 July 1984, pp. 40–1; Rogan, *The Smiths*, pp. 83, 87; Rogan, *Morrissey and Marr*, p. 71. See also the matrix messages on 'William, It Was Really Nothing' (Rough Trade, 1984), *Hatful of Hollow*, 'The Boy With The Thorn In His Side' (Rough Trade, 1985), and 'Bigmouth Strikes Again'.

145   Birch, 'The Morrissey collection', *Smash Hits*, 21 June–4 July 1984, p. 40. It is worth noting, though, that Morrissey made use of other Irish-related sources, not least for the song lyrics of 'This Charming Man', The Smiths' most celebrated song, which were drawn in part from a novel (Henry Green's *Loving* (1945)) that explored Anglo-Irish tensions during the Second World War. See Mat Snow, ''Ello 'andsome!', *Mojo*, Mar. 2008, p. 87.

146   See, for example, The Smiths, *Meat is Murder* (London: Smithdom, 1985), no pagination; 'I Started Something That I Couldn't Finish' (see *The Smiths – The Complete*

Picture, Warner DVD, 2000). For images of Delaney on the cover of Smiths records, see 'Girlfriend In A Coma' (Rough Trade, 1987); *Louder than Bombs*.

147   See Len Brown, 'Desecrating Wildly', *NME*, 16 July 1988, p. 10.

148   Hubbs, 'Music of the "fourth gender"', p. 269. For Morrissey's comments on his song lyrics, see John Wilde, 'The Smiths', *Jamming!*, no. 17 (1984), p. 18; Allan Jones, 'Trial by Jury', *Melody Maker*, 16 Mar. 1985, p. 26.

149   Hubbs, 'Music of the "fourth gender"', p. 289; James Hopkin, 'Jeane', in Peter Wild (ed.), *Paint A Vulgar Picture: Fiction Inspired by The Smiths* (London: Serpent's Tail, 2009), p. 181.

150   Zoe Williams, 'The light that never goes out', *Guardian*, 'Weekend' magazine, 23 Feb. 2002, p. 41.

151   See *South Bank Show*, ITV, 18 Oct. 1987; Leboff, 'Goodbye cruel world', *Melody Maker*, 26 Sept. 1987, p. 26; Rogan, *The Smiths*, p. 56; Mark Cooper, 'Smithspeak', *No. 1*, 13 Mar. 1984, p. 8. For an account of Morrissey's sartorial interests, see Iain Webb, 'This handsome devil', *NME*, 'Undress' supplement, 26 May 1984, pp. 4–5. For a visual example of such styles, see Rogan, *The Smiths*, pp. 52, 66, 69, 87.

152   Stringer, 'The Smiths', p. 22. For an account of the Wildean aspect of the daffodils, see Birch, 'The Morrissey collection', *Smash Hits*, 21 June–4 July 1984, p. 40; David Bret, *Morrissey: Landscapes of the Mind* (London: Robson Books, 1994), p. 29; Rogan, *The Smiths*, pp. 35, 45, 53; *Earsay*, Channel 4, 7 July 1984. For a visual example of this look, see Rogan, *The Smiths*, pp. 75, 97; *Top of the Pops*, BBC 1, 31 May 1984.

153   Sean O'Hagan, 'Look back in angst', *Observer*, 'Review' section, 7 Apr. 2002, p. 9.

154   Katie Neville, 'The post cool school', *The Face*, Feb. 1984, p. 33.

155   Brooker, 'Has the world changed or have I changed?'

156   See, for example, Rogan, *The Smiths*, pp. 47, 62, 79, 125, 126.

157   Rogan, *Morrissey and Marr*, pp. 142–3. For a brief discussion of synth-pop, see Moore, *Rock: The Primary Text*, pp. 133–6.

158   Graham Smith and Dylan Jones, 'Alias Smith and …', *Record Mirror*, 8 Sept. 1984, p. 12. As Laing points out, there has been 'a tendency [in popular music] to present groups as "families", to trade on an association between musical and domestic harmony' (Laing, *One Chord Wonders*, p. 43).

159   Wilde, 'The Smiths', *Jamming!*, no. 17 (1984), p. 17. Such assertions were clearly informed by the notion of the guitar as an 'authentic' instrument for unmediated self-expression.

160   Moore, *Rock: The Primary Text*, p. 133; Middleton, *Studying Popular Music*, p. 90, original emphasis.

161   For an account of 'authenticity' in rock, see Keightley, 'Reconsidering rock', pp. 131–9.

162   Ian Pye, 'Magnificent obsessions', *Melody Maker*, 26 Nov. 1983, p. 24; Worrall, 'The cradle snatchers', *Melody Maker*, 3 Sept. 1983, p. 27; Allan Jones, 'The blue romantics', *Melody Maker*, 3 Mar. 1984, p. 25. For similar comments, see Garfield, 'This charming man', *Time Out*, 7–13 Mar. 1985, p. 19; John Wilde, 'Morrissey's year', *Jamming!*, Dec. 1984, p. 24.

163   Allan Jones, 'Johnny guitar', *Melody Maker*, 14 Apr. 1984. pp. 10, 11, original emphases.

164   Stringer, 'The Smiths', p. 17.

165   See Moore, *Rock: The Primary Text*, pp. 146–53.

166 Rogan, *Morrissey and Marr*, p. 313; Scanlon, *The Pogues*, p. 9.

167 Steve Jones, 'Re-viewing rock writing: The origins of popular music criticism', *American Journalism*, vol. 9, pts. 2/3 (1992), pp. 102–3.

168 Simpson, *Saint Morrissey*, p. 102, original emphasis.

169 Marr, interview with the author; John Crace, 'Salford lad is back', *Guardian*, 'Education' section, 12 Feb. 2008, p. 2.

170 Simon Reynolds, 'Songs of love and hate', *Melody Maker*, 12 Mar. 1988, p. 34.

171 Goddard, 'Crowning glory', *Uncut*, Jan. 2006, p. 52, original emphasis; Marr, interview with the author.

172 Jake Arnott, 'A major part of me is always dark …', *Time Out*, 2 June 2004, p. 10.

173 O'Riordan, interview with the author.

174 Len Brown, *Meetings with Morrissey* (London: Omnibus Press, 2008), p. 78.

175 *Earsay*, Channel 4, 7 July 1984; Dave Fanning, 'The star who's taking the pap out of pop', *Irish Times*, 24 Mar. 1987, p. 10.

176 Nabeel Zuberi, 'Guantánamo, here we come: Out of place with The Smiths', in Campbell and Coulter, *Why Pamper Life's Complexities?*

177 Marr, interview with the author.

178 Ibid.

179 See the fan accounts cited in Kevin Cummins, 'Who do they think they are?', *Observer* magazine, 27 Nov. 2005, p. 29, and Heidemann, 'The Morrissey the merrier', *Time Out Chicago*, 10–16 May 2007, p. 96.

180 Karl Maton, 'Last night they dreamt that somebody loved them: Smiths fans (and me) in the late 1980s', in Campbell and Coulter, *Why Pamper Life's Complexities?*, original emphasis.

181 Ibid.

182 Marr, interview with the author.

183 For Morrissey's comments on black music, see Owen, 'Home thoughts from abroad', *Melody Maker*, 27 Sept. 1986, p. 16. See also Danny Kelly and Adrian Thrills, '*NME* readers' poll 1984', *NME*, 23 Feb. 1985, p. 22. For an account of the racism debate, see Rogan, *The Smiths*, p. 145.

184 Andy Spinoza, 'Morrissey: The man, the myth, the mouth', *City Life*, Nov. 1986, p. 25.

185 Danny Kelly, 'Exile on mainstream', *NME*, 14 Feb. 1987, p. 44.

186 Rogan, *The Smiths*, p. 54, 154; George Byrne, 'The tune smith', *Hot Press*, 12 Mar. 1987, p. 21; Morrissey, 'Portrait of the artist as a consumer', *NME*, 17 Sept. 1983, p. 11; Darling, 'Marr needs guitars', *BAM: Bay Area Music Magazine*, 3 July 1987, p. 18; Purden, 'Keeping up with The Smiths', *Irish Post*, 1 Sept. 2007, p. 17; McRae, 'The Smiths' Anti-Apartheid benefit', *NME*, 3 Jan. 1987, p. 28; Andrew Warnes, 'Black, white and blue: The racial antagonism of The Smiths' record sleeves', *Popular Music*, vol. 27, no. 1 (Jan. 2008), p. 147.

187 See, for example, Zuberi, '"The last truly British people you will ever know"', pp. 541, 546; Hyder, *Brimful of Asia*, p. 107; Christian, *My Word*, p. 65; Rupa Huq, 'Morrissey and me', *New Statesman*, 10 Dec. 2007 (http://www.newstatesman.com/writers/rupa_huq).

188 Zuberi, *Sounds English*, p. 34.

189 Simpson, *Saint Morrissey*, pp. 51, 180. See also Dave Simpson, 'Still doing it his way', *Guardian*, 12 Nov. 1999, p. 25. Clearly, the simple fact of being second-

generation Irish (or having experienced anti-Irish prejudice) does not preclude someone from harbouring or expressing racist thoughts or views.

190 Bracewell, *England is Mine*, p. 226; Heidi Mason, 'Morrissey and the outsider ideal', *Smiths Indeed*, no. 10 (winter 1988), no pagination.

191 Eva, 'Home sweet home?', pp. 139, 142, 144.

192 *Earsay*, Channel 4, 7 July 1984.

193 Christian, *My Word*, p. 66.

194 Rogan, *Morrissey and Marr*, pp. 142–3.

195 Boyd, 'Johnny take a bow', *Irish Times*, 'The Ticket' section, 31 Aug. 2007, p. 9. See also Boyd, 'Johnny, we never knew you', *Irish Times*, 'Arts' section, 8 May 1999, p. 6; Rogan, *Morrissey and Marr*, pp. 162–3.

196 See Laing, *One Chord Wonders*, pp. 42–3, 50. Many rock and pop musicians of Irish descent have changed their names, most notably Dusty Springfield (Mary O'Brien), Johnny Rotten (John Lydon), Elvis Costello (Declan McManus), Chas Smash of Madness (Cathal Smyth), and Boy George (George O'Dowd).

197 Rolston, '"This is not a rebel song"', pp. 64–5. See also Dave Laing cited in Bradby, '"Imagining Ireland" conference', p. 108.

198 Eamonn Hughes, '"Lancelot's position": The fiction of Irish-Britain', in A. Robert Lee (ed.), *Other Britain, Other British: Contemporary Multicultural Fiction* (London: Pluto Press, 1995), p. 143.

199 Ibid. pp. 144, 152–4.

200 Ullah, 'Second-generation Irish youth', pp. 317–19.

201 Arrowsmith, 'Writing "home"', pp. 214, 219–21, 236–7.

202 Malone and Dooley, '"Dwelling in displacement"', p. 25.

203 Savage, 'Rough emeralds', *Guardian*, second section, 17 Mar. 1995, p. 11.

204 Rogan, *The Smiths*, p. 10.

205 See Brah, *Cartographies of Diaspora*, pp. 16, 180, 193, 197.

206 Simon Reynolds, 'Songs of love and hate', *Melody Maker*, 19 Mar. 1988, p. 21. Reynolds contrasts this aspect of The Smiths with The Rolling Stones, who were 'all about leaving home'.

207 The first recording of the track was originally broadcast as part of a radio session for the *John Peel Show* (BBC Radio 1, 21 Sept. 1983), and later released on *Hatful of Hollow* (this is the version that I discuss here). The track was clearly important to the band, as they performed it frequently during their formative phase (see Rogan, *Morrissey and Marr*, pp. 316–19), and included it (albeit in re-recorded form) on their 1987 compilation, *Louder than Bombs*.

208 Moore, *Rock: The Primary Text*, p. 92.

209 Marr has often discussed the band's evocation of melancholy. See, for example, Goddard, 'Crowning glory', *Uncut*, Jan. 2006, p. 52; Marr, interview with the author.

210 Wilde, 'Morrissey's year', *Jamming!*, Dec. 1984, p. 26; Biba Kopf, 'A suitable case for treatment', *NME*, 22/29 Dec. 1984, p. 7.

211 Harte, 'Migrancy, performativity and autobiographical identity', p. 235. Niall Stokes, 'The private Kate Bush', *Hot Press*, 21 Nov. 1985, p. 37, emphasis added.

212 Bobby Gilmore cited in Tony Murray, 'Curious streets: Diaspora, displacement and transgression in Desmond Hogan's London Irish narratives', *Irish Studies Review*, vol. 14, no. 2 (May 2006), p. 239.

213   Murray, 'Curious streets', pp. 245, 248; Malone and Dooley, '"Dwelling in displace-
        ment"', p. 25, original emphasis.
214   Gray, 'Curious hybridities', p. 209.
215   The first recording of this track was originally broadcast as part of a radio session
        for the *John Peel Show* (BBC Radio 1, 17 Dec. 1986), and was later released as
        the B-side of 'Sheila Take A Bow'. The track was clearly an important one for the
        band, as it was performed live at all of the group's concerts on the *Queen is Dead*
        tour (see Rogan, *Morrissey and Marr*, pp. 329–33), and was selected as the opening
        track on the 1987 compilation, *Louder than Bombs*. 'Stretch Out And Wait' was
        first released on the 12-inch single of 'Shakespeare's Sister'.
216   This concern with 'home' has, of course, had a wider resonance in popular music
        – and popular culture generally. With this in mind, I do not wish to reduce The
        Smiths' address to 'home' to (only) this second-generation Irish context, but to
        suggest that this address might illuminate the band's negotiation of this context.
        For a theoretical account of 'home' in a wider context, see Morley and Robins, 'No
        place like *heimat*', pp. 3–31.
217   I take this term, 'home triad', from Ian MacDonald's account of The Beatles. See
        MacDonald, *Revolution in the Head: The Beatles' Records and the Sixties* (London:
        Pimlico, 1995, 2nd edn.), p. 366.
218   Sheila Whiteley, *The Space Between the Notes: Rock and the Counter-Culture*
        (London: Routledge, 1992), p. 125.
219   The first recording of this track was originally broadcast as part of a radio session
        for the *John Peel Show* (BBC Radio 1, 17 Dec. 1986), and was later released on the
        12-inch single of 'Shoplifters Of The World Unite' (Rough Trade, 1987). The track
        seems to have been important to the band, as it was performed live at all of the
        group's English shows on the *Queen is Dead* tour (see Rogan, *Morrissey and Marr*,
        pp. 331–3), and was included on the 1987 compilation, *Louder than Bombs*.
220   While rock musicians have often used acoustic, 'folksy' styles to convey a nostalgic
        yearning for 'home', they have, conversely, Moore suggests, deployed 'riff-based
        rock' to connote movement to urban centres. See Moore, *Rock: The Primary Text*,
        p. 92.
221   Hubbs, 'Music of the "fourth gender"', p. 280.
222   Gerry Smyth, *Space and the Irish Cultural Imagination* (Basingstoke: Palgrave,
        2001), p. 160.
223   Marr, interview with the author; Roach, *The Right to Imagination & Madness*,
        p. 310. The homology implied here – between a certain migrant mindset and a
        specific musical mood – is clearly one that Marr feels is valid.
224   Marr, interview with the author. See also Roach, *The Right to Imagination &
        Madness*, p. 317.
225   Marr, interview with the author. See also Roach, *The Right to Imagination &
        Madness*, p. 317.
226   Marr, interview with the author.
227   John Robb, *The North Will Rise Again: Manchester Music City, 1976–1996* (London:
        Aurum, 2009), p. 207.
228   Ibid. p. 207.
229   See Arrowsmith, 'Writing "home"', pp. 237–8.
230   See, for example, Owen, 'Home thoughts from abroad', *Melody Maker*, 27 Sept.

1986, p. 16. See also Male, 'Get the message', *Q/Mojo Classic: Morrissey and the Story of Manchester* (2006), p. 79.

231   Simon Goddard, *Mozipedia: The Encyclopedia of Morrissey and The Smiths* (London: Ebury Press, 2009), p. 281. This track was included on *The Queen is Dead*, and featured regularly in live performances to promote that album. See Rogan, *Morrissey and Marr*, pp. 331–3.

232   Stringer, 'The Smiths', p. 19.

233   See R. Day, *The Queen is Dead* (Woodford Green: International Music Publications, 1988), p. 13.

234   Goddard, 'Crowning glory', *Uncut*, Jan. 2006 pp. 60, 52; Marr, interview with the author.

235   Owen, 'Home thoughts from abroad', *Melody Maker*, 27 Sept. 1986, p. 16. Significantly, the matrix message at the end of side one of *The Queen is Dead* reads: 'Fear of Manchester'.

236   Brian Keaney, *Don't Hang About* (Oxford: Oxford University Press, 1985), p. 104, emphases added. See Goddard, *The Smiths*, p. 165.

237   The first recording of 'Miserable Lie' was originally broadcast as part of a radio session for the *John Peel Show* (BBC Radio 1, 31 May 1983), and was later included on their debut album. 'These Things Take Time' was first broadcast as part of a radio session for the *David Jensen Show* (BBC Radio 1, 4 July 1983), and was formally released on the 12-inch single of 'What Difference Does It Make' (Rough Trade, 1984).

238   Tim Jonze, 'Has the world changed or has he changed?', *NME*, 1 Dec. 2007, p. 14.

239   'A Rush And A Push And The Land Is Ours' was the opening track on the band's final album, *Strangeways, Here We Come*. For the source of 'A Rush And A Push ...', see Goddard, *The Smiths*, p. 240. Eliding this Irish context, Andrew Warnes claims that the song was born of the 'brutish field of British fascism', with Morrissey 'recapitulating Powellite [i.e. British nationalist] logic': 'he is stating a right of possession over England, is lamenting the nullification of this claim, and is naming repatriation as the means by which to correct such injustice', suggests Warnes (Warnes, 'Black, white and blue', p. 143).

240   'Pretty Girls Make Graves', *The Smiths*.

241   Goddard, 'Crowning glory', *Uncut*, Jan. 2006, p. 52.

242   See *Earsay*, Channel 4, 7 July 1984; Theodor Adorno, *The Culture Industry: Selected Essays on Mass Culture* (London: Routledge, 1991), p. 175; Murray, *Stomping the Blues*, p. 54.

243   Marr, interview with the author. See also Goddard, 'Crowning glory', *Uncut*, Jan. 2006, p. 52.

244   Marr, interview with the author.

245   Ibid.

246   Ibid. 'That Joke Isn't Funny Anymore' (*Meat is Murder*); 'Last Night I Dreamt That Somebody Loved Me' (*Strangeways, Here We Come*).

247   Marr, interview with the author. See also Roach, *The Right to Imagination & Madness*, p. 332.

248   Goddard, 'Crowning glory', *Uncut*, Jan. 2006, p. 52. Marr typically conceived musical ideas on guitar, which were subsequently passed (via audio cassette)

on to Morrissey, who would then add his song lyrics and vocal melodies. See John Harris, 'Trouble at mill', *Mojo*, Apr. 2001, pp. 58–9; *Top Ten Guitar Heroes*, Channel 4, 24 Mar. 2001; Roach, *The Right to Imagination & Madness*, p. 322.

249   *Dave Fanning*, RTÉ 2FM, 8 Nov. 2002.

250   Marr, interview with the author. 'Meat Is Murder' was the final track on *Meat is Murder*. 'I Know It's Over' appeared on *The Queen is Dead*.

251   See Goddard, *The Smiths*, p. 97.

252   'The Queen Is Dead' was the opening track on *The Queen is Dead*.

253   'How Soon Is Now?' was first released as an extra track on the 12-inch single of 'William, It Was Really Nothing'.

254   *The Tube*, Channel 4, 25 Oct. 1985. Elsewhere, the singer responded to questions about his background by insisting – somewhat anxiously – that he had had such an uninteresting and uneventful upbringing that it was not worthy of discussion. See, for example, *Earsay*, Channel 4, 7 July 1984.

255   Van Poznak, 'Morrissey: *The Face* interview', *The Face*, July 1984, p. 32.

256   Hubbs, 'Music of the "fourth gender"', p. 267.

257   Ibid.

258   This track appears on *The Queen is Dead*, and was performed at all of the band's 1986 live shows. See Rogan, *Morrissey and Marr*, pp. 328–33.

259   Brown, *Meetings with Morrissey*, p. 242.

260   Terry Eagleton, 'Mm … he was Irish, actually', *Fortnight*, vol. 277 (Oct. 1989), p. 30; Terry Eagleton, 'Introduction', in Oscar Wilde, *Plays, Prose Writings and Poems* (London: Everyman's Library, 1991), p. viii; Jerusha McCormack, 'Introduction: The Irish Wilde', in McCormack (ed.), *Wilde the Irishman* (New Haven: Yale University Press, 1998), p. 1.

261   *Earsay*, Channel 4, 7 July 1984.

262   Hoskyns, 'The Smiths', *NME*, 4 Feb. 1984, pp. 13, 41; Worrall, 'The cradle snatchers', *Melody Maker*, 3 Sept. 1983, p. 27. While such comments might be considered naive, utopian and self-serving (not least from a marketing point of view), they also point to an anti-segregationist stance that exceeds ethnic specificity.

263   The Prokofiev sequence can be heard at the beginning of the live album, *Rank* (Rough Trade, 1988), and was audibly highlighted in the televised excerpt of the group's show at Glasgow Barrowlands that was broadcast on *The Tube*, Channel 4, 25 Oct. 1985. The end-of-show 'stage invasion' was a feature of the group's live shows from as early as 1983. See Barney Hoskyns, 'Ridiculous and wonderful', *NME*, 1 Oct. 1983, p. 36; Dave McCullough, 'The Smiths ICA', *Sounds*, 15 Oct. 1983, p. 53. See also the televised version of their concert at Derby Assembly Rooms that was broadcast on *The Old Grey Whistle Test*, BBC 2, 9 Dec. 1983. A review of the group's 1986 tour noted 'a stage invasion of major proportions' (Dave Sexton, 'The Smiths, Sands, Carlisle', *Record Mirror*, 25 Oct. 1986, p. 64). For examples of such incursions, see the video recordings of shows at Wolverhampton Civic Hall (15 Oct. 1986) and Nottingham Royal Concert Hall (21 Oct. 1986) (video tapes in possession of the author).

264   Rogan, *Morrissey and Marr*, p. 225. This component of The Smiths' live show obviously constituted little more (and yet no less) than a symbolic blurring of boundaries between 'star' and 'fan', for while this moment signalled a refusal of the stage–floor distinction, the obvious economic discrepancies that shaped the

musician–spectator relationship were scarcely erased by such 'carnivalesque' features. For a brief discussion of this point, see Laing, *One Chord Wonders*, pp. 84–5.

265 John McLeod, *Beginning Postcolonialism* (Manchester: Manchester University Press, 2000), pp. 214–15.

266 Lydon, *Rotten*, p. 325; O'Riordan, interview with the author.

267 O'Riordan, interview with the author, original emphasis.

268 O'Callaghan cited in O'Connor, *The Irish in Britain*, pp. 146–7, emphases added.

269 Marr, interview with the author.

270 Nolan, 'I've something to get off my chest', *Hot Press*, 2 July 2008, p. 41.

271 Jones, 'The blue romantics', *Melody Maker*, 3 Mar. 1984, p. 35.

272 James Campbell, 'Escape from the margins', *Guardian*, 'Review' section, 19 Nov. 2005, p. 11.

273 See *Second Generation*, RTÉ Radio 1, Jan.–Feb. 2003.

274 George Byrne, 'The Manchester martyr', *Hot Press*, 11 Apr. 1986, p. 24.

275 See Rogan, *Morrissey and Marr*, pp. 242, 313, 320. For an account of Red Wedge, see John Street, 'Red Wedge: Another strange story of pop's politics', *Critical Quarterly*, vol. 30, no. 3 (autumn 1988), pp. 79–91.

276 See, for example, Tom Hibbert, 'Meat is murder!', *Smash Hits*, 31 Jan.–13 Feb. 1985, p. 41; Dave McCullough, 'Handsome devils', *Sounds*, 4 June 1983, p. 13.

277 William Graham, 'Johnny jumps up!', *Hot Press*, 11–30 May 1979, p. 17, emphases added.

278 James Henke, 'Oscar! Oscar! Great Britain goes Wilde for the "fourth-gender" Smiths', *Rolling Stone*, 7 June 1984, p. 45, original emphasis. In the group's 1985 tour programme, both Morrissey and Joyce listed Thatcher as their ultimate 'villain' (The Smiths, *Meat is Murder*, no pagination).

279 Tim Pat Coogan, *The Troubles: Ireland's Ordeal, 1966–1995 and the Search for Peace* (London: Hutchinson, 1995), p. 197.

280 Patrick Bishop and Eamonn Mallie, *The Provisional IRA* (London: Heinemann, 1987), p. 339.

281 See Trevor Kavanagh, 'Hang the IRA bombers says big *Sun* poll', *The Sun*, 19 Oct. 1984, p. 1; 'Denning calls for use of treason law', *The Times*, 18 Oct. 1984, p. 2.

282 'Moment of grief for Maggie', *Daily Mail*, 15 Oct. 1984, p. 3, emphases added. For a correct account of the operation, see Bishop and Mallie, *The Provisional IRA*, pp. 337–40.

283 Ian Pye, 'A hard day's misery', *Melody Maker*, 3 Nov. 1984, p. 31.

284 Ibid.

285 Brown, *Meetings with Morrissey*, p. 47.

286 See Jack O'Sullivan, 'All too easy to be seduced by the dangerous romanticism of Irishness', *Independent*, 26 Sept. 1996, p. 4; Lennon, McAdam and O'Brien, *Across the Water*, p. 10; Free, 'Tales from the fifth green field', p. 485.

287 Hubbs, 'Music of the "fourth gender"', p. 266.

288 See Steve Sutherland (ed.), 'Backlash', *Melody Maker*, 17 Nov. 1984, p. 16.

289 Ray King, 'Running scared?', *Manchester Evening News*, 9 Nov. 1984, p. 39.

290 Ibid.

291 Rory O'More, 'Spit in your eye', *An Phoblacht*, 22 Nov. 1984, p. 15.

292 Marr, interview with the author. While Marr recalls that he 'didn't mind [Morrissey's comments] at the time', he later felt that they were 'dubious and not totally informed, and put us in a little bit of an awkward position'.

293 O'More, 'Spit in your eye', *An Phoblacht*, 22 Nov. 1984, p. 15.

294 Stuart James cited in Rogan, *The Smiths*, p. 98.

295 Marr, interview with the author.

296 Derek Brown, 'Five men killed in Ulster "checkpoint" ambush', *Guardian*, 1 Aug. 1975, pp. 1, 22.

297 '"No music for Ulster" fear', *Melody Maker*, 9 Aug. 1975, p. 5; Smyth, *Noisy Island*, p. 49.

298 Marr, interview with the author.

299 Rogan, *The Smiths*, p. 98.

300 Ibid.

301 Glyn Brown, 'Laughter in paradise!', *Sounds*, 14 June 1986, p. 16.

302 Slee, *Peepholism*, p. 85.

303 Brown, 'Laughter in paradise!', *Sounds*, 14 June 1986, p. 16, original emphasis.

304 See, for example, Frith (ed.), *The Best of* Smash Hits, p. 121.

305 Garfield, 'This charming man', *Time Out*, 7–13 Mar. 1985, p. 19. See the Sex Pistols, 'God Save The Queen' (Virgin, 1977).

306 Pye, 'Some mothers do 'ave 'em', *NME*, 7 June 1986, p. 27. In the group's 1985 tour programme, Morrissey explained that the high point of his career was 'Not meeting Royalty.' In the same publication, Marr chose Queen Elizabeth as his 'villain' (The Smiths, *Meat is Murder*, no pagination).

307 Simon Reynolds and Joy Press, *The Sex Revolts: Gender, Rebellion and Rock 'n' Roll* (London: Serpent's Tail, 1995), p. 48; Laing, *One Chord Wonders*, p. 38.

308 Savage, *England's Dreaming*, pp. 352–3.

309 See *Melody Maker*, 'The Smiths' booklet, 23 Sept. 1989, no pagination. For Lydon's lyric, see Savage, *England's Dreaming*, p. 355.

310 Brooker, 'Has the world changed or have I changed?'. See also Alexis Petridis, 'The regina monologues', *Q/Mojo Special Edition: The Smiths and Morrissey* (2004), p. 50.

311 Bruce Dessau, 'Rebel without a cause', *City Limits*, 12–19 June 1986, p. 12.

312 Goddard, 'Crowning glory', *Uncut*, Jan. 2006, p. 60.

313 Zuberi, *Sounds English*, p. 33.

314 Ibid. p. 33.

315 Goddard, *The Smiths*, p. 177.

316 Laing, *One Chord Wonders*, p. xii, original emphasis.

317 See Colin Walsh, *Mud, Songs and Blighty: A Scrapbook of the First World War* (London: Hutchinson, 1975), p. 131; John Brophy and Eric Partridge, *The Long Trail: What the British Soldier Sang and Said in the Great War of 1914–18* (London: Andre Deutsch, 1965), p. 217.

318 John Brophy and Eric Partridge (eds.), *Songs and Slang of the British Soldier: 1914–1918* (London: Eric Partridge Ltd. at the Scholartis Press, 1930, 2nd edn.), pp. 99–100. The word 'Blighty' was 'a corruption of the Hindustani *bilaik*', meaning 'foreign country, especially England', which often occurred in the adjectival form of *bilaiti*, hence 'Blighty' (Brophy and Partridge, *Songs and Slang of the British Soldier*, p. 100). 'An alternative derivation is from *Vilayat*, Persian for strange or foreign. From this arose an Urdu corruption, *Belait*, which soldiers distorted to *Belati*, and eventually to *Blighty*' (Brophy and Partridge, *The Long Trail*, p. 86).

319 Gerard J. DeGroot, *Blighty: British Society in the Era of the Great War* (London: Longman, 1996), p. xiii.

320   See Paul Gilroy, *After Empire: Melancholia or Convivial Culture?* (London: Routledge, 2004), pp. 95–7; Jeremy Paxman, *The English: A Portrait of a People* (London: Michael Joseph, 1998). For the association of 'Dear Old Blighty' with the Second World War, see Various Artists, *There'll Always Be An England* (ASV CD, 1994); *This Happy Breed* (David Lean, UK, 1944). Observers recall that 'Dear Old Blighty' was sung during the Second World War. See 'WW2 People's War: An Archive of World War Two Memories – written by the public, gathered by the BBC', http://www.bbc.co.uk/ww2peopleswar/stories/81/a2951381.shtml

321   Gilroy, *After Empire*, p. 95.

322   Marr, interview with the author. For an account of Ireland's neutrality during the Second World War, see Wills, *That Neutral Island*.

323   Dave Simpson, 'Marr's attacks', *Guardian*, 'Friday Review' section, 18 Aug. 2000, p. 14.

324   See Goddard, *The Smiths*, pp. 50, 103; Marr, interview with the author.

325   Zuberi, *Sounds English*, p. 34.

326   See Cicely Courtneidge, *Cicely* (London: Hutchinson, 1953), pp. 130–9. The sampled version of the song is taken from the film *The L-Shaped Room* (Bryan Forbes, UK, 1962).

327   Zuberi, *Sounds English*, p. 33; Jon Savage, 'The escape artist', *Village Voice Rock 'n' Roll Quarterly* (summer 1989), p. 8.

328   See Goddard, *The Smiths*, p. 176. MC5 represented, for Hardy and Laing, 'a political strand of the underground music of the Sixties' that 'prefigured the concerns of the punk movement of the Seventies' (Hardy and Laing, *The Faber Companion to 20th-century Popular Music*, p. 629).

329   Mark Slobin, *Subcultural Sounds: Micromusics of the West* (Hanover: University Press of New England, 1993), p. 87.

330   Brooker, 'Has the world changed or have I changed?'.

331   Sean O'Hagan, 'What are your favourite songs by The Smiths?', http://blogs. guardian.co.uk/music/2007/05/what_are_your_favourite_songs.html. See also Savage, 'Rough emeralds', *Guardian*, second section, 17 Mar. 1995, p. 11.

332   Slee, *Peepholism*, p. 41.

333   Martin Dunn and Nick Ferrari, 'Smiths' "sick" royal disc rapped', *The Sun*, 16 June 1986, p. 13.

334   See, for example, Ray King, 'Stay away from us, club tells pop pests', *Manchester Evening News*, 2 Aug. 1988, p. 7.

335   Goddard, *The Smiths*, p. 180.

336   Darling, 'Marr needs guitars', *BAM: Bay Area Music Magazine*, 3 July 1987, p. 20; Kelly, 'Exile on mainstream', *NME*, 14 Feb. 1987, p. 45. One of The Smiths' road crew later informed the band: 'if I told you what we found on that stage you'd never go out and play live again' (Goddard, *The Smiths*, p. 180).

337   See Savage, *England's Dreaming*, pp. 365–7.

338   *The Filth and the Fury: A Sex Pistols Film* (Julien Temple, UK, 2000).

339   Reynolds, 'Songs of love and hate', *Melody Maker*, 12 Mar. 1988, p. 33, original emphasis.

340   Eva, 'Home sweet home?', p. 135.

341   See 'Pogues Fall from grace with government', *NME*, 19 Nov. 1988, p. 3; McIlheney, 'Celtic swingers', *Melody Maker*, 27 Oct. 1984, p. 25. The closest that

MacGowan came to an endorsement of IRA actions was a brief comment in January 1985 (three months after the Brighton bomb attack) in which he was asked about his views on Thatcher: 'Let's put it this way', he explained, 'I wish she'd been in a different room at Brighton' ('Shrink rap', *Melody Maker*, 19 Jan. 1985, p. 16).

342   Elms, 'Pogue in the eye', *The Face*, Mar. 1985, p. 32.

343   Easlea, 'Don't stand me down', *Record Collector*, Apr. 2002, p. 51; Roberts, 'Grand stand', *Uncut*, May 2002, p. 76.

344   An alternate reading might suggest that Morrissey wished to assimilate himself as English. However, this is perhaps unlikely given the ethnic signals – and attacks on England – outlined in this essay. Moreover, any such attempt to assimilate would itself have been born of a wish, as Simpson notes, 'to belong, to be loved, to be accepted by England' (Simpson, *Saint Morrissey*, p. 165). In other words, it would also have pertained to his Irish ethnicity.

345   Jon Savage, 'Androgyny: Confused chromosomes and camp followers', *The Face*, June 1983, p. 23.

346   Rolston, '"This is not a rebel song"', p. 65.

347   See Gartland, 'Terrorist ban hits pop song', *Observer*, 20 Nov. 1988, p. 4; Miller, 'The media and Northern Ireland', pp. 48, 57.

348   This background was evident in the film *A Hard Day's Night* (Richard Lester, UK, 1964), in which the character of Paul's grandfather, an ageing Irish immigrant (played by the Dublin-born Wilfred Brambell), shadows The Beatles throughout, issuing comments in a strong Irish accent. The band would also discuss their Irish background in various interviews. See, for instance, Ritchie Yorke, 'Ringo's right, we can't tour again', *NME*, 7 June 1969, p. 3; RTÉ News, 7 Nov. 1963.

349   John Lennon and Yoko Ono, *Some Time in New York City* (Apple, 1972); Jon Wiener, *Come Together: John Lennon in His Time* (London: Faber and Faber, 1985), pp. 159, 209; Ron Skoler, 'John & Yoko: Some time in New York City', *Sounds*, 2 Sept. 1972, p. 23. See also Vicki Wickham, 'Lennon backs IRA', *Melody Maker*, 19 Feb. 1972, p. 6.

350   Wings, 'Give Ireland Back To The Irish' (Apple, 1972); Michael Watts, 'Paul's protest', *Melody Maker*, 12 Feb. 1972, p. 19; Johnny Black, 'The *Mojo* interview', *Mojo*, May 2003, p. 70.

351   Lennon's investment in Irish issues extended to his attendance of formal meetings (of anti-internment committees) and his financial support of republican groups. See Liam Clarke, '"Pro-IRA" Lennon spied on by FBI', *Sunday Times*, 5 Oct. 1997, p. 10.

352   Wiener, *Come Together*, pp. 210–11, emphasis added.

353   'Mail bag', *Melody Maker*, 24 June 1972, p. 64; 'Mail bag', *Melody Maker*, 1 July 1972, p. 48.

354   Mark Lewisohn (ed.), *Wingspan: Paul McCartney's Band on the Run* (London: Bulfinch Press, 2002), p. 40; Watts, 'Paul's protest', *Melody Maker*, 12 Feb. 1972, p. 19; Adrian Tame and Peter Chippindale, 'Wings fly high', *Melody Maker*, 19 Feb. 1972, p. 18; Laurie Henshaw, 'Censored', *Melody Maker*, 11 Mar. 1972, pp. 24–5.

355   'Mail bag', *Melody Maker*, 4 Mar. 1972, p. 15; Mark Plummer, 'If Paul McCartney really wants to do something for Ireland, why doesn't he stop singing about it and come here?', *Melody Maker*, 4 Mar. 1972, p. 42.

356   Dwyer, 'Mac the mouth', *Sunday Tribune*, 'People' section, 2 Aug. 1987, p. 1.
357   Rogan, *Morrissey and Marr*, pp. 61–2.
358   Rogan, *The Smiths*, pp. 78, 97.
359   Len Brown, 'Born to be Wilde', *NME*, 13 Feb. 1988, p. 31.
360   Bracewell, *England is Mine*, p. 226.
361   See, for example, Foster, *Paddy and Mr. Punch*.
362   Brah, *Cartographies of Diaspora*, p. 209.
363   Savage, 'Rough emeralds', *Guardian*, second section, 17 Mar. 1995, p. 11.
364   I take these terms from Paul Gilroy's allusion to Rakim. See Gilroy, '"It ain't where you're from"', pp. 3–16.

Coda: *From the Margins to the Centre*

 1   *Front Row*, BBC Radio 4, 18 Feb. 2009, original emphasis.
 2   Dave Marsh cited in Savage, 'Rough emeralds', *Guardian*, second section, 17 Mar. 1995, p. 11.
 3   Jon Savage, 'How we listened then', *Observer*, *Observer* Music Monthly section, 17 July 2005, p. 30.
 4   Simon Frith, 'I am what I am', *Village Voice*, 3 Aug. 1993, p. 82.
 5   Rowland, interview with the author.
 6   See, for example, the song 'Foggy Dew' (Charles O'Neill, 1919).
 7   Marr, interview with the author.
 8   Slobin, *Subcultural Sounds*, p. x.
 9   Rowland, interview with the author, emphasis added.
10   *The Pogues: Completely Pogued* (Start Video, 1988).
11   See Clerk, *Pogue Mahone*, pp. 90, 156.
12   Jonze, 'Has the world changed or has he changed?', *NME*, 1 Dec. 2007, p. 13.
13   Leboff, 'Goodbye cruel world', *Melody Maker*, 26 Sept. 1987, p. 27.
14   Jonze, 'Has the world changed or has he changed?', *NME*, 1 Dec. 2007, p. 14.
15   David Quantick, 'The king is dead', *The Word*, Mar. 2008, p. 93.
16   See, for example, Hebdige, *Subculture*, p. 58; Noel Ignatiev, *How the Irish Became White* (New York: Routledge, 1995).
17   Dooley, *Choosing the Green?*, p. 19.
18   Ibid. pp. 19–20.
19   Ibid. p. 20.
20   *Who Put the M in Manchester?* (Sanctuary DVD, 2005). Old Trafford is the area of Manchester in which the singer was raised, while Crumlin is the part of Dublin from which his family hailed.
21   See Zuberi, *Sounds English*, p. 17; *Who Put the M in Manchester?* (Sanctuary DVD, 2005).
22   Andrew Anthony, 'A man of many words and few teeth', *Observer*, 5 Mar. 2000, p. 5. See also MacGowan, interview with the author.
23   Paul Gilroy, *Small Acts: Thoughts on the Politics of Black Cultures* (London: Serpent's Tail, 1993), p. 31.
24   MacGowan, interview with the author.
25   See Delaney, *The Irish in Post-War Britain*, p. 128.

26 Hyder, *Brimful of Asia*, p. 4.

27 Stokes, 'Introduction', p. 4.

28 Marr, interview with the author.

29 Ibid.

30 Rowland, interview with the author.

31 Marr, interview with the author, original emphasis.

32 Ibid.

33 Miranda Sawyer, 'Florence is away with the faeries and leprechauns', *Observer*, 'Review' section, 5 July 2009, p. 16.

34 See, for example, Marr, interview with the author; Savage, 'Rough emeralds', *Guardian*, second section, 17 Mar. 1995, p. 11.

35 O'Riordan, interview with the author, original emphasis.

36 See, for example, O'Connor, *The Irish in Britain*, pp. 146–7; Lydon, *Rotten*, p. 325.

37 See, for example, in an Irish migrant context, O'Connor, *Bringing It All Back Home*. For a broader address to this issue, see Kun, *Audiotopia*.

38 For an account of the notions of Irishness that have circulated in British popular discourses, see Curtis, *Apes and Angels*; Curtis, *Nothing But the Same Old Story*.

39 J.B. Priestley, *English Journey* (London: William Heinemann, 1934), pp. 248–9.

40 For a celebratory account of Priestley's book, see Sarfraz Manzoor, 'Bradford reflects on many shades of Englishness', *Observer*, 'Review' section, 5 July 2009, pp. 4–5.

41 Priestley, *English Journey*, p. 248.

42 Ibid. For an account of Irish labour in Britain, see Cowley, *The Men Who Built Britain*.

43 Friedrich Engels, *The Condition of the Working Class in England* (Oxford: Oxford University Press, 1993), p. 104.

44 Ibid.

45 E.P. Thompson, *The Making of the English Working Class* (London: Penguin, 1963), pp. 469, 484.

46 See, for example, Alan Cochrane, 'The £200m swindlers', *Daily Express*, 28 Oct. 1976, pp. 1–2.

47 Paul Johnson, 'Welfare: A monster of our own making', *Daily Mail*, 25 Apr. 1994, p. 25, emphases added.

48 Commission for Racial Equality, *Roots of the Future*, p. 119.

49 Ibid. pp. 73–8.

50 Annette Gartland, 'Irish culture display planned for Thatcher', *Irish Times*, 10 Sept. 1983, p. 6.

51 Rowland, interview with the author; Watson, 'A Pogue in the Eye with a Sharp Stick', *NME*, 27 Apr. 1985, p. 34.

52 Sharkey, 'A view of the present state of Irish studies', p. 116.

53 See, for example, Hickman and Walter, *Discrimination and the Irish Community in Britain*; Abbotts, Williams and Ford, 'Morbidity and Irish Catholic descent in Britain, pp. 999–1005; Garrett, *Social Work and Irish People in Britain*.

54 See, for example, Jack O'Sullivan, 'British Muslims are the new Irish', *New Statesman*, 3 Nov. 2003, pp. 25–6; Dooley, 'Your name could put you in jail', *New Statesman*, 4 Oct. 2004, p. 17; Christina Pantazis and Simon Pemberton, 'From

the "old" to the "new" suspect community: Examining the impacts of recent UK counter-terrorist legislation', *British Journal of Criminology*, vol. 49, no. 5 (2009), pp. 646–66.

55 Clerk, *Pogue Mahone*, p. 90.

56 Brah, *Cartographies of Diaspora*, p. 189.

57 David Stubbs, 'Combat rock', *Uncut*, Aug. 1998, p. 45.

58 Simpson, 'Why two's company', *Guardian*, 13 July 1996, p. 30.

59 Boyd, 'Johnny, we never knew you', *Irish Times*, 'Arts' section, 8 May 1999, p. 6; Marr, interview with the author.

60 See, for example, Bennun et al., 'Britpop', *Melody Maker*, 22 July 1995, pp. 32–3.

61 Bronwen Walter, 'Gendered Irishness in Britain: Changing constructions', in Colin Graham and Richard Kirkland (eds.), *Ireland and Cultural Theory: The Mechanics of Authenticity* (Basingstoke: Macmillan, 1999), p. 93.

62 *Sex Pistols – There'll Always Be An England* (Fremantle DVD, 2008).

63 See Dwyer, 'Mac the mouth', *Sunday Tribune*, 'People' section, 2 Aug. 1987, p. 1; Rowland, interview with the author.

64 Simon Jones, *Black Culture, White Youth: The Reggae Tradition from JA to UK* (London: Macmillan, 1988), p. 239.

65 Maconie et al., 'The 100 greatest British albums ever!', *Q*, June 2000, pp. 83–4.

66 Ibid. p. 61.

67 Maconie, 'Pungent spice', *Q*, Aug. 1999, p. 100.

68 Maconie et al., 'The 100 greatest British albums ever!', *Q*, June 2000, p. 88.

69 Ibid. p. 93.

70 Martin Cloonan, 'State of the nation: "Englishness", pop, and politics in the mid-1990s', *Popular Music and Society*, vol. 21, pt. 2 (summer 1997), p. 67.

71 Hesmondhalgh, 'Indie', p. 52.

72 Parekh, *The Future of Multi-ethnic Britain*, pp. 20–1, 31–2, 61, 63–4, 139. The Irish dimensions of the report were largely informed by the contributions of Mary Hickman and Bronwen Walter (p. 364).

73 Ibid. pp. 20, 32.

74 See, for example, Alan Travis, 'British tag is "coded racism"', *Guardian*, 11 Oct. 2000, p. 1; Richard Ford, 'The argument for becoming nation without a name', *The Times*, 12 Oct. 2000, p. 6.

75 Brah, *Cartographies of Diaspora*, pp. 208–10.

Bibliography, Interviews, Discography, Films & TV/Radio Programmes

Bibliography: Books, Journals, Ph.D. Theses, Communications

Abbotts, Joanne, Rory Williams and Graeme Ford, 'morbidity and Irish Catholic descent in Britain: Relating health disadvantage to socio-economic position', *Social Science & Medicine*, vol. 52, no. 7 (2001), pp. 999–1005

Adorno, Theodor, *The Culture Industry: Selected Essays on Mass Culture* (London: Routledge, 1991)

Aizlewood, John, 'Thankfully not living in Yorkshire it doesn't apply', in Aizlewood (ed.), *Love is the Drug* (London: Penguin, 1994), pp. 21–37

Akenson, Donald H., *The Irish Diaspora: A Primer* (Belfast: Institute of Irish Studies, 1996)

Akenson, Donald H., 'Let's stop talking about Irish emigration: Some constructive alternatives', inaugural lecture, the Beamish Research Professorship of Migration Studies, Institute of Irish Studies, University of Liverpool, 23 Nov. 1998

Althusser, Louis, *Lenin and Philosophy and Other Essays*, trans. Ben Brewster (London: New Left Books, 1971)

Ambrose, Joe, e-mail to the author, 12 Mar. 2009

Anonymous, 'UK Commentary: The Guildford Four: English justice and the Irish community: An interview with Gareth Peirce', *Race and Class*, vol. 31, no. 3 (1990), pp. 81–90

Arrowsmith, Aidan, 'Writing "home": Nation, identity and Irish emigration to England' (unpublished Ph.D. thesis, University of Staffordshire, 1998)

Arrowsmith, Aidan, 'Plastic Paddy: Negotiating identity in second generation Irish-English writing', *Irish Studies Review*, vol. 8, no. 1 (Apr. 2000), pp. 35–44

Bagley, Christopher and Gajendra K. Verma, 'Inter-ethnic attitudes and behaviour in British multi-racial schools', in Gajendra K. Verma and Christopher Bagley (eds.), *Race and Education Across Cultures* (London: Heinemann, 1975), pp. 236–62

Barclay, Tom, *Memoirs and Medleys: The Autobiography of a Bottle Washer* (Leicester: Edgar Backus, 1934)

Behan, Brendan, *Borstal Boy* (London: Hutchinson, 1958)

Bennett, Andy, '"Village greens and terraced streets": Britpop and representations of "Britishness"', *Young: Nordic Journal of Youth Research*, vol. 5, no. 4 (Nov. 1997), pp. 20–33

Bishop, Patrick and Eamonn Mallie, *The Provisional IRA* (London: Heinemann, 1987)

Blake, Mark (ed.), *Punk: The Whole Story* (London: Dorling Kindersley, 2006)

Boot, Adrian and Chris Salewicz, *Punk: The Illustrated History of a Music Revolution* (London: Penguin Studio, 1996)

Boyd, Joe, *White Bicycles: Making Music in the 1960s* (London: Serpent's Tail, 2005)

Bracewell, Michael, *England is Mine: Pop Life in Albion from Wilde to Goldie* (London: HarperCollins, 1997)

Bracken, Patrick J., Liam Greenslade, Barney Griffin and Marcelino Smyth, 'Mental health and ethnicity: An Irish dimension', *British Journal of Psychiatry*, vol. 172 (1998), pp. 103–5

Bradby, Barbara, '"Imagining Ireland" Conference, Dublin, Oct. 30th-31st 1993', *Popular Music*, vol. 13, no. 1 (1994), pp. 107–9

Bradley, Joseph M. (ed.), *Celtic Minded: Essays on Religion, Politics, Society, Identity ... and Football* (Glendaruel: Argyll Publishing, 2004)

Brah, Avtar, *Cartographies of Diaspora: Contesting Identities* (London: Routledge, 1996)

Braun, Edward, 'Introduction', *Trevor Griffiths: Collected Plays for Television* (London: Faber and Faber, 1988), pp. 1–33

Bret, David, *Morrissey: Landscapes of the Mind* (London: Robson Books, 1994)

Brooker, Joe, 'Has the world changed or have I changed? The Smiths and the challenge of Thatcherism', in Sean Campbell and Colin Coulter (eds.), *Why Pamper Life's Complexities? Essays on The Smiths* (Manchester: Manchester University Press, forthcoming)

Brophy, John and Eric Partridge (eds.), *Songs and Slang of the British Soldier: 1914–1918* (London: Eric Partridge Ltd at the Scholartis Press, 1930, 2nd edn.)

Brophy, John and Eric Partridge, *The Long Trail: What the British Soldier Sang and Said in the Great War of 1914–18* (London: Andre Deutsch, 1965)

Brown, Len, *Meetings with Morrissey* (London: Omnibus Press, 2008)

Brown, Terence, *Ireland's Literature: Selected Essays* (Dublin: Lilliput Press, 1988)

Buckley, Marella, 'Sitting on your politics: The Irish among the British and the women among the Irish', in Jim Mac Laughlin (ed.), *Location and Dislocation in Contemporary Irish Society* (Cork: Cork University Press, 1997), pp. 94–132

Burchill, Julie and Tony Parsons, '*The Boy Looked at Johnny': The Obituary of Rock 'n' Roll* (London: Pluto, 1978)

Campbell, Sean, '"Race of angels": The critical reception of second-generation Irish musicians', *Irish Studies Review*, vol. 6, no. 2 (1998), pp. 165–74

Campbell, Sean, 'Beyond "Plastic Paddy": A re-examination of the second-generation Irish in England', *Immigrants and Minorities*, vol. 18, nos. 2 & 3 (1999), pp. 266–88

Campbell, Sean, 'Review of Paolo Hewitt, *Getting High*', *Popular Music*, vol. 18, no. 1 (1999), pp. 158–60

Campbell, Sean, 'Review of Michael Bracewell, *England is Mine*', *Journal of Popular Music Studies*, vols. 11 & 12 (1999/2000), pp. 193–6

Campbell, Sean, '"Britpop: The importance of being Irish" – the relevance of ethnicity for understanding second-generation Irish musicians in England', in Tony Mitchell and Peter Doyle (eds.), *Changing Sounds: New Directions and Configurations in Popular Music* (Sydney: University of Technology Sydney, 2000), pp. 234–43

Campbell, Sean, 'Sounding out the margins: Ethnicity and popular music in British cultural studies', in Gerry Smyth and Glenda Norquay (eds.), *Across the Margins: Cultural Identities and Change in the Atlantic Archipelago* (Manchester: Manchester University Press, 2002), pp. 117–36

Campbell, Sean, 'Qualifying "nation": Plasticity, diaspora and the Republic of Ireland', *M/C Reviews* e-journal, 'Mediating football's World Cup' (http://www.media-culture.org.au/reviews), July 2002

Campbell, Sean, '"What's the story?": Rock biography, musical "routes" and the second-generation Irish in England', *Irish Studies Review*, vol. 12, no. 1 (2004), pp. 63–75

Campbell, Sean, 'Ethnicity and cultural criticism: Evocations and elisions of Irishness in the British music press', *Celtic Cultural Studies: An Interdisciplinary Online Journal*, no. 1, 'Music and Identity' (2007)

Campbell, Sean, 'Popular music-making amongst the Irish diaspora in England', in Barra Boydell and Harry White (eds.), *Encyclopedia of Music in Ireland* (Dublin: University College Dublin Press, forthcoming)

Campbell, Sean and Mairtin Mac an Ghaill, 'Dancing at the crossroads: Immigration and popular music in Ireland and abroad', *Asyland: Magazine of the Irish Refugee Council*, no. 10 (autumn/winter 2004), pp. 7–8

Campbell, Sean and Gerry Smyth, *Beautiful Day: Forty Years of Irish Rock* (Dublin: Atrium Press, 2005)

Campbell, Sean and Gerry Smyth, 'From shellshock rock to ceasefire sounds: Popular music in Northern Ireland', in Colin Coulter and Michael Murray (eds.), *Northern Ireland After the Troubles: A Society in Transition* (Manchester: Manchester University Press, 2008), pp. 232–52

Canavan, Bernard, 'Story-tellers and writers: Irish identity in emigrant labourers' auto-biographies, 1870–1970', in Patrick O'Sullivan (ed.), *The Irish World Wide: The Creative Migrant* (Leicester: Leicester University Press, 1992), pp. 154-69

Casey, Maude, *Over the Water* (London: Livewire, 1987)

Chance, Judy, 'The Irish in London: An exploration of ethnic boundary maintenance', in Peter Jackson (ed.), *Race and Racism: Essays in Social Geography* (London: Allen & Unwin, 1987), pp. 142–60

Chapman, Anthony J., Jean R. Smith and Hugh C. Foot, 'Language, humour and intergroup relations', in Howard Giles (ed.), *Language, Ethnicity and Intergroup Relations* (London: Academic Press, 1977), pp. 137–69

Chevron, Philip, e-mail to the author, 30 May 2006

Christian, Terry, *My Word* (London: Orion, 2007)

Clarke, John, 'The skinheads and the magical recovery of community', in Stuart Hall and Tony Jefferson (eds.), *Resistance Through Rituals: Youth Subcultures in Post-war Britain* (London: Hutchinson, 1976), pp. 99–102

Clarke, Stuart, public interview with Johnny Marr, Trinity College, Dublin, 2 Oct. 2007

Clarke, Victoria Mary and Shane MacGowan, *A Drink with Shane MacGowan* (London: Sidgwick & Jackson, 2001)

Clayton-Lea, Tony and Richie Taylor, *Irish Rock: Where It's Come From, Where It's At, Where It's Going* (Dublin: Gill & Macmillan, 1992)

Cleary, Joe, *Outrageous Fortune: Capital and Culture in Modern Ireland* (Dublin: Field Day Publications, 2006)

Clerk, Carol, *Pogue Mahone: The Story of The Pogues* (London: Omnibus Press, 2006)

Clifford, James, 'Diasporas', *Cultural Anthropology*, vol. 9, no. 3 (1994), pp. 302–38

Cloonan, Martin, 'State of the nation: "Englishness", pop, and politics in the mid-1990s', *Popular Music and Society*, vol. 21, pt. 2 (summer 1997), pp. 47–70

Cloonan, Martin, 'What do they know of England? "Englishness" and popular music in the mid-1990s', in Tarja Hautamaki and Helmi Jarviluoma (eds.), *Music on Show: Issues of Performance* (Tampere: University of Tampere, 1998), pp. 66–72

Cloonan, Martin, 'Pop and the nation-state: Towards a theorisation', *Popular Music*, vol. 18, no. 2 (1999), pp. 193–207

Cohen, Phil, 'Subcultural conflict in a working class community', *Working Papers in Cultural Studies*, no. 2 (1972), University of Birmingham, pp. 5–51

Cohen, Sara, *Decline, Renewal and the City in Popular Music Culture: Beyond The Beatles* (Aldershot: Ashgate, 2007)

Commission for Racial Equality, *Roots of the Future: Ethnic Diversity in the Making of Britain* (London: Commission for Racial Equality, 1996)

Coogan, Tim Pat, *The Troubles: Ireland's Ordeal 1966–1995 and the Search for Peace* (London: Hutchinson, 1995)

Coogan, Tim Pat, *The IRA* (London: HarperCollins, 2000, revised edn.)

Cosgrove, Stuart, 'Refusing consent: The "Oi for England" project', *Screen*, vol. 24, no. 1 (Jan.–Feb. 1983), pp. 92–6

Courtneidge, Cicely, *Cicely* (London: Hutchinson, 1953)

Cowley, Ultan, *The Men Who Built Britain: A History of the Irish Navvy* (Dublin: Wolfhound Press, 2001)

Cronin, Mike and Daryl Adair, *The Wearing of the Green: A History of Saint Patrick's Day* (London: Routledge, 2002)

Cummins, Kevin, *The Smiths and Beyond* (London: Vision On, 2002)

Cummins, Kevin, *Manchester: Looking for the Light through the Pouring Rain* (London: Faber and Faber, 2009)

Curtis Jr., L.P., *Apes and Angels: The Irishman in Victorian Caricature* (Newton Abbot: David & Charles, 1971)

Curtis, Liz, *Nothing But the Same Old Story: The Roots of Anti-Irish Racism* (London: Information on Ireland, 1984)

Davis, Leith, 'Irish bards and English consumers: Thomas Moore's "Irish Melodies" and the colonized nation', *Ariel: A Review of International English Literature*, vol. 24, no. 2 (Apr. 1993), pp. 7–25

Day, R. *The Queen is Dead* (Woodford Green: International Music Publications, 1988)

Deane, Seamus, *Celtic Revivals: Essays in Modern Irish Literature, 1880–1980* (London: Faber and Faber, 1985)

DeGroot, Gerard J., *Blighty: British Society in the Era of the Great War* (London: Longman, 1996)

Delaney, Enda, *The Irish in Post-War Britain* (Oxford: Oxford University Press, 2007)

Devereux, Eoin, 'Being wild(e) about Morrissey: Fandom and identity', in Mary Corcoran and Michel Peillon (eds.), *Uncertain Ireland* (Dublin: Institute of Public Administration, 2006), pp. 235–45

Dexys Midnight Runners, *Intense Emotion Review* tour programme (1980)

Dexy Midnight Runners, *Coming to Town* tour programme (1985)

Dooley, Brian, *Choosing the Green? Second Generation Irish and the Cause of Ireland* (Belfast: Beyond the Pale, 2004)

Dunne, Catherine, *An Unconsidered People: The Irish in London* (Dublin: New Island, 2003)

Dunphy, Eamon, *The Unforgettable Fire: The Story of U2* (London: Viking, 1987)

Eagleton, Terry, 'Mm … he was Irish, actually', *Fortnight*, vol. 277 (Oct. 1989), pp. 29–30

Eagleton, Terry, 'Introduction', in Oscar Wilde, *Plays, Prose Writings and Poems* (London: Everyman's Library, 1991), pp. vii-xxiii

Eagleton, Terry, 'A different sense of who I was', *Irish Reporter*, no. 13 (1994), pp. 14–15

Eagleton, Terry, *Heathcliff and the Great Hunger: Studies in Irish Culture* (London: Verso, 1995)

Eagleton, Terry, *The Gatekeeper: A Memoir* (London: Allen Lane, 2001)

Eddington, Richard, *Sent From Coventry: The Chequered Past of Two Tone* (London: Independent Music Press, 2004)

Edgar, David, 'Bitter harvest', in James Curran (ed.), *The Future of the Left* (Cambridge: Polity Press, 1984), pp. 39–57

Elliott, Marianne, *The Catholics of Ulster: A History* (London: Allen Lane, 2000)

Ellis, Catherine, *Aboriginal Music: Education for Living* (St Lucia: University of Queensland Press, 1985)

Engels, Friedrich, *The Condition of the Working Class in England* (Oxford: Oxford University Press, 1993)

Eva, Phil, 'Home sweet home? The "culture of exile" in mid-Victorian popular song', *Popular Music*, vol. 16, no. 2 (1997), pp. 131–50

Fanon, Frantz, *Black Skin, White Masks*, trans. Charles Lam Markmann (London: MacGibbon & Kee, 1968)

Feldman, Allen, *Formations of Violence: The Narrative of the Body and Political Terror in Northern Ireland* (Chicago: University of Chicago Press, 1991)

Flood, J.M. *Ireland: Its Saints and Scholars* (Dublin: Talbot Press, 1917)

Foster, J.H., 'The Irish alcohol misuser in England: Ill served by research and policy? Some suggestions for future research opportunities', *Drugs: Education, Prevention and Policy*, vol. 10, no. 1 (Feb. 2003), pp. 57–63

Foster, R.F. *Paddy and Mr Punch: Connections in Irish and English History* (London: Allen Lane, 1993)

Free, Marcus, '"Angels" with drunken faces? Travelling Republic of Ireland supporters and the construction of Irish migrant identity in England', in Adam Brown (ed.), *Fanatics! Power, Identity and Fandom in Football* (London: Routledge, 1998), pp. 219–32

Free, Marcus, 'Tales from the fifth green field: The psychodynamics of migration, masculinity and national identity amongst Republic of Ireland soccer supporters in England', *Sport in Society*, vol. 10, no. 3 (May 2007), pp. 476–94

Frith, Mark (ed.), *The Best of Smash Hits: The 80s* (London: Sphere, 2006)

Frith, Simon, *Music for Pleasure: Essays in the Sociology of Pop* (Cambridge: Polity Press, 1988)

Frith, Simon, 'Music and identity', in Stuart Hall and Paul du Gay (eds.), *Questions of Cultural Identity* (London: Sage, 1996), pp. 108–27

Frith, Simon and Angela McRobbie, 'Rock and sexuality', *Screen Education*, no. 29 (winter 1978/79), pp. 3–19

Gabriel, John, *Racism, Culture, Markets* (London: Routledge, 1994)

Gallagher, Paul and Terry Christian, *Brothers: From Childhood to Oasis – the Real Story* (London: Virgin, 1996)

Garrett, Paul Michael, *Social Work and Irish People in Britain: Historical and Contemporary Responses to Irish Children and Families* (Bristol: The Policy Press, 2004)

Gibbons, Luke, 'Unapproved roads: Postcolonialism and Irish identity', in Trisha Ziff (ed.), *Distant Relations: Chicano/Irish/Mexican Art and Critical Writing* (New York: Smart Art Press, 1995), pp. 56–67

Gibbons, Luke, *The Quiet Man* (Cork: Cork University Press, 2002)

Gilroy, Paul, *'There Ain't No Black in the Union Jack': The Cultural Politics of Race and Nation* (London: Hutchinson, 1987)

Gilroy, Paul, '"It ain't where you're from, it's where you're at": The dialectics of diasporic identification', *Third Text*, vol. 5, no. 13 (1991), pp. 3–16

Gilroy, Paul, *The Black Atlantic: Modernity and Double Consciousness* (London: Verso, 1993)

Gilroy, Paul, *Small Acts: Thoughts on the Politics of Black Cultures* (London: Serpent's Tail, 1993)

Gilroy, Paul, *After Empire: Melancholia or Convivial Culture?* (London: Routledge, 2004)

Goddard, Simon, *The Smiths: Songs that Saved Your Life* (London: Reynolds & Hearn, 2004, 2nd edn.)

Goddard, Simon, *Mozipedia: The Encyclopedia of Morrissey and The Smiths* (London: Ebury Press, 2009)

Gray, Breda, 'From "ethnicity" to "diaspora": 1980s emigration and "multicultural" London', in Andy Bielenberg (ed.), *The Irish Diaspora* (London: Longman, 2000), pp. 65–88

Gray, Breda, 'Curious hybridities: Transnational negotiations of migrancy through generation', *Irish Studies Review*, vol. 14, no. 2 (May 2006), pp. 207–23

Gray, Peter, 'Our man at Oxford', *History Ireland*, vol. 1, no. 3 (autumn 1993), pp. 9–12

Greenslade, Liam, Maggie Pearson and Moss Madden, 'A good man's fault: Alcohol and Irish people at home and abroad', *Alcohol and Alcoholism*, vol. 30, no. 4 (1995), pp. 407–17

Hall, Stuart, 'Encoding/decoding', in Stuart Hall, Dorothy Hobson, Andrew Lowe and Stuart Willis (eds.), *Culture, Media, Language: Working Papers in Cultural Studies, 1972–79* (London: Hutchinson, 1980), pp. 128–38

Hall, Stuart, 'What is this "black" in black popular culture?', in Gina Dent (ed.), *Black Popular Culture* (Seattle: Bay Press, 1992), pp. 21–33

Hanafin, Sara, 'The idea of Ireland as "home": Place, identity and second generation return migration', conference of the British Association of Irish Studies, University of Liverpool, 15 Sept. 2007

Harding, Seeromanie and Rasaratnam Balarajan, 'Patterns of mortality in second generation Irish living in England and Wales: Longitudinal study', *British Medical Journal*, vol. 312, no. 7043 (1 June 1996), pp. 1389–92

Hardy, Phil and Dave Laing, *The Faber Companion to 20th-century Popular Music* (London: Faber and Faber, 1995, revised edn.)

Harte, Liam, 'Migrancy, performativity and autobiographical identity', *Irish Studies Review*, vol. 14, no. 2 (May 2006), pp. 225–38

Haseler, Stephen, *The English Tribe: Identity, Nation and Europe* (Basingstoke: Macmillan, 1996)

Haskey, John, 'Mortality among second generation Irish in England and Wales', *British Medical Journal*, vol. 312, no. 7043 (1 June 1996), pp. 1373–4

Hawkins, Stan, *Settling the Pop Score: Pop Texts and Identity Politics* (Aldershot: Ashgate, 2002)

Hayden, Tom, *Irish on the Inside: In Search of the Soul of Irish America* (London: Verso, 2001)

Healy, John, *The Grass Arena: An Autobiography* (London: Faber and Faber, 1988)

Heaney, Seamus, *Finders Keepers: Selected Prose, 1971–2001* (London: Faber and Faber, 2002)

Hebdige, Dick, *Subculture: The Meaning of Style* (London: Methuen, 1979)

Hebdige Dick, *Cut 'N' Mix: Culture, Identity and Caribbean Music* (London: Comedia, 1987)

Hebdige, Dick, 'Digging for Britain: An excavation in seven parts', in *The British Edge* (Boston: Institute of Contemporary Arts, 1987), pp. 35–69

Hesmondhalgh, David, 'Indie: The Institutional Politics and Aesthetics of a Popular Music Genre', *Cultural Studies*, vol. 13, no. 1 (1999), pp. 34–61

Hesmondhalgh, David, 'British popular music and national identity', in David Morley and Kevin Robins (eds.), *British Cultural Studies: Geography, Nationality and Identity* (Oxford: Oxford University Press, 2001), pp. 273–86

Hewitt, Paolo, *Getting High: The Adventures of Oasis* (London: Boxtree, 1997)

Hickman, Mary J., *Religion, Class and Identity: The State, the Catholic Church and the Education of the Irish in Britain* (Aldershot: Avebury, 1995)

Hickman, Mary J., 'The religio-ethnic identities of teenagers of Irish descent', in Michael P. Hornsby-Smith (ed.), *Catholics in England, 1950–2000: Historical and Sociological Perspectives* (London: Cassell, 1999), pp. 182–98

Hickman, Mary, J., 'Hybrid and hyphenated', *Catalyst: Debating Race, Identity, Citizenship and Culture* (London: Commission for Racial Equality, 2007)

Hickman, Mary and Bronwen Walter, *Discrimination and the Irish Community in Britain* (London: Commission for Racial Equality, 1997)

Hickman, Mary J., Sarah Morgan and Bronwen Walter, *Second-generation Irish People in Britain: A Demographic, Socio-Economic and Health Profile* (London: Irish Studies Centre, University of North London, 2001)

Hickman, Mary J., Sarah Morgan, Bronwen Walter and Joseph Bradley, 'The limitations of whiteness and the boundaries of Englishness: Second-generation Irish identifications and positionings in multiethnic Britain', *Ethnicities*, vol. 5, no. 2 (2005), pp. 160–82

Higgins, Michael D., address to the 'Economy of the Arts' conference, Temple Bar, Dublin, Dec. 1994

Hillyard, Paddy, *Suspect Community: People's Experience of the Prevention of Terrorism Acts in Britain* (London: Pluto Press, 1993)

Holmes, Michael, 'Symbols of national identity and sport: The case of the Irish football team', *Irish Political Studies*, vol. 9 (1994), pp. 81–98

Hope, Henry Gerald, untitled, *Notes and Queries*, s7–ix (Jan.–June 1890), pp. 335–6

Hopkin, James, 'Jeane', in Peter Wild (ed.), *Paint A Vulgar Picture: Fiction Inspired by The Smiths* (London: Serpent's Tail, 2009), pp. 181–91

Hornsby-Smith, Michael P. and Angela Dale, 'The assimilation of Irish immigrants in England', *British Journal of Sociology*, vol. 39, no. 4 (1988), pp. 519–44

Hubbs, Nadine, 'Music of the "fourth gender": Morrissey and the sexual politics of melodic contour', in Thomas Foster, Carol Siegel and Ellen E. Berry (eds.), *Bodies of Writing: Bodies in Performance* (New York: New York University Press, 1996), pp. 266–96

Hughes, Eamonn, '"Lancelot's position": The fiction of Irish-Britain', in A. Robert Lee (ed.), *Other Britain, Other British: Contemporary Multicultural Fiction* (London: Pluto Press, 1995), pp. 142–60

Hutton, Chris and Richard Kurt, *Don't Look Back in Anger: Growing Up With Oasis* (London: Simon & Schuster, 1997)

Hyder, Rehan, *Brimful of Asia: Negotiating Ethnicity on the UK Music Scene* (Aldershot: Ashgate, 2004)

Ignatiev, Noel, *How the Irish Became White* (New York: Routledge, 1995)

Jones, Simon, *Black Culture, White Youth: The Reggae Tradition from JA to UK* (London: Macmillan, 1988)

Jones, Steve, 'Re-viewing rock writing: The origins of popular music criticism', *American Journalism*, vol. 9, pts. 2–3 (1992), pp. 87–107

Joyce, James, *Ulysses* (London: Penguin, 1986)

Keaney, Brian, *Don't Hang About* (Oxford: Oxford University Press, 1985)

Kee, Robert, *Trial and Error: The Maguires, the Guildford Pub Bombings and British Justice* (London: Penguin, 1989, 2nd edn.)

Keightley, Kier, 'Reconsidering rock', in Simon Frith, Will Straw and John Street (eds.), *The Cambridge Companion to Pop and Rock* (Cambridge: Cambridge University Press, 2001), pp. 109–42

Kelleher, David, 'A Defence of the use of the terms "ethnicity" and "culture"', in David Kelleher and Sheila Hillier (eds.), *Researching Cultural Differences in Health* (London: Routledge, 1996), pp. 69–90

Kells, Mary, 'Ethnic identity amongst young middle class Irish migrants in London', Occasional Papers Series, no. 6 (London: University of North London Press, 1995)

Kelly, Kevin, *The Longest War: Northern Ireland and the IRA* (Dingle: Brandon, 1982)

Keohane, Kieran, 'Unifying the fragmented imaginary of the young immigrant: Making a home in the post modern with the Pogues', *Irish Review*, vol. 9, no. 1 (1990), pp. 71–9

Kruks, Sonia, 'Fanon, Sartre, and identity politics', in Lewis R. Gordon, T. Denean Sharpley-Whiting and Renée T. White (eds.), *Fanon: A Critical Reader* (Oxford: Blackwell, 1996), pp. 122–33

Kun, Josh, *Audiotopia: Music, Race, and America* (Berkeley: University of California Press, 2005)

Laclau, Ernesto and Chantal Mouffe, *Hegemony and Socialist Strategy: Towards a Radical Democratic Politics* (London: Verso, 1985)

Laing, Dave, *One Chord Wonders: Power and Meaning in Punk Rock* (Milton Keynes: Open University Press, 1985)

Lambert, Sharon, *Irish Women in Lancashire, 1922–1960: Their Story* (University of Lancaster: Centre for North-west Regional Studies, 2001)

Lambert, Stephen, *Channel Four: Television with a Difference?* (London: British Film Institute, 1982)

Lennon, Mary, Marie McAdam and Joanne O'Brien, *Across the Water: Irish Women's Lives in Britain* (London: Virago, 1988)

Lewisohn, Mark (ed.), *Wingspan: Paul McCartney's Band on the Run* (London: Bulfinch Press, 2002)

Lipsitz, George, *Dangerous Crossroads: Popular Music, Postmodernism and the Poetics of Place* (London: Verso, 1994)

Lydon, John, *Rotten: No Irish, No Blacks, No Dogs* (London: Hodder & Stoughton, 1994)

Mac an Ghaill, Mairtin, 'What about the lads? – Emigrants, immigrants, ethnics and transnationals in late 1990s diaspora', in Ronat Lentin (ed.), *Emerging Irish Identities: Proceedings of a Seminar Held in Trinity College Dublin, 27 November 1999* (Dublin: Trinity College Dublin, 2000), pp. 44–57

MacDonald, Ian, *Revolution in the Head: The Beatles' Records and the Sixties* (London: Pimlico, 1995, 2nd edn.)

MacGowan, Shane, *Poguetry: The Lyrics of Shane MacGowan* (London: Faber and Faber, 1989)

Mac Laughlin, Jim, 'The new vanishing Irish: Social characteristics of "new wave" Irish emigration', in Mac Laughlin (ed.), *Location and Dislocation in Contemporary*

Irish Society: Emigration and Irish Identities (Cork: Cork University Press, 1997), pp. 133–57

Maguire, Meg, 'Missing links: Working-class women of Irish descent', in Pat Mahony and Christine Zmroczek (eds.), *Class Matters: 'Working-Class' Women's Perspectives on Social Class* (London: Taylor & Francis, 1997), pp. 87–100

Malone, Mary E. and John P. Dooley, '"Dwelling in displacement": Meanings of "community" and *sense* of community for two generations of Irish people living in north-west London', *Community, Work and Family*, vol. 9, no. 1 (Feb. 2006), pp. 11–28

Marshall, George, *The Two Tone Story* (Glasgow: Zoot, 1990)

Masterson, Eugene, *The Word on the Street: The Unsanctioned Story of Oasis* (Edinburgh: Mainstream, 1996)

Maton, Karl, 'Last night they dreamt that somebody loved them: Smiths fans (and me) in the late 1980s', in Sean Campbell and Colin Coulter (eds.), *Why Pamper Life's Complexities? Essays on The Smiths* (Manchester: Manchester University Press, forthcoming)

McCann, Eamonn, *War and an Irish Town* (Harmondsworth: Penguin, 1974)

McCormack, Jerusha, 'Introduction: The Irish Wilde', in McCormack (ed.), *Wilde the Irishman* (New Haven: Yale University Press, 1998), pp. 1–5

McGovern, Mark, 'The "craic" market: Irish theme bars and the commodification of Irishness in contemporary Britain', *Irish Journal of Sociology*, vol. 11, no. 2 (2002), pp. 77–98

McLaughlin, Noel and Martin McLoone, 'Hybridity and national musics: The case of Irish rock music', *Popular Music*, vol. 19, no. 2 (2000), pp. 181–200

McLeod, John, *Beginning Postcolonialism* (Manchester: Manchester University Press, 2000)

McLoone, Martin, *Irish Film: The Emergence of a Contemporary Cinema* (London: British Film Institute, 2000)

McLoone, Martin, *Film, Media and Popular Culture in Ireland: Cityscapes, Landscapes, Soundscapes* (Dublin: Irish Academic Press, 2008)

Merrick, Joe, *London Irish Punk: Life and Music ... Shane MacGowan* (London: Omnibus Press, 2001)

Middleton, Richard, *Studying Popular Music* (Milton Keynes: Open University Press, 1990)

Miller, David, 'The media and Northern Ireland: Censorship, information management and the broadcasting ban', in Greg Philo (ed.), *Glasgow Media Group Reader, Volume 2: Industry, Economy, War and Politics* (London: Routledge, 1995), pp. 45–75

Miller, Kerby, *Emigrants and Exiles: Ireland and the Irish Exodus to North America* (New York: Oxford University Press, 1985)

Mitchell, Tony, *Popular Music and Local Identity: Rock, Pop and Rap in Europe and Oceania* (London: Leicester University Press, 1996)

Moore, Allan F., *Rock: The Primary Text. Developing a Musicology of Rock* (Buckingham: Open University Press, 1993)

Morley, David and Kevin Robins, 'No place like *heimat*: Images of home(land) in European culture', in Erica Carter, James Donald and Judith Squires (eds.), *Space and Place: Theories of Identity and Location* (London: Lawrence and Wishart, 1993), pp. 3–31

Morton, Stephen, *Gayatri Chakravorty Spivak* (London: Routledge, 2003)

Mullen, Kenneth, Rory Williams and Kate Hunt, 'Irish descent, religion, and alcohol and tobacco use', research report, *Addiction*, vol. 91, no. 2 (1996), pp. 243–54

Mullin, Chris, *Error of Judgement: The Truth about the Birmingham Bombings* (London: Chatto & Windus, 1986)

Murray, Albert, *Stomping the Blues* (London: Quartet Books, 1978)

Murray, Tony, 'Curious streets: Diaspora, displacement and transgression in Desmond Hogan's London Irish narratives', *Irish Studies Review*, vol. 14, no. 2 (May 2006), pp. 239–53

Nagle, John, '"Everybody is Irish on St. Paddy's Day": Ambivalence and alterity at London's St. Patrick's Day 2002', *Identities: Global Studies in Culture and Power*, vol. 12, no. 4 (Oct.–Dec. 2005), pp. 563–83

Nehring, Neil, *Flowers in the Dustbin: Culture, Anarchy, and Postwar England* (Ann Arbor: University of Michigan Press, 1993)

Ó Cinnéide, Barra, *Riverdance: The Phenomenon* (Dublin: Blackhall Publishing, 2002)

O'Connor, Joyce, *The Young Drinkers: A Cross-National Study of Social and Cultural Influences* (London: Tavistock Publications, 1978)

O'Connor, Kevin, *The Irish in Britain* (Dublin: Torc Books, 1974)

O'Connor, Nuala, *Bringing It All Back Home: The Influence of Irish Music* (London: BBC Books, 1991)

O'Connor, Patrick and Seán Daffy, 'On the importance of not-being earnest: A dialogue with Terry Eagleton', *Irish Studies Review*, vol. 16, no. 1 (Feb. 2008), pp. 55–69

O'Connor, Ulick, *Brendan Behan* (London: Hamish Hamilton, 1970)

O'Doherty, Ian, *Shane MacGowan: Last of the Celtic Soul Rebels* (Dublin: Blackwater Press, 1994)

O'Leary, Brendan, 'Mission accomplished? Looking back at the IRA', *Field Day Review*, no. 1 (Dublin: Field Day Publications, 2005), pp. 217–46

O'Mahoney, Bernard, *Soldier of the Queen* (Dingle: Brandon, 2000)

O'Malley, Donogh, address to the National University of Ireland Club, Grosvenor House, London, 17 Mar. 1966. NAI DT 96/6/437

O'Sullivan, Patrick, 'The Irish joke', in Patrick O'Sullivan (ed.), *The Creative Migrant. the Irish World Wide Series: History, Heritage, Identity. Vol. 3* (London: Leicester University Press, 1994), pp. 57–82

Pantazis, Christina and Simon Pemberton, 'From the "old" to the "new" suspect community: Examining the impacts of recent UK counter-terrorist legislation', *British Journal of Criminology*, no. 29 (2009), pp. 646–66

Parekh, Bhikhu, *The Future of Multi-ethnic Britain* (London: Profile Books, 2000)

Paxman, Jeremy, *The English: A Portrait of a People* (London: Michael Joseph, 1998)

Pearce, Kevin, *Something Beginning with O* (London: Heavenly, 1993)

Philo, Greg, 'Television, politics and the rise of the new right', in Philo (ed.), *Glasgow Media Group Reader, Volume 2: Industry, Economy, War and Politics* (London: Routledge, 1995), pp. 198–233

Poole, Mike and John Wyver, *Powerplays: Trevor Griffiths in Television* (London: British Film Institute, 1984)

Pratt, Mary Louise, *Imperial Eyes: Travel Writing and Transculturation* (London: Routledge, 1992)

Prendergast, Mark J., *Irish Rock: Roots, Personalities, Directions* (Dublin: O'Brien Press, 1987)

Priestley, J.B., *English Journey* (London: William Heinemann, 1934)

Redhead, Steve, *The End of the Century Party: Youth and Pop Towards 2000* (Manchester: Manchester University Press, 1990)

Rex, John, 'Immigrants and British labour: The sociological context', in Kenneth Lunn (ed.), *Hosts, Immigrants and Minorities: Historical Responses to Newcomers in British Society, 1870–1914* (Folkestone: Dawson, 1980), pp. 22–38

Reynolds, Simon and Joy Press, *The Sex Revolts: Gender, Rebellion and Rock 'n' Roll* (London: Serpent's Tail, 1995)

Reynolds, Simon, *Rip It Up and Start Again: Post-Punk, 1978–84* (London: Faber and Faber, 2005)

Roach, Martin, *The Right to Imagination & Madness: An Essential Collection of Candid Interviews with Top UK Alternative Songwriters* (London: Independent Music Press, 1994)

Robb, John, *The North Will Rise Again: Manchester Music City, 1976–1996* (London: Aurum, 2009)

Rogan, Johnny, *Morrissey and Marr: The Severed Alliance* (London: Omnibus Press, 1992)

Rogan, Johnny, *The Smiths: The Visual Documentary* (London: Omnibus Press, 1994)

Rolston, Bill, '"This is not a rebel song": The Irish conflict and popular music', *Race and Class*, vol. 42, no. 3 (2001), pp. 49–67

Ryan, Liam, 'Irish emigration to Britain Since World War II', in Richard Kearney (ed.), *Migrations: The Irish at Home and Abroad* (Dublin: Wolfhound Press, 1990), pp. 45–67

Savage, Jon, *England's Dreaming: Sex Pistols and Punk Rock* (London: Faber and Faber, 1991)

Savage, Jon, *The England's Dreaming Tapes* (London: Faber and Faber, 2009)

Scanlon, Ann, *The Pogues: The Lost Decade* (Omnibus Press, 1988)

Shapiro, Nat, *An Encyclopedia of Quotations About Music* (Newton Abbot: David & Charles, 1978)

Sharkey, Sabina, 'A view of the present state of Irish studies', in Susan Bassnett (ed.), *Studying British Cultures: An Introduction* (London: Routledge, 1997), pp. 113–34

Shepherd, John, 'Music as cultural text', in John Paynter, Tim Howell, Richard Orton and Peter Seymour (eds.), *Companion to Contemporary Musical Thought*, vol. 1 (London: Routledge, 1992), pp. 128–55

Shuker, Roy, *Key Concepts in Popular Music* (London: Routledge, 1998)

Simpson, Mark, *Saint Morrissey* (London: SAF, 2004)

Slee, Jo, *Peepholism: Into the Art of Morrissey* (London: Sidgwick & Jackson, 1994)

Slobin, Mark, *Subcultural Sounds: Micromusics of the West* (Hanover: University Press of New England, 1993)

Smiths, The, *Meat is Murder* (London: Smithdom, 1985)

Smyth, Gerry, 'Who's the greenest of them all? Irishness and popular music', *Irish Studies Review*, vol. 1, no. 2 (1992), pp. 3–5

Smyth, Gerry, *Space and the Irish Cultural Imagination* (Basingstoke: Palgrave, 2001)

Smyth, Gerry, 'The isle is full of noises: Music in contemporary Ireland', *Irish Studies Review*, vol. 12, no. 1 (Apr. 2004), pp. 3–10

Smyth, Gerry, *Noisy Island: A Short History of Irish Popular Music* (Cork: Cork University Press, 2005)

Stanton, Michael, 'Pupils' views of national groups', *Journal of Moral Education*, vol. 1, no. 2 (Feb. 1972), pp. 147–51

Stokes, Martin, 'Introduction: Ethnicity, identity and music', in Stokes (ed.), *Ethnicity, Identity and Music: The Musical Construction of Place* (Oxford: Berg, 1994), pp. 1–27

Stokes, Martin and Philip V. Bohlman, 'Introduction', in Stokes and Bohlman (eds.), *Celtic Modern: Music at the Global Fringe* (Lanham, MD: Scarecrow Press, 2003), pp. 1–26

Stokes, Martin and Philip V. Bohlman (eds.), *Celtic Modern: Music at the Global Fringe* (Lanham, MD: Scarecrow Press, 2003)

Street, John, *Rebel Rock: The Politics of Popular Music* (London: Basil Blackwell, 1986)

Street, John, 'Red Wedge: Another strange story of pop's politics', *Critical Quarterly*, vol. 30, no. 3 (autumn 1988), pp. 79–91

Stringer, Julian, 'The Smiths: Repressed (but remarkably dressed)', *Popular Music*, vol. 11, no. 1 (1992), pp. 15–26

Thompson, E.P., *The Making of the English Working Class* (London: Penguin, 1963)

Ullah, Philip, 'Second-generation Irish youth: Identity and ethnicity', *New Community*, vol. 12 (summer 1985), pp. 310–20

Ullah, Philip, 'Rhetoric and ideology in social identification: The case of second generation Irish youths', *Discourse and Society*, vol. 1, no. 2 (1990), pp. 167–88

Vallely, Fintan (ed.), *The Companion to Irish Traditional Music* (Cork: Cork University Press, 1999)

Vignoles, Julian, 'What is Irish popular music?', *The Crane Bag*, vol. 8, no. 2 (1984), pp. 70–2

Walsh, Colin, *Mud, Songs and Blighty: A Scrapbook of the First World War* (London: Hutchinson, 1975)

Walsh, John, *The Falling Angels* (London: HarperCollins, 1999)

Walter, Bronwen, 'Gendered Irishness in Britain: Changing constructions', in Colin Graham and Richard Kirkland (eds.), *Ireland and Cultural Theory: The Mechanics of Authenticity* (Basingstoke: Macmillan, 1999), pp. 77–98

Walter, Bronwen, '"Shamrocks growing out of their mouths": Language and the racialisation of the Irish in Britain', in Anne J. Kershen (ed.), *Language, Labour and Migration* (Aldershot: Ashgate, 2000), pp. 57–73

Walter, Bronwen, *Outsiders Inside: Whiteness, Place and Irish Women* (London: Routledge, 2001)

Walter, Bronwen, Sarah Morgan, Mary J. Hickman and Joseph Bradley, 'Family stories, public silence: Irish identity construction amongst the second-generation Irish in England', *Scottish Geographical Journal*, vol. 118, no. 3 (2002), pp. 201–17

Walter, Bronwen, 'Invisible Irishness: Second-generation identities in Britain', *Association of European Migration Institutions Journal*, vol. 2 (2004), pp. 185–93

Walter, Bronwen, 'Voices in other ears: "accents" and identities of the first- and second-generation Irish in England', in Guido Rings and Anne Ife (eds.), *Neo-colonial Mentalities in Contemporary Europe? Language and Discourse in the Construction of Identities* (Cambridge: Cambridge Scholars Press, 2008), pp. 174–82

Warnes, Andrew, 'Black, white and blue: The racial antagonism of The Smiths' record sleeves', *Popular Music*, vol. 27, no. 1 (Jan. 2008), pp. 135–49

Waters, John, *Race of Angels: The Genesis of U2* (London: Fourth Estate, 1994)

Whelan, B.J. and J.G. Hughes, *EEC Study of Housing Conditions of Migrant Workers: Irish Contribution – A Survey of Returned and Intending Emigrants in Ireland* (Dublin: ESRI, 1976)

White, Harry, *The Keeper's Recital: Music and Cultural History in Ireland, 1770–1970* (Cork: Cork University Press, 1998)

White, Richard, *Dexys Midnight Runners: Young Soul Rebels* (London: Omnibus Press, 2005)

Whiteley, Sheila, *The Space Between the Notes: Rock and the Counter-Culture* (London: Routledge, 1992)

Whiteley, Sheila (ed.), *Sexing the Groove: Popular Music and Gender* (London: Routledge, 1997)

Widgery, David, *Beating Time: Riot 'n Race 'n Rock 'n Roll* (London: Chatto & Windus, 1986)

Wiener, Jon, *Come Together: John Lennon in His Time* (London: Faber and Faber, 1985)

Wilcox, Claire, *Vivienne Westwood* (London: V&A Publications, 2004)

Wills, Clare, *That Neutral Island: A Cultural History of Ireland During the Second World War* (London: Faber and Faber, 2007)

Wiseman-Trowse, Nathan, *Performing Class in British Popular Music* (Basingstoke: Palgrave, 2008)

Ziesler, Kaja Irene, 'The Irish in Birmingham, 1830–1970' (unpublished Ph.D. thesis, University of Birmingham, 1989)

Zuberi, Nabeel, *Sounds English: Transnational Popular Music* (Urbana and Chicago: University of Illinois Press, 2001)

Zuberi, Nabeel, '"The last truly British people you will ever know": Skinheads, Pakis and Morrissey', in Henry Jenkins, Tara McPherson and Jane Shattuc (eds.), *Hop on Pop: The Politics and Pleasures of Popular Culture* (Durham: Duke University Press, 2002), pp. 539–56

Zuberi, Nabeel, 'Guantánamo, here we come: Out of place with The Smiths', in Sean Campbell and Colin Coulter (eds.), *Why Pamper Life's Complexities? Essays on The Smiths* (Manchester: Manchester University Press, forthcoming)

Bibliography: Newspapers, Magazines & Websites
[anonymous] 'Mail bag', *Melody Maker*, 4 Mar. 1972
_____ 'Mail bag', *Melody Maker*, 24 June 1972
_____ 'Mail bag', *Melody Maker*, 1 July 1972
_____ '"No music for Ulster" fear', *Melody Maker*, 9 Aug. 1975
_____ 'Irish skateboard', *Sounds*, 19 Nov. 1977
_____ 'Rat again (like we did last week)', *Sounds*, 8 July 1978
_____ 'Farewell the Seventies', *Irish Post*, 5 Jan. 1980
_____ 'The 1980s', *Irish Post*, 5 Jan. 1980
_____ 'Ireland now', *Irish Post*, 26 Jan. 1980
_____ 'Nipped in the bud', *Sounds*, 8 Mar. 1980
_____ 'Tour news', *Melody Maker*, 26 July 1980
_____ 'A sense of Ireland', *Irish Post*, 17 Nov. 1979
_____ 'Young soul rebels play Old Vic', *NME*, 31 Oct. 1981
_____ 'UK singles', *NME*, 7 Nov. 1981
_____ '*The Sun* says', *The Sun*, 26 May 1982
_____ 'The Pope amid the ferment', *Guardian*, 28 May 1982
_____ 'Cap'n Kevin on the bridge', *NME*, 11 Sept. 1982

____ 'Anderson's people', *Irish Post*, 2 Oct. 1982

____ 'UK singles', *NME*, 20 Nov. 1982

____ Jak cartoon: 'Typical of the gutter press', *Irish Post*, 4 Dec. 1982

____ 'The Smiths: Message understood', *Rorschach Testing*, Dec. 1983

____ 'Music', *Time Out*, 9–15 Feb. 1984

____ 'Music', *Time Out*, 16–22 Feb. 1984

____ 'Music', *Time Out*, 23–29 Feb. 1984

____ 'Music', *Time Out*, 8–14 Mar. 1984

____ 'Music', *Time Out*, 15–21 Mar. 1984

____ 'T-zers', *NME*, 24 Mar. 1984

____ 'Music', *Time Out*, 29 Mar.–4 Apr. 1984

____ 'Music', *Time Out*, 24–30 May 1984

____ 'Smiths go to Ireland', *Melody Maker*, 13 Oct. 1984

____ 'Denning calls for use of treason law', *The Times*, 18 Oct. 1984

____ 'Talk, talk, talk', *Melody Maker*, 24 Nov. 1984

____ 'Tour news', *Melody Maker*, 8 Dec. 1984

____ 'Shrink rap', *Melody Maker*, 19 Jan. 1985

____ 'Whistle test', *Irish Times*, 4 June 1985

____ 'Naval lark', *Sounds*, 10 Aug. 1985

____ 'Desperately seeking attention', *Record Mirror*, 21 Dec. 1985

____ 'Pogues fall from grace with government', *NME*, 19 Nov. 1988

____ 'Shane McGowan [*sic*] diaries', *Melody Maker*, 10 Dec. 1988

____ 'Questionnaire', *Q*, Jan. 1995

____ 'Kevin Rowland: The early years', *Keep on Running*, no. 6 (Jan. 1997)

____ WW2 people's war: An archive of world war two memories – written by the public, gathered by the BBC', http://www.bbc.co.uk/ww2peopleswar/stories/81/a2951381.shtml

Adams, Nick, 'Johnny too bad', *No. 1*, 25 Aug. 1984

Aitken, Kit, 'String driven thing', *Uncut*, Dec. 1999

Aizlewood, John, 'Bullish', *Q*, Aug. 1996

Aizlewood, John, et al., '100 greatest singers and their 1,000 greatest songs', *Q*, Apr. 2007

Anthony, Andrew, 'A man of many words and few teeth', *Observer*, 5 Mar. 2000

Archer, Kevin, 'Hello goodbye', *Mojo*, July 2009

Arnot, Chris, 'Marie Gillespie: A good sense of humour', *Guardian*, 'Education' section, 7 Nov. 2006

Arnott, Jake, 'A major part of me is always dark …', *Time Out*, 2 June 2004

Bailie, Stuart, 'The Pogues', *Record Mirror*, 19 Dec. 1987

Bailie, Stuart, 'The first thing people think …', *Record Mirror*, 29 Dec. 1987

Baker, Danny, '"Oo you patronising, John? …"', *NME*, 26 July 1980

Barron, Jack, 'Band of unholy joy', *Sounds*, 13 Dec. 1986

Bell, Max, 'Kevin Rowland', *SFX*, 12–24 Aug. 1982

Bennun, David, Paul Lester, Taylor Parkes, Dave Simpson and Ian Watson, 'Britpop', *Melody Maker*, 22 July 1995

Birch, Ian, 'The Morrissey collection', *Smash Hits*, 21 June–4 July 1984

Black, Antonella, 'Me no pop eye', *Sounds*, 6 Apr. 1985

Black, Antonella, 'Sorrow's native son', *Sounds*, 20 Apr. 1985

Black, Bill, 'Serious drinking', *Sounds*, 12 Oct. 1984

Black, Johnny, 'The *Mojo* interview', *Mojo*, May 2003

Blake, John, 'Rock's swastika revolution', *London Evening News*, 7 May 1977

Bowcott, Owen, 'Concern over health of Irish immigrants', *Guardian*, 9 Feb. 1998

Boyd, Brian, 'Johnny, we never knew you', *Irish Times*, 'Arts' section, 8 May 1999

Boyd, Brian, 'Paddy Englishman', *Irish Times*, 'Arts' section, 20 Nov. 1999

Boyd, Brian, 'Johnny take a bow', *Irish Times*, 'The Ticket' section, 31 Aug. 2007

Boyle, P.J., 'The Pogues an insult to Irish music', *Irish Post*, 26 Oct. 1985

Breen, Joe, 'Staking their claim', *Irish Times*, 22 Feb. 1985

Breen, Joe, 'Getting the lash', *Irish Times*, 23 Aug. 1985

British Market Research Bureau, 'Top 75 singles', *Music and Video Week*, 2 Oct. 1982

Britten, Fleur, 'Siobhan again', *Sunday Times*, 22 Nov. 2009

Brown, Derek, 'Five men killed in Ulster "checkpoint" ambush', *Guardian*, 1 Aug. 1975

Brown, Glyn, 'Laughter in paradise!', *Sounds*, 14 June 1986

Brown, Len, 'Born to be Wilde', *NME*, 13 Feb. 1988

Brown, Len, 'Desecrating wildly', *NME*, 16 July 1988

Brown, Len, 'Morrissey', *Guardian*, 'Review' section, 30 Dec. 1988

Burchill, Julie, 'Julie Burchill', *The Face*, Mar. 1983

Burchill, Julie, 'Greeneland revisited', *The Face*, Aug. 1983

Burchill, Julie, 'Thermometer 3', *The Face*, Oct. 1983

Burke, Kathy, 'Kathy comes home', *Observer*, 'Review' section, 1 Feb. 2004

Burke, Ray, 'GLC seeks assurance on Irish voting rights', *Irish Post*, 4 Dec. 1982

Byrne, George, 'The Manchester martyr', *Hot Press*, 11 Apr. 1986

Byrne, George, 'The tune Smith', *Hot Press*, 12 Mar. 1987

Cameron, Keith, 'Pogues on the ropes', *Sounds*, 29 July 1989

Cameron, Keith, 'Kevin, Kevin and Kevin go large!', *NME*, 7 Oct. 2000

Cameron, Keith, 'Who's the daddy?', *Mojo*, June 2004

Campbell, James, 'Escape from the margins', *Guardian*, 'Review', 19 Nov. 2005

Carr, Roy, 'Dexys: Funky butt fassst!', *NME*, 12 Jan. 1980

Casey, Norah (ed.), 'You Say: The forum for the Irish in Britain', *Irish Post*, 13 Feb. 1999

Chevron, Philip, 'BP Fallon/RTÉ interview 1985', http://www.pogues.com/forum/
    viewtopic.php?f=24&t=9639

Christian, Terry, 'The Smiths forever', unpublished piece for the *Daily Mail*, May 2004

Christian, Terry, 'The outsiders will have their day', *The Times*, 12 Feb. 2010

Cigarettes, Johnny, 'Five go mad for it', *NME*, 17 Aug. 1996

Clarke, Liam, '"Pro-IRA" Lennon spied on by FBI', *Sunday Times*, 5 Oct. 1997

Clarke, Victoria, 'The Pogues: The sweet smell of excess', *Melody Maker*, 1 June 1991

Clarke, Victoria, 'The hardest thinking man in showbiz', *Q*, Aug. 1993

Clerk, Carol, 'Sore heads and fairy tails', *Melody Maker*, 28 Nov. 1987

Cochrane, Alan, 'The £200m swindlers', *Daily Express*, 28 Oct. 1976

Cooper, Mark, 'Smithspeak', *No. 1*, 13 Mar. 1984

Cordery, Mark, 'Shamrock it', *Record Mirror*, 27 Oct. 1984

Corrigan, Susan, 'What's to be done with her?', *Smiths Indeed*, no. 10 (winter 1988)

Cosgrove, Stuart (ed.), 'Glamour bag', *NME*, 9 Nov. 1985

Cosgrove, Stuart and Sean O'Hagan, 'Gael force: Two nations under a groove – an A to
    Z of partisan pop', *NME*, 2 May 1987

Courtney, Kevin, 'Midnight run', *Irish Times*, 'The Ticket' section, 13 Nov. 2003

Crace, John, 'Salford lad is back', *Guardian*, 'Education' section, 12 Feb. 2008

Cross, Diane, 'Status quo? Great!', *Record Mirror*, 30 Nov. 1985

Cummins, Kevin, 'Who do they think they are?', *Observer* magazine, 27 Nov. 2005

Cunningham, Michael, 'BP Fallon Orchestra', *Irish Times*, 21 Sept. 1985

Cunningham, Niall, 'Celebrate all that makes us distinct', *Irish Post*, 3 June 2000

Daily Mail Reporters, 'Moment of grief for Maggie', *Daily Mail*, 15 Oct. 1984

Dalton, Stephen, 'Getting away with it', *Uncut*, Apr. 1999

Darling, Cary, 'Marr needs guitars', *BAM: Bay Area Music Magazine*, 3 July 1987

Deevoy, Adrian, 'Married to the Murphia', *Q*, Sept. 1989

Dessau, Bruce, 'Rebel without a cause', *City Limits*, 12–19 June 1986

Dexys Midnight Runners, 'Geno', *Sounds*, 22 Mar. 1980

Dooley, Brian, 'Your name could put you in jail', *New Statesman*, 4 Oct. 2004

Dovkants, Keith, 'My plot to assassinate Ken Livingstone on the Tube', *Evening Standard*, 1 Nov. 2006

Dunn, Martin and Nick Ferrari, 'Smiths' "sick" royal disc rapped', *The Sun*, 16 June 1986

Du Noyer, Paul, 'The burning of Southall', *NME*, 11 July 1981

Du Noyer, Paul, 'Van still the man', *NME*, 6 Mar. 1982

Du Noyer, Paul, 'Oh, such drama!', *Q*, Aug. 1987

Dwyer, Michael, 'Mac the mouth', *Sunday Tribune*, 'People' section, 2 Aug. 1987

Dwyer, Róisín, 'Saint Patrick', *Hot Press*, 26 Jan. 2005

Easlea, Daryl, 'Don't stand me down', *Record Collector*, Apr. 2002

Ellen, Mark, 'Midnight express', *Smash Hits*, 22 July–4 Aug. 1982

Elms, Robert, 'Pogue in the eye', *The Face*, Mar. 1985

Elms, Robert, 'Death to dull rock', *The Face*, Nov. 1985

Evers, Paul, 'Dexys Midnight Runners', *Oor*, 17 Nov. 1982

Fanning, Dave, 'The Smiths at the SFX', *Irish Times*, 23 May 1984

Fanning, Dave, 'The star who's taking the pap out of pop', *Irish Times*, 24 Mar. 1987

Fay, Liam, 'I drink therefore I am', *Hot Press*, 10 Aug. 1989

Ferguson, Neil, 'Ain't that a Shane', *Philadelphia Weekly*, 14–20 Mar. 2007

Fletcher, Tony, 'The wild-hearted outsider: A profile of Kevin Rowland', *Jamming!*, Oct. 1985

Foley, Michael, 'Awareness and interest in music that is Irish', *Irish Times*, 4 Aug. 1977

Ford, Richard, 'The argument for becoming nation without a name', *The Times*, 12 Oct. 2000

Foyle, John, 'BP Fallon/RTÉ interview 1985', http://www.pogues.com/forum/viewtopic. php?f=24&t=9639

Fricke, David, 'Keeping up with The Smiths', *Rolling Stone*, 9 Oct. 1986

Frith, Simon, 'The Specials/The Selecter/Dexys Midnight Runners', *Melody Maker*, 8 Dec. 1979

Frith, Simon, 'I am what I am', *Village Voice*, 3 Aug. 1993

Garfield, Simon, 'This charming man', *Time Out*, 7–13 Mar. 1985

Gartland, Annette, 'Irish culture display planned for Thatcher', *Irish Times*, 10 Sept. 1983

Gartland, Annette, 'Terrorist ban hits pop song', *Observer*, 20 Nov. 1988

Goddard, Simon, 'Crowning glory', *Uncut*, Jan. 2006

Goddard, Simon, and Paul Lester (eds.), 'The uncut 100', *Uncut*, Sept. 2005

Goldman, Vivien, 'WOMAD', *NME*, 24 July 1982

Gordon, Stephen, 'Raw rags at midnite', *NME*, 17 June 1978

Gore, Joe, 'Johnny Marr', *Guitar Player*, Jan. 1990

Graham, Bill, 'New wave a Paddy plot?', *Hot Press*, 23 June 1977

Graham, Bill, 'The hard stuff', *Hot Press*, 21 Sept. 1984

Graham, Bill, 'The king and I', *Hot Press*, 27 Mar. 1986

Graham, Bill, 'Pogues off the air', *Hot Press*, 15 Dec. 1988

Graham, Bill, 'Get your yeah yeahs out!', *Hot Press*, 15 Dec. 1988

Graham, Bill, 'State of grace', *Hot Press*, 28 Jan. 1988

Graham, William, 'Johnny jumps up!', *Hot Press*, 11–30 May 1979

Granuaille, 'Asses to asses', *Zigzag*, Dec. 1985

Green, Jim, 'Dexys Midnight Runners', *Trouser Press*, Nov. 1980

Green, Jim, 'This man believes', *Trouser Press*, May 1983

Halliwell, David and Ste Mack, 'The Johnny Marr interview', *The Official Oasis Magazine*, no. 1 (winter 1996)

Harris, John, 'Trouble at mill', *Mojo*, Apr. 2001

Haviland, Julian, 'Attack on "enemy within"', *The Times*, 20 July 1984

Heath, Chris, 'Albums', *Smash Hits*, 11–24 Sept. 1985

Heidemann, Jason A., 'The Morrissey the merrier', *Time Out Chicago*, 10–16 May 2007

Henke, James, 'Oscar! Oscar! Great Britain goes Wilde for the "fourth-gender" Smiths', *Rolling Stone*, 7 June 1984

Henshaw, Laurie, 'Censored', *Melody Maker*, 11 Mar. 1972

Hewitt, Paulo, 'Cheapo, Dexys!', *Melody Maker*, 16 Aug. 1980

Hewitt, Paolo, 'Keeping up', *Melody Maker*, 7 Aug. 1982

Hibbert, Tom, 'Meat is murder!', *Smash Hits*, 31 Jan.–13 Feb. 1985

Hoggard, Liz, 'Playboy of the West End world', *Independent*, magazine section, 15 June 2002

Hoskyns, Barney, 'Ridiculous and wonderful', *NME*, 1 Oct. 1983

Hoskyns, Barney, 'The Smiths: These disarming men', *NME*, 4 Feb. 1984

Hughes, Sarah, 'Surgical spirit', *Observer*, *Observer* Music Monthly section, 20 Nov. 2005

Huq, Rupa, 'Morrissey and me', *New Statesman*, 10 Dec. 2007 (http://www.newstatesman.com/writers/rupa_huq)

Hurr, Gary, 'The Dexys soul-ution', *Record Mirror*, 19 June 1982

Hurt, Andy, 'A whip round with the Pogues', *Sounds*, 17 Aug. 1985

Hutcheon, David, 'Rides up with wear', *Mojo*, May 2002

Hutcheon, David, '10 questions for Kevin Rowland', *Mojo*, Oct. 2003

Irvin, Jim, 'Regrets? I've had a few', *Mojo*, Sept. 2000

Irwin, Colin, 'The other side of midnight', *Melody Maker*, 3 July 1982

Irwin, Colin, 'A parcel of rogues', *Southern Rag*, 1 Oct.–31 Dec. 1982

Irwin, Colin, 'Pursuing Poguemahone', *Southern Rag*, 1 Apr.–30 June 1984

Irwin, Colin, 'The thorn birds', *Melody Maker*, 6 Oct. 1984

Irwin, Colin, 'Stand and deliver', *Melody Maker*, 7 Sept. 1985

Irwin, Colin, 'Pogueology', *Folk Roots*, Aug. 1987

Jak, 'The Irish: The ultimate in psychopathic horror', *Standard*, 29 Oct. 1982

Janes, Andrew, 'The 1.5 generation', *The New Zealand Listener*, 17–23 July 2004

Jennings, Zane/Dave, 'A gig too fleadh', *Melody Maker*, 8 June 1991

Johnson, Derek, 'Dexys divide', *NME*, 15 Nov. 1980

Johnson, Derek, 'Dexys' passion runs dry', *NME*, 14 Mar. 1981

Johnson, Paul, 'Welfare: A monster of our own making', *Daily Mail*, 25 Apr. 1994

Jones, Allan, 'Rotten!', *Melody Maker*, 4 June 1977

Jones, Allan, 'The healing festival', *Melody Maker*, 25 Feb. 1984

Jones, Allan, 'The blue romantics', *Melody Maker*, 3 Mar. 1984

Jones, Allan, 'Johnny Guitar', *Melody Maker*, 14 Apr. 1984

Jones, Allan, 'Trial by jury', *Melody Maker*, 16 Mar. 1985

Jonze, Tim, 'Has the world changed or has he changed?', *NME*, 1 Dec. 2007

Katz, Robin, 'Hear the one about a group of Irish superstars …?', *Sounds*, 19 Mar. 1977

Kavanagh, Trevor, 'Hang the IRA bombers says big Sun poll', *The Sun*, 19 Oct. 1984

Kelly, Danny, 'The further thoughts of Chairman Mo', *NME*, 8 June 1985

Kelly, Danny, 'Pogues gallery', *NME*, 17 Aug. 1985

Kelly, Danny, 'Triumph of the swill', *NME*, 20/27 Dec. 1986

Kelly, Danny, 'Exile on mainstream', *NME*, 14 Feb. 1987

Kelly, Danny and Adrian Thrills, 'NME readers' poll 1984', *NME*, 23 Feb. 1985

Kelly, Nick, 'The spirit is willing', *Hot Press*, 19 Oct. 1984

Kent, Nick, 'National anthems', *Melody Maker*, 14 June 1986

Kent, Nick, 'The band with the thorn in its side', *The Face*, Apr. 1987

Kent, Nick, 'Isolation', *Q/Mojo Classic: Morrissey and the Story of Manchester* (2006)

King, Ray, 'Running scared?', *Manchester Evening News*, 9 Nov. 1984

King, Ray, 'Stay away from us, club tells pop pests', *Manchester Evening News*, 2 Aug. 1988

Kopf, Biba, 'A suitable case for treatment', *NME*, 22/29 Dec. 1984

Lass, Frances, 'Would you let these people drink in your bar?', *Sounds*, 21 Jan. 1978

Leach, Edmund, 'The official Irish jokesters', *New Society*, 'The Books People Buy' section, 20/27 Dec. 1979

Leboff, Gary, 'Goodbye cruel world', *Melody Maker*, 26 Sept. 1987

Le Page, John, 'Pogue mahone', *The Face*, Oct. 1983

Lester, Paul, 'The Pogues: The last gang in town', *Melody Maker*, 25 Mar. 1989

Lester, Paul, 'Titanic!', *Uncut*, Mar. 2000

Lewis, Alan, 'Singles', *Sounds*, 7 May 1977

Lock, Pete, 'Breaking down the walls of art-ache', *Sounds*, 10 May 1980

Lowe, Steve, et al., 'Now my chart is full', *Q/Mojo Special Edition: The Smiths and Morrissey* (2004)

Lynch, Declan, 'A Dubliner and the quare 'oul times', *Hot Press*, new year special 1987

Lynskey, Dorian, 'Songs about drinking', *Guardian*, 'Film and Music' section, 16 Dec. 2005

Lynskey, Dorian, 'Songs about London', *Guardian*, 'Film and Music' section, 7 July 2006

Lynskey, Dorian, 'Readers recommend goodbye songs', *Guardian*, 'Film and Music' section, 11 Apr. 2008

Mac Anailly Burke, Molly, 'Cool Cait', *Sunday Independent*, 31 Jan. 1988

MacGowan, Shane, 'Singles', *Melody Maker*, 6 July 1985

MacGowan, Shane, 'Heroes', *Melody Maker*, 18 Oct. 1986

Mackey, Liam, 'The leader of the band', *Hot Press*, 8–23 Oct. 1982

Maconie, Stuart, 'Pungent spice', *Q*, Aug. 1999

Maconie, Stuart, et al., 'The 100 greatest British albums ever!', *Q*, June 2000

Magee, Matthew, 'Pogues pogo on', *Sunday Tribune*, 'Artlife' section, 19 May 2002

Male, Andrew, 'Get the message', *Q/Mojo Classic: Morrissey and the Story of Manchester* (2006)

Manzoor, Sarfraz, 'Bradford reflects on many shades of Englishness', *Observer*, 'Review' section, 5 July 2009

Marcus, Greil, 'Elvis Costello explains himself', *Rolling Stone*, 2 Sept. 1982

Marr, Johnny, 'It's our most enduring record', *Uncut*, Mar. 2007

Martin, Gavin, 'Overnight bag sensations', *NME*, 14 June 1980

Martin, Gavin, 'A folk hero of the 80s: The Kevin Rowland interview', *NME*, 3 July 1982

Martin, Gavin, 'Pogue mahone', *NME*, 15 Jan. 1983

Martin, Gavin, 'Mahone ranger's handbook', *NME*, 13 Aug. 1983

Martin, Gavin (ed.), 'Gasserbag', *NME*, 20 Aug. 1983

Martin, Gavin, 'Angst', *NME*, 26 Sept. 1987

Martin, Gavin, 'Once upon a time in the west', *NME*, 2 Jan. 1988

Martin, Gavin, 'Anarchic in the UK', *Uncut*, Oct. 2000

Mason, Heidi, 'Morrissey and the outsider ideal', *Smiths Indeed*, no. 10 (winter 1988)

McAnailly-Burke, Molly, 'Pogues' gallery', *Hot Press*, 5 July 1985

McAnailly-Burke, Molly, 'Pogue lore', *Hot Press*, 30 Jan. 1986

McCann, Eamonn, 'Celtic soul brotherhood', *Hot Press*, 28 Jan. 1988

McCaughey, John, 'Mixed-up kids!', *Irish Post*, 23 Dec. 1970

McCormick, Neil, 'All men have secrets', *Hot Press*, 4 May 1984

McCormick, Neil, 'Elvis Unmasked', *Hot Press*, 23 Feb. 1989

McCrohan, Maurice, 'From Beethoven to The Pogues', *Irish Post*, 16 Nov. 1985

McCrystal, Cal, 'Emigration "poses huge danger to Irish health"', *Observer*, 9 June 1996

McCullough, Dave, 'Death to art rock!', *Sounds*, 19 May 1979

McCullough, Dave, 'The return of Kevin Rowland', *Sounds*, 24 July 1982

McCullough, Dave, 'Morrison at midnight', *Sounds*, 24 July 1982

McCullough, Dave, 'Handsome devils', *Sounds*, 4 June 1983

McCullough, Dave, 'The Smiths ICA', *Sounds*, 15 Oct. 1983

McDaid, Carol, 'He chopped up a piano with Dylan', *Observer*, 'Review' section, 20 May 2001

McGrath, Bernard, 'Angst of the Irish in Britain', *Irish Post*, 24 Apr. 1999

McGreevy, Ronan, 'Award shows Pogues' glory days are gone', *Irish Post*, 4 Feb. 2006

McIlheney, Barry, 'Celtic swingers', *Melody Maker*, 27 Oct. 1984

McIlheney, Barry, 'The thoughts of Chairman Marr', *Melody Maker*, 3 Aug. 1985

McIlheney, Barry, 'Burning the midnight oil', *Melody Maker*, 2 Nov. 1985

McIlheney, Barry, 'All I want for Christmas is my two front teeth', *Melody Maker*, 21/28 Dec. 1985

McKenna, John, 'The Smiths: These charming men', *Hot Press*, 27 Jan.–9 Feb. 1984

McNeill, Phil, 'Gift from a flower to a garden', *NME*, 31 July 1982

McNeill, Phil, 'A man out of time', *The Hit*, 21 Sept. 1985

McNeill, Phil, 'Let's get this straight from the start', *The Hit*, 28 Sept. 1985

McRae, Donald, 'Blithe spirits', *NME*, 21/28 Dec. 1985

McRae, Donald, 'The Smiths' Anti-Apartheid benefit', *NME*, 3 Jan. 1987

Melody Maker, 27 Oct. 1984

Melody Maker, 'The Smiths' booklet, 23 Sept. 1989

Miles, 'Cannibalism at Clash gig', *NME*, 6 Nov. 1976

Miller, Andrea, 'Everything's gone green!', *NME*, 28 Sept. 1985

Morris, Terence, 'The divisions that will welcome a Pope', *Guardian*, 28 May 1982

Morrissey, 'Portrait of the artist as a consumer', *NME*, 17 Sept. 1983

Morrissey, 'Never turn your back on Mother Earth', *Blitz*, May 1985

Morton, Tom, 'Dexys Midnight Runners', *Melody Maker*, 9 Nov. 1985

Mueller, Andrew, 'Johnny Marr', *Melody Maker*, 30 Sept. 1989

Mulvey, John, 'Rogue Man star', *NME*, 10 Jan. 1998

Mulvey, John, 'The third coming', *Uncut*, May 2002

Murphy, Peter, 'The unbearable lightness of being Morrissey', *Hot Press*, 8 Apr. 2009

Murray, Charles Shaar, 'Tom Jones/Hammersmith', *NME*, 16 Mar. 1974

Murray, Charles Shaar, 'We didn't know it was loaded …', *NME*, 9 July 1977

Murray, Charles Shaar, 'John, Paul, Steve and Sidney: The social rehabilitation of the Sex Pistols', *NME*, 6 Aug. 1977

Neville, Katie, 'The post-cool school', *The Face*, Feb. 1984

Nicholls, Mike, 'Fiddler's dream', *Record Mirror*, 31 July 1982

Ni Scanlain, Grainne, 'A reflection of reality', *Irish Post*, 21 Dec. 1985

Nolan, Paul, 'I've something to get off my chest', *Hot Press*, 2 July 2008

O'Brien, Glenn, 'Pogues gallery', *Spin*, June 1986

O'Hagan, Andrew, 'Cartwheels over broken glass', *London Review of Books*, 4 Mar. 2004

O'Hagan, Sean, 'Tangled up in blue', *NME*, 7 Sept. 1985

O'Hagan, Sean (ed.), 'Utensil', *NME*, 17 Jan. 1987

O'Hagan, Sean, 'Wild rovers' return', *NME*, 21 Mar. 1987

O'Hagan, Sean (ed.), 'Angst', *NME*, 23 May 1987

O'Hagan, Sean, 'In the heat of the night', *NME*, 2 July 1988

O'Hagan, Sean, 'It's all in the bollocks ...', *NME*, 9 July 1988

O'Hagan, Sean and James Brown, 'The Three Horsemen of the Apocalypse', *NME*, 25 Feb. 1989

O'Hagan, Sean, 'Look back in angst', *Observer*, 'Review' section, 7 Apr. 2002

O'Hagan, Sean, 'What are your favourite songs by The Smiths?', http://blogs.guardian.co.uk/music/2007/05/what_are_your_favourite_songs.html

O'More, Rory, 'Spit in your eye', *An Phoblacht*, 22 Nov. 1984

O'Sullivan, Jack, 'All too easy to be seduced by the dangerous romanticism of Irishness', *Independent*, 26 Sept. 1996

O'Sullivan, Jack, 'British Muslims are the new Irish', *New Statesman*, 3 Nov. 2003

O'Toole, Fintan, 'Nowhere man', *Irish Times*, 'Weekend' section, 26 Apr. 1997

Owen, Frank, 'Home thoughts from abroad', *Melody Maker*, 27 Sept. 1986

Parsons, Tony, 'Letters', *The Face*, Oct. 1983

Parsons, Tony, 'A divine spark in the British Soul', *Daily Mirror*, 17 May 1999

Petridis, Alexis, 'The regina monologues', *Q/Mojo Special Edition: The Smiths and Morrissey* (2004)

Petridis, Alexis, 'Electro-pop? New folk, you mean', *Guardian*, 'Film and Music' section, 22 Feb. 2008

Pilgrim, Dee, 'Nightshift', *Sounds*, 10 Aug. 1985

Plummer, Mark, 'If Paul McCartney really wants to do something for Ireland, why doesn't he stop singing about it and come here?', *Melody Maker*, 4 Mar. 1972

Price, Simon, 'A dark knight of the soul', *Independent*, 'Friday Review' section, 5 Apr. 2002

Price, T., 'From Beethoven to The Pogues', *Irish Post*, 16 Nov. 1985

Pringle, Gill, 'Dexys Midnight Runners', *Record Mirror*, 16 Aug. 1980

Purden, Richard, 'Mancunian Marr is still proud of his Irish roots', *Irish Post*, 'Rí-Rá' section, 7 July 2007

Purden, Richard, 'Keeping up with The Smiths', *Irish Post*, 1 Sept. 2007

Push, 'Collecting the empties', *Melody Maker*, 28 Nov. 1987

Pye, Ian, 'Magnificent obsessions', *Melody Maker*, 26 Nov. 1983

Pye, Ian, 'A hard day's misery', *Melody Maker*, 3 Nov. 1984

Pye, Ian, 'Some mothers do 'ave 'em', *NME*, 7 June 1986

Quantick, David, 'Pogue Mahone', *NME*, 24 Sept. 1983

Quantick, David, 'The quare fellow', *NME*, 24 Mar. 1984

Quantick, David and Sean O'Hagan, 'For a few ciders more', *NME*, 11 Aug. 1984

Quantick, David, 'Too-rye-eh?', *NME*, 23 Nov. 1985

Quantick, David, 'The king is dead', *The Word*, Mar. 2008

Reed, John, 'A tale of two Kevins', *Record Collector*, July 2009

Reel, Penny (ed.), 'Gasbag', *NME*, 25 May 1985

Reynolds, Simon, 'Not for sale in S.A!', *Melody Maker*, 20/27 Dec. 1986

Reynolds, Simon, 'How soon is now?', *Melody Maker*, 26 Sept. 1987

Reynolds, Simon, 'Songs of love and hate', *Melody Maker*, 12 Mar. 1988

Reynolds, Simon, 'Songs of love and hate', *Melody Maker*, 19 Mar. 1988

Reynolds, Simon, 'Whatever happened to Britpop?', *salon.com*, http://www.salon.com/ent/music/review/2007/12/08/britbox/

Richardson, Andy, 'The battle of Britpop', *NME*, 12 Aug. 1995

Roberts, Chris, 'Stand and deliver', *Sounds*, 7 Sept. 1985

Roberts, Chris, 'The midnight's hour', *Sounds*, 12 Oct. 1985

Roberts, Chris, 'Stairway to Kevin', *Melody Maker*, 9 Apr. 1988

Roberts, Chris, 'Grand stand', *Uncut*, May 2002

Robertson, Sandy, 'Do you sincerely want to be rich?', *Sounds*, 17 Dec. 1977

Rogan, Johnny, 'Rebel yell', *Irish Post*, 'The Craic!' section, 26 Sept. 1998

Rogan, Johnny, 'Dexys Midnight Runners', *Record Collector*, Sept. 2000

Rogan, Johnny, 'Dexys Midnight Runners, *Searching for the Young Soul Rebels*', *Mojo*, Sept. 2000

Rogan, Johnny, 'Don't stand me down', *Record Collector*, Apr. 2002

Rogers, Malcolm, 'The 100 most influential Irish people', *Irish Post*, 22 Aug. 1998

Rogers, Malcolm, 'Tommy made it', *Irish Post*, 'The Craic!' section, 1 May 1999

Rom, Ron, 'Rum runaway', *Sounds*, 29 Mar. 1986

Romhany, 'Dexys: Let's get this straight from the start', *Jamming!*, no. 14 (1983)

Rouse, Rose, 'Brutabilly', *Sounds*, 24 Mar. 1984

Rouse, Rose, 'Pogue-o-schtick', *Sounds*, 6 Oct. 1984

Rowland, Kevin, 'A day full of Dexys', *Melody Maker*, 21 Nov. 1981

Rowland, Kevin, 'Profile', *Record Mirror*, 17 July 1982

Rowland, Kevin, 'Kevin Rowland replies to Julie Burchill', *The Face*, Sept. 1983

Rowland, Kevin, 'Inside track', *Uncut*, Oct. 2000

Salewicz, Chris, 'Anarchy in the UK: The reality', *NME*, 18 July 1981

Savage, Jon, 'Androgyny: Confused chromosomes and camp followers', *The Face*, June 1983

Savage, Jon, 'The escape artist', *Village Voice Rock 'n' Roll Quarterly* (summer 1989)

Savage, Jon, 'Rough emeralds', *Guardian*, Second section, 17 Mar. 1995

Savage, Jon, 'How we listened then', *Observer*, *Observer* Music Monthly section, 17 July 2005

Sawyer, Miranda, 'Florence is away with the faeries and leprechauns', *Observer*, 'Review' section, 5 July 2009

Scanlon, Ann, 'The rogues of Tralee', *Sounds*, 28 Nov. 1987

Scanlon, Ann, 'Celtic soul rebels', *Mojo*, Sept. 2004

Sedgwick, Harry, 'Dexys Midnight Runners: *Don't Stand Me Down*', *Jamming!*, Oct. 1985

Sexton, Dave, 'The Smiths, Sands, Carlisle', *Record Mirror*, 25 Oct. 1986

Shapero, Lindsay, 'New riders of the purple sage', *Time Out*, 22–28 Mar. 1984

Shapero, Lindsay, 'Red devil', *Time Out*, 17–23 May 1984

Sheehan, Martina, 'On the road: The Pogues', *Time Out Chicago*, 1–7 Mar. 2007

Shelley, Jim, 'Kevin Rowland and Dexys Midnight Runners', *Smash Hits*, 14–27 Oct. 1982

Silverton, Pete, 'When Irish eyes are bloodshot', *Mail on Sunday*, 'You' magazine, 13 Mar. 1988

Simpson, Dave, 'Why two's company', *Guardian*, 13 July 1996

Simpson, Dave, 'Still doing it his way', *Guardian*, 12 Nov. 1999

Simpson, Dave, 'Marr's attacks', *Guardian*, 'Friday Review' section, 18 Aug. 2000

Simpson, Dave, 'Old habits die hard', *Guardian*, 'Friday Review' section, 26 Nov. 2004

Simpson, Dave, 'The kindness of strangers', *Guardian*, 'Film and Music' section, 24 Aug. 2007

Sinker, Mark, 'Look back in anguish', *NME*, 2 Jan. 1988

Skoler, Ron, 'John & Yoko: Some time in New York City', *Sounds*, 2 Sept. 1972

Smash Hits, 'Morrissey', *Smash Hits*, 3–16 Jan. 1985

Smith, David, 'Time out at 40', *Observer*, 10 Aug. 2008

Smith, Graham and Dylan Jones, 'Alias Smith and …', *Record Mirror*, 8 Sept. 1984

Smiths, The, 'Bigmouth Strikes Again', *Smash Hits*, 4–17 June 1986

Snow, Mat, 'The sweet smell of success', *NME*, 22 Mar. 1986

Snow, Mat, "'Ello 'andsome!', *Mojo*, Mar. 2008

Spinoza, Andy, 'Morrissey: The man, the myth, the mouth', *City Life*, Nov. 1986

Stand, Mike, 'Hearts full of soul', *The Face*, May 1980

Staunton, Terry, 'It's the Shane old song', *NME*, 2 Dec. 1989

Stokes, Dermot, 'Dexys Midnight Runners', *Hot Press*, 14–28 Aug. 1980

Stokes, Dermot, 'Singles', *Hot Press*, 30 July–12 Aug. 1982

Stokes, Dermot, '82 45s', *Hot Press*, 16 Dec. 1982

Stokes, Dermot, 'Kiss of life', *Hot Press*, 16 Nov. 1984

Stokes, Dermot, 'The long run', *Hot Press*, 10 Oct. 1985

Stokes, Niall, 'The private Kate Bush', *Hot Press*, 21 Nov. 1985

Strickland, Andy, 'Pogue mania!', *Record Mirror*, 21 Sept. 1985

Stubbs, David, 'Combat rock', *Uncut*, Aug. 1998

Stud Brothers, 'Sham rock', *Melody Maker*, 21/28 Dec. 1985

Sullivan, Jim, 'Pogues throw more in the mix', *Boston Globe*, 3 Oct. 1989

Sunie, 'Singles', *Record Mirror*, 13 Mar. 1982

Sutcliffe, Phil, Caroline Coon, Vivien Goldman, Jon Savage and Pete Silverton, 'It can't happen here', *Sounds*, 25 Mar. 1978

Sutcliffe, Phil, 'The dexedrine gang', *Sounds*, 19 Jan. 1980

Sutcliffe, Phil, 'This is my confession', *Q*, Aug. 1993

Sutherland, Alastair, 'The Pogues: Féach amach!', *Graffiti*, vol. 4, no. 9 (1988)

Sutherland, Steve (ed.), 'Backlash', *Melody Maker*, 17 Nov. 1984

Sutherland, Steve (ed.), 'Backlash', *Melody Maker*, 24 Nov. 1984

Sutherland, Steve, 'See! Hear! Now!', *NME*, 20 Sept. 1997

Sweeting, Adam, 'The Nips', *NME*, 22 Mar. 1980

Tame, Adrian and Peter Chippindale, 'Wings fly high', *Melody Maker*, 19 Feb. 1972

Taylor, Neil, 'Singles', *NME*, 14 Dec. 1985

Terry, Helen, 'Singles', *Melody Maker*, 27 Oct. 1984

Thomson, Gordon, 'My team', *Observer Sport Monthly*, 2 Nov. 2003

Thrills, Adrian, 'Ears of a clown', *NME*, 27 Oct. 1979

Thrills, Adrian, 'In search of the passion patrol', *NME*, 24 Sept. 1983

Thrills, Adrian, 'L'uomo Pogue', *NME*, 4 Jan. 1986

Tickell, Paul, 'Reds, white and blue: The politics of colour', *NME*, 17 Apr. 1982

Torres, Jennifer, 'Morrissey has strong bond with Latinos', *Stockton Record*, 'LENS' section, 27 Apr. 2007

Townsend, Martin, 'The secret life of a Pogue', *The Hit*, 21 Sept. 1985

Travis, Alan, 'British tag is "coded racism"', *Guardian*, 11 Oct. 2000

Udell, Phil, 'The Radiators at Oxegen: Video interview', *hotpress.com*, http://www.hotpress.com/oxegen/2743930.html

Van Poznak, Elissa, 'Morrissey: *The Face* interview', *The Face*, July 1984

www.jmarr.com, 'Q&A', no. 4 (2000) (http://jmarr.com/qanda4.html)

www.jmarr.com, 'Q&A' (Mar. 2001)

www.mikejoyce.com/start.html ('Smiths Photographs II')

Walsh, Nikki, 'The house that Dad built', *The Dubliner*, June 2008

Walters, Dave, 'Albums', *Time Out*, 4–10 Oct. 1984

Warburton, Neil, 'It was August 1997 ...', *Keep on Running*, no. 9 (Oct. 1997)

Waters, John, 'Those charming men', *Irish Times*, 'Weekend' section, 25 Apr. 1992

Watson, Don (ed.), 'Gasbag', *NME*, 3 Sept. 1983

Watson, Don, 'A Pogue in the eye with a sharp stick', *NME*, 27 Apr. 1985

Watts, Michael, 'Paul's protest', *Melody Maker*, 12 Feb. 1972

Webb, Iain, 'This handsome devil', *NME*, 'Undress' supplement, 26 May 1984

White, Lesley, 'Fact and fiction', *The Face*, Sept. 1982

Wickham, Vicki, 'Lennon backs IRA', *Melody Maker*, 19 Feb. 1972

Wilde, John, 'The Smiths', *Jamming!*, no. 17 (1984)

Wilde, John, 'Morrissey's year', *Jamming!*, Dec. 1984

Wilde, Jon, 'Listening to England', *Livewire*, Feb./Mar. 1995

Wilde, Jon, 'My story: Kevin Rowland', *Dazed and Confused*, June 1999

Williams, Zoe, 'The light that never goes out', *Guardian*, 'Weekend' magazine, 23 Feb. 2002

Worral, Frank, 'The cradle snatchers', *Melody Maker*, 3 Sept. 1983

Yates, Robert, 'Looking back in anger', *Observer*, 'Review' section, 7 Mar. 1999

Yorke, Ritchie, 'Ringo's right, we can't tour again', *NME*, 7 June 1969

Interviews

Shane MacGowan, interview with the author, Royal Garden Hotel, Kensington, 18 Dec. 2006

Johnny Marr, interview with the author, Manchester Night and Day café, 4 Dec. 2006

Cáit O'Riordan, interview with the author, Dublin, 24 Nov. 2005

Kevin Rowland, interview with the author, Brick Lane, London, 18 Sept. 2007

Discography

Costello, Elvis, *Almost Blue* (F-Beat, 1981)

Dexys Midnight Runners, 'Dance Stance' (EMI/Oddball Productions, 1979)

_____, 'There, There, My Dear' (EMI/Late Night Feelings, 1980)

_____, *Searching for the Young Soul Rebels* (EMI/Late Night Feelings, 1980)

_____, 'Keep It Part Two (Inferiority Part One)' (EMI/Late Night Feelings, 1980)

_____, 'Liars A To E' (Mercury, 1981)

_____, 'Celtic Soul Brothers' (Mercury, 1982)

_____, *Too-Rye-Ay* (Mercury, 1982)

_____, 'Jackie Wilson Said' (Mercury, 1982)

_____, 'Celtic Soul Brothers' (Mercury, 1983 [re-release])

_____, *Don't Stand Me Down* (Mercury, 1985)

_____, 'This Is What She's Like' (Mercury, 1985)

_____, 'Because Of You' (Mercury, 1986)

_____, 'Come On Eileen' (Old Gold, 1989)

_____, *Don't Stand Me Down* (Creation CD, 1996)

_____, *Searching for the Young Soul Rebels* (EMI CD, 2000)

_____, *Too-Rye-Ay* (Mercury CD, 2000)

_____, *Don't Stand Me Down: The Director's Cut* (EMI CD, 2002)

_____, *Too-Rye-Ay* deluxe edn. (Mercury CD, 2007)

Lennon, John and Yoko Ono, *Some Time in New York City* (Apple, 1972)

Marr, Johnny and the Healers, *Boomslang* (New Voodoo Limited, 2003)

Morrison, Van, *Veedon Fleece* (Warner Brothers, 1974)

_____, *Beautiful Vision* (Mercury, 1982)

Oasis, *(What's the Story) Morning Glory?* (Creation, 1994)

Pogues, The, 'Dark Streets Of London' (Pogue Mahone, 1984)

_____, 'Boys From The County Hell' (Stiff, 1984)

_____, *Red Roses for Me* (Stiff, 1984)

_____, 'Sally MacLennane' (Stiff, 1985)

_____, 'A Pair Of Brown Eyes' (Stiff, 1985)

_____, *Rum, Sodomy and the Lash* (Stiff, 1985)

_____, 'Dirty Old Town' (Stiff, 1985)

_____, *Poguetry in Motion* (Stiff, 1986)

_____, *If I Should Fall from Grace with God* (Pogue Mahone, 1988)

_____, *Peace and Love* (WEA CD, 1989)

Pogues, The, with The Dubliners, 'The Irish Rover' (Stiff, 1987)

Sex Pistols, 'God Save The Queen' (Virgin, 1977)

Smiths, The, 'This Charming Man' (Rough Trade, 1983)

_____, *The Smiths* (Rough Trade, 1984)

_____, 'Heaven Knows I'm Miserable Now' (Rough Trade, 1984)

_____, 'William, It Was Really Nothing' (Rough Trade, 1984)

_____, *Hatful of Hollow* (Rough Trade, 1984)

_____, *Meat is Murder* (Rough Trade, 1985)

_____, 'Shakespeare's Sister' (Rough Trade, 1985)

_____, 'Barbarism Begins At Home' (Rough Trade, 1985)

_____, 'The Boy With The Thorn In His Side' (Rough Trade, 1985)

_____, 'Bigmouth Strikes Again' (Rough Trade, 1986)

_____, *The Queen is Dead* (Rough Trade, 1986)

_____, 'Panic' (Rough Trade, 1986)

_____, 'Ask' (Rough Trade, 1986)

_____, *Louder Than Bombs* (Sire, 1987)

_____, 'Girlfriend In A Coma' (Rough Trade, 1987)

_____, *Strangeways, Here We Come* (Rough Trade, 1987)

_____, *Rank* (Rough Trade, 1988)

Talking Music, *The Interview: The Smiths* (Speek CD, 1998)

Various Artists, *There'll Always Be an England* (ASV CD, 1994)

Wings, 'Give Ireland Back To The Irish' (Apple, 1972)

Films & TV/Radio Programmes

A Hard Day's Night (Richard Lester, UK, 1964)

Alexei on Dexys, BBC Radio 2, 14 Feb. 2004

BP Fallon Orchestra, RTÉ Radio 2, 21 Sept. 1985

Bringing It All Back Home (Hummingbird Productions, 1991)

Dave Fanning, RTÉ 2FM, 8 Nov. 2002
Dexys Midnight Runners: The Bridge (Spectrum Video, 1983)
Dexys Midnight Runners: Live in Concert, BBC Radio 1, 16 Mar. 1983
Dexys Midnight Runners: It Was Like This (ILC DVD, 2004)
Earsay, Channel 4, 7 July 1984
The Filth and the Fury: A Sex Pistols Film (Julien Temple, UK, 2000)
Front Row, BBC Radio 4, 18 Feb. 2009
Granada Reports, Granada Television, 21 Feb. 1985
The Great Hunger: The Life and Songs of Shane MacGowan, BBC 2, 4 Oct. 1997
If I Should Fall from Grace: The Shane MacGowan Story (Sarah Share, Ireland, 2001)
The Irishman (Philip Donnellan, UK, 1964)
The Long Road (Marion Urch, Kent Institute of Art & Design, 1991)
The L-Shaped Room (Bryan Forbes, UK, 1962)
Mean Streets (Martin Scorsese, USA, 1973)
The Old Grey Whistle Test, BBC 2, 9 Dec. 1983
Only Fools and Horses, BBC 1, 14 Mar. 1985
On the Waterfront (Elia Kazan, USA, 1954)
The Pogues: Completely Pogued (Start Video, 1988)
Poguevision (Warners Video, 1998)
Punk in London (Wolfgang Büld, Germany, 1978)
Punk Rock Movie (Don Letts, UK, 1978)
The Quiet Man (John Ford, USA, 1952)
Right Here, Right Now, BBC 1, 20 Aug. 1997
RTÉ News, 7 Nov. 1963
Saturday Live, BBC Radio 4, 21 Apr. 2007
Second Generation, RTÉ Radio 1, Jan.–Feb. 2003
Sex Pistols – There'll Always Be An England (Fremantle DVD, 2008)
The Smiths – the Complete Picture (Warners Video, 1992)
South Bank Show, ITV, 18 Oct. 1987
South of Watford, London Weekend Television, 30 Mar. 1984
The Story of … Fairytale of New York, BBC 3, 19 Dec. 2005
This Happy Breed (David Lean, UK, 1944)
Top of the Pops, BBC 1, 31 May 1984
Top Ten Guitar Heroes, Channel 4, 24 Mar. 2001
The Tube, Channel 4, 18 Mar. 1983
The Tube, Channel 4, 11 Oct. 1985
The Tube, Channel 4, 25 Oct. 1985
Two Tone Britain, Channel 4, 29 Nov. 2004
Who Put the M in Manchester? (Sanctuary DVD, 2005)
Young Guns Go For It, BBC 2, 13 Sept. 2000

Index